THE MOST IMPORTANT ART

THE MOST IMPORTANT ART

Soviet and Eastern European Film After 1945

Mira Liehm • Antonín J. Liehm

University of California Press

Berkeley • Los Angeles • London

University of California Press
Berkeley and Los Angeles, California

University of California Press, Ltd.
London, England

Copyright © 1977 by
The Regents of the University of California

First Paperback Printing 1980
ISBN 0-520-04128-3
Library of Congress Catalog Card Number: 75-40663
Printed in the United States of America

1 2 3 4 5 6 7 8 9

FOR MOTHER

O, changes of times,
O, hope of the people.
—BERTOLT BRECHT

CONTENTS

INTRODUCTION

Heinrich Heine once pointed out that during Germany's romantic era, a great deal of suppressed political and social energy found its expression in art and philosophy. Similar observations regarding the Russia of Tsar Nicholas I were made by the critics Belinsky, Chernyshevsky, and Dobrolyubov.

A century later, the Hungarian poet Gyula Illyés noted that from their very inception the literatures of Poland, Hungary, and the Balkans had been literatures of political dissent. "Whenever one of our organs is paralyzed," Illyés declared, "another begins, for better or worse, to do the job." Little needs to be added to what has already been written about the relationship between the collapse of tsarist Russia and the Revolution on the one hand, and the explosion of avant-garde artistic activity on the other.

But when the Russian Revolution, in the words of Lenin, declared film to be "the most important art," it reaffirmed a relationship between the arts, society and politics that had existed from the days of Peter I. In the spirit of the old utilitarian concept of literature and art, film was seen as one of the main instruments of education, enlightenment, and propaganda. Having come to believe in the influential force of the cinema, the Revolution, sooner or later, had to subject it to strict regulations. The more concentrated political power became, the more a handful of its representatives at the top level of the Communist Party and government—and sometimes a single representative—became the prime and supreme "Spectator." This Spectator decided on the fate of individual films, film artists, and tendencies with a ruthlessness quite different from—and yet in many ways similar to—the ruthlessness of using box-office results in the West as practically the sole measure of a film's success. Of course, the fact that the Eastern European film-maker has no choice, that he cannot select another producer, that he has no possibility of attempting an independent production, that he is faced with a state monopoly and hence has nowhere to turn—all this intensifies the pressures within a nationalized film industry. And naturally, these pressures also provoke a counter-pressure, which is apparent in the film-makers' efforts to change the situation, in their increased feeling of collective responsibility for the overall state of affairs, in their efforts to achieve a greater decentralization and establish more independent production groups, and, ultimately, in the strengthening of the role played by film-makers and their organizations within the entire system.

The personal union between the Spectator and political power binds the film artist to politics. Every word uttered by the artist unavoidably initiates a political dialogue, every attempt to step out of line leads to a political conflict, every show of nonconformism results in political ostracism, or worse. For film artists in Eastern Europe, repeated encounters with the Spectator turned into a veritable political training school. Many lesser talents soon realized that absolute conformism would open doors that would have been tightly closed to them had they relied only on their abilities. As for those with talent, as long as they refused to betray their talents, sooner or later they found themselves in conflict with the powers that be. And then, all of them together learned the lesson—and many learned it well—of the cynicism of day-to-day politics, maneuvering, and trickery, under the motto "the end justifies the means." On the other hand, in moments of political crisis when centralized power became temporarily weak, film took advantage of its role and prestige as the "most important art" to start speaking for the real spectators, the film audience at large.

The original conception of a nationalized film industry—backed in many countries of Eastern Europe by a majority of the film artists—grew out of the conviction that film cannot become an equal partner with other arts unless it is placed on a par with, for example, the repertory theater, which has always been a publicly subsidized cultural institution in that part of the world. Even those who were not interested in the social implications of film, but primarily in its formal aspects, were gradually brought over to the political camp by the progressive distortion of this original conception and attempts to transform film into an instrument of state propaganda. First they encountered the effort to place each and every formal discovery, each and every experiment, into the "service of the Idea," which shortly became the demand to give up all searching in the area of form, "in the name of the Idea." Consequently, even the problem of form became political, and all efforts to assert new formal approaches became political efforts, as did all subsequent efforts to consciously sidestep political issues through form. Film language and film form did not develop smoothly in a single one of the Eastern European countries, not even in the most favorable periods, but was instead dependent on many extra-artistic influences. No analysis of the formal structures of Eastern European film and their development, no analysis of the best works of Eastern European film, is complete unless one takes into consideration the close connection between film art and the development of society and politics that is characteristic of a nationalized film industry—sometimes as its boon, sometimes as its bane.

When we decided to write a critical history of Eastern European film, we were aware that a task of these dimensions, within the framework of a single book, brings with it the need to make innumerable choices and define limitations. That it would be, to date, the first attempt of its kind, East or West, also meant the need to provide the reader with factual information that he could, for other areas of world cinema, find for himself in a variety of reference books. We chose to concentrate on the period following 1945, in part because data about film before that date are more accessible. This is why the directors' dates of birth and film titles in the original language are given only for the period after 1945. And because we believe that the director bears full responsibility for a film, we limited ourselves mostly to directors. When possible, we give the year of production of films and not the year of release, since the latter is often delayed.

The English titles of films are in keeping with those used for American or British distribution. In cases where this was not possible, we quoted either the titles used in English-language publications from the producing countries or our own translations.

It was also patently necessary to limit the scope of the book to fiction film. Marginal note is taken of documentary film, short film, and animated film only where it seems essential for a comprehension of the overall context of film-making at that time and place. This by no means implies any underestimation of these fields.

We are fully aware of the inexactness of the term "Eastern Europe," which we use to signify the countries in that part of the world which found themselves within the Soviet sphere of influence after World War II, and which as a result underwent profound social changes. Equally inexact are terms like "people's democracies" and "socialist," which we use simply as a matter of convenience, since more precise definitions of their meanings in the individual countries and in the given context are beyond the scope of this book.

We intentionally omitted a chapter on Albanian cinema for the simple reason that we would have had to rely almost exclusively on second-hand data, which would not have been in keeping with our basic concept.

Part One, which is a single chapter, is offered as a preface to the text proper for readers who do not have at their disposal sufficient data concerning the history of the film industries of Eastern Europe and their social context before 1945. For that reason, we were obliged to limit it only to essentials, fully aware of the danger of such a limitation—for example, the need to summarize the history of Russian and Soviet cinema in less than two dozen pages. This initial chapter does not contain a review of prewar German cinema. In the first chapter on the GDR (German Democratic Republic), the reader will find information relevant to those specific traditions of prewar German film that East German film-makers felt they had fallen heir to.

The critical appraisals of individual films and personalities in this volume are our own, unless stated otherwise. We have seen about 90 percent of the films made after 1945 that are mentioned in the book. The Bibliography is quite selective, and we have consulted many secondary sources (books, interviews, critical journals, newspaper reviews, and so forth) that would have been burdensome to list in their entirety.

We wish to thank the John Guggenheim Memorial Foundation, whose fellowship made the writing of this book possible; the National Endowment for the Arts, which assisted in its editorial preparation; Ernest Callenbach, who so strongly believed in it against all the odds; Sidney Hollister, who edited and did revision work on the manuscript; Joseph Esposito, who was there when we needed him; and all those friends in Eastern and Western Europe and the United States, without whose wisdom, knowledge, and generous and devoted help and cooperation, we would hardly have been able to bring such an undertaking to an end. Because we cannot name some of them for political reasons, it seems unfair to spell any of their names.

Our gratitude also goes to the Museum of Modern Art and the Lincoln Center Film Society in New York, to the British Film Institute, La Cinémathèque Royale de Belgique, La Cinémathèque Suisse, La Cinémathèque Française, La Fédération Française des Ciné-Clubs, Gesamtdeutsches Institut-Filmabteilung, and Die Freunde der deutschen Kinemathek for all the assistance they have provided.

This book was written in Czech and then translated by Káča Poláčková-Henley to whom we are deeply grateful. Because it will probably be some time before it can appear in our own language, this English text is therefore the first and authorized edition.

New York, Summer 1974

PART I: Before . . .

Eastern Europe. Soviet Armenia and Georgia, which are important film-producing republics, lie to the east of the map border.

FILM IN EASTERN EUROPE BEFORE 1945

There is a certain similarity to the origins of motion pictures in all the countries of Europe: each had its Lumière, its *Workers Leaving the Factory,* its *Cabiria,* its Lillian Gish, its Canudo. Although the development of cinema in each country was directly or indirectly related to that country's economic development, cultural vitality, and particular traditions, very early in the century film traditions emerged that would cut across national boundaries, influencing the development of cinematography in individual countries for decades to come.

The new medium of expression found the soil more fertile in countries where there was a mature literary and journalistic tradition than it did elsewhere. It was clear even then that film would develop in and be subject to the same influences as other elements of the culture, that it would respond to all social changes, and often foretell them.

In the section of the world that is often inaccurately referred to as Eastern Europe (it would be more precise to speak of Eastern and Central Europe), motion pictures sooner or later became a significant component of the cultural scene, influencing the political sphere through an outspokenness that was characteristic of the arts in that section of the world where they often complement or supplement autonomous politics.

Early in the century, the countries of Eastern and Central Europe could be classified into two clear-cut categories. One of them consisted of Russia, Poland, Bohemia, and Hungary (all countries that were to become republics after World War One), where the values of the Parisian and Viennese film worlds were generally accepted; the other, made up of Bulgaria, Romania, and some sections of what today is Yugoslavia, responded only weakly to signals that came through from Western Europe and then frequently faded or died out completely in the stifling native atmosphere. Significantly for the history of film as a whole, the traditions of the initial two decades remained a foundation for later development. In countries such as Yugoslavia, with a very heterogenous culture, however, the lack of such traditions became immediately evident as soon as social transformations opened the door to independent growth in the field of motion pictures.

RUSSIA

Numerically speaking, Russian film production had the strongest beginnings. The cultural world there reacted to the final stage in the struggle against tsarism with a lofty wave of nonconformism. As early as 1908, Alexander Drankov founded the first film company, which followed the example of others all over Europe by producing short documentaries and reports on current events (for example, *Tolstoy's Eightieth Birthday*). That same year, the first fiction films appeared, initially as adaptations of literary works (*Taras Bulba, Peter the Great*), later as romantic dramas based on foreign models, and finally as historical films. A total of more than 1,200 films had been produced in Russia by 1917.

Cinema became part of the extremely active prewar cultural scene in Russia. Many of its leading personalities saw in motion pictures an opportunity to apply the innovative artistic theories of the times. Stage director Vsevolod Meyerhold elaborated on his experiments in the theater with his films *Picture of Dorian Gray* (1915) and *Strong Man* (1916).

Two other directors, Boris Shushkovich and Ryszard Boleslawski of Poland (both active at the Moscow Art Theater) also turned their talents to the cinema. In 1914, Stanislavsky attempted to formulate the relationship between stage and screen. Two years later, Yakov Protazanov completed an excellent adaptation of *Queen of Spades*, with Mozhukhin playing the role of Herman. In 1917, Protazanov adapted Tolstoy's *Father Sergius*, once again casting Mozhukhin in the leading role. At the outset, Protazanov leaned heavily on his actors, thus paying the then required homage to theatrical pathos. On the other hand, he was one of the first directors in this part of the world to take his actors out of the studio for actual location shooting.

Aside from Protazanov and several other stage personalities, the most significant figure in Russian prewar and wartime cinematography was Wladyslaw Starewicz, who originally came from Poland and was an innovator in animated puppet films. After shooting several documentaries, he made a number of animated films for a Russian company, films noteworthy for their exceptional artistic inventiveness and their satirical originality. Starewicz's films (*Beautiful Leukanida, The Cameraman's Revenge, The Dragonfly and the Ant* and others) were the only products of the prolific Russian film industry, except for the productions of the Pathé Moscow Studio, that were shown to any great extent in the West. Later, Starewicz began to combine live film with animation, using film techniques, as Méliès did, to create dreamlike poetic sequences and a romantic unreality. Of particular significance are his experiments with multiple exposures, fade-outs and fade-ins, and montage.

Contrary to widespread opinion, the development of Soviet film after 1919 was not a miracle that grew out of a vacuum. It was the logical outgrowth of the innovative efforts carried out in all the arts during the preceding 20 years. These efforts were for the most part practical ones—for example, experiments with the film material as such. In contrast to the situation in the Czech and Hungarian cinema, there was in Russia at that time little theoretical analysis of the film medium. For the most part, Russian theoreticians focused their attention on theater and literature. Some theoretical work in films was done, however, by Lev Kuleshov, whose studies on cinema art appeared in periodicals before 1919. But except for Kuleshov, and aside from ordinary criticism, the only items published in film columns and periodicals were occasional opinions by people active in the other arts, and even then it was more a case of appeals in the spirit of Canudo's "Manifesto." Thus, for example, the writer Leonid Andreyev published essays called "Letters on Theater," in which he considered the strong influence that the film medium is capable of exerting and its role in international relations. In 1913, Mayakovsky published an impassioned appeal in *Kine-Journal* calling for cinema to take to the streets and revolutionize people's opinions and relationships: "It is not necessarily just what remains to be discovered that is new in this drab world of ours; it is rather the novel relationship between the individual things that surround us, things that have long since been transformed by the impact of the powerful and new life in the metropolis."

FIRST THEORETICIANS

But in Hungary at that time, film theory was blossoming. As far back as 1912, a number of well-known Hungarian writers displayed an interest in motion pictures. Regular columns on film appeared in the newspapers. One of them, in the daily *Világ,* was written by Sándor Korda, at that time a young journalist. Only a year after Ricciotto Canudo delivered his "Manifesto of the Seventh Muse" at the Ecole des Hautes Etudes in Paris, thereby launching a campaign in the press that called for film to be considered an art, the Hungarian press began printing articles in the same vein. Between 1912 and 1919 Sándor (Alexander) Korda edited several film magazines which published articles by a number of outstanding Hungarian cultural figures. Foremost among them was Zsigmond Móricz, one of Hungary's greatest writers.

Between 1907, when the first of them was published, and 1920, some 17 periodicals devoted to film had appeared in Hungary—all of them on a good professional level. A particularly noteworthy contributor to these periodicals was Jenö Török, who, without any doubt, anticipated the theories that Béla Balázs expressed in 1924 in his book *Der sichtbare Mensch* (The Visible Man). Török, a discovery of Korda's, stressed the point that film was dependent on time, and considered rhythm to be a factor equal in importance to music in a film. Clearly, Török, who died prematurely in 1918, was striving for a definition of montage which was not to be formulated until much later.

Nor was Török's work an isolated example. The theories of Rudolf Arnheim were anticipated in Budapest, for example, by the philosopher Cecil Bognár, who wrote of film's significance as a means of communication, demanding for it an autonomous position, independent of the theater and literature. In the same vein, Lajos Biró, later a successful scriptwriter for a number of British and American films, stressed the importance of original scripts.

Both in Poland and in Czechoslovakia, film theory did not come into its own until later on. In Poland, the writer Karol Irzykowski was among the first to concern himself with the role of motion pictures. In 1913, he spoke of film as being the art of motion and suggested the term "lyricism of motion" to describe its poetic values. As a representative of the literary movement called "Young Poland," he was an impassioned opponent of Zola-type naturalism, and saw in film an opportunity to create works of art on a purely fictional basis, entirely independent of "the mirror of life."

In addition to the Hungarian studies, valuable essays in the field were published late in 1908 by Václav Tille, a professor of literature at Prague University in what was later to become Czechoslovakia. In his work entitled *Kinema,* he laid the foundations for later studies in the field of film esthetics.

Tille's articles far surpass others of his day in their overall scholarliness (he was the only Czech scholar to concern himself seriously with motion pictures), and also in their effort to apply to film the same esthetic principles and demands that were applied to other art forms. Tille succeeded in defining the elements of film, and, on the basis of an analysis of the language of motion pictures, proved that film was approaching an art form. In 1908, his conclusions about "linking shots" (montage) were entirely new, a full three years in advance of Canudo.

AUSTRIA-HUNGARY

Tille's conclusions, however, were too isolated to have any effect on Czech cinematography, which, prior to 1920, showed its strongest development in the area of technology. By 1918, three of the existing Czech film companies included within their ranks most of the directors and actors who were to become members of the first Czech film avant-garde that emerged in the twenties and thirties. In 1915, an important figure from the Czech world of the theater, Jaroslav Kvapil, made his debut in motion pictures, but his *Ahasver,* like his later film *The Golden Key* (1922), must be considered just one of many sincere efforts.

As was the case elsewhere, the first Czech films were documentaries. In 1898, an architect named Jan Křiženecký used Lumière's cinematograph to capture a number of current events (for example, *Midsummer Pilgrimage in a Czecho-Slovak Village*); together with Josef Šváb-Malostranský, a popular comedian, he created the first short comedies. The best of the 20 short films shot between 1898 and 1912 were a documentary covering the Sixth All-Sokol Convocation (a mass calisthenic display) and the nature film *The Currents of St. John,* which was awarded First Prize at the International Photographic and Film Exhibition in Vienna in 1913. That year marked the beginning of Czech feature films with an adaptation of

Smetana's opera *The Bartered Bride,* which took advantage of the popularity of a number of stage actors.

Within the Austro-Hungarian and the Russian empires, the Czechs and the Poles were kept in the role of second-class citizens, for the tolerant Germanization and the more aggressive Russification that were the order of the day blocked many of the efforts to achieve autonomous national expression. Czech and Polish businessmen had their hands tied in the area of industry, where production and investment goals had for centuries been subordinate to the interests of imperial centralism. It is not hard, then, to see why of all the Eastern European nations that belonged to the large centralized monarchies, Hungary was the one that most enthusiastically took up the new medium.

In the nineteenth century, Hungary had achieved federal status within the Austrian Empire. Its contact with Vienna, which was second only to Paris as an international film center, was so close that Hungary can be referred to as one of the cradles of European film. As opposed to ethnic Austria, which for years had been stagnating culturally, cultural life in Hungary—fortified by a constant struggle for national independence—was very active and quickly welcomed the new art. The first Hungarian fiction film, entitled *Today and Tomorrow* (1912), was probably shot by a young actor from Budapest, Mihály Kertész, known after 1919 as Michael Curtiz. The best evidence of the extent of Hungarian production is that by 1919 Kertész had made 39 films and Sándor Korda 19. At the end of World War One, 33 Hungarian directors were active in Budapest.

The rule that applied throughout the world was applicable in Hungary as well: the first film directors were former actors and journalists. Film became not only the subject of debates and theoretical discussions, but also an irresistible attraction for people in other fields.

The old competitive relationship between the stage and the screen was, to a certain degree, toned down at that time in France by the film *The Assassination of the Duc de Guise* (script by Henri Lavedan, one of the "immortals," a member of the Académie Française), which displayed the talents of a pleiad of French actors. In Germany, the conflict was somewhat eased by the film debut of Max Reinhardt, and in Russia by the interventive efforts of Stanislavsky. In 1914 Stanislavsky declared:

Many people are afraid that film will be victorious. They are irritated, they write and they argue, but no one makes any effort to truly study film. We know neither its means nor its possibilities. We don't know whether work on a film is an art or a craft to a film actor, or whether it is something entirely new that could not exist earlier. Before we accept the fears of those who cry their alarm with regard to film, we must study its laws, so that we might voice our own damnation or our own benediction.

In Hungary, where from the early days of cinema theoreticians found themselves capable of explaining the artistic significance of motion pictures in esthetic terms, both writers and actors enthusiastically involved themselves in motion pictures. Most films were cast with the very best actors of the Budapest National Theater, and famous authors were eager to affix their names to screenplays.

Korda created something of a triumvirate, together with authors Frigyes Karinthy and László Vajda, and gradually began to adapt the works of Hungarian and world literature. But rather than follow the path taken by directors in many other parts of the cinema world, Korda shunned using mere adaptations, and strove instead to create authentic works of cinema art, independent of the original story's artistic form. Korda's most famous film of that period was neither Mark Twain's *Thousand Pound Note* nor Molnár's *Nightmare,* but a farce written by two Hungarian authors and presented with great success in the United States and throughout the world under the title *Harrison and Barrison.*

Kertézs, on the other hand, preferred original scripts. The most successful films of his early career are considered to be *The Secret of Saint-Job Forest, The Colonel,* and *Lady with Sunflowers.*

THE FIRST OBSTACLES

Early in the second decade of the twentieth century, the historical genre ruled motion pictures the world over. Its crowning achievement was the Italian super-production *Cabiria,* which joined *The Assassination of the Duc de Guise* in opening the new terrain to the first steps of novelists and playwrights in the new media. (The script for *Cabiria* was the work of Gabriele d'Annunzio.)

In Yugoslavia, the first fiction film, *Karadjordje,* was also of this type, being based on the history of the ruling Serbian dynasty and the first uprising against the Turks. It was directed by Ivan Stojadinović, with the leading actors of the Belgrade Theater in the principal roles. But in spite of this crossing of boundaries between stage and screen, the struggle between the theater and the cinema continued in Yugoslavia, as illustrated by the decree that ordered every moviegoer to pay one *dinar* over and above the normal price of the ticket to subsidize the legitimate theater. As did film-makers in other countries, Yugoslav cinematographers also encountered opposition from educators. This opposition, however, was exceptionally strong in Yugoslavia, and reflected the increasing popularity of the new medium. Belgrade's teachers' magazine, *Uchitel,* printed an article in 1913 that referred to bioscopes as the "proof of the absolute nonexistence of any art whatever, offering only a misleading satisfaction of the basest sort, constituting a threat above all to young boys and girls. For that reason, we must fight it!"

Waves of opposition to motion pictures began to take shape in Bulgaria, Romania, and Poland (in the latter they were supported by the Roman Catholic Church), hindering the growth of the medium—hampered already by the dearth of movie theaters, especially when compared to Czechoslovakia and Hungary. The titles of the first films made in these countries are purely of historical interest: a documentary, *The Balkan War* (Bulgaria, 1908); a short comedy, *His First Visit to Warsaw* (Poland, 1908); Pola Negri's debut in *Slave to Her Senses* (Poland, 1912); the *Countess Walewska,* directed by Aleksander Hertz (Poland, 1914); and *War for Independence* (Romania, 1912), depicting the victorious battle against the Turks in 1877.

The director of the *War for Independence* was a young actor from the Bucharest National Theater Company, Grigore Brezeanu, who directed the first Romanian fiction film, *Fatal Love* (1911). The *War for Independence* played an important role in the cultural scene of the country. Initiative was seized by members of the National Theater, writers, journalists, and, which was quite exceptional, by the government to create a great cultural and national event. Nothing like that had ever happened before in Romania.

World War One transformed the map of Eastern and Central Europe, altering both the political and social structures of many countries in that area. Wherever these transformations took place, the year 1918 may be considered a definite landmark in the development of the national film industries, as the year 1945 later proved to be.

> You see film as a show,
> I see it almost as an attitude toward life
> Film is a conductor of motion
> Film is an innovator in literature
> Film is a propagator of ideas.
> —Vladimir Mayakovsky (reprinted in
> *Soviet Film,* No. 9, 1971, Moscow)

EASTERN EUROPE AFTER WORLD WAR ONE

Many people in nineteenth-century Central Europe, above all those who belonged to the romantic movement, yearned for a "war of nations" that would return independence to the nations of the Austro-Hungarian Empire, the Kingdom of Prussia (later the German Empire), and tsarist Russia. This end was achieved as a result of the war of 1914–1918, although it certainly was not a "war of nations." The Poles, drafted into the Austrian as well as into the German and Russian armies, fired on each other from trench to trench; the Czechs fought on the side of Austria, and the Bulgarians, bound by gratitude to the Russians for their liberation from the Turks, fought side by side with Germany.

But for most small nations, robbed of their independence early or late in history by their larger, more powerful neighbors, the outcome of the war was a godsend. The Peace Settlement of 1919 was based on the principle of nationalities. For the first time in history, politicians tried to create countries along ethnic lines, leaving the rest to the individual countries' leaders. Czechoslovakia, however, was the only nation east of Switzerland and south of the Baltic to retain its civil liberties and democratic social institutions for the next two decades.

In the first years following World War One (as was the case, again, immediately after World War Two), it seemed that the 100 million people living between Russia and Germany had finally reached their long-desired goal of a free life. Germany had been defeated. Austria-Hungary had fallen apart. Russia was the scene of civil war. The temporary weakness of the powers that for centuries had dominated Central and Eastern Europe was especially fortunate for Poland and Czechoslovakia.

PILSUDSKI

The Polish military force, the nucleus of which had been organized in 1911 by Józef Pilsudski, gradually took over Polish territory that for years had been occupied by the Russians and Germans. The Polish question was one of the first to be discussed at the Versailles Peace Conference within the framework of President Woodrow Wilson's Fourteen Point Program.

The first Polish National Assembly to go into session following free elections declared Poland a republic, with Pilsudski as its acting head. But the government of the reestablished Polish state had to cope with the heritage of the past. Despite relative progress, the country was plagued by inflation. A country where 80 percent of the 20 million inhabitants were employed in agriculture, Poland found itself in an economic crisis that forced many Poles to emigrate.

Pilsudski, having left the political arena in 1922, headed a military coup in 1926, setting up the so-called "government of colonels." His coup was at first welcomed by both liberals and socialists, but gradually the new government took up positions increasingly to the right. After Pilsudski's death in 1935 the freedom of the political parties was curtailed, elections were controlled, and the so-called "national front" became the sole decisive force in the land.

All the same, Poland cannot be referred to as a totalitarian regime in the sense that Eastern and Central Europe were to know such regimes in later years. The opposition press could and did attack the failures of the system, and the universities retained their independence from government. The Communist Party was declared illegal in Poland (the only country in this part of the world where the Communist Party was legally recognized was Czechoslovakia), but a radical, left-oriented artistic avant-garde was able to come into existence. It was mainly within this group that the first efforts emerged to create worthwhile Polish films, and it was also this group that produced the film-artists whose work became the link between prewar Poland and the new postwar republic.

MASARYK

The first years of Polish independence have much in common with the beginnings of the republic of the Czechs and the Slovaks, established on

October 28, 1918. Of course, in the case of Czechoslovakia, it was two nations joining for the first time in a single state.(At that time there were 6,800,000 Czechs and 2,000,000 Slovaks.) They elected as their first president Thomas G. Masaryk, a professor of philosophy and a political representative of Czech humanistic liberalism. Like Poland, the Czechoslovak Republic took as its model the French system of a multitude of political parties. But contrary to Poland, it was an anticlerical republic. No monopolization of power was achieved in Czechoslovakia between the wars. The ruling group in Czechoslovakia merely made sure that power was in the hands of the middle class, allowing the freely elected Parliament to retain its democratic rights. Nor did the situation change after Masaryk's death in 1937, for his successor, Eduard Beneš, followed in his footsteps.

An equilibrium of political power between the bourgeoisie, the working class, and the peasants contributed significantly to the relatively stable Czech economy. In spite of sharp social conflicts, the Czechoslovak government never went so far as to prohibit demonstrations or conduct mass reprisals. To a large extent, this was due to the Czech humanistic and liberal tradition, which had its beginnings in Bohemia in the fifteenth and sixteenth centuries and was strengthened by Bohemia's unsuccessful struggle against efforts to force it to accept Catholicism and Germanic culture. This tradition served as the foundation for the exceptional cultural atmosphere which flourished in Czechoslovakia between the two World Wars and which, of course, supported new ventures in Czechoslovak cinema.

KUN AND HORTHY

Shortly after the disintegration of the Austro-Hungarian Empire, a massive rebirth of culture took place in Hungary, only to be throttled by the rightist dictatorship that followed on the heels of an attempted Soviet-style revolution. The Hungarians emerged from World War One a defeated nation. And like the Bulgarians, the defeated ally of Germany, they responded to the national tragedy with an attempt to change political structures. Two weeks before the formal capitulation of Austria-Hungary (October 16, 1918), Hungarian Prime Minister Wekerle declared the union between Hungary and Austria null and void. A new government emerged, with the liberal Count Károlyi at its head.

But as early as 1919, Károlyi turned over the reins to Béla Kun, leader of the leftist movement that soon became the Hungarian Communist Party. Kun, who had taken part in the October Revolution in the Soviet Union, proclaimed the Hungarian Councils' Republic in March 1919. One of its first acts was to nationalize the film industry, the first nationalization of film in the world. Simultaneously, Kun's government confiscated the property of the Catholic Church, nationalized all firms employing more than 25 people, and revamped the educational and judiciary systems.

In 1919, however, Romania sent an army to intervene in Hungary and Kun had to retreat to Slovakia, where he encountered the Czechoslovak army. After the failure of a socialist uprising in Vienna, Kun, unable to bring himself to make a full alliance with Russia, resigned and fled to the Soviet Union. He was liquidated in the Stalinist purges of the thirties.

The months that followed were filled with terror and revenge, adding to the atmosphere of violence that is a marked trait in Hungarian culture and above all in Hungarian film.

The new coalition government decided that Hungary would be a monarchy, but when Emperor Karl of the Hapsburg dynasty returned to Hungary, the recently named regent, Admiral Horthy, recommended that he leave. Thus, from 1920 on, Hungary was a monarchy without a monarch, administered by an admiral, although it bordered on no ocean. As the dictatorship gained in strength, it created as its ideology a nostalgia for "Great Hungary," and thus for Hungary irredenta. Nonetheless, a certain Austro-Hungarian liberalism survived among the Hungarian ruling class, permitting the intellectuals a narrow sort of freedom. Debates on philosophical and political opinions were permitted only within preset limits, meaning that everything was permitted that was not in direct conflict with the regime. Essentially, it was a matter of freedom of thought for the elite, as opposed to the situation in Czechoslovakia and to some degree in Poland. This situation remained more or less stable for the next 20 years.

In the mid-thirties, small groups of Nazis appeared on the political scene, while many of those in power made no secret of their admiration for Italian and German fascism. At the same time, one section of the intelligentsia became increasingly convinced that the only way that Hungary could survive was by means of a change in the existing social structure, which still displayed vestiges of feudalism, including medieval clericalism.

As this historical sketch of Hungary illustrates, there was little in the histories of any of the countries of Central and Eastern Europe that would indicate that these nations would collectively become the nurturing ground of "avant-garde socialism." On the contrary, their histories, the conflicts between their various national interests, and perhaps most strongly of all, the conspicuous differences in the degree of their economic and political development, all tended to separate them. Compare Czechoslovakia of that time with Bulgaria and Romania, both of which inclined to personal autocracies headed by hereditary monarchs. Neither one of these Eastern European dictatorships made even a pretense of being founded on the support of the people. Instead, they used the police as their mainstay, and thus found themselves entirely lacking that mystical historical link between ruling class and "nation" which can indisputably be said to have existed in fascist Germany and Italy. Bulgaria and Romania were typical semifeudal monarchies, their authority buttressed by the police, the army, and the bureaucracy. Both countries had mainly rural populations that were backward and apathetic, working classes that were far from organized, and weak and frightened middle classes. There was no one to organize the widely scattered rural agricultural populations, which were stagnating without contact or communications, into a true political force. That was the main reason for the failure of the attempted revolution in Bulgaria.

STAMBOLIISKI AND BORIS

Alexander Stamboliiski, a popular Bulgarian leader who was imprisoned by King Ferdinand for having criticized the war against Russia, made an attempt to form a republic in Radomir in 1918. He took command of the "Republican" army and marched on Sofia. Though abortive, the attempt nevertheless resulted in Ferdinand's abdication in favor of his son Boris. Stamboliiski emerged victorious from the elections of 1919, and became premier. He attempted to put through a number of democratic reforms and stayed in power for almost four years, during which time the influence of the Communist Party significantly increased. It appeared that a constitutional change would be possible in the elections of 1923.

But the military coup of that same year shattered all hopes of such change for the next 20 years. Stamboliiski's army, consisting of ill-armed peasants, was crushed; Stamboliiski himself was arrested and tortured to death. The Communist Party went underground, having been declared illegal, and in spite of brutal persecution, stood up to the regime until the end. Since only the elite among the Communists had any familiarity with the works of Marx and Lenin, Communist Party propaganda in backward regions based its appeal on two ideas that everyone could understand: social justice and revolution.

Over the years, the Bulgarian Communist Party gradually fell heir to the national good will felt toward Russia, which played an incomparably stronger role in Bulgaria than in Yugoslavia or Czechoslovakia. But in Hungary and above all in Poland, the traditional antipathy toward Russia blocked any possibility of the Communist Parties there bringing to fruition their aspirations to represent national interests. The same was true of Romania, where the Communist Party did not really become the recognized national party until the 1960's, when it incorporated independence from the Soviet Union as an unwritten element in its political program.

CAROL II

It was Romania that made the most of the general fear of Bolshevism after 1918. Shortly before the truce, Romania signed a separate peace treaty, declared war on her former allies, and took her place at Versailles as one of the victorious states. Since the politicians of Western Europe welcomed everyone who was willing to become a part of the "cordon sanitaire," Romania was given significant material aid during the 20 years that followed.

King Carol II gradually liquidated all opposition and established a dictatorship that ended in economic disaster. This was so in spite of the fact that in 1918 Romania had doubled its territory, had a large store of natural resources, notably oil, and a number of able politicians. Nonetheless, the king suppressed all voices that seemed even remotely to threaten his regime, and in so doing reduced to a minimum the space available to the French-oriented cultural elite. He encouraged terrorist gangs led by the Iron Guard and strove to imitate the fascist states of Western Europe with his Front of National Rebirth.

Although the postwar land reform liquidated large feudal estates, Romanian farmers and peasants had much lower living standards than their counterparts in Hungary, and their cultural level was lower as well. The intelligentsia, which was concentrated in Bucharest, was oriented toward the West, and for the most part, lived in complete isolation from the people. Romanian culture was being created for export, while the wellsprings of talent in the nation remained untapped. Many artists lived more in France than at home, if they had not already been forced into permanent exile.

The disastrous collapse of King Carol's regime, and the fall of other Eastern European dictatorships, had long-lasting consequences (which will be extensively discussed later in this book) that could be characterized by these lines from Goethe: "The spirits I once evoked / Today I cannot shake them off."

ALEXANDER AND PAUL

Profound differences existed not only between Czechoslovakia, in the heart of Europe, and the dictatorships southeast of it, but the very center of the Balkans housed neighboring monarchies that were poles apart in their historical traditions.

The atmosphere in Romania and Bulgaria seemed, at least superficially, to be completely calm, the result of thorough and effective dictatorial rule. In neighboring Yugoslavia, on the other hand, King Alexander never quite succeeded in installing a monolithic autocratic regime, though it cannot be said that he did not try his best. The nations that constitute Yugoslavia are among the most "politically conscious" and the most determined in their struggle for freedom and independence (frequently synonymous here with sheer survival) of all the nations in Eastern Europe.

Because a prime requisite for a successful dictatorship is cohesive organization, the controversies between the five main nations, and especially between the Serbs and the Croats, served to weaken the regime. There was also an intensification of the generational discord, fortified both by the political vacuum and by the economic distress of a land to which the war had wrought havoc. As was the case with the Czechs prior to 1914, a younger generation was emerging in Yugoslavia that was weaned on the principles of freedom, on patriotic national literature, and on the liberal culture of

France. The Slav in them tended to bring about an orientation more toward the traditionally liberal Czechs than toward the Russians. As members of this generation became increasingly aware of the fact that the old national parties were driving their country down a blind alley, they rejected any compromise solution. Some of these young people were in fact Communists or Marxists, and most of them were considered to be so.

A deep faith in the necessity of a new order was stronger in Yugoslavia than elsewhere. This faith could not be destroyed by the repressive tactics that the government began to employ after 1929, the first year of the active royal dictatorship. Alexander tried to apply the same methods as his neighbors Boris and Carol (such as prohibition of the Communist Party, which had won 54 seats in Parliament in 1921), but his fundamental strategy, which was to feed the corruption among politicians in all parties, brought only partial and temporary results, or—in the case of Croatia—no results whatsoever.

Croatian opposition became particularly intense after 1928, when a member of the Montenegrin opposition shot and killed Croatian parliamentary leader Ante Radić during a session of Parliament. The idea of a Yugoslav state (which translated verbatim means a state of the southern Slavs), which had been the basis of the formation of an independent Yugoslavia in 1918, gradually became transformed in the hands of the ruling Serbian monarch into the idea of "Great Serbism." Meanwhile, the monarchistic autocracy that Alexander kept trying to superimpose on the five constituent nations became increasingly anti-Croatian in nature. It was no surprise, therefore, that Croatian nationalists were behind the assassination of Alexander by a Macedonian terrorist, an act that increased tension and chaos even after Alexander's cousin Paul became regent. These phenomena also affected the cultural sphere, already divided by the interests of the individual regions and groups, and ultimately became most apparent in the newest and hence most sensitive art, that of film—or to put it more bluntly, in the virtual nonexistence of film.

INNOCENCE UNPROTECTED

The first Serbian sound fiction film, *Innocence Unprotected,* directed by an amateur, D. Aleksić, was not shot until 1942. The primary reason for this late development of Yugoslavian talkies was the corrupt methods used to wage the fight for Balkan film markets. Unlike other small countries, Yugoslavia had no legislative measures that would limit the import of foreign films, and domestic films were taxed exactly the same way as foreign films. The production of silent films—with historical themes predominating—centered on Belgrade (*Fire in the Balkans,* 1933). In Zagreb, a group of documentarists emerged, among whom Octavian Miletić received international acclaim for his remarkable experimental films.

Slovenia was least productive; only a handful of nature documentaries have been preserved.

In the thirties, Yugoslavia had only 338 movie theaters for a population of 16 million, and 234 of them were in urban areas. As the pioneer actor, writer, and director Tito Strozzi admitted, efforts to imitate foreign films overshadowed everything else. Prior to the opening of his six-part film *Lonely Mansions* (1925), Strozzi wrote: "I am indiscreet enough to admit that all of us who worked on the picture had our audience in mind, and as a result, we Americanized everything as much as we could, given the locations and circumstances."

All efforts at making motion pictures in Yugoslavia before World War Two were purely commercial and of no cultural interest, and were also outside the framework of national traditions. At the same time, foreign firms took advantage of the attractive Yugoslav countryside and the cheap manpower available there for shooting their own films. But even the large number of coproductions by foreign and Yugoslav film companies in the thirties could be called Yugoslav only in their geographic location or in the presence of Yugoslav actors. The most famous of these films, *Love and Passion* (1933), was made in New Jersey by Yugoslav immigrants; nonetheless it was called by some Yugoslav critics "Yugoslavia's first sound picture." The cast was made up entirely of Yugoslav actors, but the film was never shown in Yugoslavia. Bratko Kreft, a well-known playwright and the author of several film scripts, gave a typical description of the situation at that time in a 1934 article published in the literary magazine *Kniževnost*:

> I believe in the great art that film can some day become, and the source of my faith is in the films of Eisenstein, Pudovkin, Otsep, Ekk, Chaplin, Pabst, etc., those rare films that succeed in smuggling art past the criminal sieve of film commerce. I believe in the future of film, because I believe that social freedoms will carry with them an independence for film as well. The development of film as an art is for the most part linked with the liberation of the generations to come from the power of capitalism, which has bound it and cast it into Babylonian bondage. But even in slavery, torches have flamed high to show the path that film must take if it wants to aspire to art rather than to falsehood and to the spiritual and material exploitation of the broadest masses.

The tone was similar in articles by attorney and writer Aleksandar Vučo, editor of the avant-garde magazine *Naša stvarnost,* and in those by Oskar Davičo, Koča Popović, and numerous others who at that time were vocal in their support of efforts to achieve autonomous Yugoslav film production, the seeds of which were germinating most promisingly in Zagreb. After 1945, all of these men were active in establishing an independent Yugoslav film industry. (In 1946–1947, Vučo was chairman of the Film Committee of the Federal People's Republic of Yugoslavia; the poet Dušan Matić became the director of the Film and Theater Academy.) And, faithful to the old avant-garde that they represented, after 1948—as the limits on freedom of thought were gradually being relaxed—they struggled against and helped overthrow artistic schematism.

THE BALKANS: PIONEERS AND AMATEURS

In Bulgaria and Romania, it was even less a matter of the steady development of a motion picture industry than it was in Yugoslavia. Under conditions that may at best be classified as difficult, several directors made their first films, which were loaded with melodrama and marked by a considerable degree of amateurism. Film stagnated on the periphery of cultural and economic activity, its sole contact with the other arts being a few attempts at pious transcriptions of native literature.

Production outfits were set up for the most part as companies for the production of a few films, or frequently for only a single one, and they faded away as quickly as they had emerged. So, for example, Vasil Gendov (1891-1970), the most prolific of the Bulgarian generation of film directors between the two World Wars (he directed 11 of the 50 features made in Bulgaria before 1944), founded his own company, Gendov-Film, mainly on his earnings as an actor, and managed on a strictly amateur basis. Gendov was the creator and star of Bulgaria's first fiction film, made in 1915, the farce *The Bulgarian Is a Gallant Fellow,* prints of which have survived to this day. The first picture with sound was probably the melodramatic *Song from the Mountains* (1914), which was based on folklore and folk music and was directed by Peter Stoychev.

Late in the thirties, Boris Borozanov (1897-1951) appeared on the film scene. He was to become the director of the first film produced by the nationalized Bulgarian film industry after 1948, *Kalin the Eagle.* During the war, Borozanov directed a film about Bulgarian pilots under the title *Bulgarian Eagles* (1941), and in 1943 joined forces with Hungarian Frigyes Bán to shoot a coproduction with Hungary under the title *Encounter on the Beach.*

The best Bulgarian films of the thirties are considered to be Yosip Novak's *Voevoda Strahil* (1938), based on a novel by Orlin Vasilev, and Boris Greshov's *Crossless Graves* (1931), a story of the crushed uprising in 1923. Projection of this film provoked tumultuous political demonstrations.

In 1936, a Department of Film was set up in the Romanian monarchy within the framework of the National Tourist Office. It was patterned after the German and Italian examples in hopes that it would support the development of native productions. Unfortunately, however, this department did no more than produce newsreels and documentaries; fiction films continued to be rare and uninteresting. One of those working for the National Tourist Office was Romanian film pioneer Paul Călinescu (born in 1902, and the creator of the first Romanian postwar fiction film, *The Valley Resounds*), whose documentaries—such as *Bucharest* (1936), *How to Do a Radio Report* (1942), *How to Do a Film Report* (1943)—included the exceptional *The Country of Motzi* [*Țara Moliţor*], which was honored at the Venice Film Festival in 1938.

Another director who worked in documentaries was Nicolae Barbelian, who began in 1911 as the owner of a mobile movie theater and between 1912 and 1944 shot several dozen newsreels and documentaries, first as a cameraman and later as a director. Nevertheless, Romania could not boast of a single fiction-film director whose development had not been significantly disrupted. In spite of the establishment in 1934 of the National Film Fund, financed by a tax on film admissions and set up to build film studios and produce fiction films, the basic conditions for the development of a Romanian film industry simply did not exist. Thirty fiction films had been shot during the silent era of 1923–1930, but most of them were patterned after the popular and patriotic *War for Independence*. Of the 20 Romanian talkies shot before 1944, almost all were so-called "Romanian versions" of well-known foreign films, made with Romanian casts in studios in Paris, Prague, or Budapest.

For lack of other opportunities, this adaptation work was the vehicle chosen by the most talented of Romania's silent film directors, Jean Mihail (1896–1963), the author of the stirring *Lia* (1927), which concentrates on the poverty of mean streets as opposed to the oppulence of salons.

Another well-known Romanian creator of fiction films, Jean Georgescu (b. 1904), a romantic lead of the silent era who was also a director and photographer, did not find fertile artistic soil in his homeland, and worked as a cameraman and director in France between 1929 and 1940. On the eve of the war he returned home, and in 1942 was given the job of directing the film *Stormy Night* (1942), based on the stage play by the nineteenth-century Romanian author I. L. Caragiale. The administrators of the National Tourist Office mobilized the best forces of Romanian cinematography, from actors to musicians and designers; no effort or funds were spared— they even called in foreign technicians—but the result once again did not measure up to similar films produced in cinematically more "developed" European countries. Caragiale's farce about a night full of errors and surprises was weighted down in the film version by the theatricality of the conception, the sets, and the acting. It remains, however, the key Romanian film of that period.

What is probably more interesting is the existence of very early efforts in the sphere of animated films, which were to become the most noteworthy facet of Romanian cinema after the war. As far back as 1920, Aurel Petrescu and Marin Iorda had been experimenting in this field, and there still exist today about 15 of their small compositions in which drawings and caricatures come to life.

CZECHOSLOVAKIA: INDUSTRY AND AVANT-GARDE

Avant-garde art trends were carried rapidly from France to the countries of Central and Eastern Europe, surfacing most visibly in Czechoslovakia. There, film was greeted by the theatrical and literary avant-garde with the same passionate enthusiasm as in the land of its origin. A manifesto written by members of the Czech avant-garde in 1922 said in part: "How happy we will be to allow ourselves to be carried away by astonishing stories and films, because they all touch on the nerve of our intellect, they best satisfy our burning desire for the exciting, full, active life . . . In our judgment, movies and westerns are not damaging to school children, but rather are educational."

While the older generation of writers had certain reservations about motion pictures, almost all their younger colleagues stood fully behind the new art, turning out article after article on the reviving influence of film on the other arts.

In the first comprehensive Czech work on film esthetics, *Film* (1925), Karel Teige, a leading theoretician of the Czech avant-garde, used as his point of departure the functionalist concept of art. In opposition to objectivity in film, he stressed "pure cinematography," a mobile optical poem. To him, film was not a means of depicting the outside world, but rather a self-sufficient poetic language, the supreme criterion of which was a "photogenic" quality. Even though later development has not entirely confirmed his opinions, his study belongs among the major pioneering efforts in film esthetics, if only for helping to establish cinema as an independent art.

But even in the liberal and industrially advanced Czechoslovakia of the twenties, the dreams of the postwar avant-garde were not to be realized. For the first time, Czech businessmen felt like the real masters in their native land, and they started to search for quick and easy profits. Film seemed to be a very promising source of such profits. Besides, the traditional symbiosis of German and Czech art in the cultural climate of Prague seemed to predestine the "golden city" to become a film center for Central Europe. This hope, however, was only partially fulfilled.

After 1919, a number of film companies were indeed established there, producing an average of 25 feature films and 150 shorts annually until the end of the silent era, and, from 1924 on, 60 weekly newsreels. But although this quantity was far from negligible, as time passed the films grew to display an increasing provincialism, oriented more and more solely to the domestic viewer's desire for cheap entertainment and even cheaper nationalism.

A significant but weak counterbalance was the quality of the Czech theater, whose best actors became staunch supporters of the new art. Moreover, the quality of Czech cinematography soon became known all over Europe through the work of such cameramen as Jan Stallich, Otto Heller, Václav Vích, Jan Roth, and others. But as for the hope for substantial and successful cooperation between Czech and German film artists, it only bore fruit in a few films: for example, those of Karel Lamač, the creator of the first and best film version of Hašek's *Good Soldier Schweik* (1926); those of novice director Gustav Machatý; and those of German director Karl Junghans, who filmed the fine but neglected *Such Is Life*

(1929) in Prague with Czech actors. This film, with its socially significant subject and a realistic conception, achieved a strength that was comparable to that of the films created at the same time by G. W. Pabst or Piel Jutzi. Undoubtedly, Czech film owes a debt of gratitude to German influences for one of the most ambitious endeavors of the silent era, the depiction of the Prague underworld in the film *Battalion* (1927), directed by Přemysl Pražský.

The onset of sound accelerated the development of Czech cinema (the annual number of features increased to 35, the number of movie theaters multiplied from 490 in 1919 to 1254 in 1939), for the spoken word emerging from a film screen meant, together with political developments, the end of Czech-German cooperation. Its last significant products were Machatý's films *Erotikon* (1929) and *Ecstasy* (1932).

As Hitlerism grew stronger in Germany, émigrés from the ranks of the German artistic avant-garde began to filter into Czechoslovakia, forming, after the Russian formalists and structuralists, the second major leftist émigré influence on Czech culture. As a result, Prague became a center of avant-garde innovations in Central Europe for the remainder of the prewar period. At the same time, the cultural atmosphere in Prague became rapidly and increasingly political under the influence of international developments.

The general cry for political commitment did not remain unanswered. True to the traditions of the nineteenth century, it was the theater that reacted most quickly, with the theatrical avant-garde represented by Jiří Frejka, E. F. Burian, and Jindřich Honzl. Honzl, a director at the Liberated Theater in Prague, led its founders, Jiří Voskovec and Jan Werich, to work in film.

Voskovec and Werich had created the Liberated Theater as a center of avant-garde poetic humor and satire. It became the country's most important cultural forum against fascism. Their second and best movie, *Your Money or Your Life* (1932), constituted the birth of the Czech film comedy of the Chaplin and Clair variety. Later, much more political films were made by "the duo V & W," as they were called—*Heave-Ho!* (1934) and *The World Is Ours* (1937)—and these are still surprising in their maturity. The latter films were directed by Martin Frič (1902–1968), one of the central figures of Czechoslovak cinema and its most prolific artist. His *Janoshik* (1935), a Robin Hood-type legend from the mountains of Slovakia, was the direct outgrowth of the new ambitions of Czechoslovak film, and brought Frič international recognition.

Commercially oriented productions for the home market continued to prevail, however, though pressure from artists in all fields gradually increased. Consequently, the rapidly growing and modernizing studios began to open their doors to increasingly worthwhile projects. On the one hand, there was the profound lyricism of Josef Rovenský's *The River* (1933), and on the other, there were the efforts of the literary avant-garde to influence and control the language of motion pictures. Vladislav Vančura, an outstanding Czech writer who codirected *Before Matriculation* (1932) and directed *On the Sunny Side* (1932), and poet Vítězslav Nezval were both leaders of the aforementioned literary avant-garde and were also Communists.

Within the film industry itself, Otakar Vávra (b. 1911), although younger than these artists by a full generation, outspokenly declared his ambition to place film on a level with literature. In *Virginity* (1937), based on Marie Majerová's novel, and *The Guild of the Virgins of Kutná Hora* (1938), Vávra, a student of Renoir and Feyder, was reaching for international laurels.

In the Baťa footwear manufacturing metropolis of Zlín (to become Gottwaldov in the fifties), a studio for documentary film was established (Jiří Lehovec, born 1909, and Elmar Klos, born 1910, both worked here), as well as the first laboratory for animated films. A new generation of film documentarists was also emerging in Prague, its most promising members being Alexander Hackenschmied and Jiří Weiss (born 1913).

The situation in Slovakia was different. In spite of promises and good intentions at its inception in 1918, the Czechoslovak Republic developed increasingly into a centralist state. These tendencies, concentrating power in Prague, naturally nourished Slovak nationalism and separatism. The crisis in the relations between the Czechs and the Slovaks developed into a permanent one in the thirties, ultimately leading to the division of the republic under Hitlerite pressure in 1939.

The world of Czechoslovak cinema reflected this situation. In the beginning of the twenties, there were a few efforts to set up independent film production centers—generally financed by capital investments from Slovak-Americans—but all of them were drowned in a sea of provincialism. Of the more than 1,200 movie theaters in Czechoslovakia late in the thirties, only one-tenth of them were in Slovakia and only a few of those were in daily operation. Yet the population of Slovakia made up almost one-third of the nation's population.

Even the highly photogenic Slovak landscapes were not used, and Czech film-makers more often than not swelled the ranks of those who went in search of wild mountain exteriors in Yugoslavia. The only true breakthrough in this situation was made by ethnographer and photographer Karel Plicka, who shot a number of nature shorts in Slovakia. His main endeavor in this sphere, however, was the full-length lyrical documentary, *Land of Song*, which attracted exceptional attention at the Venice International Film Festival in 1934. One other, though less successful, effort of this sort was Josef Rovenský's attempt to repeat the success of *The River* with *A Tatra Romance* (1934), inspired by the Slovak countryside.

All the prerequisites were there for Czechoslovak cinema to enter the international film arena in the late thirties; there was the bond with the literary, artistic, and theatrical avant-garde, with all its creators and theoreticians, as well as its youth; and there were good technicians and good technical facilities—the Barrandov studios in Prague were at that time among the most modern in Europe. But history had other plans. In 1938, a new Czech film, directed by the outstanding Czech actor, Hugo Haas, opened in Prague. Entitled *The White Plague,* it was based on the militantly anti-fascist play by Karel Čapek that was making the successful rounds of European theaters. Shortly after the film opened, the Munich agreements were signed. As a result, it was not long before Hugo Haas emigrated from Czechoslovakia, as did Karel Lamač, Otto Heller, Jiři Weiss, Alexander Hackenschmied (active in the United States under the name of Alexander Hammid), Jiři Voskovec (who became, after World War Two, a stage, screen, and TV actor in the United States under the name of George Voskovec), Jan Werich, and others. A number of them never returned to their homeland.

Another loss was the sudden and premature death of Karel Čapek at Christmas 1938, literally hounded to the grave by Czechs who had embraced fascism. During the Nazi occupation, one of the heads to fall under the Nazi axe was that of Vladislav Vančura. With that occupation the first attempt of Czechoslovak film to become a component of international motion picture culture was violently crushed.

The 1939 German occupation and the development of film in the Nazi-established Protectorate of Bohemia and Moravia brought with it a number of paradoxical consequences. It was in Hitler's interest that what remained of Czechoslovakia continue to function, and become the quiet hinterland of the anticipated German eastward expansion. During the seven years of occupation, a total of 124 fiction films were shot in Bohemia. The unavoidable decrease in production as compared with the period directly preceding the war resulted in an interesting phenomenon: in a situation where the very existence of the nation and its culture were in supreme danger, producers gave priority to films of "cultural worth" over those made as cheap entertainment. Consequently, films with artistic ambitions represented a much larger portion of film production than had been the case before the war.

Another paradox was engendered by the Nazi shutdown of the universities in 1939: many young people who would have sought fulfillment in other fields had conditions been different, found their places in the film industry, discovered new interests, and as the years passed, acquired the necessary technical background to continue working and eventually make names for themselves.

Finally, the Germans greatly expanded the studios at Barrandov aiming at transforming postwar Prague into a major European film center. Thus, after the war ended, Czechoslovakia found itself, in the middle of war-ravaged Europe, with what was practically the largest undamaged film-studio complex, and with a production capacity that was equalled, at that time in Europe, only perhaps by Italy or France.

Naturally, after Munich, politically committed art vanished. The work of the avant-garde group of the thirties, however, gradually began to make itself felt throughout the industry. Emil F. Burian (1904–1959), a representative of the theatrical avant-garde, transported his unique lyricism to the screen in the story of a young couple growing up, *Věra Lukášová* (1939). Writer Václav Krška (1900–1969) made his debut on a similar note. His first film, *Fiery Summer* (1939), was codirected by František Čáp (born 1913), who joined Vávra and Frič during the war to become a leading figure in Czechoslovak film.

Frič continued making comedies, outstanding among which was *Kristian* (1939), while Vávra concentrated on sophisticated adaptations of both older and modern literature. One of his best films is *Happy Journey* (1943), a contemporary story about the life of salesgirls in a large department store that is a forerunner of postwar film realism.

The Zlín studios continued with experiments in form within the sphere of short subjects. Hermína Týrlová (b. 1900) left Prague for Zlín when Karel Dodal, a pioneer in the area of animated film, emigrated to the United States. She was joined there by Karel Zeman (b. 1910), then a young advertising artist. An experimental studio for animated films was also set up in Prague, producing *Wedding in the Coral Sea*, its first full-length cartoon, late in the war.

In the last years of the war, the community of Czech film-makers formed a group on a broad political foundation that—working underground—came up with a detailed proposal for a new organization of the film industry. Entirely in keeping with the nation's nineteenth-century traditions, which declared art and culture to be public activity and subsidized them with public funds (state-subsidized theater was taken entirely for granted in Czechoslovakia and elsewhere in Central Europe at the end of the last century), the underground proposal presumed the nationalization of film, administered by the film-makers themselves.

POLAND: TO BE OR NOT TO BE

The film industry in prewar Poland developed almost totally independently of the literary community, attracting artists and musicians rather than writers. Perhaps the reason lies in the traditionally specific role played by Polish literature. During the long years when there was no autonomous national political movement in Poland, literature became the highest form of achievement. As a consequence, film, in its early days, was relegated to the category of entertainment—and not very demanding entertainment at that—and was considered incapable of speaking for the Polish nation. Another reason might well have been the chaos among the avant-garde artists and poets, from whose ranks in other countries came the first film enthusiasts. The sole exception was the romantic revolutionary novelist, Andrzej Strug, who wrote several scripts and presided over the Council for Film Culture.

Representatives of Polish protest poetry and avant-garde theater (such as Bruno Jasienski, Ryszard Stande, and Witold Wandurski) emigrated, after the "colonel's coup," to the Soviet Union, where they disappeared in Stalinist camps during the purges of the thirties. (In 1956, they were posthumously "rehabilitated.") In the period prior to World War Two, the Polish Communist Party—in its efforts to adapt to specific demands and because of its large Jewish following—never truly won the confidence of the Soviet Union, and in 1938, after Stalin had its leaders executed in Moscow, it was dissolved by the Comintern.

In spite of the fact that about 20 features were produced annually before the war, avant-garde efforts originated for the most part outside the framework of regular production. The shaky economic and political situation defeated any attempts to develop stable production facilities. Those that were established would fold from year to year, leaving behind only three or four films as evidence of their ever having existed.

Two of the most interesting endeavors of the silent era were Leon Trystan's *Revolt of Blood and Steel* (1927)—the center of its rather hackneyed adventure plot was a locomotive travelling without a crew—and *Hurricane* (1928), directed by the foremost director of the day, Józef Lejtes, and inspired by the Polish uprising of 1863. Also worthy of note was the brief Polish career of Boleslaw Srednicki, who had worked in Russia until 1918, and after 1933 worked in Hollywood under the name of Richard Boleslavski. His most notable work as a director in Poland is the film, *Miracle on the Visla* (1921).

The film avant-garde that entered upon the scene after 1930 was strongly influenced by French motion pictures, with their treatment of social problems, their succinct naturalism, and their political commitment.

The strongest personality of his time was Aleksander Ford (b. 1908), a director, an organizer, and, like some other Polish directors, originally a student of art history. He brought with him into his new field a sense of pictorial language and little faith in any help from literature. His first films were structured on the idea of tying picture to music, which gave dramatic accent to the political impact of the films.

Ford's *Łódź, the Polish Manchester* (1930) remains a classic among Polish documentaries, capturing as it does the life of the working-class districts in the director's birthplace. The shorts of Eugeniusz Cękalski (1905–1952) were in the same vein: for example, *June* (1933), based on the contrast between the city and the country, and *We're Building* (1934), a reportage made in collaboration with Wanda Jakubowska (b. 1907) on the construction of housing projects for workers.

Jakubowska joined with Jerzy Bossak, (b. 1910), Wohl, Cękalski, Jerzy Zarzycki (1911–1971), Ford, and Jerzy Toeplitz to become one of the organizers of the avant-garde society START (Society of the Devotees of Artistic Film), founded in 1929. The START group at first made only short documentaries and reportages, its directors refusing to allow themselves to be limited by commercial requirements. Many of them did not make their debuts in fiction film until after 1945, when they helped to lay the foundations for the nationalized film industry. Worthy of mention among the feature films in the early thirties is Ford's *The Legion of the Street* (1932), a social study of the life of Warsaw newsboys that is linked to his documentary work in both its use of film techniques and in its subject matter.

The efforts of Polish film artists were not too different from those of several Polish writers with a leftist orientation who in 1933 formed a group that called itself "City Outskirts." Their aim was to call attention to the realities of society. The artistic level of their nonfiction literature was not as high as that of the other genres of Polish literature, but all the same it left a pronounced mark on the novelists who were to make their debuts shortly before the outbreak of the war. The work of Leon Kruczkowski and Jerzy Kornacki was especially typical of this literary tendency, which inspired Ford in 1937 to make an adaptation of the novel *Vistula* by Kornacki and Helena Boguszewska. Ford came up with the striking *People of the Vistula,* depicting the life of people who made their living as laborers on the Vistula River. It was codirected by Zarzycki.

Most Polish literature of the time was characterized by oppressive presentiments of impending tragedy, apocalyptic visions, futile struggles, and Kafka-like descriptions of the absurdity of day-to-day life. (See, for example, the work of Bruno Schulz and S. I. Witkiewicz-Witkacy.) The film avant-garde rejected this revolt against "vulgar naturalism," and, until the end of Polish independence, followed the path it had started on in the late twenties. Ford shot *The Path of Youth* (1936), a medium-length reportage on a sanitarium for Jewish children that was banned as a vehicle for the "dissemination of Communist propaganda." Incidentally, the only country where it was shown was in France, where it was released thanks to Jean Painlevé. The story was based on the solidarity of Polish and Jewish children at the time of a mine strike. Quite an important production of films in Yiddish existed in prewar Poland. Among the best known was W. Waszynski's *Dybukk* (1938), inspired by the enigmatic tales of Jewish folklore.

In 1939, most of the Polish avant-garde went into exile, some emigrating to England, some to the Soviet Union. Ford and Wohl headed the Film Group of the Polish Army on the Soviet Front, where from 1943 to 1945, they made a series of documentaries, among which were *Our Oath to Poland, Poland in Battle, Maidanek.* Beginning in 1944, under the direction of Jerzy Bossak, they made the regular *Polish Film Journal* newsreels. The Polish exiles in Great Britain included Eugeniusz Cękalski (*Diary of a Polish Flyer, White Eagle*) and Stefan Themerson. In occupied Poland, Bohdziewicz and Zarzycki shot newsreels of the 1944 Warsaw Uprising. All in all, Polish film-makers shot about 100 documentary films during the war.

HUNGARY: FIRST NATIONALIZATION—FASCISM

In Polish, Czechoslovak, and even Yugoslav cinema, we can trace a line of development linking the efforts of the prewar avant-garde with the nationalization of the film industry after 1945. Taking a closer look, we can see that this nationalization was the consequence of much that had happened in the cultural world in these countries, a more or less logical outgrowth of the past.

In Hungary, on the other hand, the radical postwar change in the film industry was imported from abroad. People who had once been in favor of the nationalization had long since left the country, and the ones who replaced them for the most part had different ideas. They saw in a state-owned film industry simply another form of the rigid control to which Hungarian cinematography had been subjected under the Horthy regime. Only a handful of prewar Hungarian film-makers remained to continue working after the war. Just as the nationalization in 1919 had been the result of a spontaneous movement on the part of a majority of film intelligentsia of the time, the 1948 nationalization (almost three years later than those in Czechoslovakia, Poland, and Yugoslavia) was the consequence of the Soviet occupation of Hungary and of the efforts of the regime that the Soviets installed.

The first nationalization of the Hungarian motion picture industry took place four months prior to the nationalization of film in the Soviet Union and lasted from April 1919 until August of the same year. This pathetically brief period produced a total of 31 fiction films, the culmination of the wealthy prehistory of Hungarian film. In December 1918, Sándor Korda, the foremost representative of the Hungarian film industry of his era, published an editorial in his film magazine *Mozihét* stating, in part: "Those who represent the ruling class would do better to cease their desperate defense of their endangered positions. . . . No one should oppose socialism!"

Korda, Vajda, and Kertész headed the central film organization, which joined together all the extant production companies and also prepared the unified dramatic plan. Films that were made in the new republic strove toward social criticism, turned against backwardness in the most varied spheres of existence, and stood opposed to class differences and religious dogma. The organizers devoted systematic attention to adaptations of both world literature and Hungarian writings, and made every effort to obtain the cooperation of as broad a stratum of writers as possible. In the period of white terror that followed the revolution of 1919, 31 films were produced, but 30 have disappeared. The only one to survive was of mediocre quality, having been shot hastily in eight days. Entitled *Yesterday* and directed by Dezsö Orbán, it told a straightforward tale of conflicts between workers and a factory owner whose wife had had a brief love affair with the leader of the workers.

Béla Balázs, the Korda brothers (Alexander—known as Sándor at home—and Zoltán), Mihály Kertész (Michael Curtiz), Paul Fejös, Géza v. Bolváry, László Vajda, Peter Lorre, László Benedek, Josef von Baky, Géza Cziffra, Paul Czinner, Charles Vidor, László Moholy-Nagy—these were only a few of the better-known artists who left to enrich the film industries of other countries. Practically every Hungarian cameraman worth his salt, as well as such early experimenters in the field of animated film as George Pál, ended up abroad.

Except for extended voluntary silence, what other result was possible in a country where many of those who refused to go into exile were imprisoned? What else could have emerged after the violent repression of politically committed art, except for production aimed exclusively at light entertainment, which fortunately had a long and excellent tradition to fall back upon in Hungary.

The resulting situation was truly a tragicomedy—one that lasted until another war, with its attendant destruction, so altered Hungary's political and social structure that a second burst of creative cinema was possible. Although Hungary had been producing feature films since 1912, not a single one of the pioneers in the field was still active in 1925. By the end of the twenties, all production companies had gone bankrupt. There was a dearth of directors and technicians, and only occasionally did a good craftsman turn up. In the meantime, German and other foreign staffs took over the deserted studios.

The advent of sound was a bit of a boost. Responding to audience demand for films in their own language, the government took various steps to revive film production. Unfortunately, one of the steps involved establishing the Film Industry Fund, which censored all scripts and which had to give its approval before any film could go into production. And so, for example, it was forbidden in any Hungarian film of that day for horses' hooves to raise a cloud of dust on the road ("Our roads aren't dusty!") nor could high-level Hungarian officials be shown running up or down stairs in a hurry ("A representative of our country never behaves in an undignified manner").

Early in the thirties, István Székely (Steve Sekely) began work in Hungarian film, having spent years as an apprentice in Germany. His first film was a huge box-office success. Entitled *Hyppolit the Butler,* it took its story from Molière's *Le Bourgeois Gentilhomme* and its inspiration from Lubitsch's comedies, using Budapest suburbs inhabited by typical period characters as its backdrop.

The path that Hungarian motion pictures would take was suddenly clear. Half the films produced in the thirties were coauthored by Károly Nóti, the scriptwriter for *Hyppolit,* a quarter of them were directed by Székely, and the star of *Hyppolit,* the outstanding actor Gyula Kabos, went from film to film. After the popular comedies came traditional operettas, musical revues (such as *Ball at the Hotel Savoy* directed by Székely), and idealized views of national history (such as *Rákóczi March,* also directed by Székely), while every effort to achieve worthwhile film expression ended in a fiasco.

Paul Fejös's *Spring Shower,* made after the director had returned home from exile in the early thirties, received a shattering response from critics. Fejös, who had begun to work in motion pictures during the Hungarian Councils' Republic and had made several films late in the twenties in America, brought to the screen in *Spring Shower* a Hungarian legend in which a mother prays to God for a rainstorm in order that uninvited suitors not bring shame on her daughters.

The critics were indignant over the ostensible "disparagement of life in Hungary" that they claimed to have found in Fejös's noteworthy film. "It is not true that Hungarian villagers would disown the seduced girl; it is not true that the only decent people to be found are among owners of disreputable taverns; nor is it true that the state would tear the child mercilessly out of its mother's arms and place it in an orphanage," wrote a critic in *Budapesti Hirlap,* about the only motion picture of its day that followed in the best traditions of Hungarian cinema (István Nemeskürty: *Word and Image,* pp. 82–83).

Fejös made another attempt—*The Verdict of Lake Balaton*—which was apparently as important a work as *Spring Shower,* but it, too, was attacked by the critics, and Fejös went abroad once again.

Another émigré who returned home was László Vajda, the son and namesake of Korda's scriptwriter. In the four years that he spent in Hungary, he made 10 films, the best of them being *Three Dragoons* (1936), an attempt at mild criticism of the small provincial nobility. Other directors who did significant work included Fejös's assistant, Márton Keleti (1905–1973), who made *Bride of Torockó* (1937), and Viktor Gertler (1901–1969), who directed *Stolen Wednesday* (1933).

Aside from Székely, the most called-upon director of the day was Béla Gaál, who in the years between 1932 and 1938, when he fell victim to the fascist race laws, shot a total of 18 films, some of which more or less overtly supported the ruling ideology.

The advent of war was not completely negative for Hungarian cinema. On the one hand, it helped it achieve economic stability by forcing the replacement of foreign films by domestic ones and by facilitating the considerable increase in the export of motion pictures, mainly to the Balkan states. On the other hand, however, it brought about the emigration of even more film artists—for example, Székely and Vajda.

Thanks to the increase in production, however (205 features were shot in Hungary between 1939 and 1943), young film-makers found a much larger market for their talents, as well as more range for experiment, while a solid technical base for postwar development was being formed. (A comparable situation comes to mind here: in Italy, where in 1942 Visconti made *Obsession,* the fascists unwittingly helped to bring about a new film trend that was later to be called neorealism.)

In 1941, a young director named István Szöts (b. 1912) shot a film called *People from the Alps*, about which the Italian avant-garde film magazine *Cinema* said:

"Hungary's achievement of *People from the Alps*, shot by a young director little over 20, is of great importance. It proves that young people have a new message to convey by means of cinema. They want to, and do, create and fight in the spirit of art, because they reject all mercenary claim. Let us leave the serious task of criticism to others, but without forgetting the lesson to be learned from the Hungarian director István Szöts; the fresh instinct brought by Hungarian films into Europe's superannuated film production. . . . The time has come to try ourselves. Hungary has shown the way." (István Nemeskürty: *Word and Image*, pp. 130–131).

Though using unconventional camerawork, Szöts directly and simply told a dramatic tale, based on József Nyiró's short stories, of the lives of impoverished mountain people who live at the mercy of those who own the local forests. A social message, borne by the attempt to achieve sheer realism, mingles here with a romantic, pantheistic love of nature and a faith in the strength of the simple life. The hero finally kills the landowner, a symbol of the governing class. In spite of the fact that it is the gendarmes who ultimately represent justice, the last few shots of the film, capturing the hate-filled glances of the men, indicate that the injustice will not be easily forgotten. The film did not appeal to the powers-that-be, who denied Szöts permission to make a film of Ranódy's adaptation of Ferenc Móra's pacifistic novel, *Song of the Cornfields*. The refusal came at the same time that *People on the Alps* was being honored at the Film Festival in Venice in 1942.

In April of 1945, Szöts published a pamphlet in Budapest entitled *An Appeal in Defense of Hungarian Film*, in many ways paralleling the declarations made by young Italian film artists of the same period. Szöts attacked film magnates who fence film in with conventions. He called for freedom to create, proposed the establishment of a film school, and entirely in the spirit of neorealism, maligned studio shooting in favor of authentic locations. He did not, however, say one word about the possibility of nationalizing the film industry.

During the war, three directors whose work considerably influenced the development of postwar Hungarian cinema made their first films. Frigyes Bán (1902–1969), originally a journalist, actor, and assistant director, shot a total of 15 films, mostly in the sphere of pure entertainment. They included the Hungarian-Bulgarian coproduction mentioned earlier, *Encounter on the Beach*. Imre Jeney directed *And the Blind Can See*, the only Hungarian sound film of the period that took as its subject matter the life of the working classes—even though it displayed substantial period opportunism. Géza von Radványi (b. 1907) returned home on the eve of the war after a stay abroad and in several thematically conventional films used modern editing techniques and a mobile camera.

By 1943, the second boom in Hungarian cinema had come to a close, along with an entire epoch for the country. The changes that the defeated fascist Hungary would encounter in the years that followed were to be more drastic, more unexpected and, in their way, more deeply felt than those experienced by the other countries of Eastern Europe.

THE SOVIET UNION: FROM AVANT-GARDE TO SOCIALIST REALISM

Four months after the nationalization decree of the Hungarian Councils' Republic, on August 27, 1919, V. I. Lenin signed the second nationalization law in film history. Those who stood behind the first decree were later scattered to the four corners of the world, gradually becoming bulwarks of the same type of commercialized cinema against which they had once revolted in their native Hungary. Those who were involved in the second decree gave birth to an epoch. Their work wrote a new chapter of film history and carried out the artistic revolution of which the European avant-garde had been dreaming. The essence of this revolution was the attempt to wrench film from the grasp of the market, to transform cinema from a consumer good produced solely for profit to an art underwritten by society.

The Soviet film reflected from the beginning the two faces of the Revolution that brought it into existence: the first was a movement for political revolution, a determination to change the balance of power, to shift it to a new class; the second was a movement for an artistic revolution. The spokesman for the first movement was Lenin, the political leader who had to ensure the permanence of the new revolutionary government and lead an immense, backward, and largely illiterate country in its efforts to cope with civil war, foreign intervention, and industrialization.

"The People's Commissariat [for Enlightenment]," he said, "should register . . . and mark by number all films shown in the Russian Soviet Federal Republic. The contents of every film performance must be established as follows: (a) films of entertainment, shown mainly for purposes of advertisement and for commercial reasons (naturally not counterrevolutionary), and (b) under the label 'from the lives of all nations', films with exclusively propagandistic content, e.g., on the British colonial policy in India, the activity of the League of Nations, hunger in Berlin, etc. . . . Within these limits, a broad range should be left for initiative [of producers and film-artists]. Propaganda and pedagogical films must be submitted to experienced Marxists and literary men for evaluation, in order that we never once find ourselves in the unfortunate situation where propaganda achieves results exactly opposite to those intended. . . ." (From Lenin's "Memorandum for Comrade Litkens" dated January 17, 1922; *Lenin o kino,* Moscow 1963, p. 37).

In February of that year, Lenin again stressed the importance of film in a conversation with A. V. Lunacharsky: "You are considered the protector of the arts. For that reason you must bear firmly in mind the fact that to us, film, of all forms of art, is the most important."

The second force, the movement for an artistic revolution, had been smoldering in the innards of old Russia, just as it had in the core of old Europe. It was proclaimed by Apollinaire in France:

Where was it my youth has gone
See the flame of the future flash
Know that I am speaking out today
To announce to all the world at large
The birth of the art of precognition.

In Russia its spokesmen were futurists and cubists like the poet Mayakovsky and the painter Malevich. Speaking of this period, the English critic John Berger has said: "The union of cubist example and Russian revolutionary potential made the Soviet Art of this period something unique" (*Art et Revolution*, Denoël, Paris 1970).

Lenin was not much concerned with art, certainly not with art above all else. Fifty years later, he would have declared the most significant art to be television. But once he had spoken, his words took on a life of their own. First in Russia and later throughout Eastern Europe, film became "the most important art," with all the consequences implied by that term.

The artistic avant-garde was intensely concerned with the Revolution, feeling, consciously and subconsciously, that they were linked to it by their very livelihood. The explosion of the past was their "water of life," forming along with anarchy and chaos, an amalgam in which the outlines of new forms slowly began to appear. The avant-garde advanced with the Revolution, the Revolution became its "most important art." It did not take long for the two of them to come to an agreement about their interest in film.

In the beginning, naturally, were newsreels, agitprop shorts, and many foreign and prerevolutionary films. The Soviet viewer also encountered the cinema of the world (films by D. W. Griffith, American comedies, etc.).

But new production centers for cinema gradually emerged, state firms and cooperative firms, as well as private ones: Moskovsky Kinokomitet, Agitfilm, Burevestnik, Kinoplakat, the collectives called Tvorchestvo, Rus and Slon, Kinosektsia Mossoveta, Sevzapkino, Art-Ekran, Proletkino, Kino-Moskva, Goskino, Mezhrabpomfilm, and so on. And of course, production centers were built in the various republics. Revolutionary decentralization and the multitude of workshops brought about a variety of approaches, styles, genres, and theoretical opinions. As early as 1921, Dziga Vertov (D. Kaufman, 1896–1954), created a montage film on the history of the civil war, and a year later issued the manifesto of Kino-Eye. The workshop of Lev Kuleshov (1899–1970) gave birth to the first theory of film montage, as well as to the "Naturshchiks," the first group to take a stand on the issue of the emancipation of film acting from stage acting and to declare their preference for nonprofessional actors. In Leningrad, FEKS (Workshop of the Eccentric Actor) came into existence headed by Grigori Kozintsev (1905–1972) and Leonid Trauberg (b. 1902). In 1924, Fridrich Ermler (1898–1967), established KEM (Workshop for Experimental Film) and directed the eccentric comedy, *Scarlatina*. Soon the first Soviet revolutionary action films were produced, the most notable being Ivan Perestiani's *Red Imps* (1923); shortly thereafter names emerged that were to signify an epoch—Eisenstein (1898-1948), Pudovkin (1893-1953), and in the Ukraine, Dovzhenko (1894-1956).

The new government placed at the disposal of these groups facilities that the avant-garde had never dreamed of. It accepted the support of serious film artists, and took cognizance of the art produced in its workshops—not enthusiastically, but then again not intolerantly. Here the new power followed the example of Lenin, who made no secret of his dislike of Mayakovsky's poetry, but who nevertheless did not take it upon himself to judge it, and certainly not to take administrative action against it.

In the second half of the twenties, the avant-garde moved from searching for comprehensive forms to creating and employing them. Eisenstein's *Battleship Potemkin,* Pudovkin's *Mother,* Dovzhenko's *Zvenigora,* Ermler's *Fragment of an Empire,* Kozintsev and Trauberg's *The Cloak*—each examined new possibilities for cinematic expression. Early Soviet cinema explored and developed film as a new language independent from theatre and literature. Through montage, new theories of acting and scriptwriting, and new documentary techniques, the young Soviet film-makers made a place for themselves in the history of cinema.

But the clouds of political conflict were already beginning to form over the Soviet film world. Its politically active members could not remain indifferent to the struggle for power that was breaking out in the form of Stalin's conflict with the opposition. Stalin's efforts to achieve a new centralization and to harness art to the wagon of power politics, along with his intolerance and the support he gave to artists who were willing to pay homage to the old tastes, all aroused a strong reaction from many artists. On the heels of many representatives of prerevolutionary art and those who had been connected with the February revolution, new exiles left their homeland; this time they were representatives of the avant-garde who had stood up for the Bolshevik revolution or at least had accepted it. Writers, artists, and musicians fled from Russia in droves, to continue to develop the artistic revolution of the twentieth century abroad. For the most part, the artists who rejected exile were those belonging to the avant-garde theater and those working in film. Their art was indivisibly joined to the conditions under which they worked, conditions that the Revolution had created for them. For that reason, they were more willing than the others to gauge the political struggle primarily by these conditions. And that is why so many of them supported Stalin, and why there were among them fewer direct victims of the despotism that followed. They would pay their debt to the times elsewhere, and in different coin.

Simultaneously with the struggle for political power, another fight was going on—the conflict over which of the artistic groups would take the lead, would become the "spokesman" for the Party, that increasingly potent central power structure. The diversification and heterogeneity that gave birth to the successes of the avant-garde were progressively reduced to a single artistic point of view; the artistic revolution was more and more called upon to think with a single brain. Paradoxically, both the political power structure and numerous artists and theoreticians eventually agreed on this point. In the late twenties, the group called RAPP (Russian Association of Proletarian Writers) became the cultural spokesman for the Party. It was a leftist, intolerant, and condescending group, closely linked with the efforts of the avant-garde, and firm in its insistence on the esthetic autonomy of art and culture. But the political intolerance of the RAPP group was forcing the other groups and individuals directly into Stalin's embrace. In principle, the group's only power was over literature, but in fact its influence went far beyond the written word.

After liquidating the Trotskyite opposition, Stalin began to construct his legendary system of "gears and levers." Those in the artistic world who opposed RAPP unwittingly helped him to undermine their own autonomy. When in 1932 the appeal finally sounded to dissolve all groups and to establish a unified Union of Writers, the RAPP magazine, ironically, was the only one that pointed out the danger of such a move and made the last public protest against Stalin's dictate. In 1934, at the founding congress of the Writers' Union, Gorky and Zhdanov proclaimed the doctrine of socialist realism.

At this time, the work of Soviet silent film and its esthetics had reached their high point. From the revolutionary explosion, the ensuing chaos, the fight against foreign intervention, civil war, and famine, from the pathos of the times and ideas and from the policy lines that were slowly forming the outlines of the new Stalinist Russia—from all this a new poetic language was born that we have yet to analyze and define completely. It was not the language of intimate poetry, nor was it that of a poetry of metaphysical symbols and the human subconscious; rather it was the poetry of the folk epic—the only poetry capable, in its unlimited imagination, of capturing the spirit and scope of an era that produced many nameless heros and countless historical and apocalyptic changes.

S.M. Eisenstein wrote in 1929:

The representation of objects in the actual (absolute) proportions proper to them is, of course, merely a tribute to the orthodox formal logic. A subordination to an inviolable order of things.

Both in painting and sculpture there is a periodic invariable return to periods of the establishment of absolutism. Displacing the expressiveness of archaic disproportion for regulated "stone tables" of officially decreed harmony.

Absolute realism is by no means the correct form of perception. It is simply the function of a certain form of social structure. Following a state monarchy, a state uniformity of thought is implanted. Ideological uniformity of a sort that can be developed pictorially in the ranks of colors and designs of the Guards regiments . . . (Film Form, pp. 34–35, The World Publ. Co., New York 1968)

As the Russian Revolution was gradually turning into a bureaucratic dictatorship, new developments were emerging in the field of film tech-

nology. Sound in film demanded a change in esthetics. One of the theoreticians of the avant-garde, Viktor Shklovsky, wrote of this moment 30
years later:

The most important contribution of sound was the [spoken] word, presenting the
art of film with innumerable opportunities for depicting man and opening the
door to the world of his thoughts and emotions. . . . It called for a transition from
summary characterizations of heroes to a true, realistic typification, the transmission
of all the wealth of life's content by means of vitally specific individualized characters
and figures. . . . Attention was turned to the person who breathed life into the figure
on the screen, the film actor, who was called upon to show greater virtuosity and a
familiarity with the wealth of the traditions of realistic theater" (*Ocherki istorii
sovetskogo kino,* Moscow 1959, Vol. II, Pt. 1, pp. 36–50).

Leaders of the avant-garde sensed the danger connected with "opening
the door to the world of . . . thoughts and emotions" of contemporary
Soviet man. They were well aware that a call for realism sounded in the
name of technical progress was a mortal threat to the endeavors of the
avant-garde and to the autonomy of film art, and was a bulwark for the
traditionalists. Eisenstein, Pudovkin, and G. Alexandrov (b. 1903) even
went so far as to publish a manifesto against the emerging language of the
talkies and, together with a number of others, retreated only step by step
in the face of increasing pressure. The main battle was fought early in the
thirties between the avant-garde advocates of the trend labeled "poetry" and
the advocates of what was called "prose"—that is, the new realistic line,
party-supported and leading directly into what was to be called socialist
realism. The center of the debate and the turning point in Soviet film was
Counterplan (1932), the work of Sergei Yutkevich (b. 1904) and Fridrich
Ermler, envisioned and shot as a "moralistic comedy with dialogues, in
the outdated style of Korshevsky's theater" (according to Ilya Ehrenburg,
at the First Congress of Soviet Writers). Although it was the subject of
long and exhaustive disputes, *Counterplan* was considered to be the first
success of the new line, which was confirmed by the great official and
popular success of *Chapayev* (1934), a realistic portrait of an exemplary
hero for the years to come, directed by Sergei (1900–1959) and Georgi
Vasiliev (1899–1946).

The avant-garde of Western Europe, generally sympathetic to its
Soviet counterparts, took a stand for the most part in support of the Soviet
opposition during Stalin's rise to power. This stand was a logical product
of the principles proclaimed by the Western European progressive artists,
principles inherent in their movement, principles that had brought it to
stand up in support of the Soviet Revolution. In fact, it was these very
principles that were vitally threatened by the advancing wave of Stalinism.
Because from the outset of Stalin's campaign the Soviet avant-garde had
been suspect (generally justifiably) of being in sympathy with the opposition,
the position taken by their colleagues in Western Europe in the thirties was
mere confirmation of as yet unformulated official accusations. Thus the
debate between the proponents of "prose" and the proponents of "poetry"

was really a further aspect of the political power struggle. Its end was marked by the nationwide creative conference of film workers in 1935, at which socialist realism in the area of film was canonized and the verdict with regard to the avant-garde was confirmed. (See Appendix A: Some Definitions of Socialist Realism.) This background may make it easier to understand why, in the ensuing decades, the Soviet cultural establishment was not satisfied with the mere distaste every reinstated traditionalistic and academic power displays toward avant-garde movements, but rather considered it essential to fight them tooth and nail as a basic evil. Even under Khrushchev's relative liberalism, the adjective "avant-garde" on Nikita Sergeyevich's lips was literally an adjective of abuse.

Under the conditions that existed in the Soviet Union in the thirties, following the definitive installation of Stalinism and the return to artistic academism, the manipulation of the arts was a difficult and complex process, the traces of which were apparent in literature, music, and theater for a long time to come. Not so in film. Here the artist was far more dependent on political power, not only when the finished product was presented for censorship, but throughout the entire process of creation. Thus, films bearing traces of the smoldering conflict either did not come to be, or else were stifled halfway to creation. That is why it might appear that the heritage of the avant-garde had retreated overnight to make room for moralistic stories and their simplistic heroes.

Soviet reality appeared to be divided into areas of black and white, marked clearly with the red pencil of artistic councils and ideological authorities wherever film appeared to be "opening the door to the world of . . . thoughts and emotions."

And yet these years in the development of Soviet film were a period of great human dramas—with both successes and failures. First of all there was the drama of Eisenstein, who, after the mediocre success of the second version of *Old and New,* felt it impossible to continue in the manner of the twenties. He left for America, was obliged to drop his gigantic Mexican project, and temporarily retired from film-making to devote himself to theoretical work and to teaching, after being forced to go through a severe self-criticism for *Bezhin Meadow* (1936), the sole though incomplete print of which was destroyed.

Another is the drama of Pudovkin, who was shattered by the reception of his films *A Simple Case* and *Deserter*, and who gradually became a front-line proponent of Zhdanovism and the creator of pompous spectaculars.

There is the drama of Dovzhenko, who made his *Shchors* (1939) at Stalin's request, and was persecuted as a result by political authorities and by L. Beria, chief of the Soviet secret police.

There is the drama of two of the founders of the avant-garde, Kozintsev and Trauberg, who after years of struggle toward socialist realism, made *Maxim Trilogy*—apparently the most worthwhile film of the revolutionary and patriotic series.

There is the drama in the success of another pair, Alexander Zarchi (b. 1908) and Iosif Heifitz (b. 1905), the young favorites of the avant-garde, who finally achieved recognition after they had succeeded in taming their talents in the films *Baltic Deputy* and *Member of the Government.*

There is drama in the artistic career of the man who created the classics of Soviet film comedy—*Jolly Fellows, Volga, Volga,* and *Circus*—Grigori Alexandrov, a collaborator of Eisenstein's who finally became one of the foremost proponents of superficial conventionalism.

The drama of an oeuvre that was never completed is the story of one of the most talented directors, Yevgeny Chervyakov, who waged heroic but often futile struggles for each of his projects—*Aristocrats, The Poet and the Tsar, Cities and Years*—only to perish on the battlefield during the war.

But in addition to the successes achieved as a result of innumerable ideological and artistic compromises, in addition to the real-life dramas that ultimately destroyed talents and lives, there were also the immediate successes of the advocates of "prose." Many of them, however, are associated with only a single opus, for example the Vasilievs with *Chapayev,* Yefim Dzigan (b. 1898) with *We from Kronstadt,* Alexander Medvedkin (b. 1900) with *Happiness,* Vladimir Legoshin (1904-1956) with *Lone White Sail,* Nikolai Ekk (b. 1902) with *Road to Life,* and in his own way Boris Barnet (1902-1965) with *Outskirts*—known in the United States as *Patriots.*

At this time the controversial and noteworthy film career of Mikhail Romm (1901-1971) began (*Lenin in October; Lenin in 1918*). He was the first to create the simplistic films that anticipated those of "the personality cult," and the first to present Stalin on the screen as Lenin's most faithful pupil and follower—only to become, 20 years later, one of the most determined de-Stalinizers of Soviet cinema. Parallel with Romm's beginnings, Yutkevich (*Man With a Gun*) and Ivan Pyriev (1901-1968) (*Tractor Drivers*) were just strengthening their positions. And at about the same time, Mark Donskoy (b. 1901) was working on his *Gorky Trilogy,* a vivid example—from the first to the third film—of the road followed by the "prosaists" from film realism to socialist realism. The mid-thirties was also the period of the first successes of Soviet historical films which, after the liquidation of the historiographic school of Pokrovsky, began to emphasize the patriotism and Great Russian chauvinism that are evident to this day. The stage was set, so to speak, for the creation of the cult of Stalin as the direct heir of the tsars. While the film *Stenka Razin,* directed by Olga Preobrazhenskaya and I. Pravov, was already suffering from the official distaste for films about folk rebels, Vladimir Petrov (1896-1966) was receiving the highest praise for his two-part *Peter the Great,* a thoroughly idealized portrait of the despot who tried to modernize barbarian Russia with his own barbarian methods. A young talented Georgian, Mikhail Chiaureli (b. 1894), was also active. Although still overshadowed to some degree by Petrov, he created *Arsen,* a film about the nineteenth-century

Georgian uprising against the native aristocracy, and *The Last Masquerade,* a story about the beginnings of the Georgian Soviet Republic.

A new film hero—a voluntary secret police agent—was born simultaneously with the production of the spectacular historical motion pictures, and a new villain as well—the enemy within the ranks, the traitor, the agent of foreign powers. Upon the suggestion of Stalin himself, the film *Komsomolsk* was made, and it solidified the position of young Sergei Gerasimov (b. 1907). But it was not until the late thirties that a film about the years of terrorism and mass persecution following the murder of S. M. Kirov was made; its director was Fridrich Ermler.

Ermler was the most talented of the "prosaists." His Workshop for Experimental Film set as its goal "the creation of revolutionary film" and in *Fragment of an Empire* (1929), mentioned earlier, he succeeded in turning out one of the classics of silent film. Always more attracted by the specifics of building socialism than by history and great historical cataclysms, Ermler made *Counterplan,* creating, without a tract of opportunism and with absolute conviction, a solid realistic opus that would for years be used as an argument against the avant-garde. His *Peasants* (1934) was once again an agitprop film in the purest sense of the word, but the means he used to create it were the means of an artist who relied more on his experience and imagination than on theoretical directives and political brochures. Ironically, Maxim Gorky stood at the head of those who censured him for it, even at a time when the victory of "prose" was becoming the bureaucratic dictate of socialist realism. Then came the greatest social "commission" of Ermler's career, a film about the murder of Kirov and the internal conspiracy against Soviet power. Ermler took on the task with the same enthusiasm with which he had approached his previous films. The result was *A Great Citizen,* in two parts. Just as Leni Riefenstahl served the consolidation of the myth of Adolf Hitler without allowing this propagandistic goal to weaken the artistic quality of her work, so in the late thirties, Ermler served—with lesser talent—the creation of the myth of justified purges and terrorism with a motion picture that belongs artistically (mainly its first part) among the better ones made during that period.

Today we will not find *A Great Citizen* in any historical film retrospective, for Soviet and Eastern European film archives (and maybe Western European film libraries as well) guard the existing prints jealously. The last time they were released for showing in the East was during the trials and purges of the fifties.

Against the background of these dramas, conflicts, and successes, the infinite drabness and the contrived lifelessness of socialist realism began to become apparent. With the approach of the end of the decade, and with the destruction of the lives of many of the best artists (including the most devoted among the revolutionaries), vitality began to vanish from motion pictures, to be replaced by brochure illustrations, posters of May Day slogans, and official rosy-hued optimism. Yet for some reason the purges were felt less in film than in literature or the theater. The leaders of the Lenfilm Party organization and other Leningrad communists, however, were arrested as early as 1937—and some of them never returned—for "sabotaging" the shooting of *A Great Citizen*. But the atmosphere of mistrust and fear dominated the world of cinema as well, and eventually heads rolled: Elena Sokolovskaya, the art director of Mosfilm; A. I. Piotrovsky, head of the Mosfilm script department; A. F. Dorn, author of the film chronicle on the October Revolution; film director K. Eggert; Alexandrov's director of photography and author of *The Cinema as a Graphic Art*, V. Nilsen; Kyrlia, the unforgettable Mustafa from N. Ekk's *Road to Life*; the writers and scenarists I. Tinyanov and I. Babel; and last but not least Eisenstein's political executioner, B. Shumyatsky, who, according to *Sovietskoe Iskusstvo* (1.1.1938), was struck by "political blindness" which permitted "savage veteran Trotskyist and Bucharinist agents and hirelings of Japanese and German fascists to wreck the movie industry." *Izvestya*, two months later, on March 26, 1938, was more explicit:

Wreckers who had built themselves a nest in the Main Administration of the Movie-Photo-industry and in movie studios have deliberately disrupted plans, delayed the release of films, squandered the people's money, increased spoilage, run up production costs, and intentionally failed to fulfill even modified plans. . . . Instead of the 60 or more art films per year as planned, of late only 20 to 25 films have been released annually. Spoilage has reached fantastic proportions. In 1935, 34 films were rejected, and in 1936, 55. . . . It has become the usual thing to exceed the budget on individual pictures. . . . The whole "work" system of the film industry was laid out with evil intent so as to hamper the development of the Soviet movie. . . . The variety and vividness of our Soviet reality found all too little reflection in the "plans." As a result, the country did not get films on the most vital themes of life . . . (Quoted in John Rimberg and P. Babitsky, *The Soviet Film Industry*, New York, Praeger, 1955).

Early in 1939, at the Conference of Theater Directors where he was expected to make a public self-denouncement or self-criticism, 65-year-old Vsevolod Meyerhold declared:

Where once blossomed an intense, constantly renewed artistic vitality, where great artists sought, experimented, erred and found new paths to take, creating some bad productions and some absolutely splendid ones, there today we find only depressing mediocrity, full of good intentions, it is true, but entirely lacking hope. And along with hope, displaying an increasing lack in talent as well. Is this what you wanted? If it is, then you have committed a horrible deed. You poured out the baby with the bath water, and in your effort to uproot formalism, you have destroyed art!

The following day, Meyerhold was arrested; he was indicted as a German spy and tortured to death within a matter of days.

Soviet cinema sank to unprecedented depths just when it was called upon to mobilize the masses for imminent war. *If War Comes Tomorrow, Depth Air Raid, Squadron Five,* and *Tank Crews* are proof of how official esthetics, enforced optimism, and strict police control result in absolute artistic impotence. But the mobilization of patriotism at the moment war threatened also enabled Eisenstein to return to film directing: the year 1938 was the year of the success of *Alexander Nevsky*. And a year and a half after Meyerhold perished in the dungeons of Lubyanka, as a "German spy," the treaty between the Soviet Union and Germany enabled Eisenstein to make his debut as an operatic director. The performance was Wagner's *Die Walküre,* performed at the Bolshoi Theater in Moscow on November 21, 1940.

The thirties had presented new material conditions to Soviet film-makers. The large and small workshops, the birthplaces of avant-garde masterpieces, had been replaced by well-equipped studios, generously subsidized by public funds. On the other hand, innumerable small groups and collectives had been supplanted by such centralized giants as Mosfilm, Lenfilm, and Soyuzdyetfilm, and above them all was the "main administration" which insured strict control over every phase of the artistic process. A parallel organization had been set up for each of the national republics.

The war changed this situation entirely. Production was withdrawn to the peripheral regions of the Soviet Union, where conditions were difficult and primitive; the need arose once again for improvisation and inventiveness, and for the substitution of talent for the missing technology and facilities. Central control gradually weakened:no longer was every shot in every script under the censor's eye, and the autonomy of the artist in the distant provinces, with respect to the central government, reverted to some extent to what it had been before the purges and their aftermath. In addition, as a result of the horrors of the war, Soviet film regained some of the rights of which the socialist realism of the late thirties had stripped it: the right to depict death, the right to show suffering, misery, hunger, misfortune, and grief. Along with death, life returned to Soviet films. Naturally, the academism of the late thirties had become a hard canon, and primitive production conditions did not permit the use of realistic displays of advancing military might or impressive naval battles. Still, the pathos of these imperfect films (*His Name is Sukhe-Bator, Russian People, Georgi Saakadze, She Defends her Country, Days and Nights, Girl No. 217, The Unconquered, Rainbow,* etc.) rang true. Along with these films and following them, the best traditions of the past were resurrected. Eisenstein's *Ivan the Terrible* Part I, Zarkhi's and Heifitz's *Malakhov Hill,* and Ermler's *The Great Turning Point* seemed to indicate that once again anything was possible.

PART II: Hope and Reality

Ivan the Terrible, Part II

THE ZHDANOV YEARS:
The Soviet Union, 1945–1955

On the threshold of the postwar period, Soviet film-makers knew far more about the gap between the dream of a free socialist cinema and its reality than did their counterparts elsewhere in Eastern Europe who were preparing to duplicate their experience. But let us bear in mind the fact that during the war the Soviet Union and its leadership had survived the hardest of trials. Victory seemed to justify or at least push into the background the persecutions and tragedies of the past. For a moment it was almost as if they had been erased from memory, in the name of 20 million casualties of the war, the razed countryside and the red banner over the Reichstag.

But it was not long before those who had originated and carried out the policies of the prewar period once again began their attacks. The first warning sign appeared even before the end of the war: the criticism of Ilya Ehrenburg in April 1945, the condemnation of Zarkhi's and Heifitz's poetic *Malakhov Hill*, Stalin's speech of February 9, 1946, in which he spelled out the tough policy line that would be followed for years thereafter, and much more.

ZHDANOV

All of a sudden the thunderbolt struck—"Resolutions on the Journals *Zvezda* and *Leningrad*," dated August 14, 1946. On the heels of this attack on literary figures the main targets of which were poet Anna Akhmatova and writer Mikhail Zoshchenko, there came two weeks later a resolution "On the Repertoire of the Dramatic Theaters and Measures for Its Improvement." Film in turn was attacked on September 4, in a resolution of the Central Committee of the All-Russian Communist Party entitled, "On the Film *A Great Life*." The man responsible for the implementation of this resolution and the principal author of the accompanying government decrees was a member of the Politburo, the former Secretary of the Leningrad Committee of the Party, A. A. Zhdanov.

What was demanded of art in these resolutions and decrees was in essence no different from what was called for in the resolutions of the First Congress of Soviet Writers in 1934: adherence to ideology, fidelity to the Party, and proximity to the people. But at that time, in the name of the struggle against modernism and the avant-garde, it was still a matter of asserting first artistic methods, then tastes. After experiences with the purges, and the publication of Stalin's fundamental works *Short Course in the History of the All-Russian Communist Party* and *Questions of Leninism*—the party ideology had become so oversimplified, especially in the fields of art and culture, that the Zhdanov resolution showed little concern for esthetics or the relationship between art and reality. All that was asked of art was that it be a weapon of day-to-day political work. The language had also undergone a change. In 1934, Zhdanov still attempted to speak about literature in language similar to that of the ill and aging writer, Maxim Gorky. But now that an important part of the Soviet revolutionary intelligentsia and its art had perished in the dungeons of Lubyanka and the *taigas* in the north, now between 1946 and 1948, Zhdanov spoke in the language of the creator of the pantheon of shades, A. J. Vyshinsky. His speech abounds in adjectives that prosecutors spat out at the accused in the trials of the late thirties: "disseminators of the poison of zoological hostility toward the Soviet order . . . vulgar and base little soul . . . rascal . . . disgusting lecherous beasts . . . thoroughly rotten and putrid political physiognomy . . . publicly flogged mocker . . . reactionary literary slime . . . [Akhmatova] is a whore and a nun at the same time, blending sin with prayer."

The writer, the artist, was no longer just "an engineer of human souls." Now he was expected to be a soldier, disciplined in obeying orders, seeing to it that those under him obeyed him too. And not only that: it was assumed that he would unmask, disclose, and denounce—in short, that he would do the jobs required of a good citizen late in the thirties and in the last years of Stalin's rule.

And yet Stalin and those surrounding him were sorely mistaken when they saw the spontaneous cultural liberalization as a symptom of the weakening of the Soviet system. After years of purges, terrorism, and the apocalypse of war, Soviet intellectuals and artists once again began to speak out—an act expressing their faith that a victorious regime need no longer fear enemies within, and that it would now be willing to become a true government of the people. Those who organized persecutions of cultural figures, however, were thinking of something else: the need to quiet non-Russian national minorities and to strengthen the central military oligarchy that had definitively established itself during the war.

It was clear that the leaders were not joking. One simply had to remember the hundreds of thousands of Soviet prisoners of war who had disappeared—straight from Hitler's camps to Stalin's. Immediately after Zhdanov's attack on the publications and writers of Leningrad came another "Leningrad affair": almost the entire committee of the Leningrad party organization was arrested, along with thousands of leaders of political, economic, and cultural life in the Leningrad region. The repression widened to encompass those who represented the Communists of Leningrad in the central party agencies as well as those who belonged to the generation that had advanced from the ranks in 1936-1937. Led by the Vice-Chairman of the Council of Ministers of the USSR and member of the Politbureau, N. A. Vosnesensky, some were executed, after long periods of internment and imprisonment.

An atmosphere of terror and silence once again settled on the Soviet Union. But what was demanded of art?

A GREAT LIFE

The resolution on film gives some indication. Its main target was the film *A Great Life* (*Bolshaya zhizn*–1946), directed by Leonid Lukov (1909–1963). This was a sequel to a film of the same title that had received the Stalin Award in 1939, devoted to work and life in the Donets coal basin in the Ukraine in the thirties. In this sequel, Lukov depicted the destiny of his heroes during the reinstitution of production after the Germans had been chased out. In order to comprehend the resolution, we must bear in mind that this was the area where the fighting had been the bitterest, through which the front had passed several times—not to mention the partisan war, the nationalist raids, and the Ukrainian nationalist problem itself.

The resolution says in part:

The film *A Great Life* gives a false and distorted picture of Soviet people. The workers and engineers restoring the Donets Basin are portrayed as backward people of little education and culture and with very low moral standards. The heroes of the film spend a great deal of their time loafing, chattering idly, and drinking. The very best people, according to the film, turn out to be drunkards. The main characters are people who served in the German police. One character is represented who is obviously alien to the Soviet order, who has stayed in the Donets Basin with the Germans, and whose corruption and provocative activities remain unpunished. The film endows Soviet people with traits entirely alien to our society: Red Army men, wounded in the fight for the liberation of the mine, are left without any help on the field of battle, and a miner's wife exhibits a complete indifference and insensibility when passing by the wounded. The attitude toward young women workers arriving at the Donets Basin is callously contemptuous. They are housed in dirty, half-destroyed barracks and put under the supervision of an arrant bureaucrat and rascal. The mine administrators do not show the least concern for their welfare. Instead of repairing the damp, leaky quarters in which the new workers are housed, the managers, as if in mockery, send them entertainers with harmonicas and guitars . . .

Lukov's film was only a timid and not too successful attempt to follow up the realism of the twenties and the early thirties. An emasculated version of it was shown in a limited number of theaters late in 1958.

Why then, was it so disturbing? Why did it become the symbol of all sin? There is only one answer, and the documents of the Khrushchev period confirm it fully: during the war, Stalin had become completely accustomed to the reality of the Soviet Union being presented to him exclusively through film and official reports. Just as reports on battles and military operations transformed the war in his mind into an impassioned symphony, guided by the genius of a single leader, postwar reality was expected to be in keeping with his centralist ideas of reality. For many years to come, it became the task of artists—as well as of party bureaucrats—to guess at the "Supreme Spectator's" idea of reality, and to present that reality in their works. Most of them were successful—ultimately, even Lukov himself.

FINISHING OFF THE AVANT-GARDE

But why were Eisenstein and his *Ivan the Terrible,* Part II (Ivan Grozny, II–1946), Pudovkin and his *Admiral Nakhimov* (1946), and Kozintsev and

Trauberg and their *Plain People* (*Prostiye lyudi*-1945) damned along with Lukov and *A Great Life*? Although the sins of Kozintsev and Trauberg and their film are not specifically mentioned in the resolution—we can assume, from the edited version of *Plain People* released in 1956, that the subject here—the evacuation of industry from Leningrad during the war—was, as in *A Great Life,* simply treated too realistically. *Admiral Nakhimov* was summarily condemned in a single sentence for the crime of devoting more attention to "balls and dances" than to the victory of the Russians over the Turks in the battle at Sinope—a shortcoming that Pudovkin immediately remedied in his second version. But it seems that much more annoying was the depiction of class conflicts within the Russian navy, conflicts that did not fit into the postwar emphasis on national unity. Pudovkin, who had been on the rack several times since the early thirties, was ultimately broken by the criticism of *Admiral Nakhimov.*

Finally, "the author of *Ivan the Terrible II* displayed his ignorance of historical facts by portraying the progressive army of *oprichniki* as a band of degenerates similar to the American Ku Klux Klan, and Ivan the Terrible, a man of strong will and character, as a man of no will and little character, like Hamlet." The attack in this instance is the most comprehensible of all: doubts about the use of cruelty in the name of a historical goal, the portrait of an autocrat not as a man with "a will of iron" but chased by the Furies . . . At the first private showing Stalin uttered just one word of comment: "Smyt!" (Wash it off!)

At the time of the resolution's publication, Eisenstein was recovering from a heart attack. After some delay, when he found out what was going on, he tried to defend himself; but his self-criticism here differs sharply from the self-debasement after *Bezhin Meadow* was banned. He even insisted on an audience with Stalin.

None of his efforts, however, could save from destruction the rushes of Part III, shot simultaneously with Part II, of which four reels were already edited. After this major disappointment, Eisenstein could no longer summon enough strength for creative film work and died of another heart attack, alone in his apartment, on the night of February 10, 1948.

With Eisenstein's death a second aim was achieved, for along with all memories of the realism of the early thirties, all memories of the avant-garde were destroyed as well.

THE GREAT TURNING POINT AND THE VOW

Where were the models for new films? One possibility was Ermler's *The Great Turning Point* (*Veliky perelom*-1946). It had all the qualities desired by the Soviet spectator "whose increased cultural demands and whose taste and high standards with respect to artistic productions the state will foster," as he was described in the resolution. But this singular spectator, who determined success or failure, and decided in general whether other real spectators would ever have a chance to see the film, was in fact the party and state leadership, namely J. V. Stalin. *The Great Turning Point* showed the war of the generals, the war of the staffs, contact with the people being primarily represented by contact with chauffeurs and orderlies, and the war of the battlefronts, a massive war, beautiful and uplifting. Even the theme of the conflict was correct: the clash between generals of two generations, two schools, one of which was losing the war and the other winning it, thanks to the new methods, grasped with foresight by the great leader.

All this was shown within the framework of the Battle of Stalingrad—the great turning point. Ermler never avoided political propaganda, and hence also so-called urgent subject matter. But Ermler was and remained an artist. The characters of *The Great Turning Point* (script by Boris Chirskov) were real and the conflicts and background genuine. Under

The Great
Turning
Point

Ermler's direction, the acting was good and as a result the sentiments rang true. In short, the outlines had found life to fill them.

The Spectator was not dissatisfied, it is true, but all the same he wanted something else. Simultaneously with pronouncements of the resolutions on film, he found the new model: *The Vow* (*Klyatva*-1946), directed by the Georgian Mikhail Chiaureli. In many ways, Chiaureli was predestined for the role that he played. Actor, sculptor, film director, from the beginning of his work he tended to stylize reality into sharp, frequently grotesque forms (the influence of the traditions of Georgian theater) and to employ a monumentality that had already appeared in his earlier historical films, the best of which was *Arsen*. At the height of the prewar purges, he received the Stalin Award for the film *The Great Dawn* (*Velikoye zarevo*-1938), which was the first film in Soviet cinema that clearly placed Stalin in the forefront of the Revolution as Lenin's closest collaborator and successor. After the two-part historical epic *Georgi Saakadze* (1942-1943) came *The Vow*. In it Petrov, an old Bolshevik, and his wife, Varvara, travel to Moscow in 1924 to present Lenin with a letter from the farmers. Petrov is killed by kulaks on the way, and Varvara arrives too late: Lenin is dead. On Red Square, Stalin is taking the vow, the oath, before the dead leader, and Varvara presents him with the letter addressed to Lenin. The individual destinies of Varvara and her children are then blended with the fate of the land under Stalin's leadership until their reunion in the Kremlin after the victorious war.

The Vow

It was now no longer a matter of filling the outline with life, but rather of expressing the outline by means of a system of monumental pictures. In this sense Chiaureli was undoubtedly closer to the avant-garde of the twenties than to the realists. But in the new cinema, history was no longer an avalanche of events, tumbling along on the tail of the comet of ideas, but rather a precisely cataloged black-and-white sequence of moralistic tales—with every trace of life meticulously removed—told in a pictorial language as realistic as calendar illustrations, and with the figure of Stalin always at their center. Thus a style was born that fulfilled Zhdanov's requirements entirely, was precisely in keeping with the Spectator's taste, and so became the model for other film-makers.

THE YEAR 1946

In 1946, a total of 20 feature fiction films were made. Some of the most notable were the second to last film that Zarkhi and Heifitz made together, *In the Name of Life* (*Vo imya zhizni*), the story of a trio of young doctors whose lives take them on different paths after the war; the poetic biographical film *Glinka,* directed by Lev Arnshtam (b. 1905); the patriotic saga about the destruction of the cruiser *Varyag* (*Kreyser Varyag*) during the Russo-Japanese War in 1905, in which director Viktor Eysimont (b. 1904) took as his inspiration a song that was immensely popular in the tsar's navy (the song had been prohibited after the Revolution, but the ban was lifted during the war). Also, at the studio in Sverdlovsk, Alexander Medvedkin, one of the *poètes damnés* of Soviet film, finished *The Liberated Earth* (*Osvobozhdennaya zemlya*).

Of the films that originated at that time in the rebuilt or newly established national studios, several that are worthy of note include the charming fairy tale *Nasreddin* (*Pokhozhdenia Nusreddina*), made at the Tashkent studio by Nabi Ganiev (1904–1953) and *The Sons* (*Synoviya*), the first film to be made in the Latvian studio in Riga by the unjustifiably overlooked director Alexander Ivanov (b. 1898). Alexander Ptushko (b. 1900) completed another of his expansively staged fairy tales in a pompous, artificial style, combined with paper-mâché realism, *The Stone Flower* (*Kamennitsvetok*), and in the Stereokino studios, the first postwar three-dimensional film, *Robinson Crusoe*, was made by Alexander Andricvsky (b. 1899). And finally, the year 1946 was also the year that the film *In the Mountains of Yugoslavia* (*V gorakh Yugoslavii*) was made by director Avram Room (b. 1894), together with the Yugoslav director V. Afrić and the great cameraman E. Tisse. This film was shown in movie theaters in October 1946, but in 1947 it was withdrawn from circulation, and never reappeared. (Stalin's clash with Tito became public only in the summer of 1948.)

Two years after the war, the production of feature fiction films reached the prewar level and the prewar production level of raw film was surpassed. In addition, production of animated films was revived (7 were produced in 1946), and several experimental stereoscopic (three-dimensional) films were completed. In 1947, a total of 27 fiction films were produced, but the creative atmosphere that had existed during the war and had accompanied Soviet film into the postwar period had vanished. Nonetheless, the Spectator was still confronted with films that had originated before the resolution of 1946, and he was dissatisfied.

DOVZHENKO AND MICHURIN

The greatest victims of this dissatisfaction were no less a personage than Alexander Dovzhenko, and along with him, two first-rank directors, Sergei Yutkevitch and Sergei Gerasimov.

Dovzhenko had not made a fiction film since *Shchors*. Now, however, he had material that he considered ideal. It was his own play *Life in Blossom* (*Zhizn v tsvetu*), about the life and work of the Russian agro-biologist, Ivan Michurin. The film was to be a lyrical poem about life amid nature and about enchantment with its beauty. But just when work on the film began, Michurin's theories became the object of a political controversy. Biologist Trofim Lysenko, with Stalin's support, led an attack on Soviet genetics in the name of Michurin's theories. It culminated in 1948 and 1949 with the campaign against "cosmopolitanism." The story of Ivan Michurin—a simple man whose life revolved around his garden, his experimental fields, and his provincial town—had to be adapted to legend, pedagogic purpose,

Life in Blossom

and editorial clichés. Dovzhenko entered a new purgatory; the film that ended up on the screen in 1949 was only partly his work, and bore only traces of his genius. In his diaries, Dovzhenko himself wrote about it in April 1947:

"Life in Blossom had been dragging on for several years. I wrote it both as a short story and as a play. It was a hard road that I walked before I made a color film of the play. I literally pulled the film out of the barren ground, I suffered, exhausted by heart attacks and the insults of dull bureaucratism. Then, after superhuman efforts, when the film finally began to show signs of life, and excited even contemptuous snobs, I stumbled into a fantastic experience when it was judged by the Supreme Arts Council. Then the Minister ran around with it someplace, and they showed it to the Great Leader, supreme among mortals. And the Supreme One proscribed my work. . . . Now the film agency had me on the rack again. I spend days sitting at my desk. I have to throw away everything that I have written, turn against everything I was enthusiastic about, which is composed of many delicate elements, and create a hybrid—an old poem about his work and a new story about selection. And my heart bleeds. I often get up from my desk after a day's labor and look over what I have written, I see how mournfully little of it there is. And I am exhausted as if I had been dragging heavy rocks around all day long."

Dovzhenko lived almost 10 years after that, but he never made another film. Between heart attacks, he prepared scripts for other films—*Taras Bulba, Opening of the Antarctic, The Enchanted Desna*—but his heart stopped on November 25, 1956, the evening before shooting began on *Poem of the Sea* (*Poema o more*).

YOUNG GUARD—GERASIMOV AND THE OTHERS

Late in the thirties, Gerasimov was considered to be among the most talented directors. During the war, he was in charge of the Moscow studio for documentary film. His first postwar fiction film, *Young Guard* (*Molodaya gvardiya,* I and II–1948), based on the novel of that name by Alexander Fadeyev, was found lacking for two reasons. The first was due to the "mistakes" of the novel, which described the origins of anti-Nazi youth organizations in the Ukraine as spontaneous, without the Party playing

Young Guard

any role in it; and the second was that there was no traitor in the story. The errors were corrected both in the novel and in the film. (Later, after Stalin's death, the novel was returned to its original version; even the "traitor" was rehabilitated.) But the director had also committed other sins, most especially a realistic depiction of the retreat of Soviet troops from the Ukraine. This error was also corrected; Part I was reshot, and Part II set up in the spirit of Zhdanovian esthetics. Gerasimov learned his lesson and soon became the official socialist realist and the spokesman for Soviet cinema.

And finally Yutkevich, a member of the prewar avant-garde, who was one of the first to join the "prosaists." A cultured man, he was always fully aware of what was going on around him. In 1945, he made the musical comedy *Greetings, Moscow* (*Zdravstvuy Moskva*), and then immediately went to work on the film adaptation of the officially much-lauded play by Nikolai Pogodin, *Kremlin Chimes* (*Kremlevskiye kuranty*), which was about Lenin's plan for introducing electricity throughout Russia. But the film *Light Over Russia* (*Svet nad Rossiei*) was never publicly shown and is not to be found in any official filmography. (Its scenario was recently published in Moscow, but with no explanation of what happened to the film itself.) We are not certain just what led to its prohibition. Rumor had it that the Spectator, accustomed to seeing Boris Shchukin or Maxim Straukh in the role of Lenin, did not approve of Maxim Kolesnikov in the role. One thing is certain: in the late forties, Nikolai Pogodin rewrote the play to give Stalin an important part in it. Later on, he was to return it to its original form.

The attack on *Plain People* meant the end of the collaboration between Kozintsev and Trauberg. They each came out with a new film in 1947, but the spark was gone. In Lithuania, Trauberg wrote *Life in the Citadel* (*Zhizn v tsitadeli*), directed by H. Rappaport (b. 1908). A small-town drama about a family that was separated by the war, the occupation, and the conflict between fascism and communism, it was a film like innumerable others that were being shot in the newly occupied countries and regions of Eastern Europe at that time. Kozintsev fled into the past and made a biographical film about the nineteenth-century Russian surgeon, *Pirogov.*

The movie theaters were also showing the new comedy by Grigori Alexandrov called *Spring* (*Vesna*), which had been filmed in Prague with Lyubov Orlova in a double role. The critics were uneasy; Alexandrov was a respected director, Orlova still a very popular actress, but the film was rather heavy handed and lacked the spark and humor of their previous works—besides, it spoke in the voice of an entirely different epoch, the joyful mood characteristic of the end of the war, a mood that was beyond recall by then. The next two comedies, *The Train Goes East* (*Poezd idet na vostok*-1947), directed by Yuli Raizman (b. 1903), and *Tales of the Siberian Land* (*Skazaniye o zemlye sibirskoi*-1947), directed by Ivan Pyriev, were more in keeping with the requirements of the times, with respect to both their sentimental content and their picture-book esthetics.

ROMM AND DONSKOY

The optimism that characterized the immediate postwar period was soon replaced by the icy atmosphere of a new conflict, the cold war. The first film of the cold war was *The Russian Question* (*Russkiy vopros*-1947), in which Mikhail Romm transposed the agitprop stage piece by Konstantin Simonov into cinematic language. The hero was an American journalist who returns home from the Soviet Union and refuses to become a sounding board for an anti-Soviet campaign, a stand that ends with his social destruction.

The
Russian
Question

This was the first of a series of films of the so-called "publicistic genre." Its basic esthetics were that the verisimilitude of details is not important, nor is the probability of the plot or the credibility of the individual characters; all that matters are the truth of the idea and the interpretation of the fundamental tendencies of world development. The problem with "publicistic films," however, was that instead of being convincing, their pathos, their naïveté, and their obvious superficiality evoked doubts about the truth of everything they were trying to propagandize. As for Romm and Simonov, we find reliable indications—the better part of their oeuvres and their later participation in the struggle for de-Stalinization—that the film was not just a product of their opportunism. The atmosphere created by the Zhdanov campaign and cold-war propaganda was simply such that—as in the United States during McCarthyism—too many were ready to believe anything they were told.

A Village Schoolteacher (*Selskaya uchitelnitsa*-1947), directed by Mark Donskoy, remains the best film of the year. It is the simple story of a woman who comes to a rural village before the Revolution, loses her husband during the civil war, and devotes her life to the education of a generation for a new life.

1948: "ARTISTIC DOCUMENTARIES"

The year 1948 is, on the surface at least, the year of the real entrenchment of Soviet sovereignty in Eastern Europe, the full onset of the cold war despite all efforts to continue postwar cooperation. It was also the year of the Yugoslav rebellion against the dictates of Stalin, which provided the final impetus for the start of real "witch hunts." Enough time had elapsed since the Resolutions on Culture for their results to become apparent. That year, they were supplemented by another resolution, this one concerning V. Muradeli's opera *The Great Friendship*. The entire musical world, especially its leading figures, were the subjects of crushing critiques in the name of the principles of simplicity, comprehensibility, patriotism, etc. Control over script approval and film production was tightened, and the newly appointed Deputy Minister of Cinematography, the critic V. Shcherbina, declared that it was a mistake to sacrifice the quality of films for their quantity. As a result the number of films produced annually began to drop—hitting 17 in 1948.

Lukov went to work in children's film, and made *Red Scarf* (*Krasnii galstuk*). The Zharkhi and Heifitz team broke up, with Zarkhi turning out a contemporary film about a young woman editor of a small-town newspaper at harvest time, under the title *Precious Grains* (*Dragotsenniye zerna*). Alexander Stolper (b. 1907) came to the forefront with a film based on the best-seller by Boris Polevoi, *Story of a Real Man* (*Povest o nastoyashchem cheloveke*), which told the story of the pilot Maresyev, who returned to the battlefront after the amputation of both his legs.

The first of a series of so-called "artistic documentaries" on World War Two was then made in the Ukraine. Entitled *The Third Blow* (*Tretiy udar*), this film introduced another genre, born of a combination of reconstructions of wartime operations and acted portrayals of staff members, members of the high command, and selected characters from the people. Here, the Spectator was finally given a picture of the war the way he wanted it, and the way he believed it. *The Third Blow* is the first, and the best, of the series of artistic documentaries. Its director, Igor Savchenko (1906–1950) was one of the foremost Ukrainian directors, and in many ways a true successor to Dovzhenko.

AGAINST COSMOPOLITANISM

Just as *The Russian Question* had come on the scene a year before, another film appeared to illustrate the new political line and the subsequent campaign, *Court of Honor* (*Sud chesti*-1948), directed by Avram Room, based on a stage play of the same title by A. Stein. The subject is the rejection of the international nature of science and the condemnation of a young talented scientist who has written an article for an American publication (the play was based on an actual event). The film ends with a rejection of cosmopolitanism and of kowtowing to the West, a proclamation of the superiority of Soviet science, and an affirmation of the irreconcilable conflict between them.

The campaign against cosmopolitanism, bourgeois objectivism, and kowtowing to the West this time had clearly anti-Semitic overtones. Shcherbina led the attack against the group of "estheticizing cosmopolitans" in the film industry, starting with Leonid Trauberg, and going on to the scenarist Mikhail Bleiman (coauthor of the script for *The Great Citizen*), and other "homeless and nameless cosmopolitans of the cinema" and "base spokesmen of reactionary estheticism" who had conducted "an organized slander campaign. . . . They are the ones who have created the myth of a decline in the contemporary Soviet film and of its loss of poetic force." What had happened? We discover that the Zhdanov line and its consequences encountered opposition inside the film world. Credits (including those on older films) suddenly were conspicuously without the name of A. Kapler, the scenarist for Romm's films, *Lenin in 1918* and *Lenin in October;* Yutkevich and Kozintsev also found themselves in bad grace, as did Eisenstein.

The campaign against cosmopolitanism was followed by an attack on the founder of the Russian comparatist school in literary criticism, Alexander Vesclovsky, and by an attempt to force Russian literary historians and critics to prove that Russian literature had evolved practically uninfluenced by the literature of the rest of the world. Parallel to the campaign against film (which also concerned critics above all—Trauberg and Bleiman were attacked specifically for their critical and historiographical activity), a campaign was launched against cosmopolitanism in theatrical criticism and musicology. The beginnings were always the same: the crushing of any attempt to take a stand in opposition to the most extreme consequences of the Zhdanov line. And so were the results: the official indictment of people whose characteristic trait was, as Konstantin Simonov commented at that time, "the desire to undermine the roots of national pride, because people without roots are easier to defeat and sell into the slavery of American imperialism."

And who are the traitors? It was not for cultural figures to give the answer, this was up to Beria's police. On January 27, 1949, came the arrest (and later the execution) of the leading Soviet Jewish poet, Perets Markich, along with other Jewish cultural leaders. The Jewish Anti-Fascist Committee was dissolved, its leaders arrested, and, for the most part, liquidated. These included the director of the Moscow Jewish Theater, a great actor in his own right, S. M. Michoels.

WORLD WAR II: MEETING ON THE ELBE

In 1949, only 15 films were made.

Grigori Alexandrov's *Meeting on the Elbe* (*Vstrecha na Elbe*) was a publicistic film of the first rank. It begins with the great scene of the meeting of the American and the Soviet troops on the Elbe River in 1945, and then goes on, in rough outline, to show the Soviet view of the origins of the cold war. There is the divided city of Altenstadt, with Americans looting while the Soviet Army aids its section of the town in rebuilding itself; the Soviets support the antifascists while the American administration seeks the aid of notorious Nazis. The film is still in black and white, the photography by Eisenstein's cameraman, E. Tisse, is incredibly drab, and the direction—aside from the crowd scenes—clearly puts the dialogue above any cinematic values, ensuring that the principal players are immediately recognizable as good or bad.

Meeting on the Elbe

Ermler emerged once again with a timely topic. *Great Power (Velikaya sila)* was quick to present on the screen the events that became known as "the Lysenko affair." The setting of the conflict between a proponent of the ideas of Mendel and a follower of Michurin and Lysenko was a scientific institute headed by an indecisive director. One aspect of the film was new but soon became routine—the scientists in the institute and their party organization were not capable of resolving the matter by themselves. The solution was produced by a *deus ex machina,* a member of the Central Committee of the Communist Party.

THE FALL OF BERLIN

The zenith was reached with Chiaureli's *The Fall of Berlin (Padeniye Berlina)*, a two-part monumental "artistic documentary" in color that is actually a textbook summation of the history of the Soviet participation in World War Two. The hero of the film is a simple worker-soldier, striding victoriously through all the stages of a historical epoch, from the mobilization to the capture of the Reichstag. In addition to Stalin, leading roles were given to members of the Soviet command, as well as to Hitler, Goering, Goebbels, and their generals, and of course to Roosevelt and Churchill, all adapted to fit the images that the Soviet propaganda machine gave to them at that time. The acting and individual shots were stylized so that each image simplistically expressed the historical aspects of the moment, and by means of the general arrangement also expressed their ideological interpretation. Clearly, the film followed the worst aspect of Napoleonic painting, generously imitated at the court of the Russian tsars. But the Spectator was satisfied: history was shown on the screen exactly as he wanted to bequeath it to posterity.

The Fall
of Berlin

The Battle of Stalingrad (*Stalingradskaya bitva*), directed by Vladimir Petrov, with a script by another of the leading figures of Stalinist literature, Nikolai Virta, remained in the shadow of *The Fall of Berlin*. The creator of *Peter the Great* was simply unable to handle the new esthetics. The history of the Soviet artistic documentary ended with this film. The style, however, proved to be an important influence on film work in the years that followed.

BIOGRAPHIES AND OPERETTAS

Academician Ivan Pavlov (*Akademik Ivan Pavlov*-1949), directed by Grigori Roshal (b. 1899), and *Alexander Popov*, directed by Herbert Rappaport, who took over the material from Trauberg, were the first in the series of biographical films aimed at proving the superiority of Russian and Soviet science and art over that of the West. Under the influence of the pompous realism of the period, these films established their own type of didactic theater, overwhelming in the pomp of its sets, the splendor of its costumes, and the perfect demonstration of the Stanislavsky method of acting on the film screen. This style did not develop fully until the color biographical superfilms of subsequent years.

The Zhdanov eulogy of the joyful Soviet life came to a peak, after several attempts, in Ivan Pyriev's film, *The Cossacks of Kuban* (*Kubanskiye kazaki*-1948). This kolkhoz operetta filmed in color in the richest grain country of the Soviet Union, exemplifies the official taste of the period. The plot is familiar from dozens of other films: two collective farms, one better, one worse, competition; a man from the worse *kolkhoz* falls in love with the woman who is the head of the better one. The characters are reincarnations of the vaudeville and operetta personages presented in the nineteenth century by Russian provincial touring companies. The music (by Isaac

The Cossacks
of Kuban

Dunaevsky) is a montage of themes inspired by third-rate traditional operettas and folk music. The collective farmers' tables are bountifully laden; life is a beautiful promenade through a landscape of plenty where the "merely good" encounters the "even better." Half a decade later, Nikita Khrushchev was to point out in many of his speeches about the situation of Soviet agriculture, that in the late forties and early fifties, the Soviet farmer was literally starving, and faced the most elementary production problems.

On the other hand, Mark Donskoy was subjected to criticism for the film version of the much-lauded novel by T. Semushkin, *Alitet Leaves for the Hills* (*Alitet ukhodit v gory*-1949). The way in which he depicted the local kulaks and American fur merchants in post-Revolutionary Chukotka apparently did not sufficiently conform to the Spectator's notions about the enemies of the Revolution. And besides—it was simply a poorly made film.

THE STAR

The really exceptional film made during this period was immediately shelved and withheld from public viewing until the fall of 1953. Entitled *The Star* (*Zvezda*-1949), it was produced by Lenfilm and directed by Alexander Ivanov from a short story of the same title by E. Kazakevich. It is a tragic story of a group of army reconnaissance men who are surrounded by German troops but whose transmitter keeps on working for four days before it is finally silenced. This noteworthy work of wartime literature was to inspire a wave of written and filmic works 10 years later. It speaks in a whisper of the tragedy of a group of nameless heroes who overcame their individual destinies through a profound conviction about the meaning of their existence. It was in this tone, entirely out of keeping with everything that Soviet cinema was expected to be at the time, that Ivanov made the film version. Only the optimistic ending was tacked on.

FIVE FILMS A YEAR

The reconstruction of the Soviet Union continued: Some of the wounds of the war began to heal, the economy to consolidate. But film production dropped sharply: first to 10 feature fiction films annually, then to nine, and finally, in 1952, to five. In an editorial published as late as 1954 in *Literaturnaya Gazeta* (confirming that by then a decisive change was under way), the situation prevailing in the early fifties was described:

"The number of examinations through which a scenario must pass makes cinema work very difficult for writers . . . A scenario goes to an editor of the scenario department and to the editor-in-chief. Then the editorial board of the scenario department and afterwards the art council of the studio discuss it. The decision of the art council must be approved by the director of the studio. The studio is not entitled to sign a contract with the author, however, until the Main Administration of Cinematography gives its consent. And so at this point, the scenario is sent there.

Again it goes to an editor of the scenario department and to the editor-in-chief, and from them to the assistant chief [of the Main Administration]. Then straight to the chief himself, whose signature authorizes the studio to make its arrangements with the author. And finally, the court of last instance is [in 1954] the collegium of the Ministry of Culture of the USSR. A verdict is rendered at 10 levels and at each stage revisions are made and instructions given. . . ."

In 1950, Lukov was permitted to atone for the errors of *A Great Life* through the making of *The Donets Miners* (*Donetskiye shakhteri*). This was a film in color about the utopian lives of miners in the Donets coal basin, which had been renewed and rebuilt with the aid of modern technology. Not a thing in the film is truthful and Khrushchev again, shortly after, confirmed that fact officially. Leonid Lukov—who by then was a Stalin Prize laureate—was completely ruined as an artist. He made a few more films, all of which were mediocre. He died in 1963 of a heart attack at the age of 54—a way of death for many artists who shared his destiny.

The Donets
Miners

STALINIST REALISM

Two other directors with better reputations can be classified alongside Lukov. Yuli Raizman, author of *The Last Night,* made a super-production of the Zhdanov-line Stalinist novel *The Dream of a Cossack* (*Kavalier Zolotoy Zvezdy*-1950) by Semion Babayevsky: it tells the story of Sergei Tutarinov (played by Sergei Bondarchuk) who returns after the war wearing the gold star of a Hero of the Soviet Union on his uniform jacket. He becomes the head of a kolkhoz, and, with the support of the party organization, sets out to put into effect a plan for bringing together all the collective farms in the region and for constructing an electrical power plant. (In this respect it was an illustration of the then current party directives.) A comparison of this naïve piece of calendar art with Eisenstein's *General Line,* another dream of a future Soviet village, reveals to us the changes that had occurred in less than a quarter of a century. In the spirit of *The Donets Miners, The Dream of a Cossack* ends with a vision of complete electrification, including electrical tractors, forecast by party resolutions. But how to put them on the screen when reality was limping behind literature and art? What would the tractors look like? Thus the final scenes of the film follow the hero's misty gaze over the broad steppes, the tractors in his field of vision dragging behind them cables that are connected somewhere off-screen. We are supposed to find out where these cables end someday in the future—the day when life catches up with the reality of art.

Another work of this type is *Far From Moscow* (*Daleko ot Moskvi*-1950), directed by Alexander Stolper and based on another Zhdanov-line novel by Vasili Azhaev. The subject here is the difficult construction of an oil pipeline in the Far East, with all its attendant problems—the establishment of a large working collective, the development of competition, conflicts with saboteurs, and above all, of course, the inspiring leadership of the true Stalinist hero, Batmanov, the organizer of the construction project, whose life and work methods became compulsory study material for Communists and youth leaders from Vladivostok to Berlin. This story was also based on fact; Azhaev had really visited such a construction project at an unidentified location. The difference between fiction and fact was in keeping with the times: the oil pipeline was actually built by political prisoners from camps in the Far East, and the man who served as the model for the legendary Batmanov was V. A. Barabanov, the former commander of the notorious concentration camp at Vorkuta.

Mikhail Kalatozov (1903-1973) filmed another portrait of reality, but this time reality was not only that decreed by party resolutions, it was the reality of police-manufactured court protocols. His *Conspiracy of the Doomed* (*Zagovor obrechyonnikh*-1950), is a publicist film about an imperialist conspiracy within an unnamed Eastern European people's republic. In it, we find historical elements of the falsified conspiracies and trials of Romania, Hungary, Bulgaria, Poland, and Czechoslovakia, without even the slightest effort being made to establish credibility. The triumph of its genre, this film was so blatant that it encountered opposition even among governing circles in Eastern Europe.

In the latter half of 1948 Zhdanov disappeared from the scene. According to Khrushchev, he fell victim to alcohol, although others contend that Stalin feared the growth of his authority. Official reports indicate that Zhdanov died of a heart attack in 1949. Later on, his death inspired the final convulsion of Stalin's rule, the affair of the "assassins in white blouses." The head of the hospital in the Kremlin and several Soviet specialists, for the most part Jews, were arrested in 1952 and accused of assassinating

Zhdanov and conspiring against the lives of other Soviet leaders. After Stalin died in March of 1953, the accusations were rescinded, the accusers held responsible, and the accused rehabilitated.

BIOGRAPHICAL FILMS AND *THE UNFORGETTABLE YEAR*

The filming of biographies continued, and one by one, film theaters showed, among others, *Zhukovsky* (1950), Pudovkin's next to last—and truly bad—film about the pioneer airplane builder; *Mussorgsky* (1950), directed by G. Roshal; *Taras Shevchenko* (1951)—the director, I. Savchenko, died in the course of the shooting, and the film was completed by his assistants, Alexander Alov (b. 1928) and Vladimir Naumov (b. 1927); *Belinsky* (1951) directed by G. Kozintsev; *Przhevalsky* (1951) directed by S. Yutkevich; *Glinka* (*Kompozitor Glinka*-1952), in which director G. Alexandrov corrected L. Arnshtam's recent version of the composer's biography in the new spirit of the times; *Dzhambul* (1952), directed by Y. Dzigan; *Rimsky-Korsakov* (1952), directed by G. Roshal; *Dzerzhinsky* (*Vikhry vrazhdebnye*), directed by M. Kalatozov (this film was completed in 1953 but not distributed until 1956, with the figure of Stalin vanishing from the final version); and finally, *Admiral Ushakov, I and II,* directed by V. Petrov. The individuality of the creators—their personality, their handwriting—had all but disappeared, leaving only a bland uniformity of style. This series finally ended in 1953.

Taras Shevchenko   Rimsky-Korsakov

A number of films in the cold-war spirit were made during that period, among them *Secret Mission* (*Sekretnaya missiya*-1950), directed by Mikhail Romm, and *In Days of Peace* (*V mirnye dni*-1950), directed by Vladimir

The
Unforgettable
Year,
1919

Braun. The cold-war atmosphere even dominated children's films, filling them with instructions to be watchful.

Other films dealt with the life of collective farmers and socialist competition. Gerasimov returned from China and made *The Country Doctor* (*Selskiy vrach*–1951) with Tamara Makarova. He was criticized for this film, the accusation this time being a lack of conflict—times had changed. And finally, there was the last of the super-productions of Mikhail Chiaureli, *The Unforgettable Year, 1919* (*Nezabyvayemiy 1919 god*–1951), giving to Stalin sole credit for suppressing an anti-Bolshevik uprising in Leningrad and attempting to trace Stalin's military genius to his early years (as had already been done in *Defense of Tsaritsin,* 1942, by S. and G. Vasiliev).

The cinema of individual Soviet republics developed in a similar fashion. Immediately after the war—particularly in the Baltic region—the first films were made under Russian directors and for a time even with Russian actors. In the late forties and early fifties, however, regional production was carried out by regional artists. Nonetheless, scripts and finished films still had to be approved in Moscow, a practice that was discontinued after Stalin's death but reinstituted in the early seventies.

COLOR FILM

In 1951, the directive to convert production to color began to be carried out on a wide scale. Fulfilling this order was made considerably easier by the drop in annual production. It seems probable as well that the effort to make a required percentage of color films was also one of the reasons for the sudden drop in production. But color—limited by the poor quality of Sovcolor (Agfacolor)—was an important stylistic element in monumental calendar-art films, which avoided a halftone in any context, and were perfectly adaptable to the narrow range and simple color scale the material had to offer.

Starting in 1951, film records of theatrical productions began to be important in Soviet cinema. They were cheap to produce and there were no problems with the scripts. But this was not the only reason. The Spectator loved the theater, and considered himself a connoisseur. At his urging certain performances were kept in theater repertoires for decades, even with the cast unchanged, thereby blocking a new generation of actors from the stage. But as the Spectator fell victim increasingly to his dread of the public, he practically gave up going to the theater. In order not to deprive him of his favorite cultural experience, it was decided that selected performances must be recorded for posterity on 35mm film, allowing audiences outside Moscow, Leningrad, or Kiev to see them, as well as viewers outside the Soviet Union. Ultimately, the sole merit of these "faithfully filmed" performances was to record the art of some outstanding actors. In 1953, some 20 films of this sort were made.

EMBARRASSMENT

In 1952, the cultural situation relaxed somewhat. It is difficult to say what had the strongest influence here—the fact that the Soviet Union had its own atom bomb, the end of the Korean War, the apparent consolidation of the situation in Eastern Europe, the fact that there was no Zhdanov any longer, or just that as Stalin's health deteriorated he shifted his focus away from cultural affairs. The alarming economic situation was in direct conflict with the screen image of reality; both the quantity and quality of cultural creativity had been dropping dangerously.

No matter what the cause, the proposed solution in the film world was explicit: a new campaign, this time against schematism, and "a lack of conflict." At the Nineteenth Congress of the Soviet Communist Party, A. Mikoyan called for satire, for new Gogols, and Shchedrins. "But they should not scare us and they should be nicer to us," I. Ehrenburg commented ironically. A resolution was adopted calling for an increase in production of feature fiction films, which meant a twofold fundamental change: a gradual return to black-and-white films, and, above all, a slight opening of the door to younger film artists. It was not yet opened wide, but it had been tightly closed since the thirties.

No one knew what was going to happen. The past was dead, both figuratively and literally—Stalin died in March 1953—and the future was yet to be born. In spite of the slight increase in production (17 fiction films), the year 1953 was the least interesting year of postwar Soviet cinema. S. Yutkevich made a coproduction with Albania, a rather unfortunate attempt at a historical spectacle entitled, *The Great Warrior* (*Velikiy voin Albanii Skanderbeg*); Room made yet another cold-war horror film in

Lithuania, *Silver Powder* (*Serebristaya pyl*); more children's films were made; Chekov appeared again (*Nalim*), this time in a stereo-film by S. Ivanov; and all studios began producing short satires. The latter, however, did not surpass the safe and secure level of so-called "communal satire." In addition, a wide variety of story ideas (for example, the difficult service of a border guard, foreign attempts to sabotage a cooperative of horse breeders) was used to create something like a Soviet "western", particularly by Konstantin Yudin (1896-1957), the director of *Brave People* (*Smelye lyudi*) and *Flag in the Mountains* (*Zastava v gorakh*).

At that time, Vsevolod Pudovkin made his last film, *The Return of Vasili Bortnikov* (*Vozvrashchenie Vasilie Bortnikova*), an adaptation of Galina Nikolayeva's novel *The Harvest*. For a short time, the novel was considered a pioneering feat, the first to fulfill the directive to return real conflict to literature: a man who had been thought dead returns from the war to find his wife with another man. But the moralistic, shallow treatment, as well as the conventional framework, was made even more pronounced in the film version. Pudovkin, who had, in the last years of his life, become a mere decoration for peace assemblies and congresses, had identified completely with the style of the epoch. He died three months after the film opened, on June 30, 1953.

The Return
of Vassili
Bortnikov

COMRADE STALIN, EVEN IF YOU WERE GOD . . .

Dovzhenko was the only one of the giants of the twenties still living. At the end of 1952 he had completed the cold-war script entitled *Farewell, America* (*Proshchai, Amerika*), which was never filmed (like similar scripts of Bleiman and Ermler, Ehrenburg and Kozintsev, Katayev and Kalatozov, *et al.*). But Dovzhenko's desk also contained diaries that even by the sixties had only been partially published. In one of them is an entry dated July 27, 1945:

Comrade Stalin, even if you were God, I would not take your word that I am a nationalist who should be branded and dragged in the mud. When there is no hate as a matter of principle, and no scorn and no ill will for a single people in the world, not for any people's fate, or for its happiness, or for its achievement or prosperity, is love for my own people nationalism?

Or is it nationalism to be short-tempered with the stupidity of bureaucrats, with cold fault-finders, or to be incapable as an artist of restraining tears when people are suffering?

Why have you turned my life into torment? Why did you take joy away from me? Why did you trample my name?

Still I forgive you, for I am a part of the people. And therefore I am greater than you.

Since I myself can be very small, I forgive you your smallness and malice. You also are imperfect, even though people pray to you. God exists. But his name is chance.

THE END OF THE ZHDANOV LINE

Stalinism and Zhdanovism played several fundamental roles in Soviet culture and, particularly, in Soviet film: they destroyed the heritage of the old avant-garde, branding it un-Soviet and hostile; they made of the nineteenth century an esthetic norm and a standard of taste, simplifying its romantic view of the people, of folklore, and of traditions, its descriptive, narrative realism, and transforming them into a sort of vulgar pseudoromanticism and pseudorealism; they introduced practices whereby culture and art, particularly film, became an affair of the state. In so doing, they gave it an importance so heavy and overwhelming that frequently neither society nor the artist knew how to deal with it.

The end of Stalinism and the Zhdanov line did not resurrect the dead. Talent, enthusiasm, and creativity could not be infused into people who were tired and broken; but the new regime did return civil honor to the dead and to the living, and to the latter it gave more bearable living conditions. What could not be revived, however, was the feeling of liberty and freedom that had enabled Soviet art, at one time, to continue in the tradition of the prerevolutionary avant-garde and become the avant-garde of world art. After years of terrorism, cultural terrorism included, the aims were far more humble: if not the truth, then at least no lies; if not an advance with the artistic avant-garde of the world, then at least not a retreat to the ranks of the reactionaries of art; if not reality as it is, then at least not a reality painted pink; and if reality could not be changed, then at least an effort could be made to make it bearable for decent people.

We must also bear in mind that it was Stalin and not Zhdanov who was condemned in the Soviet Union. The postwar cultural resolutions were never officially revoked, though their victims more or less received satisfaction. And no one ever rescinded Zhdanov's declaration at the First Congress of Soviet Writers nor its canonization of socialist realism. Thus, in the years that followed, it was not the negation of socialist realism but rather its most flexible interpretation that became the order of the day.

Nevertheless, there was one fundamental change. At least at the outset, police rule over culture vanished, as did fear of Lubyanka and of the camps. Some of the method and the fear, though, was to return later on.

The goal of the Communist Party was to produce 150 feature fiction films annually. This aim was far from realized, but the loosening of ideological criteria, the studios' increased independence in approving scripts, and the nonexistence of the sole Spectator and the uncertainty as to who was now the Spectator—all led to an increase in production to 40 films in 1954.

THE NEW GENERATION

Eight film records of theatrical performances were still made that year. One of them, the concert revue, *Holiday Evening* (*V prazdnichnii vecher*), was directed by Yuri Ozerov (b. 1921). The credits of the Kiev studio's fairy tale, *Andriesh*, showed Armenian Sergei Paradzhanov (b. 1923), as co-director. Graduates of the VGIK (All-Union State Film Institute) Yakov Segel (b. 1923) and Vasili Ordynsky (b. 1923) made, as their graduation film project at the Gorky studio, the medium-length fiction film *Alarm* (*Perepolokh*), based on a story by Chekhov. Alexander Alov and Vladimir Naumov made their first feature film, *Restless Youth* (*Trevozhnaya molodost*), with Bleiman returning as scenarist, and Vladimir Basov (b. 1923) made his debut with *School of Courage* (*Shkola muzhestva*). In both cases, the subject matter was youth in the Revolution, based on noncontroversial, tried and tested, safe literary sources. And yet the first changes began to be apparent: rather than omniscient leaders in parade uniforms, there were nameless heroes: the Revolution was no longer the work of one or several geniuses, but rather the product of a romantic rebellion. Cameramen less frequently used the monumentalizing pose and abandoned a single camera viewpoint for each scene. Instead, they shot a scene from several angles, trying to capture the rhythm of the story, though they could not shed completely the limits of their training and education.

The greatest success of the year was achieved by two films based on short stories by Chekhov, *Anna Around the Neck* (*Anna na sheye*), directed by Isidor Annensky (b. 1906), and *Swedish Matchstick* (*Shvedskaya spichka*), directed by K. Yudin, and by the contemporary comedy directed by Mikhail Kalatozov entitled *True Friends* (*Verniye druzya*). It is almost incredible how fresh and new this last film seemed to be, with its tame satirical tale of the reeducation of an academician during a vacation trip down the Volga on a raft with his friends. Although the script for the film had been lying around the Ministry of Culture waiting for approval for two and a half years, production was not approved until 1954, after Stalin had died.

True Friends   The Big Family

Pathos and monumentality acquired a new countenance as well. Heifitz filmed his epic *The Big Family* (*Bolshaya semya*) in color and in a basically traditional manner, but once again there was an effort to put some life into the approved outline and to eulogize "simple folks."

"THE THAW"

What had slowly begun to find its way to the forefront of Soviet cinematography, as a result of both the change in the political atmosphere and the drastic increase in production, was of course part of a far broader movement. The publication of the first part of Ehrenburg's *The Thaw* in 1954 marked the appearance of a minor work that was to give its name to the entire period. Approved for performance after sharp debate, Shostakovich's Tenth Symphony restated the artist's right to communicate a tragic sense of existence. The repertoire of the theaters was opened to unproduced classics as well as to new productions and to more recent critical plays, such as those by Leonid Zorin and more sentimental variants by Viktor Rozov. The first rehabilitation of writers and artists who had been condemned in the resolutions of 1946–1948 then occurred. Anna Akhmatova took part in the Second Congress of Soviet Writers, convened—after a 20-year lapse—at the end of 1954. A report stated that in 1954, 231 million copies of works of literature had been printed. "And what did readers find in this avalanche of printed matter?" asked Ehrenburg in the discussion that followed. He answered his own question, "Communal apartments painted in gold, workshops in factories looking like laboratories, kolkhoz clubs resembling palatial mansions—a world of stage properties, of tinsel trinkets inhabited by primitives or model children made of wax. . . ."

All that was also true of film. "There is no branch of our complex art industry that is not in need of a complete overhauling. We have ahead of

Othello

us years of demolition, years of building, years of hard construction work,"
wrote Mikhail Romm in September 1954.

Everyone began shooting new films, except the ailing Dovzhenko. The
filming of stage performances continued (13 in 1955), ending with the first
orders for television in 1956. Another name, Eldar Ryazanov (b. 1927),
appeared among the directors of the filmed records of stage plays.

Following the sensational return to the Soviet stage of Mayakovsky's *The
Bath,* after an absence of 25 years, the filming of the stage program, *They
Knew Mayakovsky* (*Oni znali Mayakovskovo*), took place, a product of the
collaboration of such proscribed "modernists" as the painter A. Tishler,
and the composer R. Shchedrin.

Ermler's and Raizman's films, *An Unfinished Story* (*Neokonchannaya
povest*) and *Lesson of Life* (*Urok zhizni*), tried to introduce emotional
conflict into the traditional Soviet subject matter, and met with immense
popularity.

Classics were also put on film: Chekhov, Kuprin, Lermontov, and even
the first Shakespeare—Yutkevich's version of *Othello.* The number of films
for young people increased, and many contemporary films displayed real
conflicts and admitted the existence of crime—for example, Heifitz's *The
Rumyantsev Case* (*Delo Rumyantseva*). There were more first directorial
efforts as well: Samson Samsonov (b. 1921) directed *The Cricket* (*Popri-
gunya*) based on a Chekhov story; Stanislav Rostotski (b. 1922) made *The
Land and the People* (*Zemlya i lyudi*), and Yuri Ozerov *The Son* (*Syn*); both
shot in black and white. The resistance to color gradually came to express
the rejection of academicism.

Not all these directors making their first films at that time were young
men—only Alov and Naumov were under 30 when their films came out.
Thus, the motto "make room for youth" must be viewed in context, for
during the preceding two decades it was almost impossible for the younger

The
Rumyantsev
Case

generation to begin their own film-making careers. An exception was Moisei Schweitzer (b. 1920), who had made his debut in 1949 and later returned to Lenfilm, via documentaries, to make in 1955 his best film, *Strange Relatives* (*Chuzhaya rodnya*), an unusually realistic film in black and white about kolkhoz and family life that was based on a story by Vladimir Tendryakov, who was to become one of the most important writers of the following period.

Film studios in the non-Russian regions of the Soviet Union grew even busier, coming up with two successful action films, *Saltanat* (1955), directed by Vasili Pronin (b. 1905) and *The Defeat of the Emirate* (*Krusheniye emirata*), directed by Vladimir Basov (b. 1923). But the most revealing work was the medium-length film in black and white by two Georgian directors, Tengis Abuladze (b. 1924) and Revaz Chkheidze (b. 1926), *Magdana's Little Donkey* (*Lurdzha Magdany*). For the first time in years there was an authentic cinematic expression of a non-Russian national culture. From that time on cinema of the non-Russian nations remained a significant force in Soviet cinema.

Now the great unanswered question was: who would be the first to try to carry on the heritage of the Soviet film classics? Mark Donskoy with *Mother* (*Mat*–1956) and Alexei Masliukov (1904–1962) and Mechislava Mayevskaya (b. 1904) with *Pedagogic Poem* (*Pedagogicheskaya poema*)—this time based on A. S. Makarenko's novel of the same name—made unsuccessful remakes of classical works by Pudovkin and Ekk. It was evident that the color realism of Soviet film of the fifties could not compare to the poetic language of the black-and-white cinema of the founding fathers. The way back—which was to open the road for the way forward—led along other paths.

Magdana's Little Donkey

OUT OF RUINS—DEFA: German Democratic Republic, 1945–1956

On November 17, 1945, a meeting was held in an old Berlin hotel on a bombed-out plain, amid rubble, a few steps from the bunker where Adolf Hitler ended his life in April 1945, and where 16 years later the wall between East and West Berlin was built.* The hotel was the Hotel Adlon—once the most pretentious of hotels in Berlin, site of many meetings of imperial and fascist dignitaries—and the meeting was to decide about the founding of a film organization on Soviet-occupied German soil. The main spokesman, Hans Klering, originally an actor, had returned a month earlier after spending 14 years in the Soviet Union as a citizen. The 40 people attending included photographer Kurt Maetzig (b. 1911), directors Wolfgang Staudte (b. 1906), Georg C. Klaren (b. 1900), and Boleslaw Barlog, playwright Friedrich Wolf, and writer Hans Fallada—who together formed the six-member group that was the nucleus of what was to become DEFA (Deutsche Film Aktien-gesellschaft).

THE ANTIFASCIST DEMOCRATIC PERIOD

The Soviet administration gave the new company the largest German studios in Babelsberg, the property of the former Tobis firm in Johannistal, and the administration building of what used to be UFA (Universum Film Aktien-gesellschaft). At the presentation of the license, the Soviet advisor in matters of culture, Colonel Sergei Tulpanov, declared: "The DEFA Film Company is faced with great tasks. The greatest is the struggle for the democratic construction of Germany, the effort to educate the German people, above all young people, in the meaning of true democracy and humanism."

Thanks to this comparatively liberal directive, a number of interesting films, infused with the idea of antifascism, originated in the Soviet zone in the first years following the war. Colonel Tulpanov, like so many other representatives of Soviet power in eastern Germany, was said to belong to the advocates of the so-called Leningrad group, the more liberal segment of the Soviet cultural, technical, and economic intelligentsia that was scattered to the winds by Stalin in 1947.

Understandably, East German film production followed Soviet cultural policy from the very beginning, and, along with it, took advantage of the brief moments of relative freedom. DEFA was under the jurisdiction of the German Central Administration for Popular Education, but the Soviet administrators saw to it that there was dual control. All scripts and finished films had to be approved both by the Soviet military administration and by

---

*This account of the origins of DEFA is based on a report by Heinz Kersten (see Selected Bibliography).

76

Sovexportfilm, the Soviet distribution agency for the Soviet zone. In addition, the films were presented for final approval to a commission consisting of members of the Soviet military administration and members of SED (the Socialist Unity Party of Germany).

In the summer of 1947, after the liquidation of the Leningrad group and after the visit of the Soviet Minister for Cinematography, basic changes took place. DEFA became a Soviet stock company (SAG), and Major Rozanov, the new censor of the Soviet military administration, declared that he would "take care of the last remnants of the Leningrad group." Soviet director Ilya Trauberg (Leonid Trauberg's brother), at that time the artistic advisor to DEFA, was in favor of making socially critical films, and wanted to invite certain Western directors to come and work in the Soviet zone (he had negotiated, for example, with William Dieterle and Roberto Rossellini), but he died in 1948 at the age of 43.

At that time, the management of DEFA changed from month to month. In the spring of 1949, Klering was removed from his post as Personnel Chief. The only one of the founders of DEFA to remain in his post was Maetzig, who decided, after clashing with the management, to give up his intention of trying to make socially critical films, and in mid-1949 took over the direction of the propaganda film, *Council of the Gods* (*Rat der Götter*).

After systematic reorganization and the placement of "reliable people" in all responsible jobs, DEFA was once again placed in German hands. Roughly speaking, that was the end of what is called the "antifascist-democratic" period in East German cultural policy, and the beginning of a period of socialist realism, a cultural line that was imposed more rigorously on DEFA films than on films made in any other country in Eastern Europe.

BEGINNING AND END OF A TRADITION

And yet it seemed, after 1945, that East German culture would continue in the tradition of the pre-Hitler avant-garde, becoming a focal point for those German artists who for years had been striving for a change in the capitalist conditions for artistic activity. There were more than enough starting points for the new culture. Pre-Hitler film and theater presented fertile soil that did not go fallow even after 13 years of Nazi dictatorship. There was the rich heritage of the so-called "second blossoming" of 1929–1932, when many artists joined forces for a last-ditch struggle against the imminent dictatorship. At first it seemed that DEFA would at least partially continue in the line started in those years by the films *Mother Krausen's Journey to Happiness* (*Mutter Krausens Fahrt ins Glück*-1929), *Comradeship* (*Kameradschaft*-1931), and *Kuhle Wampe* (1932), and by people like G. W. Pabst, Slatan Dudow, Piel Jutzi. Above all, Jutzi's *Mother Krausen's Journey to Happiness* tried to capture the situation of the German proletariat through the aid of the stylistic techniques borrowed from the expressionistic graphic art of George Grosz and Heinrich Zille. The achievements of expressionism, based on pictorial objectivity, primarily Ruttmann's *Berlin,*

The Blum Case   Beaver Coat

Symphony of a Great City (*Berlin, Symphonie einer Grosstadt*-1927), were
to some extent followed through by Jutzi in his second film, *Berlin,
Alexanderplatz* (1931), a picture of the city before the Nazis took over.
In this case, one can hardly agree with György Lukács, who in 1955 referred
to the "new objectivity" as "apologetic," and felt that it "could have led to
fascism" (*Probleme des Realismus,* Berlin, 1955). On the contrary, it may
be concluded that a film like *People on Sunday* (*Menschen am Sonntag*),
made in 1928 by four young film enthusiasts (Robert Siodmak, Fred
Zinnemann, Billy Wilder, and Edgar Ullmer) was among the best to come
into being in Germany in the period immediately prior to the onset of
Nazism.

Only a few of the many directors who had left Germany in the thirties
returned, and none of them went to the East. For the most part (Max
Ophüls, Otto Preminger, Billy Wilder) they stayed abroad, or else (William
Dieterle, Frank Wisbar, Fritz Lang, Richard Oswald, Robert Siodmak)
they did not return until later, when the political and cultural lines in East
and West Germany were clearly drawn. And so DEFA recruited its first
directors from among people who had worked under the Nazis in German
studios, with greater and lesser compromises.

Two notable members of the pre-Hitler avant-garde who continued to
work in East Germany were Erich Engel (1891–1966) and Slatan Dudow
(1903–1963), both collaborators with Bertolt Brecht, both avid supporters
of the avant-garde ideals of the twenties and thirties, both men with unsatisfied ambitions, and finally, both totally disillusioned men who gradually
became resigned to the defeat of everything that they had fought for in their
youth. Engel, who had worked with Max Reinhardt, was more a man of
the theater than of film. In 1928, he had directed Brecht's *Threepenny
Opera* in Berlin, and after a number of film comedies and revues, tried to
take up where he left off when East Germany offered Brecht a theater and
Brecht invited Engel to join him as director. He first began working with
DEFA in 1948 when he filmed the story of a miscarriage of justice under
the Weimar Republic, *The Blum Case* (*Affäre Blum*), and a year later,
Beaver Coat (*Der Biberpelz*-1949), after a play by Gerhardt Hauptmann.

NOTE: All stills in this and following GDR chapters courtesy DEFA.

DUDOW

The Bulgarian director Slatan Dudow was among those who left Bulgaria after the murder of Stamboliiski. A student of the Dramatic Arts at Humboldt University in Berlin, full of admiration for the Soviet avant-garde theater, he worked on the crew of Lang's and Pabst's films. In 1930 Dudow had directed Brecht's play *Measures Taken* and Brecht's adaptation of Gorky's *Mother*, two major works of the German agitprop theater, the two Brecht plays that encountered the most conflicting interpretations. Although almost everyone involved in the production of *Measures Taken* was a Communist, the Communist Party of Germany was sharply critical of the play, foreshadowing words that 20 years later were to be spoken at the Fifth Plenary Session of the Central Committee of the SED by Politbureau member Fred Oelssner concerning *Mother*: "I ask you: is it truly realism? Are those typical figures in a typical environment? I won't speak of form. In my opinion it isn't theater at all. In this *Mother* of Brecht's, there are also scenes that are historically untrue, and politically damaging."

In the early fifties when Oelssner and the others selected Brecht as their target in the campaign to crush formalism and to silence a great tradition, Dudow was one of the most widely recognized directors working for DEFA. Other members of the former leftist avant-garde who represented the culture of East Germany at that time were Johannes R. Becher and Friedrich Wolf; Hans Eisler, who composed the music for many of Brecht's plays; and Gustav von Wagenheim (b. 1895), a director in the important "1931" theatrical group and the son of Eduard von Winterstein, an actor in Reinhardt's theater. They were all attracted to the Soviet zone by Brecht's theater, and a hope for the freedom to work; but in the fifties, none of them had the courage to stand up to totalitarian power for the second time. All the more emphatic is the ring of the words that Brecht addressed to one of the leaders of the German Democratic Republic in 1956, shortly before he died: "Write that I made you uncomfortable, and that I intend not to stop making you uncomfortable. After I die there will still be a lot of opportunities."

In 1929, Brecht—together with Ernst Ottwald—wrote the script for Dudow's *Kuhle Wampe*, which has since become a film classic. Backed by the communist movement, the authors elaborated on the story of a Berlin laborer's family that was forced to move from an apartment into an emergency colony called Kuhle Wampe, and succeeded in capturing the mood of the depression years.

Dudow tried to continue his work in 1933, when he still managed to make a satire on the German bourgeoisie entitled *Soap Bubbles* (*Seifenblasen*). A year later, he fled to Paris to avoid arrest. After the war broke out, he was interned, but he succeeded in escaping and he spent the rest of his wartime exile in Switzerland.

His way back led to East Berlin, to the very heart of the newly founded DEFA, where he remained among the leading figures until his death. He did not make his first film for DEFA until 1949—having been active until then as a literary adviser—a time when the era of postwar liberalism was fading and the year when the line followed by film production was changed by the birth of the German Democratic Republic (October 7, 1949). Dudow's *Our Daily Bread* (*Unser täglich Brot*-1949), with music by Eisler, is marked by Zhdanov's schematism, which allows the author's obvious talent to show through only in occasional flashes of a free approach to the so-called "Reconstruction" subject matter (the term "Reconstruction" used both literally and figuratively).

Our Daily Bread

In a certain sense, it might be said that *Our Daily Bread* picks up where *Kuhle Wampe* left off, and that Dudow undoubtedly meant the film that way. Once again we see the worker's family and its encounters with day-to-day problems. The young son, a black-marketeer, ends up committing suicide, while the older one helps build up his homeland. At the outset the father is suspicious of the socialist tendencies of the new era, but even he becomes convinced by the motto "it's not a matter of socialism, but of the reconstruction of our new Republic." This film, like all the others until then, still made no mention of any political aims, nor of any direct enemies—the niece, who loved American soldiers, was only a peripheral character.

STAUDTE

The best of the so-called "Trümmerfilme"—films from the rubble—was
DEFA's very first film, presented as the first German postwar fiction film
on October 15, 1946, in what was then the Admiralpalast. Wolfgang
Staudte's *Murderers Are Among Us* (*Die Mörder sind unter uns*) logically
followed the expressionism that was the last artistic style prior to the Nazi
takeover. The silhouette of a city in ruins symbolizes the mental state of
the hero, the play of light and shadow reflects his inner struggle, dialogues
frequently take place against a background of bombed-out houses with
broken windows; the entire film is infused with the irrevocable sensation

The Murderers Are Among Us

of a terrible catastrophe and perhaps also a terrible mistake. One of millions
of Germans returns to Berlin, and decides that he will administer justice
to a superior who was responsible for the execution of hostages. Staudte
takes a sharp stand against war criminals, many of whom hurried to blend
with postwar life, but he allows his hero to arrive at a philosophical form
of accusation—although he does not make him forget or forgive.

At the end of the war, Staudte had three fiction films to his credit, all
of them light social comedies. He did not get to work independently until
1941, at the age of 35, when representatives of the Tobis firm selected him
in a competition to find talented young directors and "forgave" him his

past as a member of the Volksbühne, the leftist Berlin theater, and his collaboration with Piscator. In 1945, he was one of the few film-makers who remained in bombed-out Berlin. His first job was to direct the dubbing for *Ivan the Terrible.* DEFA's management treated him as some sort of representative artist, allowing him to work more freely than the other directors; as a result the films that he made for DEFA in the first 10 years following the war are undoubtedly more important than the work he did in West German studios. At that time, there was still more room in the East than in the West for Staudte's aggressive antifascism and his hatred for the German bourgeoisie.

In 1947, Staudte returned to the West to finish the film he had started at the end of the war, *The Man Whose Name Was Stolen* (*Der Mann, dem man den Namen stahl*), a satire on bureaucratism and the petty bourgeoisie, a theme that was to remain nearest to his heart throughout his life, and that was also the subject of his second film in East Germany, *The Strange Adventures of Mr. Fridolin B.* (*Die seltsamen Abenteuer des Herrn Fridolin B.*-1948). In it, Staudte did a thorough job of combining his talent as a realistic raconteur, experienced in the pre-Nazi theater, with his continuing attraction to expressionist film techniques. In the character of Herr Fridolin, he created a dignified predecessor to his *The Kaiser's Lackey* (*Der Untertan*-1951).

The Strange Adventures of Mr. Fridolin B.

The Kaiser's Lackey

Rotation

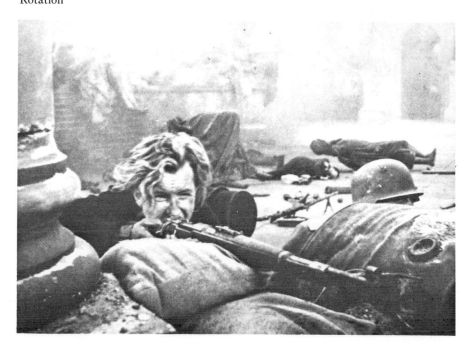

In *Rotation* (1948) he went even further, both as to form and to content. From the personal tale of an apolitical worker whose destiny was formed by politics, Staudte created a social fresco, a further indictment of the Nazi past of Staudte's homeland. Always striving to avoid abstraction, Staudte developed the hero's transformation into a resistance worker by intermingling subjective observation and objective reality. The subjective side culminates at the moment that the father is denounced, in the spirit of the times, by his own son, a member of the Hitlerjugend (Hitler Youth). The objective action peaks at the end of the film: the work of destruction done, the father and son meet, one returning from prison, the other from the battlefront. "I will never put on a uniform again," says the younger man. Later, these words were cut as being pacifistic.

KLAREN

Similarly to Staudte, the versatile director, Georg G. Klaren, saw an opportunity to further develop the language of film in the revived forms of expressionism. In a free adaptation of Büchner's *Wozzeck* (1947), he set the heightened social conflict and an antimilitaristic note as an antithesis to Büchner's existential tragedy. The formal qualities of Klaren's film prove without a doubt that the heritage of pre-Nazi film was by no means exhausted. Klaren, however, was one of the first to capitulate to the management of DEFA. Both his *Semmelweis—Savior of Mothers* (*Semmelweis—Retter der Mütter*-1949) and his *Sonnenbrucks* (1950) were merely illustrative elaborations of themes determined by the political line of the new republic.

Wozzeck

INTERFERENCE OF THE NEW STATE

Extensive records, statements, resolutions, and articles reflect on the history of East German film. Here, more frequently than elsewhere it seems, party functionaries and state dignitaries had a great deal to say about film; perhaps this was in part a substitute for their lack of opportunity to be heard on domestic and foreign policy, a lack that, for obvious reasons, was more evident here than in other Eastern European countries. Problems of cinema were treated with true German thoroughness in many newspapers and magazines. Long articles were written about every film, analyzing their social and political impact.

We should not be surprised that the old forces tried to influence new German film and to force it into a false line. The strong influence of the traditions of UFA were apparent in DEFA's films *Don't Dream, Annette* (*Träum nicht, Annette*-1948), or *The Girl Christine* (*Das Mädchen Christine*-1949), the tenor of which was false and deceptive. These obvious influences were joined by the erroneous standpoints of progressive artists falling prey to formalism or neglecting the story line. Such deviations came about because the necessary bond between film artists and the interests of the popular masses was not formed. In addition to these deviations, intentional efforts were undertaken to make films that had nothing to say to the present, and that crossed over to a platform of neutrality between East and West. An example of these efforts were the films *The Beaver Coat* and *The Marriage of Figaro* (*Figaros Hochzeit*-1949) . . . We also overcame these disruptive efforts. But in so doing, DEFA had to relinquish some of its collaborators (Sepp Schwab, *Auf neuen Wegen,* Deutscher Filmverlag, Ost-Berlin, 1951).

That is in brief the declaration of DEFA's chief, Sepp Schwab, who from 1938 to 1945 had worked as an editor in the German division of Moscow Radio, and after the war, until taking his new job in film, was deputy editor-in-chief of the SED's daily *Neues Deutschland.*

One of the first to leave for West Germany after Schwab assumed his position in 1949 was Arthur Maria Rabenalt, one of the most prolific directors of the Nazi era. Rabenalt was active after the war as superintendent of the East Berlin Metropol Theater and made several undemanding films for DEFA. They included the aforementioned *The Girl Christine,* an impressive success (four million tickets sold) in the movie houses of East Germany, which were flooded almost exclusively with Soviet films. Gerhard Lamprecht, a veteran of German film industry and a collector of old films (in 1965, his collection became the basis of the West Berlin film archives), also left East Germany in 1949. By 1945, Lamprecht had made 25 fiction films in Germany, and had directed one of DEFA's first films, *Somewhere in Berlin* (*Irgendwo in Berlin*-1946), about the destiny of children in the rubble of the former metropolis.

Another to leave was Erich Engel, who returned several years later at the age of 60 to make a crude propagandistic film about the French war in Vietnam, *Fledermaus Squadron* (*Geschwader Fledermaus*-1958).

Others left, too, including one of the founders of DEFA, Boleslaw Barlog, who had sat with Maetzig at the meeting in the Hotel Adlon, and who was caricatured six years later in the latter's *Story of a Young Couple* (*Roman einer Ehe*–1951) in the character of the West Berlin superintendent, Möbius.

As in all the countries of Eastern Europe, a so-called Arts Council was formed under DEFA that had to approve any proposed film before it could go into production. And, as in all the Eastern European countries, this pre-censorship resulted in a drastic reduction of film production. In 1949, DEFA produced 12 fiction films; for 1950, 1951, and 1952 the figure dropped to 10, 8, and 6 films per year.

In June of 1952, Party Secretary Walter Ulbricht spoke at the Second Congress of the SED: "DEFA should concentrate on the production of films telling of the struggle for the building of the foundations of socialism, it should devote greater attention to the questions of the villages, and make more films that show the significant figures of our history."

Later in the same month, the Politbureau of the Central Committee of the SED published a resolution "For the Development of a Progressive German Film Art," which said, in part: "The socialist consciousness of the working people must be developed, the people must be convinced of the need to defend the peace, to fight for a peace treaty, to increase vigilance with regard to agents, spies and saboteurs, of the need for the defense of our country and for hatred of the imperialist war mongers, militarists, and traitors to the homeland. . . ."

So political goals were now established that were fundamentally different from the line that Colonel Tulpanov had once set for DEFA. Simultaneously, the management of DEFA once again underwent a reorganization, and a State Committee for Cinematography was set up, patterned on the Soviet model, with a strong centralized authority. Even more changes took place early in 1954. The Committee was dissolved, and its chairman, Sepp Schwab, was replaced by Anton Ackermann at the head of the newly formed Main Film Administration. (Ackermann had been predestined, as a leading ideologist of the SED, for higher posts, but he was a victim of the purge after the workers' demonstrations in June 1953).

MAETZIG

Not long after the 1952 resolution, shooting was started on the two-part film about German labor leader Ernst Thälmann, which was to go on for three years: *Ernst Thälmann, Son of His Class* (*Ernst Thälmann, Sohn seiner Klasse*) and *Ernst Thälmann, Leader of His Class* (*Ernst Thälmann, Führer seiner Klasse*). The direction was entrusted to the most ambitious of all the East German film-makers, Kurt Maetzig, who had proven himself several times over both as to his unqualified fidelity to the immediate political line and to his film talent. Maetzig started his postwar career with one of the best German films of that era, *Matrimony in Shadows* (*Ehe im Schatten*–1947), inspired by the life of the well-known actor Joachim Gottschalk, who chose voluntary death at the side of his Jewish wife under

(Above) Ernst
Thälmann, Son of
His Class

(Right) Matrimony
in the Shadows

the Nazis. (Maetzig was the son of a mixed marriage himself.) His second
film, *Life in the Ticking* (*Die Buntkarierten*–1949), a saga of a family of
laborers from 1884 until the present, also met with considerable acclaim.
In this film, Maetzig again used broadly conceived episodes to tell the story
of a marriage in the shadow of poverty, unemployment, war, and suffering.
Toward the end of the film, the man, a social-democratic labor-union
leader, speaks to his granddaughter, the first member of the family to study
at the university, calling on her always to fight for peace and to respect the

achievements of the new German state. This schematic ending foreshadowed Maetzig's next film, *Council of the Gods* (script by Friedrich Wolf), which was intended to be a propaganda super-production of the type being made at that time in the Soviet Union by Mikhail Chiaureli. *The Council of the Gods* cost almost three million marks; the Soviet Union donated the necessary material from the Nuremberg trials and the director attempted to prove that the German IG-Farben concern collaborated throughout the war with the Americans and was helping them prepare another confrontation.

The Council of the Gods

Maetzig's *Story of a Young Couple* was another almost classical example of a propaganda film. Its heroes were an actor and an actress, separated by the line between West and East Berlin. The wife acts in the East, the husband in the West, the conflict between them arising at the point where the man accepts a role in Jean-Paul Sartre's play *Dirty Hands,* while the wife is performing in Konstantin Simonov's cold-war propaganda play *The Russian Question.* It seems that divorce is inevitable, but the husband finally comes to the conclusion that the truth lies only in the East, and he enters the courtroom with a symbol of peace—a paper dove—in his hand.

SLATAN DUDOW'S LATER FILMS

In 1950, Maetzig and Dudow led a group of young film-makers in shooting *Family Benthin (Familie Benthin)*, which was discussed in the East Berlin *Neue Filmwelt* magazine (No. 10, 1950) as follows:

The greatness of this film rests in its realization of the greatness of our life today, built on the foundation of the difficult past and finding firm soil in the GDR. But we also see the other side. We see people on the other side of artificially created frontiers, and we see forces whose interest lies in the destruction of West German youth by means of unemployment and the black market. There, it is not a matter of creating new, free people. There, people are processed for service as mercenaries in the war that the imperialists are preparing.

Women's Fate   Stronger than the Night

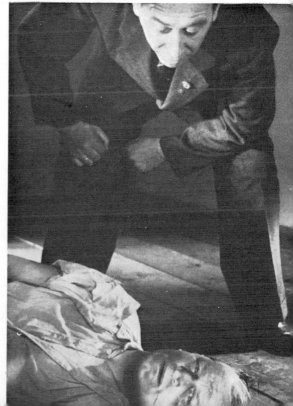

The theme of West Germany as the center of evil and destruction is also evident in Dudow's film *Women's Fate* (*Frauenschicksale*-1952). Once again, Dudow's experienced direction of this second DEFA film in color makes palatable the story of young girls who cross over to West Berlin and become the victims of its night life. Dudow did not neglect to stress human aspects of this otherwise not too inventive tale, so that this film was also rather an exception to the prevailing fathomless ocean of schematism.

Dudow's best postwar film is *Stronger than the Night* (*Stärker als die Nacht*-1954), in which the director escaped from the obligations of the present to the past, and in effective film language depicted the fate of a communist couple under Nazism. The husband is arrested in 1933, returns after seven years, organizes a resistance group, and ends up being executed. In this film, Dudow turned away from the usual clichés and fortified a straightforward story of a unique human destiny by means of strong images of ordinary human heroism.

HELLBERG AND THE COLD WAR

One of the pinnacles of the propaganda art of its time was Martin Hellberg's (b. 1905) clever film *The Condemned Village* (*Das verurteilte Dorf*-1951), with a script by Jeanne and Kurt Stern. Hellberg, originally an actor, worked with strong emotional effects, and did not miss a single opportunity to stress the cold-war line in this story of a West German village that opposes the construction of an American airfield. His characters are excellent bearers of the political ideas of the time. The hero, for example, is a simple

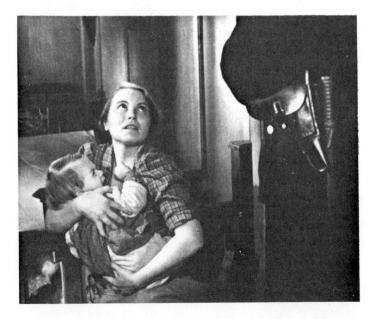

The
Condemned
Village

German soldier who returns from a Russian P.O.W. camp to tell of a better life in the East, organizes the opposition to the Americans, and is arrested; one of his antagonists is a German officer, who sings fascist songs and can't wait for the day that he is in uniform again. In spite of being faithful to the political line demanded of East German cinema at that time, Hellberg's direction manages to circumvent the complete artificiality typical of the corresponding variety of Soviet film.

For several years, Hellberg remained an adept depictor of theses and antitheses, as is evident in the film *The Solvay Dossier* (*Geheimakten Solvay*-1952), which was inspired by the trial of several directors of the West German Solvay-Werke. *Neues Deutschland* (January 27, 1953) called it a film that "at the right moment fortifies the vigilance of our working people and their revolutionary preparedness."

After the criticism of *The Girl Christine* and *Don't Dream Annette,* the production of nontendentious entertainment films came to a halt. The last film of this type was the fairy tale, *The Cold Heart* (*Das kalte Herz*-1950), DEFA's first color film, directed with considerable craftsmanship by film veteran Paul Verhoeven (b. 1901). In the next four years, the only films made were variations on themes determined by party resolutions. They were centered on a "positive hero" ("the good guy"), a member of the working class and a party member who worked to convince the "doubters" and to win them over to the fight against the "reactionaries." Representatives of other social strata, as well as non-party workers, could also be on the good side, but only in auxiliary roles. "Negative heroes" ("the bad guys") were depicted as former Nazis, spies, and saboteurs. DEFA became a massive "dream factory."

For the most part, these films did not approach the level of Maetzig's, Hellberg's, and Dudow's films. For that matter, directors did not even try for anything more than straightforward stories filmed in the simplest ways. For instance, in the film *By Mandate of Högler* (*Der Auftrag Höglers*-1949), Gustav von Wagenheim shows how the West German capitalists try to sabotage nationalized industries in East Germany; in *The Oceans Are Calling* (*Die Meere rufen*-1951), Eduard Kubat tells the story of a defector from East Germany who returns home after having foundered in the West; *Dangerous Load* (*Die gefährliche Fracht*-1953), also directed by von Wagenheim, is about West German harbor workers who succeed in their refusal to unload American weapons; *Shadows over Islands* (*Schatten über Inseln*-1952), directed by Otto Meyer, shows how capitalist merchants threaten the health of the people; *The Undefeatable* (*Die Unbesiegbaren*-1953), directed by Arthur Pohl, returns to the history of the German labor movement and brings two of its leaders, Karl Liebknecht and August Bebel, onto the screen.

THE DEPARTURE OF WOLFGANG STAUDTE

At that time, Staudte wrote a script based on Arnold Zweig's novel, *The Axe of Wandsbeck* (*Das Beil von Wandsbek*-1950), and Falk Harnack took over the direction. The story of the Hamburg butcher who became an executioner under the Nazis, and later committed suicide with his wife, was banned shortly after it opened. The film was accused of "objectivism," the reason being that it did not show the role of the working class in the struggle against Nazism. Another reason, though not stated as such, was the subject itself. It was not shown until 1962, on the occasion of the 75th anniversary of Zweig's birth.

The Axe of
Wandsbeck

Staudte was more fortunate in deciding to film Heinrich Mann's novel *The Kaiser's Lackey* (*Der Untertan*-1951). Although, according to *Neues Deutschland* (September 2, 1952), he did not show "the militant working class that at the turn of the century achieved great political successes," he did succeed in creating a sharp satire of the German bourgeoisie and the German sense of obedience, and in so doing made one of the best postwar German films. The director took Mann's precise style and transformed it into ironically stylized images, composed with an exceptional sensitivity for period detail and atmosphere. The result was an elliptical parable of a certain type of human mentality.

Staudte tried in vain to avoid the demands of the new line by looking to "accepted" literature. He made two other films for DEFA—the fairy tale *Little Mook* (*Die Geschichte vom kleinen Muck*-1953) and *Lighthouse*

Mother Courage

(*Leuchtfeuer*-1954), a story from the life of fishermen on the North Sea, but his conflicts with the administration continued to worsen. Finally, when he encountered difficulties in 1956 with the film version of Brecht's *Mother Courage* (which was never completed), Staudte crossed over to the West.

LOVE UNDER SOCIALISM

The drop in production early in the fifties evoked extensive debates in the press. Artists and journalists, along with party leaders, sought a way out of the blind alley. The unfortunate condition of production and attendance was explained, in part, by a lack of comedies and of films about love. In the end, *Neues Deutschland* summarized the long discussions, publishing a recipe for the production of socialist love stories:

Conflicts in love in a socialist society originate as a result of the fact that people's [political] awareness does not grow equally fast, that for example one partner lags behind the other. Those are conflicts of human development, whereas bourgeois love conflicts are conflicts of human degeneracy . . . What is typical of human relations in socialism is that they cannot be considered apart from an inner relationship to society. Personal and social happiness blend into one . . . It is impossible to make a film that is a pure love story if it is to be a realistic film, because love does not exist abstracted from social relationships. (June 5, 1953.)

In 1953, Martin Hellberg made a film according to this formula, *Little and Big Happiness* (*Das kleine und das grosse Glück*). Although Goethe Prize laureate Paul Wiens wrote the script, it took the director two years to carry out all the instructions of the Arts Council and receive permission to start shooting. The film shows the conflict between sweethearts—a youth brigade leader and a model worker—in their efforts to fulfill a production plan. The worker is somewhat careless, but the party group talks it over with him, and after he decides to give it his all, his girl forgives him. The plan is fulfilled ahead of the deadline. Not surprisingly, the film was a flop.

"NEW COURSE"

DEFA did better with light operettas and revues than with these "new" love films. The musical films began to appear in increasing numbers after Stalin's death when the "new course" was introduced.

The milder "new course" had its roots in the crushing of the first Eastern European workers revolt by Soviet tanks. The Soviet occupation army put a quick end to a widespread outburst of popular anger that originated in a peaceful demonstration of construction workers on the Stalin Avenue (Stalinallee) in Berlin on June 16, 1953. Responding to the slogan of the revolt, "We want to live like free men, not like slaves," Walter Ulbricht promised: "The Party will abandon its erroneous line and will move ahead along new paths." In the following weeks some of the leaders of the revolt were executed, the Soviet Union granted a large amount of economic aid, the Party proclaimed a "new course," and the German Democratic Republic never experienced the kind of prolonged political and ideological "thaw" that followed Stalin's death in other Eastern European countries.

DEFA was encountering competition not only from the revivals of old German films, but to an increasing degree from West German television. This problem was attacked by the production of films like *Whoever Loves His Wife* (*Wer seine Frau lieb hat*-1955), directed by Kurt Jung-Alsen (b. 1915), an adaptation of Strauss's *Fledermaus* called *Swelling Melodies* (*Rauschende Melodien*-1954), directed by E. W. Fiedler, and *Tsar and Carpenter* (*Zar und Zimmermann*-1956), directed by Hans Müller.

In 1955, annual production once again rose to 13 fiction films and the programming of movie theaters was changed. German films from the Nazi era were shown much more frequently (only one of them was shown in 1951, 12 in 1954, as well as West German films (two in 1951, 14 in 1954). In 1952, one British film was shown, one French film, and three Italian films; in 1955, three British films, nine French films, and 10 Italian films. At the same time, the number of Soviet premieres dropped from 23 in 1950 to 11 in 1955.

Within the past few days, the old German film *Annelie* was shown in Rostock. Other movie theaters in the city were showing the DEFA films, *Council of the Gods, Semmelweis, By Mandate of Högler, Bürgermeister Anna,* all of which played to catastrophically small audiences, in spite of the fact that they were welcomed by all progressive forces. On the other hand, in the case of *Annelie,* a special late-night performance was not enough. . . . (*Neue Filmwelt,* October 1950).

There are innumerable quotations of this type, with statistics, from East Germany and the countries of Eastern Europe. They simply testify to a fact that has been repeated so often in the past: in the period of socialist realism, the education of the film audience, as called for by party resolutions, failed utterly, creating, in reaction, a disproportionate need for escape, and finally, trashy entertainment.

FROM NEW REALISM TO FAIRY TALES: Czechoslovakia, 1945–1955

Before the end of the war, proposals for the nationalization of Czechoslovak cinema prepared by Czech film-makers during the Nazi occupation were sent to London and Moscow on microfilm. The final wording of the nationalization decree, issued in Prague on August 11, 1945, was not entirely in keeping with the original, looser, conception, but film is clearly referred to in the document as "cultural activity." And when Czechoslovakia's president, Eduard Beneš, declared, "If there is anything in our country ripe for nationalization, it is film!" he was simply giving voice to the old central European conviction that financing the development of culture is the task of the state.

After the war, Czechoslovakia had a special position in this part of the world. A country with a liberal tradition, it had a well-developed industry that for the most part had not suffered the ravages of the war; the West had a bad conscience with respect to Czechoslovakia because of Munich, and the Soviet Union justifiably saw it as a country in which it was popular; the two groups of war-time political representatives, those in London and those in Moscow, had come to an agreement during the war, and thereby avoided the fratricide that took place, for example, in Poland; cultural life began to develop with the same intensity as did the revival of the economy.

For reasons similar to those that had at one time held true in the Soviet Union, film represented the most homogeneous and the most committed segment of the cultural sphere. The man who became the head of the film section at the Ministry of Information was Vítězslav Nezval, the surrealistic poet. Directors and writers had their say wherever it was a matter of artistic creation; fulfillment of the dream of the late thirties seemed within reach. The Prague studios (where Russians, Poles, and others soon came to shoot their films) were the scene of the completion of two feature films started before the end of 1945: *Rosina the Foundling* (*Rozina sebranec*) a seventeenth-century historical film directed by Otakar Vávra, and the first film that Václav Krška directed independently, *Magic of the River* (*Řeka čaruje*). In 1946, 10 feature films were completed, and 18 were produced in each of the two years that followed. For the most part they were done hastily, carried more by enthusiasm, good will, and practiced hands than by anything else. They were also wartime stories, stories from the Nazi occupation (the best was *Men Without Wings, Muži bez křídel*–1946, directed by František Čáp) or films that had originated during the war (for example, another historical film of Vávra's, *The Mischievous Bachelor, Nezbedný bakalář*–1946).

One of the things that survived from the prewar period was the ability—fortified during the war—to transpose good literature to the screen (e.g., Vávra); another thing that survived was the poetic lyricism of Čáp and Krška. Continuing this dual tradition, Vávra filmed the lyrical story of adolescence, *Presentiment* (*Předtucha*-1947), and Krška made a film of the poetically stylized biography of a Czech violinist (Paganini's contemporary, Josef Slavík) entitled *The Violin and the Dream* (*Housle a sen*-1947). But new impulses began to become evident. The strongest of them, the influence of the British new realism, was already apparent among young film artists. To begin with, these new film-makers strove to remove the theatricality from film language. A major contribution to this effort was made by Bořivoj Zeman (b. 1912) in *Dead Among the Living* (*Mrtvý mezi živými*-1946), a psychological study about fear and courage that was based on a script by Elmar Klos, who also codirected. Jiří Krejčík (b. 1918) was another film-maker who believed in documentarist approach. But he made his debut with an adaptation of some short stories by the nineteenth-century classic Czech writer, Jan Neruda, *Week in a Quiet House* (*Týden v tichém domě*-1947).

It was Jiří Weiss's first feature film, *Stolen Frontier* (*Uloupená hranice*-1947), that made the first real splash. Weiss had made two medium-length fiction films during the war in London for the British Crown Film Unit (*John Smith Wakes Up* and *Before the Rate*), but it was the Munich-inspired *Stolen Frontier,* which told the story of the inhabitants of a Czech frontier

Men Without Wings

(Above) Stolen Frontier

(Left) The Strike

village at that crucial period, which confirmed the emergence of a mature artist with an original style.

A second event was the film *The Strike* (*Siréna*-1946), directed by Karel Steklý (b. 1903), which received the first and only Golden Lion of St. Marc (at the Venice Film Festival) to be awarded to a Czech film. Even before the end of the war, Steklý, who for long years had been a scriptwriter, had finished a film adaptation of the popular novel by Marie Majerová that was to be the basis for *Strike*, a film set carly in the century in a mining area near Prague. After his initial film, the mediocre *Turning Point* (*Přelom*-1946), he brought together a number of prewar avant-garde stage and screen artists—among whom were E. F. Burian, whose music for the film also won an award at Venice, cameraman Jaroslav Tuzar, and others—to create *Strike*, a film that joined social pathos with avant-garde poetics and period color. Steklý never made a good film after that. The success of *Strike*, however, reminded Europe that there was such a thing as Czechoslovak cinema and fortified its self-confidence at a time when the period of postwar advancement was just beginning.

The third important event was Jiří Trnka's (1912-1970) first feature-length puppet film, *The Czech Year* (*Špalíček*-1947), confirming the fact that when public funds and the free development of talent meet, they can bring success to public film-making in a small country where no immediate return on the production investment can be expected. The fact that it was folk art that inspired *The Czech Year* was no coincidence—it was simply the end result of Trnka's development of one of the creative notions of the Czech prewar avant-garde, primarily represented by E. F. Burian, and also by Josef Trojan, who thereafter was Trnka's indispensable collaborator in the sphere of music.

Slovakia, which did not produce any independent feature fiction films before 1945, began to do so under the new nationalized cinema, although for a while with such Czech directors as Frič and Cikán. The first Slovak director to make a feature film was the star of the prewar *Jánošík*, the actor Palo Bielik (b. 1910), who shot *Fox Holes* (*Vlčie diery*) in 1948. (The interior scenes were shot in Prague, as the construction of the first studio at Koliba in the Slovak capital of Bratislava was not completed until 1950.)

Work at the former Baťa Studios—now the Gottwaldov Studio at Kudlov—resumed, not only with the production of documentaries and popular science films, but also with activity at the animated film studio by Hermína Týrlová and Karel Zeman.

In 1947, the first Czechoslovak film in color was made, Vladimír Borský's (1902-1962) *Jan Roháč of Dubá* (*Jan Roháč z Dubé*).

During this period, the political future of Czechoslovakia was uncertain. Czechoslovakia—along with Yugoslavia—was the only country where the Communist Party was a great political force (38 percent in the 1946 elections). Czechoslovakia also was the only country in this part of Europe with a highly developed industrial base and a democratic tradition. All this led to the idea that the advance toward socialistic development would take its own path, in cooperation of course with the Soviet Union, but without any direct interference, and without any obligation to copy the Soviet model. These ideas also survived for a short time in the leadership of the Czechoslovak Communist Party, even after the Communists took power in 1948 and forced the abdication of President Eduard Beneš.

In 1948, Vávra made a film that was for years to remain his best. After filming a parable about the danger of atomic warfare (*Krakatit*-1947), based on the prewar novel by Karel Čapek, Vávra filmed *Silent Barricade* (*Němá barikáda*-1948), which was set during the few days of the Prague uprising against the Nazis in early May 1945. For the first time Vávra

Silent Barricade

Conscience

toppled the barrier that literature had built in front of his camera and indicated that he could become a spokesman for reality, observed in all its immediacy. Also in 1948, Krejčík made his third—and very mature—film, *Conscience* (*Svědomí*). The coauthor of the script was Vladimír Valenta, who was to spend years in prison, and who would not return to film as an actor and scenarist until the sixties. Psychological realism based on the restraint of the actors' expression—that was the style that Krejčík developed in the story that was almost identical to that of the later Spanish film, J. A. Bardem's *Death of a Cyclist*. And he encountered as sharp a reaction from the establishment as did Bardem.

Martin Frič also seemed to be catching his second breath, and after *Tales from Čapek* (*Čapkovy povídky*-1947) and the interesting *Lost in Prague* (*Návrat domů*-1948), filmed from a script by Leopold Lahola, about a soldier's bitter return to his homeland, he created a successful parody of a commercial tear jerker, *The Poacher's Ward* (*Pytlákova schovanka*-1948).

THE CHANGE AFTER 1948

Illusions about "the Czechoslovak path to socialism" only lasted a few months after the February 1948 takeover, or more exactly, until the split between Yugoslavia and the Soviet Union in June of that year. During the years that followed, the Soviet Union desperately tried to impose the experience of Stalin's Russia onto an industrial, liberal, central European country. Attempts had been made even earlier to apply the Zhdanov resolutions and laws to Czech and Slovak culture. As long as there was comparatively broad freedom of speech and expression, however, the absurdity of such efforts was apparent even to those who were faced with the task of fulfilling Moscow's demands. Czech culture on the one hand followed its traditional strong socialistic inclinations, and on the other hand continued to nourish a strong individualistic avant-garde movement. But when in the latter half of 1948, the position and prestige of the Communist Party was ensured by force, freedom of expression was gradually liquidated, and an atmosphere of fear and suspicion became dominant, there was nothing to prevent Czech and Slovak culture from being measured by Zhdanov's yardstick.

Three leading representatives of the avant-garde responded to the attack on their movement and its heritage with suicide: poet Konstantin Biebl, choreographer Saša Machov, and theatrical director Jiří Frejka. Also, many talented people fled abroad, including a sole film-maker—František Čáp, who started his second successful career in Yugoslavia.

The first targets of the Zhdanov-line criticism were the best films of 1948: *Conscience* (the very title called attention to undesirable problems), the "neorealism" of *The Silent Barricade,* and the "intellectualism" of *The Poacher's Ward.* And of course the poetic melancholy lyricism of Trnka's new puppet film, *The Emperor's Nightingale* (*Císařův slavík*-1948). What followed was a swarm of schematic films. One of them, however, remains surprisingly fresh. It is *Katka* (1949), a story that encourages young girls in Slovak rural areas to leave the farms and go into industry. After it met with official rejection in Slovakia, its director, the young and avid Communist, Ján Kadár (b. 1918), went to Prague, where he was offered a helping hand by Klos.

Weiss was criticized for *The Last Shot* (*Poslední výstřel*-1950), which showed the end of the war in a large steel mill. Singled out for criticism were the film's lack of pathos and the fact that Weiss had given the leading roles to nonprofessional actors, following in the footsteps of British and Italian film-makers. At that time, and to a large extent still today, socialist realism required, among other things, theatrical acting and professional actors.

Even the most notable member of the prewar theatrical avant-garde, one who really believed in the "truth" of Stalinism—E. F. Burian—was unsuccessful. His second film, *We Want to Live* (*Chceme žít*-1950), about the unemployed before World War Two, was cut by 30 per cent in length because it was guilty of "formalism and naturalism."

The
Distant
Journey

In 1950, though, two other films were produced that had pioneering significance. The first was *The Distant Journey* (*Daleká cesta*), the work of Burian's pupil, stage director Alfred Radok (1914-1976). Radok took a dime-a-dozen story of a pleasant lad who, under the Nazi occupation, risks his life for his Jewish sweetheart, and made of it an expressionistic tale of the Terezin ghetto and the struggle for human dignity, a visionary film frequently inspired by surrealist poetics. Labeled as existentialistic, the film was banned for years. Only occasionally did it turn up in one small-town movie theater or another; but it was sold to distributors abroad, where it gained for its director a reputation as one of the great Czech postwar film talents. In 1953, Radok succeeded, under difficult conditions, in making the first Czechoslovak musical, *The Magic Hat* (*Divotvorný klobouk*), based on a classical comedy by V. K. Klicpera. But the genre and the method used were so unusual that Radok was proscribed in the film industry, to return only one more time with *Old Man Motorcar* (*Dědeček automobil*-1956)—a clever art-nouveau film about the beginnings of the automobile.

The Magic Hat

Another important debut of an entirely different sort was the feature-length graduation project by two students of the Film Academy (FAMU—Filmová fakulta Akademie múzických umění), Vojtěch Jasný (b. 1925) and Karel Kachyňa (b. 1924), *The Clouds Will Roll Away* (*Není stále zamračeno*-1950). Spending long months at a farm in the border region resettled by Czechs after the so-called Sudeten Germans were expelled to Germany following the war, they captured, in a semidocumentary manner, the struggle of man against the difficult conditions there and particularly his struggle within himself. The film was not only an expression of a unique talent, but also a confirmation of the unity of postwar artistic impulses and their esthetic solutions in different parts of Europe. But that was all that was needed to move the authorities to bury in the archives this evidence of the possibilities of a nationalized cinematography.and its film school (FAMU was established by decree on October 25, 1945). The two young directors were banished to the limbo of making propagandistic documentaries for several years.

The inconsistency of the establishment (as proven, for example, by the fate of *Distant Journey*), as well as the differences in traditions and in interpretations of dogma, led to varying applications of Zhdanovism in each of the Eastern European countries. Thus, in the 1950–1951 period, director Miroslav Hubáček (b. 1921) made his debut with a good detective film *In the Penalty Zone* (*V trestném území*). Martin Frič made a two-part intellectual comedy about the limitations of unlimited power, *The Emperor's Baker* and *The Baker's Emperor* (*Císařův pekař* and *Pekařův císař*), in the spirit of Prague's Liberated Theater of the thirties, with one of this theater's founders, Jan Werich, in the title role. Something like that would have been unthinkable in the Soviet Union, as would Weiss's film about the beginnings of the labor movement, *New Warriors Shall Arise* (*Vstanou noví bojovníci*). This picture, one of Weiss's best films, was based on the autobiographical novel by Czechoslovak president, Antonín Zápotocký, with emphasis in the film's key scene on democracy and the right to vote.

The
Emperor's
Baker

New
Warriors
Shall
Arise

The Soviet model was used in making biographical films about artists, scientists, and inventors from the period of the nineteenth-century Czech "national rebirth." The director of many of them was Václav Krška, but the best was made, again, by Martin Frič—*The Mystery of Blood* (*Tajemství krve*-1953).

The April 1950 resolution on cinema issued by the Central Committee of the Czechoslovak Communist Party attempted to combine the criteria spelled out in the original Soviet resolutions of 1946–1948 with the criticisms against schematism and lack of conflict formulated in later resolutions and policy statements. One result, of course, was not at all surprising: fewer films, but all of them heavy-handed. In 1951, only 8 films were made, as compared to 24 in 1950.

Soon a wave of arrests and trials, first of non-Communists and later of Communists hit Czechoslovakia. In November 1952, 11 death sentences were handed down in a trial in Prague in which the main defendant was the secretary general of the Communist Party of Czechoslovakia, Rudolf Slánský. Most of the defendants and the condemned were Jews. At the same time, the campaign against "cosmopolitanism" reached its peak and Czechoslovak film settled on its own Stalinist style, "national in form, socialist in content."

The first to capture the style of the times was Otakar Vávra. After *The Silent Barricade* he did not make any films for four years; at the end of this period, which was filled with struggles with others and with himself, came the color super-production *Lining Up* (*Nástup*-1953), about the Communists' battle with reactionaries between 1945 and 1948 in the Czech border area. The film was not only a political illustration of the party interpretation of recent history, but also a formally faithful imitation of the Soviet style for color films of those years. The same is true of Vávra's subsequent work, the Hussite trilogy, *John Huss* (*Jan Hus*-1955), *Jan Žižka* (1956) and *Against All* (*Proti všem*-1957), based on the Czech classic by Alois Jirásek about the struggle of adherents to the Czech Reformation in the fifteenth century against the Pope and the Emperor. Only the first part of this trilogy bears traces of Vávra's own style. By means of these films, Otakar Vávra succeeded in securing his position in Czechoslovak film, but he lost his artistic authority.

John Huss

Tomorrow There Will Be Dancing Everywhere

As is often the case in such situations, the ones to take advantage of the new trend were people of lesser talent, including Karel Steklý, who, in 1956, made the worst version to date of Hašek's *Good Soldier Schweik* (*Dobrý voják Švejk*), K. M. Walló (b. 1914), and Vladimír Vlček (b. 1919). The latter had graduated from the Soviet Film Academy shortly after the war, and, along with V. Belyayev, was codirector of one film in a series of "documentaries" about the Eastern European countries, *New Czechoslovakia* (*Nové Československo*). He made his independent debut in 1952 with *Tomorrow There Will Be Dancing Everywhere* (*Zítra se bude tančit všude*), a color film about "joyous" youth made in operetta style. Then, entirely in the spirit of Chiaureli, he filmed another autobiographical book by Zápotocký, *Red Glow Over Kladno* (*Rudá záře nad Kladnem*-1956), a film that surpassed even Vávra's *Lining Up*. After two unsuccessful adaptations of modern Czech classics, Vlček made the first Czechoslovak coproduction with France, an undistinguished film entitled *In the Currents* (*V Proudech— Liberté surveillée*-1957). Soon thereafter he became the first Czech director to emigrate to the West.

ANIMATED FILM

Might it be said, then, that no sooner had nationalization opened new possibilities for Czechoslovak film-making, than it turned around and eliminated them by establishing strong central control and stifling artistic guidelines? Yes and no. In these years, for example, great development took place in animated film, with both Jiří Trnka and Karel Zeman turning out a large portion of their life's work.

Nationalization established excellent material conditions for the successful development of animated film in the period before television, by ridding it above all of worries about profit and the market. The creators of animated films, working in well-equipped studios, felt no need to pursue lucrative contracts or commercial advertising film orders, nor to run a successful style into the ground to satisfy a passing spectator interest. On the contrary, the doors to the studios were open to the largest possible number of artists, to a multiplicity of styles, and to experimentation with new animated techniques. This was the contribution of the Prague "Bratři v triku" Studio and the animated film studio in Gottwaldov, where Hermína Týrlová created delightful puppet films for children.

TRNKA AND ZEMAN

Jiří Trnka began as a painter, a Czech heir to Odilon Redon. In the sixties, an exhibition of his paintings and graphic art created a sensation, first in Prague, and later in a number of Western European cities. But he had years of puppet-making experience as well. "The unexpected possibilities of the use of trick technique in cartoon film amazed me," he said, but at the same time they instilled a longing in me to take three-dimensional puppets on the screen where "everything's possible"—puppets that can move not only on a plane but in three dimensions. From the very beginning, I insisted on my own conception of the stylization of the puppets, always with an individual—but unchanging—facial expression, as opposed to the ones who change their expression thanks to various techniques. Which—as practice proved to us—is not so much in keeping with realism, but leads rather to naturalism, instead. Puppet film has unlimited possibilities, and would be capable of use in any of the genres of acted film. But of course there it could do no more than imitate. Puppet film is unique and original only where it oversteps the limits of acted film, wherever stylization, pathos or lyricism as presented by live actors would appear improbable, ludicrous, and uncomfortable (From an interview with J. Brož in *Czechoslovak Film* No. 6, 1955).

Trnka's best interpreter, Jaroslav Boček, who himself later became a director of animated films, wrote:

Puppet film entered the cinematography of the world with *The Czech Year* and *Song of the Prairie [Árie prérie*-1949] not as a plaything or a supplement, but as a self-sufficient poetic work. Trnka joined the ancient art of the puppeteers with the most modern art of film, and arrived at exceptional charm that soon brought him worldwide success. As to material, development covered the legendary antiquity of *Old Czech Legends [Staré pověsti české*-1953], through the recent past in the adaptation of Hašek's *Švejk [Schweik*-1955] to the present in *Obsession [Vášeň*-1961], all the way to a vision of the future in *Cybernetic Grandma [Kybernetická babička*-1962]. He worked on native themes like the fairy tale *Bayaya* (1950) or the *Czech Year,* but he also reached for foreign literature, like Hans Christian Andersen's *Emperor's Nightingale [Císařův slavík*-1948], Shakespeare's *Midsummer Night's Dream [Sen noci svatojanské*-1959], or *The Archangel Gabriel and Mother Goose [Archanděl Gabriel a Paní Husa*-1964] adapted from Boccaccio. In spite of this broad range, he is the most consistent philosopher of human destiny. He asks about the essence of Czech heroism in *Bayaya,* and finds it in a fidelity to homeland and a rejection of evil, and in *Old Czech Legends* in defense of one's country and one's heritage. And at the same time he makes fun of noisy soldiering and force and robbery. In *The Emperor's Nightingale* and in *Cybernetic Grandma,* he asks about the conflict between man and technology, and man and knowledge, and he finds the solution that will prevail over the horrors of machines. He seeks the meaning of human life and finds it in love, in work, in simplicity, and in creative enthusiasm. At a time when Czechoslovak art was answerable to temporary needs of propaganda, Trnka polarized the entire development of cinematography with his orientation toward permanent values and ideas that for years comprised both the development of national history and the essence of Czech culture (*Film a doba* No. 5, 1965, Prague).

Karel Zeman did not possess Trnka's gift of poetic vision and philosophical profundity, but inclined instead toward playfulness, experimentation with materials, and contemporaneity. His *Christmas Dream (Vánoční sen*-1945) soon became a classic of its genre, his serial about *Mr. Prokouk* (1947-1955) an example of combining art with the needs of the times, his *Treasure of Bird Island (Poklad z Ptačího ostrova*-1952), *King Lávra (Král Lávra*-1950) and *Inspiration (Inspirace*-1948) evidence of his effort to breathe life into static materials (paper, glass, etc.). In *A Journey to Primeval Times (Cesta do pravěku*-1956) he once again combined live actors (a group of boys) with puppets, using animation to bring the world of

Old Czech Legends

Midsummer
Night's
Dream

The Invention of Destruction

prehistoric flora and fauna to life. He remained faithful to this practice in all the films that followed—*Baron Münchhausen* (*Baron Prášil*-1961), *A Jester's Tale* (*Bláznova kronika*-1964). Eventually, inspired by the work of Jules Verne—the source of his major triumph, *The Invention of Destruction* (*Vynález zkázy*-1957)—he made *On a Comet* (*Na kometě*-1970) more than 10 years later.

How can we explain that in the period of the most rigid dogmatism such original talents could emerge in the sphere of animated films—and not only in Czechoslovakia—talents so ill-fitted to the image of the times? The reply is not too complicated. The nationalization presented a secure material foundation for the extant talent. Directly after the war, film production was decentralized into small, ultimately autonomous workshops, headed by experienced producers, artists, directors, or scenarists. In the creative atmosphere of these small collectives, the successes of the early postwar years were born. It was just this organization that was the first to fall victim to the Zhdanov line, which required central control over every phase of the creative and production process. This was not very feasible, however, in the sphere of animated film. Production in this area is by nature craftsman-like—work is only possible in small groups, where the responsible person is the author of the artistic concept. Scripts for animated, and particularly for puppet films, are difficult for the layman to understand, and the world of dreamlike fairy-tale fantasy in which they move is on the periphery of consciousness, difficult to measure by criteria that authorities at all levels are accustomed to using. So these authorities were presented with the finished work, which frequently received disapprobation—most of Trnka's films did—but which were defended from the consequences of disapproval both by their artistic quality and by the immediate international response that they evoked, both of which were more than rare at that time. Thus, in the sphere of animated film, a model of organization was formed that was later to facilitate the development of feature film—both in Czechoslovakia and in other Eastern European countries.

VÁCLAV KRŠKA

In the first half of the fifties, though, such things were still unthinkable. Everyone felt the influence of the prevailing Stalinist attitude. In the film world, the one who felt it most acutely was, paradoxically, the very one who rediscovered himself because of it. In the years from 1949 to 1956, Václav Krška filmed five biographical films and one opera. The times ripped him away from his poetic, imaginative lyricism, his striking pictures of the Czech countryside, and his tense sensualism. It tossed him in the direction of the biographical genre, the content and the esthetic conventions of which had clear limitations. But at the same time, in 1953 and 1954, he managed to make two films, one right after the other, based on a stage play and a novel by his compatriot from southern Bohemia, Fráňa Šrámek, an impressionistic, pacifist poet who spoke for the young people who were eventually killed on the battlefronts of World War One. The two films were *Moon Over the River* (*Měsíc nad řekou*-1953) and *Silvery Wind* (*Stříbrný vítr*-1954). Until 1950, Šrámek's position in Czech literature and film was tolerated, apparently because late in his life his pacifism had developed into a sympathy for communism. But in the early fifties, his voice was too different to be tolerated. The Spectator, with his hypocritical and puritan morality, could not help but be repelled by a nostalgia for the passing of a generation, by a sorrowful farewell to a youth that had never fully experienced life, as shown in Krška's sensitive interpretation of *Moon Over the River,* and above all by Krška's sensitivity to the awakening sensuality of adolescent youths as depicted in the film version of *Silvery Wind.* For a while, *Moon Over the River* slipped through on the weight of Šrámek's name. But *Silvery Wind* was banned straight away, and Krška returned to biography and opera.

Two years passed; *Silvery Wind* was rehabilitated. Its belated premiere late in 1956 gave notice that Czech film was entering a new stage.

FILM POLSKI:Poland, 1945–1954

Everything that happened in Poland after the war was touched by the memory of the six million people of Poland's 35 million that were killed under the Nazi occupation. This was true not only for the period immediately following the war. Even 10 and 15 years later, the years from 1939 to 1945 remained an open wound for those who had lived through them, a trauma that kept returning. There wasn't a single Polish family that hadn't lost someone: on the battlefronts, in the concentration camps, during the Warsaw Uprising, during the Nazi reprisals, or in the civil struggles at the end of the war. Nazi Germany saw in the Poles, as in the nations of Yugoslavia, a people that dared to show defiance, and as such, ought to be exterminated. And Polish film, like Yugoslav film, found its greatest inspiration in the collectively experienced tragedy; it kept returning to this period, painfully and painstakingly examining it from all points of view.

The Polish tragedy, however, was the greater of the two. It comprised the bitterness of defeat and degradation, and the collapse of the dream of a Great Poland that keeps reappearing in Polish history, only to end in repeated tragedy. "Unfortunate the nation where independence is a mere adventure," wrote the poet, Adam Mickiewicz, a spokesman for Polish freedom.

The fifties did not bring Poland the same kind of extremes and cruelties that occurred, for example, in Hungary. It was as if the proximity of the horrors of recent history had bound the hands of those who were in positions of decision at that time. Yet, in the late forties and early fifties, that did not prevent a broad and extensive settling of accounts—made possible by Soviet military presence—by means of false trials of members of the non-Communist anti-Nazi resistance, which was by far stronger than the Communist resistance element during the war, and members of the Warsaw Uprising. (We have already mentioned that the Communist Party in Poland before World War Two was very weak.)

The nationalization of film was decided before the end of the war in Lublin, the first large Polish city to be liberated and the seat of the Polish Committee of National Liberation, established during the war in the Soviet Union. The nationalization became law in November 1945, when Film Polski was established as the central organ for cinema, with a jurisdiction that included production, distribution, import, export, and film education. The director Aleksander Ford was its first chief.

As a matter of fact, however, there was nothing to nationalize: the prewar studios had been razed to the ground. The first films were shot in the hurriedly adapted sports stadium in Łódź. In 1945, a film workshop for young film-makers was founded in Cracow, where, for example, Jerzy Kawalerowicz (b. 1922), Jerzy Passendorfer (b. 1923), and Wojciech Has (b. 1925) had their beginnings. In a short time, almost 500 movie theaters were put into operation (by 1950, the number had reached over 1,300). The Film Institute was also founded in 1945, as was *Film*, the first Polish postwar film magazine. In 1948 the Film Academy was established in Łódź, from which 700 film artists would graduate within the next 20 years.

FIRST FILMS

The first director of fiction films to return to the studios was Leonard Buczkowski (1900-1967), who before the war had made nine fairly good films, mostly comedies, and had acted in several others. When his *Forbidden Songs* (*Zakazane piosenki*-1947) opened, crowds of people besieged the theaters, and well after the opening, long lines formed at the box offices. The first Polish film in a nation that had been destined for extermination was seen as simply a miracle.

It was not a good film, but its value was not related to its quality. The director's intention to film an anthology of patriotic songs sung during the occupation in defiance of the Nazis grew into a fiction film with a simple plot that placed Nazis and Warsaw patriots face to face.

Buczkowski was also responsible for the second most successful postwar film in Poland, the comedy, *Treasure* (*Skarb*-1949), which told the story of the difficulties encountered by a young couple looking for an apartment in Warsaw during the city's reconstruction.

Forbidden
Songs

There was neither the time for—not the interest in—creating new forms.
What mattered was to make Polish-language films as quickly as possible.
Not even Aleksander Ford, the most ambitious prewar director, surpassed
his earlier achievements in his first significant postwar Polish film, *Border
Street* (*Ulica Graniczna*-1949). Poland was one of the few countries where
there had been no film production during the war, where—contrary to the
situation in Czechoslovakia and Hungary—development had been violently
interrupted. And so *Border Street* returned to a prewar inspiration, French
populism, and thematically tied in with Ford's film *The Path of Youth*,
dealing again with the idea of solidarity between Poles and Jews, standing
this time together in opposition to the German occupying forces. The film
culminated with the uprising in the Warsaw ghetto in 1943, when the Jews,
supported by the Polish underground, stood up against the Nazis with
weapons in hand. Ford stratified the plot according to the structure of Polish
society at the time, telling the story through typical representatives of Polish

Border
Street

The Last Stage

social groups, whose unity under fire was to have been the source of a unified Poland. *Border Street* was shown throughout the world, together with the second most significant Polish film of the period, *The Last Stage* (*Ostatni etap*-1948), directed by Wanda Jakubowska.

Jakubowska did not leave Poland during the war, as did Ford and others. She remained in the country, was arrested, and then deported to the concentration camp at Auschwitz. She made her first fiction film, the best film she ever made, on the basis of her memories of the horror and terror that she experienced there. Death, inhuman suffering, more death, fear and cowardice; but also the power of friendship, the will to survive, hatred of the torturers, and love of fellow-sufferers—all this blends in her film with semidocumentary shots made in camps where crematory chimneys had been smoking not long before. Undoubtedly, the director's collaborators contributed to the exceptional strength of *The Last Stage*: the excellent cameraman, Borys Monastyrski, and assistant directors Jerzy Kawalerowicz and Jan Rybkowski (b. 1912).

In spite of their talents, however, the directors who created Polish film after the war—the generation of 1910—were not sufficiently prepared for the task of reviving all branches of film and setting them up on a new foundation, free of commercialism. Above all, they lacked the necessary organizational experience, being essentially theoreticians and enthusiastic debaters rather than organizers and administrators. Yet, together with the administrative and technical personnel, their first and basic task was to build a new type of film industry from scratch, and at the same time, to train a new generation of film-makers.

In their films, they carried on where they had stopped before the war, reflecting in a surprising fashion the strong roots of the tradition of the thirties. This is true not only of Ford and Jakubowska, but also of Zarzycki and Buczkowski, and of Cękalski and his film about postwar village life, *Bright Fields* (*Jasne lany*-1947), and of Antoni Bohdziewicz (1906-1970) and his occupation drama, *Others Will Follow* (*Za wami pójdą inni*-1949).

CONGRESS AT WISLA

Then, when the first difficulties were finally overcome, when Polish film-making finally stood as a consolidated organizational and artistic unit, and when finally there might have been time for more purely creative work, the 1949 Congress of film-makers was held at Wisla and proclaimed the principles of socialist realism, once again violently interrupting the development of Polish cinema.

In 1949, power in Poland had been taken over entirely by the Polish Workers' Party, which was the new name of the Polish Communist Party (dissolved by the Comintern in 1938). In the same year, its general secretary, Wladyslaw Gomulka, was removed, and shortly thereafter imprisoned. He was replaced by Boleslaw Bierut, and command of the army was taken over by a Soviet general of Polish origin, Konstanty Rokossowski. It was clearly apparent from these and other events that hard years were in the offing.

Today we are surprised to realize how much political nonsense we allowed ourselves to be talked into. We let ourselves be convinced that the feeling of generational gap is wrong. We allowed ourselves to be talked into believing that the most dangerous things in our books were free verse, 'anti-estheticisms,' 'crude language,' and that the ideal of socialist poetry is the complete sentence, noble, avoiding all inversions, emotive and humbly subservient to the rhythmical traditions of the nineteenth century. We let ourselves be convinced that continuing in this tradition was tantamount to using this rhythm and these verses, that love and wrath do not belong to the tradition, nor generosity and independence. We allowed ourselves to be convinced that some names may not be uttered, and yet that that does not mean counterfeiting history, but rather giving it a revolutionary perspective; and that there are other names that must be constantly quoted, and that that doesn't imply sycophancy but rather idealism. We allowed ourselves to be convinced that inspiration may be achieved administratively, on the occasion of some anniversary or celebration. (*Temps Modernes,* Paris, Fall 1957, p. 1107)

That was how poet and essayist Wiktor Woroszylski summarized the first years of the new regime—and not just for the field of poetry.

At the congress of film-makers in 1949, held under the aegis of the Ministry of Culture and Art at Wisla, all of the prior films were sharply criticized, including *Last Stage* and *Forbidden Songs*. Italian neorealism was condemned as a trend that "is not in the slightest in keeping with objective reality," and the film *Warsaw Robinson* (*Robinson Warszawski*-1948)—in its original version apparently the best work of its time and the film in which another member of the prewar avant-garde, director Jerzy Zarzycki, returned

Unvanquished City

to the screen— was labeled "the first product of an erroneous conception
of national solidarity."* The film had to be made over. It received a new
title, *Unvanquished City* (*Miasto nieujarzmione*-1950), and the original
story of a small group of Warsaw citizens who hid in the ruins of the city
during the uprising was transformed for the most part into the tale of the
Soviet radio-operator who helped the heroes of the film. Another film, the
debut of Jan Rybkowski, *House in the Wilderness* (*Dom na pustkowiu*-1950)
met a similar fate, its director being forced to give the intimate drama a
political reworking.

In 1951, Rybkowski was selected to direct the first costume film, a
prettied-up biography that copied the style used for such films in other
Eastern European countries (in the Soviet Union, Mussorgsky, Rimsky-
Korsakov, Glinka; in Hungary, Erkel; in Czechoslovakia, Smetana).
In *Warsaw Premier* (*Warszawska premiera*) he depicted the life of Stanislaw
Moniuszko, above all the period when the composer strove for the recognition of his opera, *Halka*. A year later, Rybkowski's *First Years* (*Pierwsze
dni*) became a model of the socialist realistic film, an example that was
used throughout Eastern Europe to prove that Polish cinematography had
taken the right path.

One of the more primitive Czech plays of the time, *Grinder Karhan's
Crew* (*Parta brusiče Karhana*), with its struggle between the "old" and
the "new," inspired the Polish film *Two Brigades* (*Dwie brygady*-1950),
which was made by the graduates of the school at Łódź under Cękalski's
guidance.

*Jerzy Plazewski in "Le jeune cinéma polonais," *Cahiers du cinéma*, Paris, 1964.

KAWALEROWICZ

Of the members of the new generation, one who called attention to himself was a former art student, Jerzy Kawalerowicz. Kawalerowicz entered postwar life burdened with the problems of his entire generation, having grown to maturity during the war, and being closely acquainted with the reality of the country from within. He and his contemporaries had in them the disillusionment of the resistance movement, the distaste for traditional Polish romanticism, the desire to maintain artistic independence, and the simultaneous fear of losing contact with the people. They were full of sympathy for the mistreated country, and at the same time full of shame for its poverty and subservience, full of defiance as well as humility. But primarily they were filled with the idea of the historic mission of art, conceived as an instrument in the struggle not only for national freedom, but also for the social revolution.

Kawalerowicz's first film, made jointly with Kazimierz Sumerski, was called *The Village Mill* (*Gromada*-1952), and spoke rather superficially about village life, collectivization, and the class struggle. Nonetheless, this film revealed qualities that were evident only rarely in the work of other directors: a good grasp of atmosphere and of the lifestyles of the heroes and a realistically perceived environment.

Two years later came Kawalerowicz's two-part work, *A Night of Remembrance* (*Celuloza*) and *Under the Phrygian Star* (*Pod gwiazdą frygijską*-1954), which remains to this day one of the best Eastern European films of the time. The life of a villager between the two World Wars, and his introduction to political underground activity, is told with a feeling for film poetry, inspired by Kozintsev's and Trauberg's *Maxim Trilogy,* and in many aspects also by neorealism. But above all, Kawalerowicz's work is supremely

Under the Phrygian Star

Polish, directly tying in with the realistic prose of the two prewar decades. The material on which he based the films, Igor Newerly's novel, *Cellulose Recollection,* made it possible for him to achieve something that had appeared impossible in socialist cinema since the beginning of the thirties: the treatment of heroes of the class struggle, organizers of the revolutionary underground, not as paper figures or outlines to be filled out by predigested ideas, but as multi-dimensional, fully human characters. True, the subject matter was still entirely traditional, but the approach to the material and the form of the work anticipated the period of passionate reaction to stylistic academism.

In its first part, the story is primarily a pretext for views of a variety of environments, poor village structures, a cellulose factory, a carpenter's workshop, the army, the underworld of a capitalist city. In the second part, the hero's personal life is in the foreground, his love for a girl who is better educated than he, his struggle for justice, culminating in the murder of an *agent provocateur,* his struggle with his own conscience.

The first efforts of Kawalerowicz's generation clearly indicated that Polish cinematography was undergoing a change, that it was turning against the traditions represented by the prewar avant-garde. At the same time, this generation tied in loosely with traditional Polish symbolism, typical for example of the work of Aleksander Ford, and elaborated on it in the spirit of their own conception.

FORD

Ford, the head of Polish Film between 1946 and 1948, went through a period of schematism without making too many compromises. In *The Youth of Chopin* (*Młodość Chopina*-1952), he joined the romantic elements of the musician's life with a contemporary interpretation of history in a less propagandistic manner than was used in other biographical films. But it was the visual strength of the film—J. Tuzar was the cameraman—that stood out in sharp relief against the artistically poor products of the Stalinist era.

Ford's next film, *Five Boys from Barska Street* (*Piątka z ulicy Barskiej*-1954), was thematically related to a number of films of the fifties that concerned themselves with juvenile delinquency. However what was entirely natural in French and American film was new and courageous in Poland or Czechoslovakia, where according to official propaganda there were no delinquent youth. Nonetheless, Ford's boys are brothers to Carné's and Brook's heroes. Only their roots are different: the young Poles steal, rob, and ultimately even kill because they were taught to by the war, because they had never known anything else, because they found themselves completely alone in the world, and because the new Polish society did not know how—or did not want—to help them.

Ford's assistant director on *Five Boys from Barska Street* was Andrzej Wajda (b. 1929), a graduate of the Łódź school; his assistant cameraman

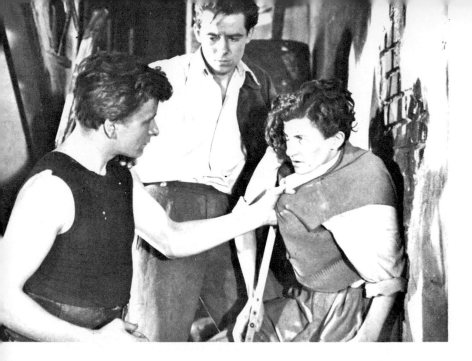

Five Boys
from
Barska Street

was Jerzy Lipman. At the time that Ford was shooting the film, a script was being written that would be turned into the first film of the new Polish school. It was *Generation* (*Pokolenie*–1955), Wajda's debut in fiction film, with Lipman as cameraman and two of the leading roles interpreted by principal actors from *Five Boys from Barska Street.*

GENERATION AND "THE BLACK SERIES"

Kawalerowicz's or Ford's partial successes were still made possible by the political establishment that backed them up. The directors that followed them were products of a new social situation in which the authority of the masses, the authority of the individual—above all of the creative individual— and the authority of truth began to grow. Between 1953 and 1956, it was as if all of Poland began slowly to take a long and candid look at itself.

Wajda's *Generation* does not appear, on first glance, to be a breakthrough film—just as, in Hungary, *Fourteen Lives in Danger* did not appear to be. And yet it contains the key to understanding the metamorphosis that occurred at the time *Generation* was being made. The novel by Bohdan Czeszko tells the story of a young Communist resistance group in Warsaw, speaks of the lives of its heroes, and shows how these lives ended. Nothing that would seem to be outside the framework of "official" literature. But on the screen, a group of boys and girls appear, moving, living and fighting in a real city, away from the synthetic reality of film studios. Neither cardboard heroes nor typical examples cut out of the textbooks of political script-writing, they are flesh-and-blood people who know how to be courageous but also know how to be afraid, and literally to die of fear. They are devoted to their cause, but they are also youthfully rash and

undisciplined. They are arrested in the end, not because there are traitors among them, but through a series of coincidences, resulting partly from a senseless accident. Against the background of schematic determinism that revolutionary epics or social dramas were only rarely capable of avoiding, Wajda created the first tragedy in Eastern European cinematography. His romantic hero dies at the moment he has overcome his own fear, another tragic figure in Polish art, for whom nothing is left but a heroic suicide, and the first figure of pathos in Polish film.

The beginning of the thaw in Polish film was a conference of film workers in September 1954, at which the principles of socialist realism were violently criticized. The first concrete signs of the political changes that this thaw was to bring about in Polish life in 1954–1956 were documentary films that were later referred to as "the films of the black series." At a time when, under public pressure, the Minister of Interior, the feared Radkiewicz, was removed from his post, when the public was learning more and more about Stalinist misgovernment, and when some members of the leadership of the Polish Workers' Party called for changes in the country's overall political orientation, documentaries about political and social realities began to appear.

Jerzy Hoffman (b. 1932) and Edward Skórzewski (b. 1930) made a film about disturbed youth, *Attention, Hooligans* (*Uwaga, chuligani*-1955); Jerzy Ziarnik (b. 1931) told the dramatic story of the depopulation of a *Small Town* (*Miasteczko*-1956); Jerzy Bossak and Jaroslaw Brzozowski (b. 1931) in *Warsaw 56* (*Warszawa 56*) showed a picture of Warsaw that was entirely different from any that had ever appeared on the screen before; and Wladyslaw Slesicki focused his *In the Sticks* (*Gdzie diabel móvi dobranoc*-1956) on the hopeless life of young people who don't have any place to spend their leisure time. Only someone who has seen the documentaries that were made under Stalinism could comprehend the significance of these films. The one who deserves the most credit for the origin of the "black series" was Jerzy Bossak, at that time the head of the documentary studio. He backed these films, supported them, and sought out new young people to work on them.

In 1955, a fundamental decentralization took place, production groups were re-established, allowing far more authority to the artists. (It was on the basis of such production groups that Ford had originally founded the nationalized film industry.) Within the groups, artists were to be responsible for a film from script to final realization, thereby fully affirming the basic principle of the nationalization of the film industry. Opposition to "orders from on high" and to "inspiration on orders" was growing stronger in all areas of artistic activity. Within this tense atmosphere of life "atop a volcano," which culminated in the events of autumn 1956, the young people were the most radical. Mostly students, they formed a grouping around the Warsaw periodical, *Frankly Speaking* (*Po prostu*), calling with increasing emphasis for the abolition of authoritative methods.

Already in 1953, the writer Jerzy Andrzejewski, who was also a Communist member of parliament, had pilloried the lack of contact between the government and the people in his satire, *The Great Lamentation of the Paper Head*; he was followed by others. Andrzejewski's story, for which he received a sharp rebuke from the Party, could not be published until 1956, but other writings were published immediately. Events leading up to the fall of 1956, events in which Polish film and its creators played such an important role, could no longer be held back. Poet Adam Ważyk wrote in his "Poem for Adults" (1955):

> I won't believe the lion is a lamb, friend,
> I won't believe the lamb is a lion, friend,
> I won't believe in magic formulations, friend,
> I won't believe brains kept under domes of glass.
> But I believe that a table has only four legs,
> I believe that the fifth leg is a figment,
> and when figments accumulate, my friend,
> the human heart slowly comes to a halt. . . .

FROM THE MOUNTAINS
TOWARD THE STUDIOS:
Yugoslavia, 1945–1955

What sort of tradition can our cinematography refer to?
The individual and completely isolated efforts of film workers
who tried, before the war, to give this country a film tradition
are entirely negligible. They are significant primarily from the
point of view of historical science. The year 1945 may be
considered the true beginning of our cinematography.

Rudolf Sremec, *Filmska Kultura,* Zagreb, 1968

Before the war, the Yugoslav film industry was practically nonexistent. And
for the world public, it did not exist, to all intents and purposes, for the
20 years that followed the war. The world discovered Yugoslav film only
thanks to the Zagreb school of animated film, for the production of features
did not become internationally known until the mid-sixties, when it had
205 films to its credit.

The first Yugoslav feature film was made in 1947, in the difficult postwar
period, when a nationalized film industry was being established in the
war-torn country. Those who established it, however, had nothing to work
with—no cameras, no studios, no experience, no people. What they did
have, was the strong support of the state, and a will that was equally strong.
There was enthusiasm and persistence. During the partisan resistance
against the Nazis, which in Yugoslavia in fact amounted to war, Yugoslavs
joined the cameramen of the allied armies in filming some military action.
Immediately after the liberation of Belgrade in 1944, within the framework
of the propaganda department of the high command of the liberation forces,
a film section was established that was later to form the foundation for the
organization of Yugoslav film. In the summer of 1945, the State Film
Enterprise (Zvezda, or Star) of the Socialist Federal Republic of Yugoslavia
was established. A year later, the Committee for Cinematography was
placed at the head of the entire film structure, with writer Aleksandar Vučo
at its head.

Yugoslav cinematography worked within this organizational structure for
more than five years. At that time, a film city—Koshutnyak—was built in
Belgrade and film centers were set up in the republics; young people were
sent abroad to study—to Prague, to Moscow, and to Rome. In Belgrade,
a film school was opened, film laboratories were organized, production
facilities for film equipment were set up, and late in the forties, a network
of movie theaters began to be developed, growing to a total of 1,326 by

1953—almost four times the number that existed in 1946. During those same years, the so-called "de-bureaucratization" of film was also being effected, cinema having originally been based on the same centralist and statist principles as "State Film" setups in other People's Democracies.

Directors, who were recruited primarily from the theater, had for the most part been in the partisan resistance, and not a single one had any film experience. The scriptwriters were also amateurs, although they included such well-known writers as Vučo, Davičo, Branko Čopić, and Vladan Desnica.

PARTISAN SUBJECT MATTER

Thus, the first Yugoslav films were primarily evidence of good will, enthusiasm, and persistence rather than works that can be measured by artistic criteria. What the genocide of the forties was to Polish film, the partisan war against the Nazis was to Yugoslav film—not only a thematic inspiration, but a key to the thought and emotions of a land where the word "national" was identified with the words "revolutionary" and "socialist." What in the other countries of Eastern Europe was to a greater or lesser degree the product of the postwar Soviet influence and ideological importation, grew up in Yugoslavia as a result of national experience. It is true that this experience pushed Yugoslav culture onto the path of "socialist realism," but ultimately it rescued it from the Stalinist-Zhdanovist consequences.

Yugoslav artists relied on their personal experience in the partisan movement for the subject matter of most of their films. The first of these were marked with clumsiness, naïveté and exaggerated pathos, but as the years passed, Yugoslav cinema worked its way toward maturity. "Traditionalistic" films, which saw the past as one great heroic deed, strictly respected the given rules of tale-telling, their achievements being exclusively in the thematic field. Everything in them was solid and tranquil, borne by the philosophy of revolutionary fatalism; they spoke for themselves, leaving the author in the background.

In the years between 1945 and 1947, some 67 documentaries were made, devoted for the most part to the reconstruction of the new republic. Gustav Gavrin (b. 1906) made the first postwar documentary, *Jasenovac* (1945), about a Nazi concentration camp; Nikola Popović (b. 1907), originally a famous actor, and during the war a partisan fighter, devoted his film *Belgrade* (*Beograd*-1945), to the history of the capital city from 1938 to the liberation; Radoš Novaković (b. 1915), who before the war had been a student of the Drama Academy and then a partisan, collected material in his film, *In the Name of the Nation* (*U ime naroda*-1946), about the brutality of the police during the German occupation; Šime Šimatović (b. 1919) made a film portrait of the Zagreb garrison on the occasion of the first anniversary of the end of the war, *Victory Day in Zagreb* (*Dan pobjede u Zagrebu*-1947); Puriša Djordjević (b. 1924), first a prisoner of war and after his escape a partisan and radio reporter, dedicated his film *Georgi Dimitrov* (1947) to the Bulgarian statesman; Fedor Hanžeković (b. 1913) depicted the new republic's attitudes and programs for maternity and child care in *New Youth* (*Nova mladost*-1947); France Štiglic (b. 1919), a journalist and actor, made a report about a youth construction site in Slovenia under the title *Youth Builds* (*Mladina gradi*-1946).

Finally, in April 1947, came the premiere of the first fiction film, *Slavica*. Its director, Vjekoslav Afrić (b. 1906), was an actor in the Zagreb National Theater before the war, then a partisan and a member of the Theater of National Revival. After the war, he became director of the Film Academy. In 1946, he worked as assistant to Soviet director Abram Room in filming *In the Mountains of Yugoslavia* (*U planinama Jugoslavije*-1946), writing the first sketch for *Slavica* during the shooting. In it, he related his own experience during the war, centering the story on a young girl, a worker named Slavica, who died in one of the guerrilla actions of his division. The story takes place in Afrić's birthplace on the Dalmatian coast of the Adriatic, where the partisans fought the Italian occupation forces. The authenticity of the Dalmatian surroundings, balances, at least in part, the melodramatic story and the theatrical acting.

Slavica remained Afrić's most significant film, for the entry upon the scene of younger, better-trained directors pushed him out of work. In 1952, he made two other films, both of them mediocre, and thereafter his name does not appear in film credits.

Slavica

It took eight years for production to become stabilized at an annual average of 14 films. Of the 38 motion pictures made between 1947 and 1954, most were on partisan themes, later on worked up in the form of thrillers and action films. In the first years, there was a strong note of pathos and a yearning for monumentality, occasionally apparent in compositions inspired by Russian cinema. In the second postwar fiction film, *This People Must Live* (*Živjeće ovaj narod*-1947), directed by Nikola Popović, efforts at a formal experiment resulted in a contrived superstructure being imposed on a straightforward plot. The story of two lovers separated by the war ends with closing shots of Marshall Tito addressing "the people that must live."

This People
Must
Live

Exceptional in its genre was the film by France Štiglic *On His Own Ground* (*Na svoji zemlji*-1948), based on the liberation struggles in Slovenia. Apparent here was both the director's sense of the richness of film language and his effort to combine the story with a real environment. His film also testified to a profound personal war experience that Štiglic was to present in the years to come by means of strong associative visions.

Two of the most productive directors,- Radoš Novaković and Vojislav Nanović (b. 1922) started out making partisan films. The story *Immortal Youth* (*Besmrtna mladost*-1948) took place in occupied Belgrade, whereas Novaković's heroes in *The Boy Mita* (*Dečak Mita*-1951) were children fighting in partisan units. Novaković had already called attention to his work with his first film, *Gypsy Girl* (*Sofka*-1948), an adaptation of Bora Stanković's classic novel of the turn of the century that told the story of a young girl sold into marriage. It remained his strongest film.

Literature was the second most important source for the young film art, which suffered from a lack of scripts along with a lack of technological experience. The quality of Yugoslav prose and drama, however, always surpassed the level of the film adaptations, in which the lack of directorial experience was more apparent than in the partisan tales. This was true of the debut of Puriša Djordjević *A Child of the Community* (*Opštinsko dete*-1953) based on the novel by Branislav Nušić, as well as of Fedor Hanžeković's first film *Monk Brne's Pupil* (*Bakonja Fra Brne*-1951). In the latter, the director retold the story by the Croatian Simo Matavulj, published in 1892, which recalled the atmosphere of Renaissance life through the story of a poor peasant who becomes a gluttonous monk. While Djordjević's effort obviously showed the director's lack of interest in the remote subject, Hauzeković did a generally successful job of dramatizing the classical narrative material.

In contrast to the majority of his peers, Vladimir Pogačić (b. 1919), one of the few directors who knew film theory and history, having graduated from the Film Academy, began with stories of contemporary life. His slice-of-life portayal of a factory disrupted by sabotage campaigns—*Story of a Factory* (*Priča o fabrici*-1949)—or his story about the attempts of former Gestapo members to harm the new republic—*The Last Day* (*Poslednji dan*-1951)—resembled in many respects the films made in other Eastern European countries: straightforward, falsely optimistic—a mixture of reality and wishful thinking.

Story
of a
Factory

THE FIRST STRUGGLES FOR FREE ART

The first Yugoslav feature films were made at a time when the party line, after allowing a brief period of postwar artistic freedom, was becoming more rigid. In 1946, leading Croatian author Miroslav Krleža wrote an article in the initial issue of the magazine *Republika* that called for a critical approach to the present and artistic independence for all; but his views, espoused primarily by surrealists (Vučo, Davičo, and others), ran up against the opposition of the so-called traditionalists. Stalinist socialist realism was never officially accepted in Yugoslavia, but the Yugoslav moderate variant—"national realism"—had many of the same attributes, particularly, artistic dogmatism and intolerance. The traditionalism persisted after Yugoslavia's 1948 break with Russia and its expulsion from the Cominform, when the country found itself in a difficult situation in both a domestic and an international sense.

At that time, official supervision of culture increased, voices that seemed excessively critical were suppressed, and a number of writers fell silent.

Early in the fifties, after an internal and an external stabilization, and in connection with a number of extensive reforms based on the idea of self-management in all strata of social activity, the flame of opposition to a "national realism" once again burned strong, this time even more vigorously. A sort of collectively spoken monologue was heard from all the republics, demanding freedom for artistic work, asking that Yugoslav culture be placed in the context of world evolution, and proposing that all art styles, from populism to the avant-garde, be granted equality. Art and culture, as has happened so often in the past, became an important field on which the battle for the democratization of Yugoslav society was waged. The strongest centers of controversy were poetry and painting, the new forms of which were to inspire Yugoslav film far more than prose. Canonized mythical reality disappeared, and simple human destinies came more and more to the forefront: man, frequently tired by the war, sometimes sceptical, and almost always helpless, seeking a relationship to life, to the world, to himself. A key work of the time was Davičo's *Man to Man,* a poem about the conflict between the prewar revolutionary dream and the day-to-day reality of socialism. Soon after its publication in 1953, the poem was withdrawn from circulation, as being a product of "Djilasism" (see pp. 243). After the plenary session of the Central Committee of the Communist Party in January 1954, which condemned the activity of journalist, author, and leading party ideologist, Milovan Djilas, the Party decided once again to set up policy guidelines for artists. But it was too late for a real dictatorial effort that would silence all the voices of resistance. Discussions did not cease, even after repeated warnings by party functionaries, and so by the end of 1954, Party Presidium member Edvard Kardelj made a declaration about the freedom to create that was to remain influential, to a greater or lesser degree, for several years.

REORGANIZATION

Along with the rest of the Yugoslav economy, the film industry underwent a decentralization of production early in the fifties, and at the same time asserted the principle of autonomy. Like individual industrial plants, individual film enterprises became autonomous, economically independent production units, with their own administrations and budgets. State control, to all intents and purposes, disappeared, as did state subsidies. Deficits were sometimes covered by financial bonuses that the individual films won at domestic festivals, by various technical jobs for foreign companies, by profits from foreign coproductions, and so on. The Committee for Cinematography was eliminated, and all production, technical, and distribution operations were turned over to film centers in the individual republics. Many film-makers ceased to be employed by the studios and became freelance artists working on the basis of contracts with individual production outfits. Whereupon they created their own coordination agency, the Union of Producers of Yugoslavia. The film law of 1956 confirmed the existing practice and right of each of the six republics to have its own national film production.

The largest company, Avala Film in Belgrade, Serbia, was founded in 1945 and produced the first postwar film, *Slavica*. In 1955, Dunav Film was established as its offshoot for the production of shorts and, later, of features as well. At the same time as Avala, Jadran Film was founded in Zagreb, Croatia, which produced as its first fiction film *This People Must Live*. Since 1953, Zagreb has also been the site of Zagreb Film, a studio for animated and documentary film. The third oldest studio of fiction film is Triglav Film in Ljubljana, Slovenia, founded in 1947. France Štiglic was one of the artists to work there. In 1956, Triglav Film was supplemented by Viba Film, specializing in shorts. In Skopje, Macedonia, Vardar Film was formed in 1947; its first fiction film was shown in 1952—the partisan story of *Frosina* by Vojislav Nanović. In Sarajevo, Bosnia, film production started in 1947 under the name Bosna Film, the first production being *Major Bauk* by Nikola Popović. The last to be founded was Lovćen Film in Budva, Montenegro, in 1949, where, after six years of documentary production, the first fiction film was made in 1955.

In addition to these production centers, independent distribution companies exist in each of the republics. Also, Vojvodina, a part of Serbia, has its own production center, Neoplanta Film, in its capital, Novi Sad.

The first results of the new structure, which differed from anything existing in any of the other nationalized film industries, were indisputably positive. Film production centers found themselves in direct competition, both economically and artistically, and the economic pressure forced them to be more flexible in the selection of both subject matter and collaborators. Artistic quality rose, amateurism disappeared, and the range of subjects expanded considerably. There were more contemporary topics, the first comedies began to appear, and the first historical films as well.

The most successful of the comedies was *Vesna* (1953), the Yugoslav debut of Czech director František Čáp, who had settled in Yugoslavia after Tito's break with Moscow in the summer of 1948. As one of the few film professionals there, he was given the job of making the first Yugoslav comedy, the story of a girl called Vesna and a group of her fellow students. An entertaining and well-made film, it brought crowds into the movie theaters. In the coming years Čáp became one of the most prolific directors of officially acceptable entertainment.

Vatroslav Mimica (b. 1923), who had been chief of Jadran Film since 1950, attempted a satirical comedy in 1955, *Mr. Ikl's Anniversary* (*Jubilej gospodina Ikla*). This story of a factory owner, whose dream that his wife and friends want to murder him becomes a reality, is a classical example of a failure in which the director, later to become a successful film artist, is testing the possibilities of his medium.

But comedies were an exception. Subject matter still centered for the most part on World War Two, and on the long struggle with the Turks. Žika Mitrović (b. 1921) became the main specialist in this field, having thoroughly mastered the method of story-telling mainly through action. He filmed a number of professionally competent stories that were enormous box-office successes—e.g., *The Echelon of Doctor M* (*Ešalon doktora M*-1954).

Echelon
of
Dr. M.

Other directors appeared. Veljko Bulajić (b. 1928), a graduate of the Centro Sperimentale di Cinematografia in Rome, made his first documentary, *The Stone and the Sea* (*Kamen i more*-1953), about the Republic of Montenegro. Branko Bauer (b. 1921) made his debut in fiction with two films for youngsters. His *Blue Seagull* (*Sinji galeb*-1953), with Nikola Tanhofer at the camera, tells about a bunch of boys who overcome a gang of smugglers, and *Millions on an Island* (*Milijuni na otoku*-1955), one of the most successful films of its time, tells about a fortune that is found and lost again.

The Sun Is Far Away

The most significant films of the first half of the fifties were those of
Radoš Novaković, and they were his best films as well. In 1953, Novaković
turned Dobrica Ćosić's novel, *The Sun Is Far Away* (*Daleko je sunce*), into
a film that played an important role in the ideological debates between the
traditionalists and the modernists. Ćosić was the first to speak of the
destiny of man and his bitter disillusionment, and the first to reject the myth
of the purity of the war of liberation. For the first time, he showed it as
a war that also destroyed and killed many who wanted to serve it most
devotedly. Ćosić's farmer Gvozden is shot by the partisans because he
refuses to submit to absurd discipline. He dies unnecessarily, his killers
as desperate as their victim.

Two years later, Novaković codirected (with Kaare Bergström) the
Norwegian-Yugoslav production, *Bloody Road* (*Krvavi put*-1955), a dramatic story set against the backdrop of Norway's snow covered and moun-
tainous countryside, frozen and desolate, where escaped Yugoslav prisoners
fight for survival. Scenes from the prison camp are shown without pathos,
the tranquil realism pointing up the inhumanity of the situation and the
absurdity of human destinies. It was not, however, just a matter of repeating
a familiar cliché, the demonstration of solidarity between the Yugoslav and
Norwegian people. Here the screen presents man, robbed of his most pro-

found dreams, caught unaware by reality like a helpless animal—man marked forever.

New Yugoslav literature, theater, fine arts, and eventually film, differed from earlier Yugoslav artistic works primarily by their approach to the question of human existence. Their basis is not an abstract situation that is realized in a half-real world, but an inner reality that is considered the only true reality. The transition from the abstract idealism characteristic of postwar culture in Yugoslavia and in the other countries of Eastern Europe, to the concreteness of individual destinies, was accompanied by the disintegration of the fixed narrative form into freely linked sequences, by the disappearance of epic symbolism, and by the replacement of eventful stories full of meaning with analyses of interior spiritual states. This change of structures and values in Yugoslav culture is based on the same foundation as the regenerative process that took place in the mid-fifties in Hungary, Poland, and Czechoslovakia.

THE PAST WEIGHS HEAVY:
Bulgaria, 1945-1956

Officially, the history of postwar Bulgarian cinema is usually begun with the first film after the nationalization (1948), shot in 1950, ignoring the years 1945-1947, when eight fiction films were made. The sparse data at our disposal concerning the films made immediately after the war indicate that film production continued along the same path in liberated Bulgaria—proclaimed a People's Republic after a plebiscite held in September 1946—as it had taken in the thirties. The first eight postwar films were made by small firms that were in existence for only a few years. Nonetheless, the topics of these films reflected an effort to respond to the changing situation in the country. Almost overnight, Bulgaria had traded her position as a supporter of fascist Germany in the struggle against Bolshevism for that of one of the Soviet Union's most devoted allies. The plots of these films include a story of a new Bulgarian village, striving, with the aid of the working classes, to liberate itself from the oppression of the wealthy farmers, *New Days Will Come* (*Shte doidat novi dni*-1945), a patriotic tale, *The Struggle for Happiness* (*Borba za shtastie*-1946), an optimistic drama of a returning soldier who is seeking a new place in society, *For a New Life* (*Otnovo v zhivota*-1947), etc.

There are no details available about these films, and all indications are that their significance comes from the fact that they were made at all.

Typical of the postwar situation in Bulgaria is the fact that the film industry was not nationalized until after the other branches of industry, which is partial proof of its occasional nature and, in the final analysis, of its peripheral importance. In 1948, film production was nationalized, and the slow process of organizing production facilities began. Bulgaria, with its population of eight million, had achieved independence only in 1878 and had few material or spiritual resources to rely on in building something as complex as a film industry. There was both a lack of industrial and administrative experience and a lack of any sort of technical outfitting. The basis of the national literature was for the most part limited by the rural nature of life in Bulgaria. Bulgarian culture had lived a life more or less isolated from the world beyond its borders, an isolation that grew even more profound during the war.

The most stable fulcrum of postwar life was Bulgaria's renewed friendship with her twofold liberator (from the Turks and the Nazis), Russia, linked also to Bulgaria by their shared Orthodox religion and Byzantine Christian tradition, an important element in the struggle against the Turks. Under the circumstances, the construction of a postwar society was hardly possible without Soviet aid, which came, but was accompanied by the demand for the payment of a bloody tribute to Stalinism.

The nationalization of the film industry, and everything that followed, was a part of this process. Soviet film-makers helped in the shooting of the first films, Bulgarian directors studied in Moscow, the first technical equipment came from the Soviet Union, and, along with it, technicians and advisors.

The first fiction film of the nationalized film industry was produced in 1950. It was *Kalin the Eagle* (*Kalin Orelut*), directed by Boris Borozanov and written by Orlin Vasilev. Both Borozanov and Vasilev were among the few film-makers who had some experience, but both lived and worked isolated from the development of film-making elsewhere in the world. *Kalin the Eagle* was a modest, naïve, old-fashioned film, reminiscent of the simple Bulgarian films of the thirties. Even the subject matter was similar. It was not World War Two, but the fight against the Turks that lived most strongly in the national consciousness and presented far more opportunities for heroism.

Kalin
the Eagle

Kalin the Eagle was conceived as a celebration of patriots who had devoted their lives to the struggle against the oppressors, a celebration of the hundred-year effort of the nation to achieve independence. Its hero, the rebel Kalin, called "Eagle," spends 15 years in exile, and upon his return finds the country entirely changed. The war with the Turks is over, Bulgaria is free, the heroes of the liberation struggle are forgotten. But the poor

Alarm

people are still oppressed, the first socialist organizations are being formed, a new struggle is being prepared.

The work of Orlin Vasilev, which imprinted the feeling of nationalistic schematism on the first Bulgarian films, never contained any complex conflicts. Events were developed in a straightforward manner, and a general characterization of social groups replaced any specific psychology of individual characters. The second film, based on a script by Vasilev, was *Alarm* (*Trevoga*–1951, inspired by Vasilev's play of the same name) which emerged from the interdependence of social phenomena. The protagonists are an officer of the royal army who tries during the war to remain aloof from the struggle against fascism; his son, an anti-communist, also an officer; and his son-in-law, a communist. This classic triangle—the communist, the anti-communist, and the reluctant intellectual—gave birth to a story with an ending that was obvious from the outset, an ending that the author arrived at by way of externally imposed dramatic tension.

Alarm was the directorial debut in fiction films of Zakhari Zhandov (b. 1911), originally a cameraman and documentarist, who in later years became a significant figure in Bulgarian cinema. In *Alarm,* as in his later films, Zhandov based his approach on a firm concept of traditionalism and on the romanticizing monumentalism typical of a majority of Eastern European films of the time.

Between 1950 and 1957, the Bulgarian film industry produced a total of 26 fiction films. Their attention was focused on educating the people and increasing the nation's political awareness, as demanded not only by the principles of Stalinist film-making but also by Bulgarian cultural tradition and by Bulgarian literature's basic function, that of "enlightenment." In this atmosphere, it was practically impossible to reflect contemporary life on the screen. One of the few who repeatedly attempted to tread this ground was Anton Marinovich (b. 1907), director of the first postwar film *New Days Will Come,* who, together with S. Sirkhadjev (b. 1912), shot several "Zhdanovist" movies dealing with the reconstruction of the new republic—notably, *Morning Over the Homeland* (*Utro nad rodinata*-1951), and *Our Land* (*Nasha zemia*-1953).

The most ambitious undertaking of this period, the screen version of the classic Bulgarian novel by Ivan Vazov, *Under the Yoke* (*Pod igoto*-1953) was made by Dako Dakovski (1919-1962) shortly after his graduation from the Moscow Film Academy. The story of a Bulgarian village at the time of the last rebellion against the Turks (1876) became the model—ideologically, thematically, and formally—for further film work. Patriotism; self-sacrifice; mistrust (mixed with exaggerated admiration) of strangers as the bearers of other faiths; monumental bathos; the ambivalent self-assurance of a small nation—all these were typical, along with the sweeping epic quality of Dakovski's work. In the six films that he made, Dakovski remained above all the spokesman for the Bulgarian peasant, the chronicler of his struggle for freedom and his effort to maintain this freedom, as illustrated, for example, by *Troubled Road* (*Nespokoyen put*-1955).

Bulgaria's first coproduction with the Soviet Union, *Heroes of Shipka* (*Geroite na Shipka*-1955), also looked back to the Russo-Turkish War. Soviet director Sergei Vasilev, who guided Bulgarian film-makers in the use of color technique, recreated in this film one of the most glorious chapters in Bulgarian history—the battle for Shipka Pass, where Bulgarian patriots defended themselves against a superior enemy force.

Song
for
Man

Song for Man (*Pesen za choveka*-1953) was filmed in the same style by another graduate from Moscow, Borislav Sharaliev (b. 1922). The life of poet Nikola Vaptsarov, executed in 1942 by the fascists, presented the opportunity to elaborate on a story from the period of the antifascist struggle and to stress traditional nationalistic ideas.

Perhaps only *Septembrists* (*Septemvriitsi*-1954), directed by Zhandov, found more in the subject than a glorification of the past. Although it was basically another official interpretation of the rebellion against the monarchy in the early twenties, scriptwriter Angel Wagenstein managed to shape the characters according to truly human dimensions. Wagenstein went on to make a significant contribution to the renaissance of Bulgarian cinema in the late fifties.

After Stalin's death, steps along the new path were hesitant and slow. In spite of the traditional Russophilia, which made the relationship with the Soviet Union far easier in Bulgaria than, say, in Romania or Hungary, the new regime was extremely suspicious of all changes, particularly in the sphere of culture and thought. And because the road to the second half of the fifties was also lined with political trials, Bulgaria entered the period of de-Stalinization on tiptoe. It was unthinkable that advances in any sphere deviate from the path laid down by the Soviet Union. We are hard put to find the names of any of the people who helped establish nationalized film in the credits of films that—beginning in 1958—attempted to find a new approach to reality, a more modern expression. The generation gap, and above all a gap in thought processes, was much more apparent in Bulgaria than elsewhere. And, unfortunately, the new generation in Bulgaria was

Septembrists

It Happened
in the Street

isolated from the rest of the world just as its predecessors were. Each movement toward change was repeatedly overwhelmed by the constant efforts to strengthen and purify national tradition, ethics, and esthetics.

The first symptom of deviation from the Zhdanov cultural policy was the effort to film subjects other than patriotic ones. In 1956 and 1957, films about historical epochs continued to dominate production. For example, another Soviet-Bulgarian coproduction, *Lesson from History* (*Urok na istoriyata*-1957), directed by Soviet director Lev Arnshtam, told the story of the Leipzig trial of Georgi Dimitrov in 1933. But in addition to this pious, craftsmanlike work, 1957 also saw the production of such films as *Labakan* and *Legend of Love* (*Legenda za lyubovta*), the aim of which were no longer just to educate the audience, but also to entertain it. Both films were the work of Czech director Václav Krška, who introduced a bit of his sense of poetry, beauty, and lyricism into the fairy tale of Labakan and into the adaptation of Turkish poet Nazim Hikmet's play, *Legend of Love*. Measured by the criteria of Czechoslovak cinema of the time, Krška's films, with their static composition, in crude color, were nothing out of the ordinary, but in Bulgaria they opened the door to new vistas, if only because of their subject matter.

The case was similar with the first contemporary comedies, *It Happened in the Street* (*Tova se sluchi na ulitsata*-1956), directed by Yanko Yankov (b. 1924), *Two Victories* (*Dve pobedi*-1956) directed by Boris Sharaliev and written by Wagenstein, and *Adam's Rib* (*Rebro Adamovo*-1956), directed by Anton Marinovich. Even Bulgarian critics, ordinarily so indulgent with regard to native production, could not avoid seeing their clumsiness and their poverty of expression. But in the brief history of Bulgarian film-making, the discovery of light comedy was indisputably a step forward.

At that time—once again following the Soviet example—production was being stepped up, and the first new names began to appear in the credits. Rangel Vulchanov (b. 1928), one of the coauthors of *Two Victories,* started work on his first independent film, and some other Bulgarian film-makers began to seek new forms for old themes. Nonetheless, the Bulgarian film industry was among the last in Eastern Europe to take advantage of the political and cultural thaw that followed Stalin's death, which was natural enough, given the history·of that country. The same could be said for Romania.

STARTING FROM SCRATCH:
Romania, 1945–1955

Nationalized cinema began its life in Romania in 1948 with even less in its favor than its counterparts in Yugoslavia and Bulgaria. And because in the first years of its difficult existence, it rejected even what little was left over from the monarchy, its further development was slower and more obstacle-ridden. The Communist Party, with only a couple of hundred members, gradually strove to take power in Romania. It succeeded, with the help of the Soviet Army, in 1948, after the abdication of King Michael in December 1947 and the proclamation of the People's Republic. But in this traditionally anti-Russian nation, the Party found little support, and was forced to seek backing in an unconditionally loyal relationship to the Soviet Union.

In addition, the Romanian Communist Party rulers, as the leaders of a defeated ally of fascist Germany, had to accept all the conditions of the Soviets—the first among them being the ceding of all production from Romanian oil fields to the Soviet Union and yielding control of the Romanian economy to newly created mixed Romanian-Soviet corporations. The Soviet Union took over the role that in years past had been played by Great Britain, France, the United States and later, Germany.

In the area of culture, there was no room for anything but the most primitive application of the teachings of Zhdanov. Another unfavorable influence on the infant Romanian cinematography was the Bucharest tradition of second-rate boulevard theater "à la Parisienne".

In contrast to nationalized film industries in the other Balkan countries, from the very outset Romanian film encountered the disinterest of the artistic community—decimated by emigration and purges—which, like the majority of prospective audiences, saw film as the prolonged arm of the unpopular regime. Unlike Bulgaria and Yugoslavia, the France-oriented Romanian culture, centered in Bucharest—"the Paris of the East"—did not have a cultural tradition of enlightenment or instruction, nor the notion of culture as an agent to "awaken" the "nation." It was this tradition and this notion that supported the initial steps of Yugoslav and Bulgarian film. The unified "nation" in Romania had always been an exceedingly foggy concept, and remained so until the new Communist establishment took control and for obvious reasons issued a call for the systematic education of the nation.

If we say that the first stage of the development of a nationalized Romanian film industry ended in 1956, as it did in the neighboring lands, it is not because Romanian film followed its neighbors to arrive at an artistic turning-point, but simply because that year marked the completion of the first stage of building the technical foundation for film in Romania, including movie theaters.

Between 1945 and 1948, a few small private Romanian firms sluggishly produced, as they had prior to the war, a number of primitive comedies and musicals—for example, *The Forest of Lovers* (*Pădurea îndrăgostiților-*1946), directed by Cornel Dimitrescu; *Two Worlds and One Love* (*Două lumi și o dragoste-*1947), a Romanian-Hungarian coproduction directed by Hungary's Viktor Gertler. The new national film organization was based primarily on the old state studio for short films, which had been founded in 1936 within the framework of the National Tourist Office. In 1949, after producing a number of documentaries, the national cinema began to produce feature films (one each in 1949 and 1950, two in 1951, five in 1952, and 27 by 1956).

The propaganda that was their sole raison d'être was primitive and ineffectual, but at a time when "not being with us" meant "being against us," a film could do nothing but fight for something or against something, and show how the expropriated classes were trying to subvert the new republic.

THE VALLEY RESOUNDS AND RURAL DRAMAS

In the early films of the Romanian nationalized industry, every sabotage attempt was foiled, every problem was solved, every construction project grew before your eyes, every tunnel was ceremoniously inaugurated—for example, *The Valley Resounds* (*Răsună valea-*1949), directed by Paul Călinescu. In those years, Romanian film created its own unmistakable "style," which it retained far into the years that followed: a style based on fragments of the "realistic" bathos of commercial silent films, on the means of expression used in provincial amateur theaters, and on dialogues of socialist-realist jargon, all this filtered through the multi-layered nets of political control.

When the attention of the ruling party concentrated on the collectivization of agriculture and the development of the semiliterate rural regions, most films looked to the farms for their subject matter. But these new rural dramas had nothing in common with the social realism of the Romanian writer Panait Istrati, one of the greatest European representatives of this literary trend, nor with the earlier Romanian rustic tragedies that told tales of tragic loves and passions in a setting of somber fatalism. In the new villages, the only ones who were allowed to entertain such emotions were the characters in the background, referred to as "atypical," people who had not yet embraced the values of the new society. In the foreground, at the center of attention, the heroes were concerned only with social justice and the happiness of all. They were people of strong moral fiber who saw the future of generations to come as more important than their own lives. They were always played by actors with strong features and an open gaze, with

The Valley Resounds

broad shoulders and manly handshakes. The actors cast in the role of the
kulaks, on the other hand, had big bellies, a number of meaty chins, and
villainous eyes. The kulaks were incorrigible schemers, full of the darkest of
passions, usually aimed in the direction of the innocent young daughter of

Mitrea
Cocor

The Mill of Good Luck

the poverty-stricken, indebted farmer. Sometimes, the hesitant young farm boy fell prey to the kulak's wiles, an innocent lad, unaware of his place; but before the words "the end" appeared on the screen, he too had joined the ranks of the new society. In short, they were replicas of the old romantic melodramas, with "socialism" taking the place of "God." Examples of these village dramas are *In Our Village* (*In sat la noi*-1951); *Mitrea Cocor* (1952), after the novel by Mihail Sadoveanu; *Development* (*Desfășurarea*-1954); and *Mill of Good Luck* (*Moara cu noroc*-1955), after a story by Ion Slavici.

Aside from *Development*, which was directed by Călinescu, the village dramas were the work of Victor Iliu (1912–1968), a graduate of the business academy, who followed his debut in short film with *In Our Village*, co-directed by Jean Georgescu. Georgescu was one of the three veteran directors who participated in the founding of nationalized film, the other two being Mihail and Călinescu. Iliu learned the fundamentals of film-making from Georgescu; he learned his job well, became one of the prime pedagogues of the Film Institute, and soon was given the title of Honored Artist. With the passage of time, he mastered some degree of film culture, and his *Mill of Good Luck* telling of the poverty of Transylvanian peasants in the nineteenth century, is considered by some Romanian film historians to be the first Romanian film to pose questions other than political ones, questions of form.

NEGREANU AND *THE BUGLER'S GRANDSONS*

In a country where the traditional antipathy to Russia was equated with anticommunism, new films were above all supposed to explain why most of the population rejected and continued to reject the dictatorship of the proletariat. In *Life Prevails* (*Viaţa învinge*-1952), directed by Dinu Negreanu (b. 1919), the new-type intellectual foils the intrigues of a member of the old intelligentsia, who sold out to a foreign power for the purpose of espionage. *Alarm in the Mountains* (*Alarmă în munţi*-1955), also directed by Negreanu, tells of life in the border regions, where peace-loving people are threatened by bandits sent by members of the expropriated classes now living abroad. As late as 1956, Negreanu made another film with the same plot scheme, *Stormy Bird* (*Pasărea furtunii*), a story of fishermen from the Black Sea during the war and after 1944. The most demanding effort of the early fifties was a two-part chronicle from the life of what Romanian critics liked to refer to as "simple folk," illustrating their struggle for social justice, and ending in the great apotheosis of the social changes yet to come, *The Bugler's Grandsons* (*Nepoţii gornistului*-1953): part one covered the period from World War One to the thirties, the second part, *The Sun Rises* (*Răsare soarele*-1954), concerned World War Two and the postwar period until "liberation." Negreanu had shot *Life Prevails* in the studios of Prague, but the *Bugler's Grandsons* and *The Sun Rises* were made in Bucharest, where work had begun on the Buftea Studios in 1950, the year IATC (The Institute of Theater and Film Art) was also founded.

Romanian film-makers educated in Moscow were very much an exception. Negreanu was the most prominent of the Moscow-trained directors. After having attended a special course at the Leningrad Theater Academy, he became chief director at both the Bucharest National Theater and the Buftea Studios. A recipient of the State Prize, he also occupied the high position of vice-president of the government's Committee for Cinema. In the sixties, he emigrated to the United States.

VETERANS AND PIONEERS

Anyone who wanted to introduce even an individual note into the symbolic schematics—the idea of an individual style was unthinkable—was suspect of "ideological confusion" and "ignorance of life." Thus, the first deviations from party orthodoxy—or better said, the first nuances—were so minute that they are indiscernible to all but the most painstaking historian. Comedies, which, together with village dramas, had been an integral part of Romanian film prior to and just after the war, began to be made again in 1952. Caragiale's farces were among them, the 1942 production of *Stormy Night* being the basis of a film that Romanian film historians consider a classic. Its director, Jean Georgescu, filmed three of Caragiale's one-act plays in 1952: *Chain of Weakness* (*Lanţul slăbiciunilor*), *The Visit* (*Vizita*) and *Romanian Farmer* (*Arendaşul român*). Georgescu also filmed the first Romanian "socialist" comedy, *Our Director* (*Directorul nostru*-1955), attacking bureaucracy, as personified by a dictatorial director. This theme, which was used at that time by all the film industries of Eastern Europe, was sharply attacked by Romanian critics, who accused the film of "generalization" and of being "atypical," and used the familiar argument that the film "does not disclose the positive attributes of the regime that removed the bourgeoisie from power."

Immediately after 1945, the new film industry welcomed back the third of the veterans, Jean Mihail, the man who had captured the life of the poor in *Lia,* one of the best Romanian films of the silent era. After a series of documentaries—*The Romanian People in the Fight for Democracy* (*Poporul român în luptă pentru democraţie*-1946)—he entered the schematic current, first of all with *The Ionutz Brigade* (*Brigada lui Ionuţ*-1954) and two years later with the wartime village drama, *The Devil's Abyss* (*Rîpa dracului*-1956), which was his last film. He died in 1963.

After 1956, when the worst excesses of socialist realism were coming to an end, the people who had breathed life into Zhdanov's teachings began to fall silent. Georgescu went on to shoot a film based on Caragiale's anecdotes and sketches, *Potpourri 1900* (*Mofturi 1900*-1964), and in 1962, made *Lantern of Memories* (*Lanterna cu amintiri*), reminiscent of the first Romanian fiction film, the 1912 picture, *War for Independence.*

Another of the pioneers, Victor Iliu, followed up his *Mill of Good Luck* with only one more film, *The Treasure of Vadu Vechi* (*Comoara din Vadul Vechi*-1964), once again concerned with sabotage, this time during the drought of the first postwar years.

FIRST GRADUATES, FIRST PROBLEMS

New directors followed the pioneering generation. Almost all of them were drawn from among the first graduates of the IATC, which graduated 140 film-makers in a brief seven years, and which had to close down some sections temporarily between 1957 and 1963 because the number of graduates exceeded the needs of Romanian film. It was not until 1958 that the Romanian film industry began to turn out 10 fiction films a year.

One of the first graduates of the IATC, Gheorghe Tobias (1926-1962) made the first Romanian color film, *The Red Water Lily* (*Nufărul roşu*-1955). It was a film for youngsters that showed the development of a little boy from a selfish individualist to a conscientious member of a youth organization.

The films made during the period that followed were also for the most part in keeping with the style and contents of *The Bugler's Grandsons.* Consequently, when Iulian Mihu (b. 1926) and Manole Marcus (b. 1928) graduated from the IATC in 1955 with the poetic *Pinching Apples* (*La mere*), filmed in a style that was unique for its individuality, within the context of Romanian culture of its day, they found themselves in conflict with the critics. Thus, from the very outset of their careers, they were prevented from taking advantage of the possibilities that had been created by the establishment of a nationalized film industry.

The creation of conditions for autonomous artistic development described in the nationalization decree was even less feasible in Romania than elsewhere, not to speak of the establishment of creative freedom. On the other hand, although for centuries one of the most backward countries in all of Europe, Romania finally possessed in 1956 the technological resources essential to large-scale film production. The Alexandru Sahia short-film studio, founded three years earlier, was working at full capacity and the studios making fiction films were well enough equipped to be able to welcome the first foreign directors and producers. Their economic and artistic contribution fulfilled an important precondition for the further development of Romanian cinema.

SOMEWHERE IN EUROPE:
Hungary, 1945–1954

Of all the countries in Europe, Hungary, for some very basic reasons, was perhaps the most likely to have followed the postwar neorealist path taken by the Italian cinema. First of all, a number of Hungarian film-makers, even before the war ended, had shown a keen interest in the theories foreshadowing the neorealist movement. And secondly, the postwar situation of Hungary bore a certain resemblance to that of Italy. Like Italy, Hungary had a nationalistic, authoritarian regime since 1919 and had been in the fascist camp during the war. As a result it shared the catastrophic Italian experience of 1943, "when our country was divided in two with foreign armies fighting on our own ground" (Alberto Moravia, commenting on the origins of Italian neorealism in *Europeo,* No. 50). Moreover, in Hungary and Italy there was a strong desire to examine the national character and to discover the truth about the war as well as about the sources of national violence and local fascism, though the latter was supported in these two countries by a smaller proportion of the population than had been the case in Germany.

Thus, it was no accident that in 1948, critics throughout the world spoke of "Hungarian neorealism" when *Somewhere in Europe* (*Valahol Európában*-1947) was shown at the Cannes Film Festival, and that they prophesied for director Géza Radványi a career like Roberto Rossellini's. But postwar Hungarian cinema had neither enough time nor enough room (compared to Italian film) to develop a substantial neorealist movement. A country that had been invaded several times by foreign armies and whose capital had been partly leveled to the ground during the three-month siege of the final winter of the war, Hungary could produce only three films a year during the immediate postwar years. The small number of movie theaters (280) also hindered any further development. In addition, the period immediately following the war was the time of another invasion, that of the American film industry, and everything that it implied. During the year and a half that followed the war, 100 American films were shown in Hungary.

Hungary also resembled Italy in the year of its capitulation (1943). During the last years of the war, young Italian film-makers were preparing the theoretical foundations for new film work, students at the film school in Rome were discussing films that were entirely different from those produced by Mussolini's Italy. In 1945, an Academy of Cinematographic Arts was established in Budapest, and under the leadership of the theorist Béla Balázs, it educated the first film-makers. Only a few films were made with the new, freer approach. By 1948, Hungarian film-makers had to submit to Zhdanov's principles, which stood diametrically opposed to the efforts of neorealism. In Hungary, neorealism, or better said, the new realism, was able to develop only in the mid-fifties, at a time when, in Italy, the neorealist movement had ended.

The most significant films produced in Hungary in the postwar period were *Somewhere in Europe* and *The Song of the Cornfields* (*Ének a búzamezökröl*–1947). Both of these films were made with the cooperation of Balázs, who had returned home after a long exile, the first years of which were spent in Germany side by side with the film and theatrical avant-garde and the later years in the Soviet Union where his direct experience with Stalinism had a fundamental influence on his later development.

In *Somewhere in Europe*, Géza Radványi found his inspiration in the fate of homeless children, and, as did De Sica in Italy with *Shoeshine*, Gerhart Lamprecht in Germany with *Somewhere in Berlin*, and Fred Zinnemann in Switzerland with *The Search* he created a shattering indictment of the world's antihumanism. Just like De Sica's little shoeshine boys, Radványi's heroes steal, pillage, and cheat, because they see nothing else around them, and because they had never encountered anything but contempt for the right to live and disrespect for human dignity. But society rejects them even when they try to make an honest living, and does everything in its power to hamper their struggle for a future. The cry for a new

Somewhere in Europe

humanism resounded from Hungary, as from Italy, inspired by neorealism and by some Soviet films of the late twenties and early thirties.

Shortly after having completed the film, Radványi left his homeland, this time for good. Balázs died prematurely shortly thereafter, having been officially attacked as one of those who were leading Hungarian cinema astray, and deprived of any possibility of working.

Postwar Hungarian literature, as well as art, continued in the tradition of native populism, a literary trend inspired by village life that stressed the decisive role of the village people as bearers of national values, all in the spirit of the nationalistic mythology. The main representatives of this trend included Áron Tamási, Péter Veres, and József Darvas. One of their predecessors was Ferenc Móra, whose 1927 novel about two rural families during World War One was made by István Szöts into the film, *Song of the Cornfields*. For Szöts, the Hungarian Dovzhenko, it was an opportunity to elaborate on the theme of *People from the Alps,* and to supplement it with an antiwar note. Szöts also shaped the story into the form of a ballad. Once again the view is of the Hungarian rural regions: cornfields, hand pumps, white gabled buildings, processions of black-garbed villagers walking dusty paths as they had for centuries, lives of drudgery and self-denial—always the strongest inspiration for Hungarian literature, and later on, for film.

People from the Alps

The Song of the Cornfields was never shown. The film was shelved as "non-Marxist" and "ideologically erroneous," and its director, the most talented in Hungary, was left without work, condemned to anonymity. The film that he had been preparing in 1948, *The Soil Under Your Feet* (*Talpalatnyi föld*) was taken over by Frigyes Bán.

The Soil under Your Feet

THE FIRST REORGANIZATION

In contrast to the other defeated countries of Eastern Europe—Bulgaria, Romania, and Germany—the decision to nationalize the cinema in Hungary was not the immediate result of postwar social and political realignments and it did not occur until after the Communist Party took power in 1948. The Hungarians knew better than anybody what state control over film meant, and so strove for a different "model."

Before nationalization, film production was in the hands of four coalition parties that formed the first postwar government: the Social Democratic Party, the Communist Party, the Peasant Party, and the largest party of all, the Smallholders' Party. Each of them tried to see to it that "its own" films were made.

The Communist Party produced *Somewhere in Europe,* while for the Peasant Party, Frigyes Bán made *Prophet of the Fields* (*Mezei próféta*-1947), a heavy-handed film based on a novel by the populist writer Áron Tamási. László Ranódy, in the same year, also wanted to make a film for the Peasant Party based on József Darvas's drama, *Abyss* (*Szakadék*). In it, Darvas, who was born into a poor village family, elaborated on his central theme, the moral problems created by fidelity to the soil and the rural environment. But there was no time for Ranódy to film his script. The Communist Party, as was the case elsewhere, took up arms against all expressions of a farmer's attachment to the soil as the greatest obstacle to the collectivization of agriculture. (Ranódy eventually did get to film *Abyss*—written during the war—in 1956, when Darvas, a former member of the Rákosi government, was awarded the Kossuth Prize for the film adaptation.)

The last film to be made before the nationalization was *The Siege of Beszterce* (*Beszterce ostroma*), another attempt on the part of Márton Keleti at a cinematic version of a national classic, this one written by Kálmán Mikszáth, a critical realist of the second half of the nineteenth century.

THE SECOND NATIONALIZATION

On March 21, 1948, the Hungarian film industry underwent its second nationalization. As compared to the first one in 1919, which came about as a result of pressure from below—its organizers having set up an extensive production plan in advance so as to be able immediately to start production on a large number of films—the first stage of the second nationalization began by reorganizing the entire industry and setting up an administrative hierarchy. The National Film Office was established as the supreme organ. Subservient to it was the Management of the Film Industry (under Dezsö Révai) and the National Enterprise for Film Production, which employed all directors, scriptwriters, and technicians. (Later on, these two organizations merged under Révai's leadership.) The original structure was very cumbersome, being subdivided into so many mutually interlinked departments that the production of fiction films remained far below the prewar, and even the wartime, level. Only six films were produced annually.

As was the case in most of the countries of Eastern Europe, the greatest contribution that nationalization made was to create a material basis for autonomous work: expansion of the network of movie theaters, schooling for a new generation of technicians and artists, and financial support for the other production branches (documentary, animation), which under capitalist control had no chance of independent development. In Hungary, the popular science film developed first, made famous throughout the world by the nature and animal films of director István Homoki Nagy (b. 1914)—e.g., *The Wild Waters* (*Nadvízorság*), *The Tale of the Woods* (*Gyöngyvirágtol lombhullásig*).

The first feature film of the nationalized industry, *The Soil Under Your Feet*, continued the tradition of rural themes. The basis for the film was once again a novel—a trilogy by contemporary author Pál Szabó—and the director was once again Frigyes Bán, who, together with Zoltán Fábri played a decisive role in reorganizing the production of fiction films and the selection of film-makers.

Frigyes Bán was always more of a prolific artist than a talented one. Together with Márton Keleti and Viktor Gertler, he belonged to the class of film-makers who are ready, willing, and able to make any film, any time. Lacking the talent of István Szöts, whose work on *Soil Under Your Feet* he took over, his effort to create a sequel to *People from the Alps* fell short of success. And yet *The Soil Under Your Feet*, which is Bán's best film, is a good realistic work whose success was due largely to the work of Bán's collaborators: director of photography Árpád Makai, cameraman György Illés, editor Félix Máriássy (1919-1975), and assistant director Károly Makk (b. 1925).

The Soil Under Your Feet is the love story of two young, poor villagers told against the backdrop of life in the thirties. The young people try in vain to keep up with their debts, try in vain to find a bit of happiness for themselves. It is inevitable that they should revolt against the situation that has been forced on them, and equally inevitable that the gendarmes respond by putting the young hero in jail. Everything had conspired against him; all he had left was his courage, and he offered it in the struggle for the common cause.

Fortunately, *The Soil Under Your Feet* was not simply a classic story of the struggle of the poor against the rich, but rather was interspersed with poetic images from rural life, and, in addition to the central couple, was filled with other well-developed characters. Although the film vacillates constantly between sentimental melodrama and schematic social realism, Bán succeeded in preserving both its integrity and that of its central characters. It ranks among the better Hungarian films of its day, which cannot be said of its so-called "optimistic sequel," *Liberated Land* (*Felszabadult föld*), which Bán shot in 1950.

Liberated Land

Optimism had become a duty in Hungary, as in the rest of Eastern Europe. Keleti, for example, made a musical comedy about the experiences of a factory choral group called *Singing Makes Life Beautiful* (*Dalolva szép az élet*-1950); Máriássy made *Full Steam Ahead* (*Teljes gözzel*-1951) about the victorious efforts of railroad workers to fulfill their production plan, and Gertler shot an optimistic drama, *Honesty and Glory* (*Becsület és dicsöség*-1951). Hollywood-type happy endings were dressed up in Hungarian clothes. During these same years (1949-1950), Minister of Interior László Rajk was arrested, although he was one of the most devoted of those who advocated and applied Communist policies. He was executed as an agent of a foreign intelligence service, along with a number of others, after a fake trial and enforced confession.

Full Steam
Ahead

Imre Jeney attempted to link his new work to his wartime film, *And the Blind Can See,* interweaving life in a factory with scenes of a drab postwar Budapest, the black market in the streets, and the daily life of a people that had been stripped of everything by the war.

But the attempt remained just that, and Jeney's film, *Woman Gets a Start* (*Egy asszony elindul*-1949) became proof of the lack of artistic vigor characteristic of Hungary at that time. Besides, the scenario was repeatedly changed in the process of shooting, so that the story of a woman from a wealthy family who goes to work in a factory after the war ended up with an espionage twist: the heroine's husband wants to flee to the West and sell plans for a new welding machine there.

Such changes were commonplace and reflected what was considered to be the only proper viewpoint. The Minister of Culture, József Révai, spoke of this viewpoint and the artist's duty in 1952, addressing his comments to Communist writer Tibor Déry, who had defended the right of the artist to his own inspiration:

Here, the writer has no such right. He has far greater rights, because he is free to speak out the truth, but it has to be *the* Truth. We do not give the writer the 'right' to deform vital truths. The state and the people are not going to adapt to his taste and his judgement. The writer is the one who has to identify his work with the interests of building socialism.

The words of József Révai, an outstanding prewar journalist and literary critic who after 1948 supported the greatly feared political leaders, Rákosi, Gerö, Farkas, were absolutely prophetic in the sphere of film. Until 1954, no motion pictures came into being that in any way deviated from the official line. As Rákosi was one of the most dedicated of Stalin's pupils, Hungarian film inevitably became a complete and thorough incarnation of Stalinist esthetics. No matter how hard we try, we can find nothing in the 31 films produced during those four years that would be worth more than passing mention.

In 1949, Révai unleashed an attack against the Marxist philosopher and esthetician György Lukács. In an organized campaign that was the ideological complement to the Rajk affair, Lukács was proclaimed a revisionist, an enemy to the party line and to Soviet literature. The roots of the evil were declared to be his acceptance of Hegel's idealism. And Lukács confessed, stating that as a result of overwork he had not kept in touch with the development of new Hungarian and Soviet literature. But he did not go much further.

In May 1956, András Kovács (b. 1925), head of the literary department of the Hungarian film industry and a future director, wrote about Hungarian film in the early fifties for the Hungarian Communist Party daily *Szabad Nép*:

We did not know the new Italian films, while in Soviet films we saw only the traditions that were not of permanent value. The mercenary traditions of old Hungarian films were also allowed to assert themselves, since they were often compatible with schematic demands, while a stiffer critical attitude precluded the appropriate espousal of the cause of such films as *People from the Alps, Somewhere in Europe,* or even *The Soil Under Your Feet,* works of high standard even though their contents may be debatable at some points. . . . When the social and political preconditions for a straightforward representation of the conflicts of reality are lacking, the strongest call for a full portrayal of life is futile. The contradictions due to the personality cult, to the formal interpretation of democracy, to criticism and self-criticism having become formal, and to the violations of legality that created deep social tensions and intrigued the film-makers even more intensively, could not be put on the screen truthfully, because any artist who exposed these contradictions in their full depth would in many fields have found himself up against the mistakes of political origins dominating the public life. There remained nothing else but to gloss matters over and speak half-truths. (István Nemeskürty's *World and Image,* p. 160.)

PUDOVKIN IN HUNGARY

In autumn of 1950, V. Pudovkin visited Hungary for the first time, as a special advisor. But the hopes with which some Hungarian film-makers had looked forward to his visit were unfounded. Only three years prior to his death, Pudovkin in 1950 was old, tired, broken. Moreover, having just completed a schematic biography of Russian aviation pioneer Zhukovsky, he was hardly in a position to give Hungarian film-makers any advice save the kind that was repeatedly drummed into their heads by party resolutions.

As Kovács wrote in the brochure "Pudovkin on Hungarian Film" ("Pudovkin a magyar filmről," Budapest, 1951), Pudovkin called on Hungarian film-makers to perfect themselves in their knowledge of Marxism-Leninism, in case of doubt to turn for advice to party representatives and to the ministry of culture, and to avoid all formalism. Concerning the production of historical films, Pudovkin declared that if a director is armed with Marxism-Leninism, he may invent historical events without damaging the authenticity of the work.

During his second visit, in the spring of 1951, Pudovkin viewed all the unreleased Hungarian films, and recommended changes in almost all of them. Thus Jeney's film *Underground Colony (Gyarmat a föld alatt),* and Máriássy's comedy *Catherine's Marriage (Kis Katalin házassága),* were imbued with an even more arid schematism. (Jeney's name eventually

The Sea
Has Risen

disappeared from the credits of *Underground Colony.*) Almost all of Pudovkin's remarks and speeches had as their guiding motif the idea that Hungarian film had improved since 1948, thanks to Soviet influence. Hungarian film had taken the right road, Pudovkin said, "It has taken the road of the working class. It has realized that people active in art must keep learning to retain the right and the means to fulfill the supreme task and the noblest duty: to support the beloved people in the building of their new life." (Georges Sadoul, *Panorama du cinéma hongrois,* Paris 1953).

The great film-maker was, fortunately, mistaken. Pudovkin's opinions, and those of the people who quoted him and wrote articles and brochures in praise of him during the Rákosi era, served only to deepen the crisis in Hungarian film. Pudovkin, for example, demanded the supremacy of script over direction. He also had the script to *The Sea Has Risen* (*Feltámadott a tenger*-1953), originally the work of the prominent Hungarian writer Gyula Illyés, rewritten 35 times until all the historical facts of the film's 1848 setting conformed precisely to the spirit of the prevalent ideology.

ZOLTÁN FÁBRI

The first to revolt against the concept of the omnipotence of script over direction (which shows up wherever producers or politicians strive to adapt film to their own taste or ideology) was Zoltán Fábri, since 1949 active as an artistic advisor for fiction films. His model was once again neorealism, together with the inspiration of the prewar social realism, represented in Hungarian literature by Zsigmond Móricz and Ferenc Móra.

In *Storm* (*A vihar*-1952) Fábri created another "film of the soil," but just two years later, in 1954, his *Fourteen Lives in Danger* (*Életjel*), sometimes considered the first work of the Hungarian film renaissance, attempted to break through the walls of Zhdanovist esthetics. The story in itself was exceptional in that, at a time when all art forms had to glorify the victory of man over nature, it admitted the possibility of a mine disaster that was not caused by sabotage. The ending still pays its tribute to the times by raising a high government official to the level of a deus ex machina who saves the miners, but Fábri's direction clearly points the way to a new esthetics. There are no alternating over-the-shoulder shots, none of the shots–reverse–shots repeated with regularity and scholastic lack of inventiveness in all the works of Zhdanovian cinematography; there are no long shots composed to match the paintings of socialist realist masters; nor are there any medium shots of characters presenting monologues from the screen to the film audience, taken with a static camera and lit to eliminate all nuances between light and shadow. Artificial sets are missing, as are polished interiors and false overall atmosphere. Fábri strove for authenticity, and, managing to circumvent the usual clichés, brought real problems to the screen.

Fourteen Lives in Danger

The silence that had settled over Hungary in the years under Rákosi began to loosen its grip. Writer and Minister of Popular Culture József Darvas encountered that silence during an election speech he made in May 1953 before 20,000 villagers. Three years later, he wrote about it in *Szabad Nép* (October 6, 1956):

The immense crowd was silent. There was no applause, no protest. That impenetrable silence aroused fear and anxiety. Several days later I went to a nearby village and walked from house to house. I encountered the same silence. In one house I found a woman alone. She didn't even answer my greeting. She was doing the laundry and she never even raised her head from work. I asked her some things, but she did not reply. She didn't even look at me. She just scrubbed and scrubbed, as if it were her job to wash the laundry of the entire world. She had a black kerchief on her head and she reminded me of my mother. She used to act that way when she was angry at me. In a while, she raised an uneasy gaze to my face. Then she walked over to the cupboard, took out a piece of black bread and threw it to me. "Here," she said, "they took everything from us. They emptied our corn-loft and they gave me this in the cooperative store." (Quoted in François Fejtö: Budapest 1956; ed. Julliard, Paris, 1962)

In June 1953, the absolute rule of Mátyás Rákosi came to an end. Hungary, so firmly controlled under Stalin, was the first of the Eastern European countries to take advantage of the changed situation after Stalin's death. The first intellectual opposition to the old regime came from the Union of Writers, which included among its members Tibor Déry,

Gyula Hay, Tamás Aczél, Zoltán Zelk, Tibor Méray, and Imre Sarkadi. They were soon joined by the film-makers.

In 1953, László Ranódy (b. 1919) and Kálmán Nádasdy finally finished the monumental historical fresco, *The Sea Has Risen,* which did a thorough job of falsifying the Hungarian revolution of 1848 and the life of the great national poet, Petöfi. But a year later, when the number of fiction films produced annually had risen to eight, it became clear that the burden of the past had been set aside. Károly Makk finally made his debut with a successful adaptation of Molnár's comedy *Liliomfi*; Zoltán Várkonyi (b. 1912) tried to find new means of expression in the screen version of Déry's story, *The Birth of Simon Menyhért* (*Simon Menyhért születése*), the fight for life of a woman giving birth to a child in a remote village cut off from the world by a snowstorm, and Máriássy created a partly traditional, partly new film, *Relatives* (*Rokonok*). At the same time, Makk was already preparing *Ward No. 9,* Fábri *Merry-Go-Round,* and Máriássy *A Glass of Beer* and *Spring in Budapest.* The Hungarian film was ready to accept and support any changes that could bring the land some relief.

PART III: Degrees of Dissent

THE REVOLT:
Hungary, 1954–1963

Four years are not a long time in the history of a country, and yet in the past four years, our homeland has changed more and progressed further than in decades past. . . . The majority of intellectuals today is convinced that the people's democracy can raise the nation from the depths. They know that our regime appreciates the work of the intelligentsia, values it, and grants intellectuals the opportunity to develop their talents that they never dreamed of under capitalism. . . . The policy of our government was fundamentally opposed to using force in the creation of agricultural cooperatives, and always based on the principle of voluntary membership. . . . Our people's democracy must be on guard against conspiracies and sabotage, which are almost always financed and organized from the USA.

Three weeks after Mátyás Rákosi made this speech on May 10, 1953, his successor, Imre Nagy, characterized the situation as follows:

Great tasks await our government, if we are to right the profound wrongs that were committed, and if law is once again to be installed . . . In the course of unjust purges, intellectuals of good will were treated in a manner unworthy of the people's democratic order, and they were denied the opportunities to utilize their specific abilities for the good of the homeland. . . . Membership in agricultural cooperatives was enforced by violence, and the violations that ensued resulted in grave unrest . . . Our authorities repeatedly violated the laws that protect the citizen's right to freedom and security. The new government will invalidate sentences passed by administrative decree, and will dissolve concentration camps. (Both quoted from Aczél-Méray: *La révolte de l'esprit*, pp. 147–151, Gallimard, Paris, 1962).

The first quotation falsifies reality just as it was falsified up to that time in Hungarian films. In the second series of quotations, the real truth penetrates to the surface, a truth that Hungarian film attempted to reflect between 1953 and 1956 and again in the sixties.

RÁKOSI AND NAGY

When in 1949 Rákosi planned the treason trial that became the starting gun for witch hunts throughout Eastern Europe, the man he singled out for the noose was not the hard-line Stalinist László Rajk, who finally ended up there, but rather the more liberal Imre Nagy. The same Nagy, who in 1953, four months after Stalin's death, returned from political limbo to become premier and then proceeded to secure the release of 10,000 political prisoners, got rid of culture's dogmatic dictator, József Révai, and turned the attention of the nation's economy—on the verge of bankruptcy and exhaustion as a result of untenable plans for building a heavy engineering industry—to the production of consumer goods and the improvement of agricultural production. In 1954, Nagy put on trial members of the state security apparatus, a security apparatus that was publicly described at that time by István Kovács, First Secretary of the Budapest Communist Party organization, as having used "criminal, reprehensible methods" in interrogations and investigations, and as having "fabricated all the charges of the prosecution in political trials."

Nagy had the support of Stalin's immediate successor, Malenkov, who had made hesitant attempts at similar reforms in the Soviet Union. But when Khrushchev replaced Malenkov in 1955 Nagy went on a leave of absence for reasons of health, and was subsequently accused of "rightist deviations."

It was too late to stop progress, though, and less than a year later, Rákosi, who still headed the Party, had to make a public declaration of the rehabilitation of the victims of the Rajk trial. The cultural arena became the focal point of political ferment, particularly the Union of Writers and the students' Petöfi Circle, originally established on the initiative of its Communist members. Attempts to hinder the development toward democracy only served to encourage the activity of the intellectuals, headed by three Communist writers, Tibor Déry, Tamás Aczél, and Zoltán Zelk, all laureates of the highest state prizes for literature. In his memoires, published in Budapest in 1969 under the title *No Verdict,* Déry wrote, "I was a bad Communist from the outset, I don't deny that. The question only is—and the answer has been sought for decades—whether anyone can be a good writer and a good Communist at the same time, in the close-fitting uniform which the Party fits him into and which he only rarely gets permission to unbutton."

In 1956, Déry published two short stories inspired by what was then referred to as the "deformations of the times." In *Niki* he told the story of a dog that dies when his master is arrested, because "no beast can withstand as much as a man." And in the story *Love,* which was filmed 15 years later, he related the story of a woman whose husband—unjustly jailed—returns unexpectedly from prison.

That was the atmosphere of the years in which Rákosi, who had spent most of the Horthy regime in prison or in the Soviet Union, and consequently whose contact with Hungarian life was at a minimum, tried desperately to prevent any reforms, thus setting the scene for an explosion. But the 20th Congress of the Soviet Communist Party and Khrushchev's pronouncements concerning Stalin's crimes meant Rákosi's end. The negligible concessions offered by his successor Ernö Gerö were no longer sufficient. The atmosphere was too tense, people were calling for radical changes. On October 6, 1956, 200,000 people attended the funeral of the rehabilitated Rajk and his co-defendants. On October 23, students stood at the foot of the statue of the Hungarian revolutionary poet of the mid-nineteenth century, Sándor Petöfi, and declaimed his poem "Arise Hungarians!" There were calls for solidarity with the Poles and for the return of Nagy, and the first shots were fired at the Radio Building. The immense statue of Stalin was toppled to the cobblestones—Stalin, whom

Révai had once referred to as the greatest figure in Hungarian history. Imre Nagy again became premier and György Lukács became minister of culture. The session of the Hungarian Communist Party Politbureau—with Soviet leaders Anastas Mikoyan and Mikhail Suslov present—emerged with a new First Secretary for the Party: János Kádár, Rákosi's former minister of the interior and later one of those jailed during the purges of the early fifties. But by then Soviet tanks had appeared on the streets of Budapest; they were welcomed with Molotov cocktails.

CRUSHED REVOLUTION

What ensued was without the slightest doubt a revolution. Its demands: (1) the establishment of Workers' Councils at the plants and factories; (2) a multiparty democracy; (3) freedom of speech and freedom of the press; (4) the departure of Soviet troops from Hungary; (5) agriculture based on private ownership of the soil by small landowners, with the retention of cooperatives only where the members voted in favor of it. Not a word about any return to conditions as they were before 1945, or of returning the land to large farmers and landholders.

The most important demands originated in the factories and the workers' districts of Csepel and Ujpest, underscoring the fact that this revolution was not just a revolution of the intelligentsia, it was a workers' revolution, a revolution of the impoverished.

The demands were accepted. On October 30, Soviet tanks withdrew from Budapest and the Soviet government issued a statement that spoke of "violations and errors in the relations between the socialist countries." Mikoyan assured Nagy that all Hungarian demands would be met and Kádár told Hungarian Communists, "We can safely say that the ideological and organizational leaders who prepared this uprising were recruited from among your ranks. . . ." The revolution had succeeded. For four days.

On the evening of November 4, Soviet tanks once again occupied all of Hungary; the Hungarian delegation was arrested as it sat down to negotiate with the high command of the Soviet forces, and a new government was established, headed by Kádár. Nagy and many of his collaborators, including Lukács, were arrested; some of them spent years in internment. It was not until June 17, 1958 that it was announced that Imre Nagy, along with a number of others, had been condemned to death in secret trial, and executed. Lukács had been released a year earlier.

After the events of 1956, about 200,000 citizens fled Hungary (some of them returned after the first amnesty), about 500 were executed, about 10,000 more deported. Leading cultural figures were arrested and sentenced to years of imprisonment (Déry, Háy, Zelk), others went into exile (Aczél, Méray). The Union of Writers and the Union of Film Workers were disbanded, as was the Hungarian Communist Party; it was replaced by the Hungarian Socialist Workers' Party, which started out with only 250,000 members.

On May 27, 1957, an agreement was signed concerning the "temporary presence" of Soviet troops in Hungary. Another chapter in Hungarian history had come to an end.

FILM IN 1954-1957

A knowledge of the facts surrounding the Hungarian revolution is essential for the comprehension of the so-called post-Stalinist period in all of Eastern Europe, no matter what the course of events during this period in the individual countries. It is essential for an understanding of the Hungarian film renaissance of the period from 1954 to 1957, and of the Hungarian film phenomenon of the sixties.

It is apparent from a glance at the records of historical events that the period of freedom of expression was very short in Hungary—as compared, for example, to Poland—and that it was suddenly and brusquely broken off, leaving time for a scarce handful of films to be made. There was no time for the emergence of the young generation, and thus the best films of this period were the work of directors of the preceding period. Nor was there time to create an autonomous structure of thought and form, which could have left a more permanent mark on the production that followed. Hungarian films of the period were more notable for their content and the manner in which they viewed reality, than for their form or the manner in which they interpreted reality. Form remained merely a link with the traditions of Hungarian populism, on the one hand, and on the other hand was simply an adaptation of Italian neorealism.

Moreover, a major hope of Hungarian film-makers perished with the suppression of the revolution: the establishment of autonomous production groups that would replace the central administration and give the artists more authority. Demands for these groups had appeared repeatedly in all resolutions drawn up by film-makers since 1953, and particularly in those issued by the Union of Film Workers.

FÁBRI AND MÁRIÁSSY

The majority of noteworthy films came into being in 1955, a year and a half after Dezsö Révai had been removed as the head of the Hungarian film industry and András Kovács had been named chief of the literary department. The effort of Hungarian film-makers to do away with the traces of the recent past, both in form and in content, had the effect of a bolt of lightning, not only at home, but also in the other Eastern European countries—and perhaps, even more strongly there than in Hungary. It was above all the films of Fábri and the Máriássys that became a symbol of faith in the possibility of speaking in a new language for the countries that had, up until then, been forced to hoe the Stalinist line.

Máriássy's film, *Spring in Budapest* (*Budapesti tavasz*-1955), based on Ferenc Karinthy's novel, was meant as a commemoration of the tenth

Spring in Budapest

anniversary of the liberation of Budapest by the Soviet Army. But Máriássy avoided some of the usual clichés, and attempted to show the end of the war as the inhabitants of the war-torn city had really experienced it. No one welcomed anyone, there were no reasons for celebrations, the land was destroyed, lives wasted, and the most valuable thing was a crust of bread. Even the love story receded into the background, although in the novel it was the center of the plot. Most important for Máriássy were the scenes of an unceremonious execution on the bank of the river, fragments of conversations, glances and gestures that the camera captured with a care generally reserved for events of significance. The same was true for *A Glass of Beer* (*Egy pikoló világos*–1955), in which Máriássy and the scriptwriter, his wife Judit, focused attention on the day-to-day events in the life of a family of workers in Budapest: their departure for work, their return home, their Sunday excursions to a garden restaurant in the suburbs. The film, undoubtedly influenced by the theories of Cesare Zavattini, captures the life of Budapest in general and in particular tells the story of a young working-class girl and her boy friend, who is doing his military service.

A Glass
of Beer

Merry-Go-Round

Simple people were also the subject of Fábri's film *Merry-Go-Round* (*Körhinta*–1955). The script was based on a short story by Imre Sarkadi, whose populist-inspired work is exceptional for its cruel view of contemporary man's morality, the very root of his selfishness. The story of *Merry-Go-Round,* which takes place on a cooperative farm, is conceived without the tragic peripatetics of populist art. The love of two young people is pursued on the basis of the systematic development of contemporary motifs, including the opposition of the parents seen this time as a part of the opposition to the forced organization of cooperatives. (Sarkadi, who had been awarded the highest literary prizes and honors, died in a fall from a window in 1961.)

Fábri filmed the exceptionally good script in a manner in which Hungarian populism had never been handled before. First of all, he more or less "rediscovered" montage and flash-backs, both of which had been prohibited by the Zhdanov esthetics of the recent past. Both Fábri's and Máriássy's films demonstrated an interest in new trends in the fine arts, an interest that accompanied the renaissance of film in other Eastern European countries as well. Neither Máriássy nor Fábri, however, were experienced enough to be able to take advantage of them as a starting point for the creation of new forms. For that matter, they did not even have enough time to tie in with the trend of modern film that was being born in world cinema. Visual influences in their films led rather to the deepening of the academic approach, which was probably most apparent in the direction of the actors.

Professor Hannibal

Fábri's next film, *Professor Hannibal* (*Hannibál tanár úr*–1956), was also based on the work of a well-known writer, a satirical short story by Ferenc Móra on the prewar Horthy regime. Fábri retained the historical background of the plot, but he elaborated on the individual motifs—selfishness, intolerance, cowardice, mob psychosis—in a manner that permitted no doubt as to their timeliness. Fábri's Professor Nyúl, whose life moves forward through musty schoolrooms and his miserable flat, seems to have just emerged from Rákosi's Hungary, with its atmosphere of fear and envy. The unfortunate author of an essay on Hannibal, the professor is persecuted by the mob for something that he did not do and sacrificed to higher interests about which he knows nothing. He is a figure as symbolic as Munk's trainman, Orzechowski, in the Polish *Man on the Track*. In the final scenes, after he is all but stoned to death, he tries to save his skin by presenting the obligatory self-criticism. Throughout this sequence, his frail build, reflecting his pitiable state, is emphasized by contrasting high- and low-angle shots. He finally concludes his presentation by praising the one who destroyed him. Although the mob understands nothing, the leader finally turns his thumb up. Professor Nyúl retreats before the unexpected clamor as he had before the stones, and his debased life ends with a step into the abyss of which he was totally unaware.

FIRST INTERVENTION

The atmosphere of *Glass of Beer* was developed further by the Máriássys in *Suburban Legend* (*Külvárosi legenda*-1957), but at the last moment, they were obliged to change the framework of the plot. The story, originally conceived as a contemporary one, had to be placed in the thirties instead, even though it was apparent from the official reaction to the film that the director did not entirely conceal the original intention. The film is once again set in a poor workers' district of the city, where two young people fight for moments of happiness in an oppressive environment. But there is no way out, and the escape from the present is sought in alcohol. The film was banned for "hopelessness and a false view of the working class," the authors of the film had to attend organized meetings where they were subjected to sharp attacks without being able to defend themselves. *Suburban Legend* remained the most influential film of the Máriássys.

Another film that was banned after 1956 was the fiction debut of Tamás Banovich (b. 1925), *The Empire Gone with a Sneeze* (*Az eltüsszentett birodalom*-1956), a fairy-tale allegory about a tyrant whose entire kingdom had to bend to his will. Banovich's career as a director of feature films (he had done short films and collaborated on scripts in the past) practically came to an end with this work. Although he later did outstanding work as a designer of Miklós Jancsó's films, the three feature films that he made in the sixties did not arouse any interest, not even on the Hungarian market. (The leading actor in *Empire*—who made his name in the role of the young farmer in *Merry-Go-Round*—Imre Soós, committed suicide after 1956.)

Nor did movie theaters get to show Zoltán Várkonyi's *Bitter Truth* (*A keserü igazság*-1956), a film that attacked Stalinist bureaucracy through the story of the corrupt manager of a large enterprise. Though politically ambitious, however, *Bitter Truth,* the product of what was known as "upside-down schematism" was in no way distinguished for its artistic quality. A similar film was *Danse Macabre* (*A tettes ismeretlen*-1956), in which László Ranódy told of the destinies of young delinquents in an ordinary manner, giving little attention to any deeper relevancies.

SZÖTS FOR THE LAST TIME

The work of István Szöts, who emerged after seven years to make films again, was among the more interesting contributions to Hungarian cinema during these years. In *Stones, Castles, People* (*Kövek, várak, emberek*-1955) he created a poetic document of the northern Hungarian hill country, where geese promenade among the ruins of castles, and where the old traditions still survive among the rural inhabitants, Szöts's great love.

Which of the Nine? (*Melyiket a kilenc közül?*-1956) is one of Szöts's purest films. The fairy tale of a poor father who has no Christmas present for his nine children except a song once again demonstrates the exceptional talent that Hungarian film lost when it lost Szöts.

Szöts was one of the 200,000 to leave Hungary after 1956. He did do some film work in Austria and France, but the essence of his work—the people, the landscape, the countryside, the atmosphere of Hungary—all remained far behind him.

Of the young generation, the one to call the most attention to himself was Károly Makk, with his film *Ward No. 9* (*A 9-es kórterem*-1955), a promising neorealistic attempt to capture the atmosphere of waiting in a hospital, and the partial destinies of several patients. The film was shot according to the excellent script of Tibor Méray, one of the leaders of the revolt of Hungarian intellectuals. Similar in its conception was Makk's next film (also after Méray's script), *Tale on the Twelve Points* (*Mese a tizenkét találatról*-1956), which took some simple characters and, against the backdrop of an accurate view of contemporary Budapest, developed into a political allegory about the Hungarian national passion: soccer.

Sunday Romance

Imre Fehér (1926-1975), a member of Makk's generation, never fulfilled the hopes that he aroused in 1957 when he filmed Sándor Hunyady's short story *Sunday Romance* (*Bakaruhában*) (first shot by Norman Taurog in 1938 in Hollywood as *The Girl Downstairs*). The main charm of Fehér's *Sunday Romance* rests in its finely drawn picture of the final years of the

Austro-Hungarian Empire. With great understanding Miklós Hubay's script sketches the small dramas of a small world—the unhappy love of a maid for an officer who visits the home where she is serving. *Sunday Romance* also attracted attention for its superb camerawork, by János Badal. (After 1956, Badal left Hungary, and the actor who played the lead, Iván Darvas, the leading star of the day, was sentenced to six years in jail.)

AFTER THE REVOLUTION

The first film that attempted to respond somehow to the events of 1956 was György Révész's (b. 1927) third feature film, *At Midnight* (*Ejfélkor*-1957). Révész, an adaptable artist and a good craftsman, used a script by journalist Iván Boldizsár that told the story of a young couple who must decide during a single night whether to flee across the border or stay at home.

The official version of the Hungarian revolution as a conspiracy on the part of imperialist agents was created by Márton Keleti in the propagandist films *Yesterday* (*Tegnap*-1959) and *To the Frontier* (*Pár lépés a határ*-1959), the type of film that had no predecessors in Hungarian production, nor, fortunately, any sequels.

The period between 1958 and 1962, when production held steady at about 15 films a year, was mostly a time of literary adaptations characterized by national academism and populism. The new chief of cinematography was the writer, József Darvas, formerly Rákosi's Minister of Popular Culture.

Fábri made an interesting film about the tragedy of a young village girl in prewar Budapest—*Anna* (*Edes Anna*-1958)—and a weaker rural drama,

Accident

The Brute (*A dúvad*-1959). As for Máriássy, he strove—both in the cinematically more successful *The Smugglers* (*Csempészek*-1958) and in *Sleepless Years* (*Almatlan évek*-1959)— to elaborate on the theme of force and the desire for freedom.

Once again, as had been the case before 1954, films of low artistic quality were in the majority, represented as before by Frigyes Bán, who directed the Hungarian-Slovak coproduction of *St. Peter's Umbrella* (*Szént Péter esernyőjé*-1958), the costume film about the mysterious robber *Fatia Negra* (*Szegény gazdagok*-1959), and *A Husband for Suzy* (*Rangon alul*-1960); Zoltán Várkonyi, who made *Pillar of Salt* (*A sóbálvány*-1958), and *Crime at Dawn* (*Merénylet*-1959), and finally Viktor Gertler, who made only two detours between 1955 and 1958 from his undemanding routine. In *Accident* (*Gázolás*-1955), he tried to use the neorealistic method to treat a social theme (reminiscent of the Czech *Conscience* and the Spanish *Death of a Cyclist*); three years later, he made what was probably his best film, *Red Ink* (*Vörös tinta*), a psychological story about children and their encounter with school discipline.

Thus, by May 1959, József Darvas was able to declare, at a meeting of Hungarian film-makers: "It is no longer a threat but a reality. Grey mediocrity prevails in the selection of subjects, there is disinterest in what people are working on, film messages stand in second place, literary adaptations are weak. . . . Efforts to create a real drama from contemporary life wind up one by one as failures."

In this situation, László Ranódy's elaborate film, *For Whom the Lark Sings* (*Akiket a pacsirta elkísér*-1959), with a script by Darvas, was highly overpraised, even abroad, although it was simply another story of a village

Two
Half-Times
in Hell

before World War One, where two young people from poor homes fight for happiness in a hostile world.

Of the films produced early in the sixties, one that stood out was Fábri's *Two Half-Times in Hell* (*Két félidö a pokolban*-1961). The original anecdote—a Nazi colonel holds a soccer match between Hungarian concentration camp inmates and his SS men in celebration of Hitler's birthday—was adapted by Fábri to include a number of indirect references to the situation in Hungary, a frequent approach in Hungarian film, though, unfortunately, rarely coupled with an adequate form. The Hungarian team wins, even though it knows that the penalty for the victory will be death.

A note of social protest, attempting to follow the best films of the period from 1954 to 1957, was reintroduced into Hungarian cinema by György Révész. But his *Land of Angels* (*Angyalok földje*-1962), which is set in the Horthy era, never did get further than a genre portrait of the outskirts of Budapest, inhabited by typical figures of the urban poor, whose lot is uncertainty and hopelessness.

Károly Makk's film *Fanatics* (*Megszállottak*-1961) was the only one to bring some thematic revival and make an attempt at a nonconformist approach to contemporary material. The camera was in the hands of one of the best Hungarian cameramen, György Illés. After *House Under the Rocks* (*Ház a sziklák alatt*-1958), another rural love tragedy, Makk, in *Fanatics,* finally abandoned populist themes, which had become a rut into which both Hungarian film and literature were falling.

The central problem of *Fanatics* is the conflict between personal initiative and bureaucratic authority: an engineer searching for water in steppe-like "puszta" is helped by the head of a cooperative farm, who thereby sins against bureaucratism. As in *The Defendant,* a Czech film of the same period, the focus is on personal responsibility in a system that is doing everything to eliminate it. Makk stresses the initiative of people who, amid general indifference, enter into the fray, risking being put on trial for overstepping the bounds of their authority. But, as in 1954, when a high government official stepped in to resolve the crisis of Fábri's *Fourteen Lives*

Land of
Angels

in Danger, Makk's protagonists are saved by the action of a member of parliament.

MIKLÓS JANCSÓ

The first director to try to systematically demystify the essence of the Hungarian character and the Hungarian situation in the sixties was Miklós Jancsó (b. 1921), who had been shooting short films ever since his graduation from the Film Academy in 1950. Three of these short works were based on materials from Jancsó's trip to China, one was devoted to Zsigmond Móricz (1879-1942), a writer whose approach to reality is close to Jancsó's. It was from him that Jancsó learned his self-confident treatment of language, as well as the structure of plots based on the interrelationship between biological and social motifs as an expression of one and the same vital force. Jancsó's documentary films were in no way significantly different from other films produced in the fifties, conforming to the general policy line. And Jancsó's first fiction film, *The Bells Have Gone to Rome* (*A harangok Rómába mentek-*1958), falls into the same category: it was a classical realistic story about some children who, during the war, try to rescue bells that are being taken to be used as metal for guns. But its filming was out of keeping with Jancsó's creative approach.

On the other hand, his second film, *Cantata* (*Oldás és kötés-*1962), is considered an overture to the Hungarian film renaissance of the sixties. The story of a crisis experienced by an ambitious young doctor who had closed himself off from reality and attempts unsuccessfully to reestablish his ties with his peasant father (the literal translation of the title is "To Untie and Retie," and the theme is rather frequent in Eastern European literature of the period) is told by Jancsó in a de-dramatized form inspired by Antonioni. Moreover, it anticipates the future texture of Jancsó's oeuvre in the complex structure of its script. The story of a man who experienced the Rákosi regime and the events of 1956 (though never mentioned in the film) is in a way symbolized by the lyrics to Béla Bartók's *Cantata Profana*—overheard on the radio at the end of the film—a popular ballad telling of a father who doesn't recognize his sons who have been transformed into deer.

In 1961, the first films of the so-called Béla Balázs Studio began to appear, the studio being something of an experimental workshop, founded three years earlier, which was to give the graduates of the Film Academy the opportunity to make their first films. The fact—unique in the world—that here young people would immediately have a chance to work independently, became a decisive factor in the further development of Hungarian cinematography. In the first films of the Studio, which was independent of official production, we encounter film-makers who would play key roles in the future of Hungarian cinema: István Szabó, Sándor Sára, István Gaál, Pál Gábor, János Rózsa, Ferenc Kardos, Judit Elek, and others.

THE POLISH SCHOOL:
Poland, 1956-1963

Poland's "October 1956," which was the culmination of a simmering crisis that had begun after 1953, started in the industrial city of Poznan with a spontaneous general strike, demonstrations, and street fighting. Later in the month, after the crisis became generalized, Soviet tanks surrounded Warsaw. But they never received the order to attack, even though Khrushchev's personal efforts to prevent a change in the governmental and party leadership of Poland had been thwarted at every turn. Khrushchev himself understood quickly enough that the newly elected First Secretary of the Polish Communist Party, Wladyslaw Gomulka, was no liberal or "revisionist." But on October 20, 1956, Gomulka stood as the indisputable leader of the nation. This leadership was affirmed when, in addressing the people of Warsaw on a city square, he began his speech by singing the first notes of the "Internationale" and was joined by a hundred thousand voices.

One of his first promises to the nation was that he would rehabilitate the victims of the wartime non-Communist anti-Nazi resistance and erect a memorial to their courageous struggle. At the same time—and for the first time—theaters were permitted to show the newsreels that Antoni Bohdziewicz and Jerry Zarzycki had shot during the Warsaw Uprising in 1944. Audiences wept. And Bohdziewicz, the only film-maker to oppose the party's cultural policy line at Wisla in 1949, was allowed to start working again after seven years of enforced inactivity.

It was not until later that the real significance of October 1956 became apparent: it did not in reality represent the beginning of a broad democratization of Polish socialism, but rather the beginning of the end for the hope that had been born several years earlier. Polish cinema became a precise reflection of this situation, moving from films that overtly contemplated Poland's bright future to films filled with sorrow and hopelessness, and finally, in the mid-sixties, to films characterized by a uniform mediocrity and inanity. The tension of these years gave birth to the "Polish School." This was its first tale:

ANDRZEJ MUNK'S POLAND

An old man, an engine driver who has been deprived of his job, dies under the wheels of a train. Did he commit suicide? Was he a saboteur? Witnesses testify before the investigation commission, and each presents his own version of the events of a rather unimportant demise. What sort of a person was the dead man? An eccentric? An opponent of the new life in Poland?

Man on the Track

A critic of the young people who had shunted him out of his job? Was he embittered and hateful, or was he, rather, too human, too vulnerable, and, ultimately, too honest to accept the hypocrisy of the society in which he lived? "The air in here is bad," says the head of the investigation commission at the end of the hearing, and he opens a window.

Andrzej Munk (1921-1961) divided the story of *Man on the Track* (*Czlowiek na torze*-1956) into three flashbacks, three subjective versions, of the dead man's life, the resultant mosaic of which not only partially answered questions concerning the life and destiny of an individual, but also a number of other questions, questions that all of Poland was posing in these years. In the light of the answers, truth was no longer consistently clear and unequivocal, mistakes and failures were not always the fault of the enemy, and the people were not the fortunate recipients of directives and resolutions. In speaking of *Man on the Track*, Munk said, "We wanted to show what a terrible injustice social circumstances can inflict on a person." It was almost as if Munk's trainman, Orzechowski, suspected, attacked, and persecuted, who perished on the railroad tracks in order to prevent a railroad disaster, was a symbol for Poland in that year of 1956, a symbol of the years when anything could be inflicted on a man—even the most brutal kind of injustice—under the name of "social circumstances." His story, filmed before the events of October 1956, seemed to illustrate the ideas Gomulka voiced at a meeting of the Central Committee on October 20, 1956, shortly after the spontaneous Poznan demonstrations:

The system of the years past broke human characters and consciences, trod on people, spat on their honor. The instrument of power was slander, falsehood, and even provocation. Tragic missteps were committed, innocent people were sent to their deaths. Others were imprisoned, many for long years. Some of them were Communists. Many people were bestially tortured. Fear and demoralization reigned. We have finished with this system, or better said, we shall finish with it once and forever.

Reality is seen and reconstructed in Munk's films through the eyes of his characters, imprisoned in certain unmistakable environments that symbolize their lack of freedom—the railway station in *Man on the Track,* Warsaw of the uprising and the prison camp in *Eroica,* the mountains in *Blue Cross,* the concentration camp in *The Passenger.*

Munk, Wajda, Kawalerowicz, and others never doubted the soundness of the socialist system, but they argued that every man had a right to select freely his own life situation and called for social conditions that would transform this right into something that was a matter of course.

Munk had graduated in 1950 from the Film Academy at Łódź where he specialized in photography and direction. His first short documentaries are informed by enthusiasm for the new way of life and by an effort to achieve a timely "objectivism"—e.g., *Science Closer to Life (Nauka bliżej życia*-1951); *Direction Nowa Huta (Kierunek Nowa Huta*-1951); *Recollections of the Villagers (Pamiętniki chlopów*-1952). But *The Word of a Railroadman (Kolejarskie slowo*-1953) clarified Munk's inclination to see objective facts in a subjective manner and to develop a kind of social reflection that aimed at eliciting the viewer's participation. *The Stars Must Shine (Gwiazdy muszą plonać*-1954), a documentary about several miners, further develops this style. The film was codirected by Witold Lesiewicz (b. 1922).

In his first feature film, *Blue Cross (Blękitny krzyż*-1955), Munk tried for an action film made with documentaristic methods. He placed the film in the mountains of the Polish-Slovak border, where at the end of the war, members of the Polish Mountain Rescue Service evacuated a partisan hospital threatened by the German offensive. The characters are delineated in such a manner that their inner lives introduce dramatic tension into the story, even though they still are not fully realized individuals. There was only one step left in Munk's full transition towards fiction film—the addition of a narrative voice, a role that in Munk's films was assumed by the writer, J. S. Stawiński, one of the cofounders of the Polish film school. Stawiński's rationalist-existentialist philosophy is dialectically linked with Munk's interpretation of the past as the outcome of variously interdependent destinies. Both Stawiński's notion of being captive, and Munk's relativism of the past—a relativism based on a person's experience of the land—were to appear repeatedly in many other Polish films. Stawiński's influence on Munk, however, should not be exaggerated, as is often done. Munk took his stories and his plots from Stawiński, but in the final

Eroica

analysis he subjugated everything to his own philosophy, and to his subjective style.

The basis of *Eroica* (1957) was two of Stawiński's stories entitled "Hungarians" and "Flight." Munk, whose entire oeuvre consists of breaking down stories into chapters (three in *Man on the Tracks,* six in *Cross-eyed Luck,* three in *The Passenger*), did not connect them. On the contrary, he wanted to add another independent story to them, a third movement in his antiheroic symphony, with its ironic Beethovenian title.* The ironic tone runs throughout the film, but is strongest in the first segment, *Scherzo alla pollacca,* where the Warsaw Uprising appears as a tragicomedy. Stawiński's rational scepticism, mercilessly attacking the "Polish standard of death," is played out in a typical Munkian environment, presented, with what appears to be noninvolvement, as a segment of everyday reality. As opposed to most other Polish directors, Munk hardly ever uses symbolism or expressionism, but instead develops his ideas through the use of the physical reality of objects and people. In *Eroica,* his basic idea is "antieroica," a refutation of the myth of heroism, and an exploration of the myth's origin.

Dzidzius, the central figure of the first story, is a Warsaw black-marketeer who arranges for contact between resistance fighters and a Hungarian unit that is fighting on the side of the Nazis, making the arrangements as if they were an ordinary business negotiation. He handles first one side and then the other with the same sceptical matter-of-factness, is more often

* This third story was shot, but Munk did not consider it good enough to be shown.

drunk than sober, and more attracted to his wife and bed than to the barricades. He embodies nothing of the traditional Polish romanticism, but instead is ludicrous and shrewd. Seen through his eyes, even the embattled city of Warsaw loses its heroic dimensions. In the end, however, Dzidzius returns to the beseiged city, in spite of his conviction that all the suffering and sacrifice is totally useless.

The second story, *Ostinato lugubre,* attacks the legend of heroism at its very core. Here, more than in any other of Munk's films, the meaning of life is dependent on concrete conditions. The more Munk's heroes adhere to the myth, and the more blindly they confuse it with the independent experience of life, the less they are free. And so a group of Polish prisoners of war, vegetating in a German camp, appears all the more grotesque when they arrive at a fanatical credulity in the heroism of one of their own number. The grotesqueness becomes farcical when the hero—who is believed by the entire camp to have escaped—appears concealed in the attic, where he takes his own life in order to allow the myth to survive.

At the conference of film-makers from the Eastern European countries that was held late in 1957 in Prague, the main spokesmen condemned the new Polish films as being hostile to the socialist system and demanded that Polish film-makers return to the idealization of national history and the present. The Prague conference was the first attempt to reinstall a unified ideological line in the countries of Eastern Europe after the 20th Congress of the Soviet Communist Party and after the events in Poland and Hungary in 1956—and their causes and consequences—had shaken the ideological foundations of Stalinism.

The films of the Polish school—namely, *Eroica, Night Train, Canal, Ashes and Diamonds, Cross-eyed Luck, Eve Wants to Sleep*—were not shown in the movie theaters of the other socialist countries until the sixties, if at all.

THE ROMANTICISM OF ANDRZEJ WAJDA

In *Canal* (*Kanal*-1957), Stawiński's rationalism was dissolved in Andrzej Wajda's romanticism and fateful tragedy. Here there was no room for farce, nor for objective analysis, here, with imminent death the only certainty, the commonplace became unique. In all of Wajda's films, the destiny of the heroes, enmeshed in the turning gears of history, is intensified by personal tragedy, for the most part unfulfilled love, which is frequently of greater interest to the director than the story itself.

Canal tells of the last desperate struggle by a group of resistance fighters in the 1944 Warsaw Uprising and their journey through the sewers from the German-occupied section of the city to areas where the fighting is still going on. As in his other films, extreme situations present Wajda with an opportunity to examine the consciousness and conscience of his heroes, all the "pros" and "cons." Stawiński saw the Warsaw Uprising as a

Canal

"military absurdity," and the journey through the sewers—which he himself had experienced when in 1944 he escaped from German imprisonment, later to be recaptured—as a "journey through the infernos." The absurdity of the situation comes to a head primarily in scenes where the images are composed to show the opposite side of the Wisla River, where the Soviet Army had halted, scenes in which the physical presence of the Soviet troops is strongly felt by audiences aware of the historical facts. The Uprising, in which 250,000 people perished, was played out before the eyes of the Soviet Army, and the orders not to come to the aid of the Polish patriots that had rebelled without first consulting Moscow were carried out to the letter.

Wajda's films, like those of Munk and other directors, wanted in part to show the antifascist resistance as it actually was. This is where we should seek the answer to why so many films on the resistance movement were made in Poland after 1956. In Poland, it was not an escape from the present, as was the case in other Eastern European countries, nor was it a last resort. It was, on the contrary, the reopening of one of the nation's unhealed wounds. Discussing the resistance movement the way Wajda and Munk did was a doubly controversial act. On one hand it revealed lies that had been spread within the past years, when the facts concerning the resistance movement were twisted and distorted, and on the other it turned against an underlying conviction held by a majority of the Polish people—a

conviction that, quite logically, uncritically glorified the resistance movement and all its myths.

"Souvenir of the sewers," says the hero of another of Wajda's films,
Ashes and Diamonds (*Popiól i diament*-1958), indicating his eyes, hidden
behind dark glasses. He too soon dies "for the cause," "for the idea."

Ashes and
Diamonds

Ashes and Diamonds was based on Jerzy Andrzejewski's novel of the same
name, written in 1948, and captures the hopelessness of so-called "moments
of truth" through the prism of the first day after the war. Maciek, a former
member of the Home Army—the principal bearer of the anti-fascist
non-Communist resistance—accepts the last order from his commander,
the order to kill a Communist functionary. The date is May 9, 1945, but
the war is not yet over in Poland, for now Pole faces Pole. Maciek (Zbigniew
Cybulski's first major role) is going to commit murder in order finally to
become free—with no expansive gesture, without conviction, without faith,
with the feeling of infinite fatigue and disgust. His victim is only an
exhausted old man, tortured by doubts and recriminations. The plot of
the film, just like the plot of the novel, covers only a few hours. In the
course of this period, Maciek has a brief love affair, commits murder
without knowing why, and perishes with equal senselessness, equally alone.

Last Day
of Summer

In 1948, Andrzejewski was obliged to change many places in the first edition of the novel, for reasons of censorship. In Wajda's film, the reality of postwar Poland appeared in its undistorted form, in which an expressionist vision blends with a complicated symbolism. The director of photography for *Ashes and Diamonds* was Jerzy Wójcik, who also filmed *Eroica, Samson, Mother Joan of the Angels, Cross of Value,* and others.

THE POLISH SCHOOL

Such a renaissance in both content and form was so apparent in almost all the Polish films produced between 1956 and 1959 that these films soon came to be identified with the "Polish film school." These new currents in Polish cinema were so broad and had such a profound effect on Polish film making that no later efforts were able to eliminate either the resultant elaborate styles of expression or the presentation of ideas through mature reflective forms. Clearly, the years between 1956 and 1959 saw the birth of a modern Polish cinema.

That was also the period when Polish production divided into two categories, the borders of which had for a long time remained fuzzy in Eastern European film-making. On one hand, there were challenging films, responding to avant-garde tendencies, on the other hand, films of pure entertainment. No longer was Polish film-making dominated by the monotonous styles and genres typical of the Stalinist era; no longer were purely entertaining or experimental films proscribed.

A subjective approach, diametrically opposed to the practice of socialist realism, reigned supreme to an increasing degree in the films of the Polish school. Polish directors approached reality more and more through the main character or characters, sometimes identifying directly with them. Their means of expression were with increasing frequency those means that best interpreted this view: a complex, frequently eclectic form with the frequent use of expressionistic and symbolic images.

Typical of this type of film was *Last Day of Summer* (*Ostatni dzień lata*–1958), the directorial debut of writer, screenwriter, and critic Tadeusz

Konwicki (b. 1926) and cameraman Jan Laskowski (b. 1928). The 60-minute story seems, on first glance, to be made up out of nothing: an ocean beach and two people who are strangers, a man and a woman. Gradually the silence and the isolation fill up with memories of the war and the past that become the actual content of the film, mingling with the present, creating an image of human solitude, documenting the impossibility of escape from one's own consciousness. The motif of the immutability of tragic experiences would return again and again, in various forms, in the Polish cinema of the years that followed, as would a view of reality by means of the past. Gradually the analysis of the relationship between two individuals replaced contemplation on the dubiousness of heroism—or, better said, just slightly amended it—that for several years had been the primary concern of Polish film-makers.

Before he had the opportunity to direct *Last Day of Summer,* Konwicki had written the script for *Winter Dusk* (*Zimowy zmierzch*-1957), a film that reflects a similar outlook. Mieczyslaw Jahoda, the cameraman for *Winter Dusk,* had, together with Jerzy Lipman and Jerzy Wójcik, a considerable influence on the pictorial quality of films of the Polish school. There is no doubt that *Winter Dusk* was primarily a scriptwriter's and cameraman's film. The name of the director, Stanislaw Lenartowicz (b. 1921), had never in the past appeared in connection with a film of such significance, and did not appear so later. Once more, against the apparently bare backdrop of a small town, we are presented with a melancholy story of people derailed by the war: of a father who is waiting for his son, a man who brings a wife home from the war, and the girl who was once his sweetheart.

A similar theme also appeared in Kawalerowicz's *The Real End of the Great War* (*Prawdziwy koniec wielkiej wojny*-1957), a film that represented a marked change from the director's prior concentration on plot-centered stories. After a noteworthy attempt at a modern thriller with a political background—*The Shadow* (Cień-1956), based on three stories by Aleksander Scibor-Rylski—Kawalerowicz used *The Real End of the Great War* to focus on the spiritual state of a person who, returning home mentally disturbed from a concentration camp, finds that his wife no longer expected him to return and is living with someone else. Kawalerowicz's inclination to structure stories on a precise pattern continued to be a strong characteristic of his work, as did his interest in sets and the symbolic significance of objects. The sophisticated form of his films, the shots composed to focus the viewer's attention on formal beauty, and the structure of his plots left no doubt that Kawalerowicz was aware of contemporary currents in world cinema.

Kawalerowicz was the only one of the older directors who found real inspiration in the new approach. Aleksander Ford also tried to join his past experiences with the new form and de-dramatized content in his *Eighth Day of the Week* (*Osmy dzień tygodnia*-1957). But his tale of two

young people vainly seeking a place where they can be alone remained more
an effort to tie in with the aspirations of the young generation of writers
and film-makers than an expression of an autonomous creative interest.
Made in coproduction with the West Germans, the film was an adaptation
of a short story by Marek Hlasko, an idol of Polish youth, whose novellas
were reminiscent of the documentary "black series." *Eighth Day of the
Week* was never shown in Poland.

Hlasko's short stories also formed the basis for the graduation project
of three students of the Łódź Academy (Pavel Komorowski, Julian
Dziedzina, and Walentyna Uszycka): *End of Night* (*Koniec nocy*-1957).
The plot of the film, made under the artistic supervision of Antoni
Bohdziewicz and with the directorial assistance of Roman Polański,
deals with the history of hooliganism and juvenile delinquency as a tragedy
that has its source in both material and psychic poverty.

The most interesting of the film adaptations of Hlasko's stories was
Wojciech Has's *The Noose* (*Pętla*-1957). In it, two people meet in a
situation of extreme desperation in a world that is deformed by the man's
determination to commit suicide—a world seen through Jahoda's strongly
expressionistic camera. The man, an alcoholic—Gustav Holoubek's first
great role—spends the last day of his life in his room with a bottle of vodka
and a noose suspended from the ceiling. The woman, who returns again
and again to pound on his door, does not know what she is rescuing him
from. (Hlasko's short stories, revealing the wounds in Polish society after
15 years of peace, soon aroused sharp official criticism, and in 1958,
Hlasko emigrated from Poland.)

In his second film, *Farewells* (*Pożegnania*-1958), Has again concentrated
on the atmosphere of uncertainty and despair in Poland in 1939, when
people, traditions, objects, memories, and relationships were doomed. An
obtrusive tone of nostalgia for something that had perhaps never existed
imbues *Farewells* with an unusual sensuous fascination.

Farewells

Tadeusz Chmielewski (b. 1927) was the only new director of the period to select comedy as his exclusive genre. His *Eve Wants to Sleep* (*Ewa chce spać*-1958) is a crazy comedy about a girl who in looking for lodgings in a small town finds herself up against the stupidity of the police apparatus. Chmielewski tried to give a view of contemporary life through a series of satirical episodes that develop from the realistically filmed environment of the film's early scenes to the absurdity of its final sequence. As to style, Chmielewski, who also wrote the script, sought his inspiration from American screwball comedies, a form that had almost been forgotten in Eastern Europe. He remained true to this form, although with a smaller degree of success, in his later films as well—e.g., *Where Is the General?* (*Gdzie jest general*-1964).

Eve Wants
to Sleep

THE FADING OF THE POLISH SCHOOL

From the middle of 1957, indications began to appear that presaged the coming limitations on the freedoms so recently gained. These indications made it increasingly clear that the development that had begun in 1956 would not go nearly so far as the representatives of the Polish intelligentsia had hoped. In September 1957, the student magazine *Po prostu,* which had become a symbol of October 1956, was banned. Shortly thereafter, party authorities confiscated the first issue of the long-awaited literary monthly, *Evropa,* and fired five members of the editorial council, including editor-in-chief Jerzy Andrzejewski. This action prompted the entire editorial council to decide not to publish the periodical at all, and all its Communist members quit the Party.

In film this change of political climate was signaled by the meticulous examination of scripts that were being prepared, by the reworking of finished films, and by the postponement of projected openings—for example, Jerzy Zarzycki's *Lost Feelings* (*Zagubione uczucia*-1957) and Czeslaw Petelski's *Damned Roads* (*Baza ludzi umarlych*-1959).

Wajda was one of the first to be caught in the changed atmosphere. His script for *We Are Alone in the World,* which tells the story of a pair of young people who close themselves off from the world, never got filmed, and Wajda, like so many others, returned to an evocation of the past, a more acceptable path. In *Lotna* (1959)—a film that was exceptionally beautiful from the pictorial point of view, and definitely one of his greatest film achievements, though not appreciated abroad—he depicted the tragedy of a nation condemned to live on after its romantic myth has turned to dust. He used as his backdrop a popular legend about the slaughter of attacking Polish cavalry by German tanks in 1939. Lipman's color photography was based on the concept of color as an expression of emotions, moods, and atmosphere.

Lotna

Early in the sixties, the number of remarkable Polish films dropped considerably, and mediocrity reigned in film production. Twenty-four fiction films were made in 1962, a figure that was to remain fairly stable for the next few years. The door was closed most firmly to the younger generation, a principal reason for the gradual stagnation, and the "great themes" of the Polish school were rehashed over and over again, increasingly diluted and cheapened.

A pair of the most successful films of this period were *Small Dramas* (*Male dramaty*-1960) and *Colored Stockings* (*Kolorowe pończochy*-1960), the first two fiction films of Janusz Nasfeter (b. 1920), who until then had worked on educational films. His stories of children's dreams and yearnings that were smashed by the adult world stood out not only for their familiarity with child psychology, but also for the high level of their imagery, inspired by primitive painting.

Another interesting new director was Kazimierz Kutz (b. 1929), Wajda's assistant. His *Cross of Valor* (*Krzyż walecznych*-1959), an adaptation of three short stories by Jósef Hen, introduced the character of the rank and file soldier into Polish film, and along with him problems that were less bathetic, so-called "plebeian" problems. From the outset, Kutz intentionally avoided motifs of "heroism and death," associated in Polish literature with the traditions of the aristocratic class. Kutz's heroes, farmers in peace time, do not experience wrenching inner conflicts, for they are tied not to the national myths but to the land and to "ordinary" life.

Kutz's first films testify to an intense search for style and inspiration. After the semi-neorealistic *Cross of Valor,* Kutz made another film on the basis of a story by Hen, *Nobody Is Calling* (*Nikt nie wola*-1960), a film that provided Wójcik with the opportunity to experiment with pictorial

Nobody
Is
Calling

composition the way Antonioni had done in his films of that period, and gave Hen and Kutz the chance to debate with *Ashes and Diamonds*: their hero is also supposed to carry out a death sentence against a Communist functionary, but he does not do it, and returns to life. At the same time, however, *Nobody Is Calling* is a metaphoric portrait of fear, a reminder of the persecution of resistance fighters, and finally also an analysis of the dilemma faced by people who are attacked from both sides. *Nobody Is Calling* was the first film to be criticized for formalism after 1960.

In his less successful *People on the Train* (*Ludzie z pociągu*-1961), Kutz continued to depict the lives of "ordinary people," showing their behavior in a stress situation—a search by German police among passengers on a train for a member of the underground.

After the detailed characterizations of *People on the Train* came the overly psychological *Silence* (*Milczenie*-1963). The least successful of Kutz's films, it was an examination of injustice, confession, and prejudice.

THE RÓŻEWICZ BROTHERS

The films of Stanislaw Różewicz (b. 1924) were typical of those years of disillusionment. Różewicz, who had for years been an assistant director, attracted the attention of the critics with his third independent film *Free City* (*Wolne miasto*-1958), a dramatic story about the first days of the war. His most successful film was *Birth Certificate* (*Swiadectvo urodzenia*-1961), which was based on three short stories by his brother Tadeusz, one of the most significant representatives of postwar Polish poetry and the theater of the absurd. The third story that is the most effective both as to form and content: Hitler's experts find typical signs of the Aryan race in a little Jewish girl. Other films by the Różewicz brothers, *Voice from Beyond* (*Glos z tamtego świata*-1962) and *Echo* (1964), were noteworthy for their brilliant dialogue, although frequently it was too literary to be used in film. They are permeated, as is all Różewicz's literary work, with the horror of human solitude, which is not limited to this world, but is perceived as man's universal condition: he lives totally alone without any metaphysical help. *Echo* was based on the theme of the mingling of the past with the present, which was becoming to an increasing degree both a substitute for timely contemporary themes and an expression of the Polish obsession with the past.

Wojciech Has succeeded in creating a good film by using this method in *How to Be Loved* (*Jak być kochaną*-1963), which was shot from a script by novelist Kazimierz Brandys. Here, as in *Noose,* Has concentrated his story on the love of a woman for a man, and ended it with the man's suicide. Has, who always saw human destiny in existential terms, conceived of life as the result of numerous causes linked together at random, causes that almost always generate tragic effects. The story of *How to Be Loved* is divided into two sections—the Nazi occupation and the present—joined together by the fatalistic relationship of the heroine to one man.

Mother Joan of the Angels

KAWALEROWICZ

One of the last significant films of the Polish school was Kawalerowicz's *Night Train* (*Pociąg*-1959), with a script by Jerzy Lutowski. The well-handled narrative structure testified to the formal mastery that Kawalerowicz had achieved and that allowed him to tell stories as dramatically accented as *Night Train*, and later *Mother Joan of the Angels* (*Matka Joanna od Aniolów*-1961). In *Night Train*, it is not merely a matter of human solitude, captured for the most part through the atmospherically isolating character of the train and the night, but also a matter of a phenomenon that accompanies emotional frustration: intolerance. All that is needed is a suspicion, and the peaceful passengers of the night train turn

Night
Train

into a hateful mob, willing to persecute a person, track him, and hunt him down.

In *Mother Joan,* which can be considered Kawalerowicz's best, as well as his most eclectic, film, the theme of intolerance and dogmatism is taken even further. The basis for the film was a novel by contemporary writer Jaroslaw Iwaszkiewicz, with its source in seventeenth-century documents about events at the convent at Loudon (which also inspired Aldous Huxley and other writers and film-makers). Iwaszkiewicz transported the action from France to Poland, and Kawalerowicz deepened the allegory of the intolerance that destroys both inquisitors and victims.

But like all Kawalerowicz's films, *Mother Joan* is a film about feelings that force a person into the most profound of conflicts, with faith on the one hand and love on the other. The relationship between the nun who is possessed by the devil and the priest who is exorcizing that devil presents Kawalerowicz with an opportunity to elaborate on parallel motifs: the frustration of people bound by political and social convictions who must conceal their desire to simply be two human beings in love.

MUNK 1959-1961

Like *Night Train, Cross-eyed Luck* (*Zezowate szczęście*-1959) was prepared in the period of the post October thaw. Munk and Stawiński once again concentrated on the problem of anti-heroism. They did now, however, present it in an analytical fashion, but chose instead to trace its development through the individual phases of the life of the leading figure. Piszczyk, a blood brother to Dzidzius of *Eroica,* is a typical careerist, coward, and opportunist, whose opinions change with the times, from the prewar republic all the way to Stalinism. The detailed, but broadly sketched satiric theme went from an excellent first half to schematic abbreviations and an exaggerated explicitness. As the film progresses, postwar Polish society becomes the primary target, but the director's hand becomes heavier and his irony less freewheeling.

Cross-Eyed
Luck

The most impressive display of Munk's talent is *The Passenger* (*Pasażerka*), during the shooting of which, in 1961, Munk was killed in an auto accident. The film had been practically finished when Munk died, but he had been unsatisfied with the scenes that take place on the ocean liner and had wanted to reshoot them. After his death, Munk's collaborators —led by Lesiewicz—respected his wishes, and instead of using the finished scenes, used still photographs for the contemporary scenes. Even in this form, *The Passenger* is an integral work, probably the artistic pinnacle of Munk's career.

The Passenger

Once again, the protagonist is a captive individual. But Marta, a prisoner in a concentration camp, does not need to create for herself a myth of freedom, for her freedom is inside her. On the contrary, the German guard Liza has no inner freedom and so becomes dependent on Marta's inner freedom, and thus a captive. Liza (the oppressor) needs Marta (the oppressed) to love her; she is convinced that she is only doing good things for her, and she considers Marta's every show of defiance to be a display of ingratitude. When Marta definitely rejects her, and voluntarily chooses death by the side of the man she loves, Liza is condemned to spend the rest of her life as a prisoner of the past and of the woman she oppressed.

The film is separated into segments that together make up a mosaic of reality. Liza is returning from South America, where she emigrated after the war, and it seems to her that she recognizes Marta, whom she had thought to be dead, as one of the passengers on the transoceanic liner. At first, memories of the camp return to her in the form of disconnected emotional images, then the return to the past is transformed into a defense of herself, addressed to her husband. And finally, reality becomes increasingly concrete as through her inner monologue she comes to ultimately stand face to face with herself as she really was.

With *The Passenger*, Munk returned to the theme of his first film, *Man on the Track*. In both films the central idea is that the past can be mystified and closed off in history, but not in an individual conscience, which remains open to the past until the moment of death.

THE REVOLT OF THE SCRIPTWRITERS AND THE VICTORY OF MEDIOCRITY

As Munk's films illustrate, most films made in Poland until the early sixties were adaptations of works of literature—though frequently quite autonomous ones—and many scripts were the product of collaboration with the writers themselves. There were several reasons for this. First of all, there was the important role that Polish literature, one of the most significant in all of Europe, had always played in the ideological rebirth of the nation, and the consequent effort of film to tie in with this tradition and, at least to a certain degree, to use it as a support. There was also, undisputably, a lack of scriptwriters capable of independent thinking, one of the phenomena produced by Stalinism. And finally, there was the writers' interest in film, particularly after 1957, when film became the worldwide symbol of the Polish cultural renaissance.

Early in the sixties, J. S. Stawiński—who had lost a congenial director with the death of Munk—published an article entitled "Exploitation in the Film Industry," in which he called for a rebellion of scriptwriters. Stawiński asked for equal rights for scriptwriter and director in shooting a film, which in practice meant allowing the writer to collaborate in the direction of a film.

Not much came of this rebellion, and even those scenarists who managed to be in on the birth of interesting films did not play particularly significant directorial roles. Only Tadeusz Konwicki, a multifaceted artist and an exceptionally talented one, made several noteworthy films. In 1961, his *Halloween* (*Zaduszki*) pursued the thematic line presented in *Last Day of Summer*—the problem of the inability of escaping from the past.

Scibor-Rylski, the scriptwriter for Kawalerowicz's *Shadow*, Lesiewicz's *First Year*, and several other films, made *Everyday* (*Ich dzień powszedni*-1963), a psychological study of a marital triangle. But though he was a good scriptwriter, he proved to be, over the years, only a mediocre director. Stawiński's debut was the comedy, *No Divorces* (*Rozwodów nie będzie*-1964), which attracted as little attention as Hen's *Weekends* (*Weekendy*-1963).

But these rather unadventurous works were not exceptional; mediocrity was the order of the day. The better part of these films was represented by the craftsmanlike dramatic action films of Jerzy Passendorfer (b. 1923), inspired mainly by the German occupation and the war: e.g., *Answer to Violence* (*Zamach*-1959), *Shadows of the Past* (*Powrót*-1960); *Surrounded by Flames* (*Skąpani w ogniu*-1964); and *The Colors of War* (*Barwy walki*-1965). Jan Rybkowski represented the official line. Since 1955, he had made a film every year, changing his genre and style according to what was called for. The best of his films are the war stories, *Hours of Hope* (*Godziny nadziei*-1955) and *Tonight a City Will Die* (*Dziś v nocy umrze miasto*-1961). Rybkowski was later joined by Ewa (b. 1920) and Czeslaw Petelski (b. 1922), both graduates of the Film Academy, who made their debut, along with Stanislaw Lenartowicz, with the 1955 film, *Three Starts* (*Trzy starty*). In the 10 years that followed, they made eight fiction films, seeking dramatic conflict in the struggle against capitalism or fascism: for example, *A Sky of Stone* (*Kamienne niebo*-1959); *Burning Mountains* (*Ogniomistrz Kaleń*-1961); and *Black Wings* (*Czarne skrzydla*-1963). Czeslaw Petelski's best film remains the aforementioned *Damned Roads* (based on the story by Marek Hlasko) which had to be repeatedly redone in 1958, but still remained an interesting work of brutal, almost naturalistic realism.

THE GENERATION OF A. FORD

One of the genres supported by the management of Polish cinematography was that of historical super-productions, the kind that were beginning to emerge at that time from Western Europe and the United States. The first to make one of these films in Poland was Ford. His *Knights of the Teutonic Order* (*Krzyżacy*-1960), an adaptation of Henryk Sienkiewicz's novel of 1900, was the most colossal enterprise that the Polish film industry had ever launched. The film, which was a success in its genre, receiving an enthusiastic audience response all over Eastern Europe, centers on the Battle at Grunwald in 1410 and the victory of the Poles and Lithuanians over the German warrior-monks of the Teutonic Order, bearers of aggressive Germanization.

Ford was the only one of the founders of Polish film to maintain acceptable artistic standards in all his films. On the other hand, Jakubowska's work of the fifties and sixties—whether it be the *Atlantic Story* (*Opowieść atlantycka*-1955), against the French war in Indochina; or the children's film, *King Mat* (*Król Maciuś*-1958); or finally the attempt to follow up *Last Stage* in *The End of Our World* (*Koniec naszego świata*-1964), which was situated in a concentration camp—were heavy, outdated social epics overloaded with "ideas." After *The Last Stage,* Jakubowska's importance was strictly limited to the fields of organization and education.

Jerzy Zarzycki's path was more successful. After his misfortunes with *Warsaw Robinson* in 1949, he attempted in 1956-1957 to tie in with a

Knights of the Teutonic Order

series of social conscience films, creating a fiction counterpart to the black documentary series with *Land* (*Ziemia*) and *Lost Feelings*. But his films once again encountered criticism, and from then on, Zarzycki simply sought acceptable subject matter. In the sixties, he worked mainly in light comedy, as did Buczkowski.

INNOCENT SORCERERS AND KNIFE IN THE WATER

Wajda finally did complete a film about the young generation, although it was in a form different from the one he had originally intended. His *Innocent Sorcerers* (*Niewinni czarodzieji*-1960), made from a script by Jerzy Andrzejewski and Jerzy Skolimowski, is at first glance far removed from his work of the past. It was a contemporary film, lacking symbolic imagery and pathetic accents, lacking a "great" theme, and, for that matter, lacking a plot—the key to the individual sequences must be sought more in the dialogue than in the visual images. But the heroes are once again young people, and the motif of undeclared love is intertwined in their story. As always, Wajda marks his *Innocent Sorcerers* with the seal of unfulfilled yearnings and vital disillusionment in which a blasé attitude replaces a heroic pose. Wajda's (and Skolimowski's) portrait of the young Polish generation, comprised of observations from a single night in Warsaw and fragments of dialogue and thoughts, was the only Eastern European film of its time to disclose certain problems of young people that the official view of reality refused to see: fear of the future, self-deception, uncertainty, the yearning for an easy life.

Innocent
Sorcerers

The very nature of *Innocent Sorcerers* aroused an immediate and negative response; so did *Samson* (1961), focusing in a powerful existential metaphor on the tragic fate of an outcast, a Polish Jew.

When Gomulka criticized film production at the Thirteenth Plenary Session of the Party Central Committee in 1963, he named *Innocent Sorcerers* as one of the films for which there was no room in Polish cinema. In addition to the Wajda film, he also named Roman Polański's *Knife in the Water* (*Nóż w wodzie*–1962). Polański (b. 1933) was the only new young director making films at that time. While a new generation was beginning to enter upon the scene in both Hungarian and Czechoslovak film—young people who were to instill new life into their national cinema enterprises—in Poland, young people were kept on the periphery of cultural life. It is clear that the reasons were a fear of the repetition of the past, of a new intellectual ferment among the young. In a speech at the Fourteenth Congress of the Union of Polish Writers in 1965, Gomulka criticized writers of so-called "accusative literature," rejecting their efforts to "settle accounts." His words were a reply to the 1964 *Freedom Manifesto* that was presented by 34 leading Polish writers and scientists to Premier Josef Cyrankiewicz. It stated, in part: "The undersigned demand that Polish cultural policy be changed to conform to the spirit of the rights guaranteed by the Polish constitution and to the national good."

Polański was the only member of the upcoming generation, then, who not only made, but showed in those years a fiction film of protest and attack. He was 28 years old, had worked for a number of years as a successful actor (*Generation, End of Night, Innocent Sorcerers, The Fat and the Lean*), had served as assistant director on several films (such as *Cross-eyed Luck*), and had directed two short films. These films had already revealed the strain of sarcastic sorrow that was to remain the most characteristic trait of Polański's work. The plight of man living in an alienated society is expressed in Polański's films, at one level, through the absurdity of common everyday experience and at a deeper level through the history of Polański's homeland and the course of his own life.

Even in one of his first films, the experimental short, *Two Men and a Wardrobe* (*Dwaj ludzie z szafa*-1958), Polański concentrated on the burden of nonconformity in a conformist society. He elaborated on this theme both in *The Fat and the Lean* (*Le Gros et le Maigre* 1961), made in France, as well as in the experimental *Mammals* (*Ssaki*-1962). Whereas in *Two Men and a Wardrobe*, the heroes share a single destiny—the vain effort to be free in a world that is not free—and must together carry a wardrobe wherever they go, in *Mammals* a shared minor advantage—a sled—becomes the object of controversy and transforms them into enemies. Polański feels that everyone has an equal chance of becoming either a lord or a slave, it is only a matter of who begins to exploit whom first.

Polański's feature debut, *Knife in the Water*, the script for which he wrote with Skolimowski, launches attacks on two generations of Poles and their common "code of honor": the middle generation, representing the new "red bourgeoisie," living in comfort, security, and conformism; and the younger generation, "our cynical generation, that still has its romantic yearnings, and yet simultaneously already craves integration" (*Barrier*, Skolimowski).

As he did later in *Repulsion* (1965), Polański placed his characters—a married couple and a student—in a confined setting, a boat on a lake, from which there is no escape. He then developed their triangular relationship in such a manner that their emptiness, their instability, and above all their selfishness, had to surface. Polański does not give his characters the slightest hope. In the final scene, the man and wife—happily married, according to social standards—drive away in their new car; they are silent, everything around them is dead, the windshield wipers move mechanically in the rain, everything is saturated with the feeling of resignation and of

Knife in the Water

the awareness that everything will in fact always be just that way, as the acceptance of the truth would destroy all the standards by which they live.

Not only in content, but also in form, *Knife in the Water* is linked to *Innocent Sorcerers,* no doubt because Jerzy Skolimowski collaborated on both scripts. First, they are the only two Polish films of the early sixties that dealt with subject matter that had direct relationship to the times. The language of *Knife in the Water* approaches that of the French new wave; visually, the film relies more on camera motion than on montage, the story is not tied together by the dramatic nature of the action but rather by its scenic and temporal continuity; and finally, it abandons the pictorial symbolism that was used by the preceding generation. In both films, social commentary is not bound up with the specific historical situation, but rather is an expression of the inner motivations of the characters.

In 1963, Polański left Poland and became one of the world's foremost directors, making *Repulsion, Cul-de-Sac, The Fearless Vampire Killers, Rosemary's Baby, Macbeth,* and *Chinatown.*

BOROWCZYK AND LENICA

Polański was the third of a number of outstanding Polish directors to leave Poland when the times negated the advances of October 1956. The first was Walerian Borowczyk (b. 1923), who—together with Jan Lenica (b. 1928) and Daniel Szczechura (b. 1930)—led the Polish school of animated film. Borowczyk, who was awarded the Polish National Prize for his graphic work in 1953, made his first internationally recognized film in 1957, in collaboration with Lenica, *Once Upon a Time* (*Byl sobie raz*). Eventually, his interest shifted from the field of experimental animation to the sphere of fiction film. His last Polish film (once again made with Lenica), *House* (*Dom*-1958) was the first to combine animation with live actors. In France, where he settled upon leaving Poland, Borowczyk

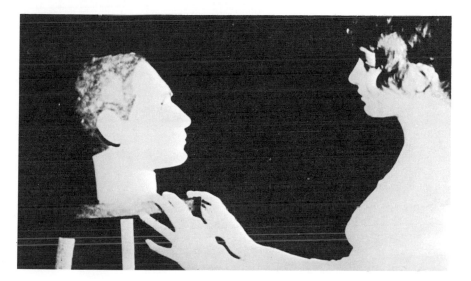

House

concentrated on experiments with graphic expression and music (*Renaissance, Diptyque, Gavotte*), and later made avant-garde feature films (*Rosalie, Goto, L'Isle d'amout, Blanche*) as well as the more commercially oriented *Les Contes Immoraux* and *La Bête*. In the first three features, as in his short films, we find a very Polish characteristic that was near to the hearts of Polański and Skolimowski as well: the acceptance of the absurdity of everyday life, which encloses people in an ever tightening vicious circle. In 1974 he shot for Film Polski in Poland an excellent full-length feature film in an entirely surrealist vein: *The Story of Sin* (*Dzieje grzechu*). Based on a minor story by Stefan Zeromski, it tells the tale of the erotic fantasies of a middle-class girl who has been raised in a bigoted atmosphere. Borowczyk, however, continues to live and work in France.

After Borowczyk's departure, Lenica made two more films in Poland, both of which used the latest trends in graphic art to examine human destiny: *New Janko Musician* (*Nowy Janko Muzykant*-1960) and *Labyrinth* (*Labirynt*-1962). When *Labyrinth* was banned from distribution for two years, Lenica finally decided not to return to Poland. Since 1963, he has been active in Western Europe, making among others, *Adam 2* (1968),

Labyrinth

and *Still Life* (*Stilleben*-1969). The international renown of Polish film posters is also linked with his name, and their artistic level has inspired numerous efforts at imitation all over the world.

The first half of the sixties, which saw throughout Eastern Europe an upsurge of national cinema, found Poland in the depths of a depression. Munk was dead, Wajda was working in Yugoslavia, three of the best film-makers had moved abroad, Kawalerowicz had not made a single film between 1961 and 1966, Kutz, Różewicz, Stawiński and Ford were suffering artistic stagnation, and the opportunities for young film artists had been stifled. The major portion of the well-equipped production facilities (about 25 fiction films annually) was devoted to the making of super-productions, which politically had become the most favored genre. Almost 10 years would pass before the Polish film industry would once again call attention to itself by producing more than one important film a year.

The Story of Sin

WHERE DID THE CRANES FLY?
The Soviet Union, 1956–1963

The October 1957 opening of Kalatozov's *The Cranes Are Flying* (*Letyat zhuravli*), marked a moment of significant transitional development in Soviet film. Critic L. Anninsky recalls that day:

The silence in the Udarnik Theater in Moscow was profound. Tatiana Samoylova (the actress who played the heroine) faced thousands of eyes to explain what the film-makers had been trying to say: 'We wanted to show people . . .' Not even the older film-makers, men who had recently passed judgment and approved the film at the session of the Arts Council of Mosfilm, succeeded in explaining it—but apologized to each other instead for illogical argumentation. A certain shift of values took place in the audience: it was as if the wall between art and living life had fallen. . . . In my mind, hundreds of international awards could not make up for the tears with which people purged themselves after this film. In truth, our tears 'unlocked the door'. (*Film A Doba,* Prague, 1971, p. 258)

THE CRANES ARE FLYING

It was film language that rejuvenated Soviet cinema, returning it to its pre-Stalinist cinematic heritage. *Cranes* was based on Viktor Rozov's *Eternally Alive,* which though in most ways a conventional play chose as its subject matter the long-taboo themes of war seen as a misfortune, death, treachery, baseness, guilt, and redemption. Kalatozov and his cameraman Urusevsky had for a number of years made films that strictly adhered to the Stalinist line. Urusevsky, however, had been a pupil of the avant-garde

The
Cranes
Are
Flying

photographer Rodchenko, and Kalatozov's early film work had been strongly influenced by Eisenstein, Pudovkin, and Vertov, particularly in his famous documentary film, *Salt for Svanetia* (*Sol Svanetii*–1930). *The Cranes Are Flying* was not so much an advance in cinematic language as it was a reminiscence on avant-garde ideas, an anthology of directorial styles, including quotations from such recent masters as Kurosawa and Carné. But the main effect of the film was to remind viewers of the emotive power of the black-and-white film image, and of montage, when they are used to describe certain tragic aspects of Soviet history that had been banished from the screen for years.

THE NEWCOMERS

It took almost five years for Soviet film to arrive at this point. But there were films along the road that had prepared the way. And with these films, new names came to the forefront, primarily as a result of the rapidly increasing volume of film production. In 1956, Vasili Ordynsky's (b. 1925) nonconformist debut, *A Man Is Born* (*Chelovek rodilsya*) introduced the unwed mother to the puritan ranks of Soviet film heroes and presented her problems to a society that, as a result of the war, had a considerable numerical preponderance of women over men. Marlen Khutsiev (b. 1925) made his debut in the Odessa Studio, stressing the now low-key style of narration that was typical of young Soviet film-makers in the film *Spring on Zarechna Street* (*Vesna na Zarechnoi ulitse*), which he co-directed with F. Mironer (b. 1927). It was an unconventional open-ended story—still uncertain in its form—about the burgeoning love of a worker and a teacher. This film called attention not only to an interesting new talent but also to the entirely different approach of the younger generation, even within the limits of a traditional theme.

Alov and Naumov's new film, *Pavel Korchagin* (1956), based on N. Ostrovsky's novel, *How Steel Was Tempered,* challenged conventions in its approach to so-called revolutionary subject matter. The tense romanticism, the ascetic, red-eared revolutionary hero, with his "pock-marked face" of the heroic period, evoked fierce debate. "Is that how steel was tempered?" asked the press, with upraised index finger. But the old masters stood behind the young ones. N. Pogodin replied, "Indisputably, this optimism is entirely different from the kind we stooped to in *Dream of a Cossack* . . . This film is a pure example of pre-Rappian socialist realism, uncrippled by later theories and unsullied by the dogmas of conflict-free plots and rose-water."*

---

*If we bear in mind that socialist realism was codified in the "post-Rappian" period, we find it easier to understand both the meaning of these words and the language that had to be used so frequently in the Soviet Union and elsewhere at that time.

The Forty-First

Grigori Chukhrai's (b. 1921) romanticism was more poetic, we might say more Russian. Mariutka, the heroine of his film, *The Forty-First* (*Sorok pervyi*-1956)—a remake based on the story by B. Lavrenev—is a member of a unit of the Red Army lost in the desert. She falls in love with her prisoner, a White Guard officer, but kills him at the moment that he is about to escape from her to join his own people. In many ways she is close to the heroines of nineteenth-century Russian literature. In this film, Urusevsky's camera was entirely free for the first time, taking repeated advantage of the possibilities offered by the—albeit imperfect—color film to photograph the sand of the desert and the foam of the ocean waves.

The year 1956 was the year of the Twentieth Congress of the Soviet Communist Party and Khrushchev's "secret report" about Stalin's crimes and the period of the "personality cult." The secret report went from hand to hand; gradually, the country learned about itself and began putting together what had risen to the surface in the years following Stalin's death, particularly reports from those who kept coming back from "far away."

Another noteworthy film of that year is the first independent film of the Georgian director R. Chkheidze, *Our Courtyard* (*Nash dvor*), which confirmed fully the anticipated reemergence of Georgian cinematic talent that had been signaled by the appearance of *Magdana's Donkey*. *Soldiers* (*Soldaty*), directed by A. Ivanov and based on V. Nekrasov's novel about the 'prose of war,' *In the Trenches of Stalingrad,* seemed to follow the mood of *Star* and its view of war, typical of the period during and immediately following the war.

Two theatrical directors also made their film debuts in 1956, Zakhar Agranenko (1912–1960) and Konstantin Voynov (b. 1918). Agranenko's *Immortal Garrison (Bezsmertniy garnizon),* which he codirected with Tisse, who was also the cameraman, returned to the early days of the war, in its attempt at an authentic wartime tragedy, but it promised more than its director could fulfill. Voynov, with his moralizing *Two Lives (Dve zhizni),* and even more so with his subsequent *Three Emerged from the Woods (Troye vyshli iz lesa*–1958), in which he strove to create a genuine cinematic realism, also aroused unfulfilled expectations.

On the other hand, a premonition of future success was suggested by the joint debut of Lev Kulidzhanov (b. 1924) and Yakov Segel, *This Is How It Began (Eto nachinalos tak),* a film about young people that was made at the active Odessa studio, like Khutsiev's debut. At that time, as was often the case in more "open" periods, the Ukrainian studios were one of the centers of things new. Alov and Naumov's first films were made at Kiev; it was also there that Vladimir Braun (1896–1957), using thematic material from Gorky, made his last and best film, *Malva* in 1956. His contemporary, Efim Dzigan, on the other hand, only copied the style of the recent past in a pompous color film *Prologue,* which was devoted to the revolution of 1905. Another veteran, the pioneer of Soviet trick film, Alexander Ptushko, created the first wide-screen film, the fairy tale *Ilya Muromets.* The film versions of popular novels by the dean of Soviet prose, K. Fedin—for example, *Extraordinary Summer* and *First Joys*—called attention to the talented Vladimir Basov's fall into the rut of academic convention.

But no sooner had the process of rebirth begun than it encountered its first obstacle—which also called attention to its limits. The Hungarian revolution was not all that the advancing Russian tanks crushed; they also put an abrupt end to the first stage of the de-Stalinization of Soviet culture. In May of 1957, Khrushchev made it perfectly clear to the leadership of the Union of Writers that the Soviet powers-that-be would never grant them the freedom that their Hungarian and Polish colleagues had enjoyed, at least for a short time, and that his hand "would not tremble" if their counterparts were to appear in the Soviet Union. *The Cranes Are Flying* was saved from the consequences of the sudden freeze only by its extraordinary international success.

The production of fiction films remained at an annual level of about 100, only one third of which were in color, but the development of directorial freedom was stalled. As in other countries of Eastern Europe, the fight for such independence became a key issue of this and the subsequent period in Soviet film. The ideological-propagandistic concept of film art, the pedagogical role that cinematography was given, and the almost mystical faith in its effectiveness determined both its exceptional position and the limitations imposed on creative effort. Artistic changes were conceived of mainly as different "pedagogical concepts," within which individual, and usually suppressed, exceptions could occasionally appear.

The urgent question in the Soviet Union in 1956 was: Will film artists be just involved in the newly programmed pedagogical activity, or will the film-makers—or at least some of them—be able to take advantage of the changed program for their own, autonomous, truly personal artistic testimony?

THE HOUSE I LIVE IN

That is why Lev Kulidzhanov's and Yakov Segel's second film, *The House I Live In* (*Dom v kotorom ya zhivu*-1957), was more the exception than the rule. Although made shortly after *The Cranes Are Flying*, its style was entirely different, revealing the influence of low key, unemotional narration (mainly in British films) and of neorealism, and a strong distaste for pomp and bathos. ("I know the impression created by the Italian films," declared M. Romm in 1962. "I can underline that this influence was real.") It told the story of the inhabitants of a house in a Moscow suburb before, during, and after the war, pursuing them with that clear interest in the ordinary— even during their severest hardships or moments of heroism—that is so characteristic of the best works of the post-Stalinist period. With the film *The House I Live In*, the approach and the viewpoint of the young generation finally took its place in Soviet cinema. Soon thereafter, inevitably, some of its members became spokesmen for the new film establishment. But among those who did not was a former concentration camp prisoner, Mikhail (Moisei) Kalik (b. 1927) who in 1958 made both *Feathers* (*Yunost nashikh otsov*) and *Ataman Kord* and who was thereafter to assume an exceptional position in Soviet cinema.

The
House
I Live
In

In addition to those named above, the young generation also includes Eldar Ryazanov (b. 1927), creator of the successful comedies *Carnival Night* (*Karnavalnaya noch*-1956) and *Girl Without an Address* (*Devushka bez adresa*-1957), and Stanislav Rostotski, who made the falsely poetic *May Stars* (*Mayskie zvezdy*-1959), inspired by the liberation of Czechoslovakia by Soviet troops in 1945. This film, along with the Soviet-Yugoslav *Oleko Dundich* (1958), the story of a Yugoslav hero of the Soviet Revolution that was directed by Leonid Lukov, introduced the era of coproductions. But coproduction was basically viewed only as a tool of international cultural cooperation; it did not give birth to any films of particular significance.

THE CLASSICS

Many of the old directors fully subscribed to the "new pedagogical concept," which included, above all, the confirmation of Lenin as the sole leader, and the "purging of the image of the Revolution from Stalin's cult." As a result of this new policy many films devoted to Lenin were produced, the first of which were Sergei Yutkevich's *Stories About Lenin* (*Rasskazi o Lenine*-1957) and *The Ulyanov Family* (*Semya Ulyanovykh*-1957), directed by Valentin Nevzorov (1918-1961). Others were Sergei Vasilev's *In the Days of October* (*V dni oktyabrya*-1958), a bad replica of Eisenstein's *October,* Fridrich Ermler's *The First Day* (*Den perviy*-1958), Yuri Ozerov's *Kotchubey* (1958), and Leonid Trauberg's *The Soldiers Marched* (*Shli soldaty*-1958). The older generation also turned to the tried and true Russian classics. In this area, G. Roshal was definitely more successful with *The Sisters* (*Sestry*-1957-59), a popular three-part version of Alexis Tolstoy's epic *The Road to Calvary* (*Sestry; 1918; Khmurnoye utro*) than was Sergei Gerasimov with his superficial illustrative version— also in three parts—of Mikhail Sholokhov's *And Quiet Flows the Don*

And Quiet Flows the Don   The Bath

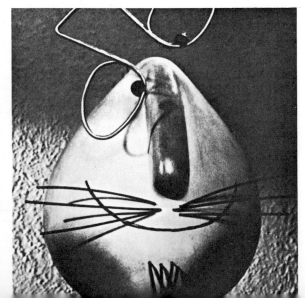

(*Tikhiy Don*-1957-1958). In 1962, Yutkevich made an animated version of Mayakovsky's *Bath* (*Banya*), but neither this nor other writings of the "greatest poet of the Soviet Revolution" eventually found their way into Soviet fiction film. Ivan Pyriev also turned to the past and was the first after decades to film Dostoyevsky—*The Idiot* (*Idiot*-1958), probably his best film, and *White Nights* (*Belye nochi*-1959). Mark Donskoy succeeded in making a real comeback with *Foma Gordeyev* (1959) after a story by Gorky, and V. Petrov made a film based on Turgenev's *On the Eve* (*Nakanunie*-1959) as a Bulgarian-Soviet coproduction. Probably the best of the new film versions of Russian classical literature was one of Gogol's *The Overcoat* (*Shinel*-1959), which was filmed with a strong sense of style by one of the most popular actors of the younger generation, Alexei Batalov (b. 1928). And there was the memorable *Lady with a Little Dog* (*Dama s sobachkoi*-1959) filmed after Chekhov by Heifitz. With *Don Quixote* (1957), Grigori Kozintsev followed, with much greater success, Yutkevich's example of seeking material for reflection about the present in the classics of world literature. He remained faithful to this approach throughout the last 15 years of his outstanding career.

Don
Quixote

In 1958, Dovzhenko's widow, Yulia Solntseva (b. 1901)—who devoted all her energy to Dovzhenko's heritage—completed *Poem of the Sea* (*Poema o more*), but its often picture-book pathos lacked Dovzhenko's

Destiny of a Man

lyricism and warm human perspective, as did her later film, *Story of the Flaming Years* (*Povest plamenykh let*-1960). Another woman director of the older generation, Vera Stroeva (b. 1903), continued filming operas with M. P. Mussorgsky's *Khovanshtchina* (1959).

SUPPORT FROM LITERATURE

The most secure support for efforts to revive Soviet film in the late fifties and early sixties was the new Soviet literature, which had taken advantage of the thaw after Stalin's death to give more than just a promising start to the younger generation. This was true in spite of the fact that even here, the icy wind of 1957 quickly chilled the atmosphere. In the fall of 1958, a scandal erupted over the Nobel Prize that was awarded to Boris Pasternak following the publication abroad of his novel, *Doctor Zhivago*. The writers' struggle for the right to a personal and individual concept of their art and of life was begun; its successes and failures proved to be characteristic of the further development of Soviet culture.

The first film-maker to seek and find support in this direction was Moisei Schweitzer, whose new cinematic view of life on a collective farm, *Sasha Enters Life* (*Sasha vstupayet v zhizn*-1957), was based on one of the first successful items of "new prose," Vladimir Tendryakov's *Hard Knot*. Vladimir Vengerov (b. 1920) filmed what might be termed one of the most noteworthy novels of the early post-Stalin years, V. Nekrasov's *Home Town*. But in this case, it became apparent that film would certainly not be permitted the same latitude as literature. On the other hand, actor Sergei Bondarchuk (b. 1920), with V. Monakhov as his director of photography, put Sholokhov's story, *Destiny of Man* (*Sudba cheloveka*-1959) on film. In it, we find a pathos and eclecticism similar to that of *The Cranes Are Flying*, but Sholokhov's story about the heroism of a Soviet prisoner of war in a German camp had a particular political importance

The
Communist

Ballad
of a
Soldier

(many of the Soviet POW's disappeared in Stalin's camps after the war, having been labelled as "cowards and traitors").

Of the most interesting films based on original scripts, we should note above all *Two Fedors* (*Dva Fedora*-1959), directed by Marlen Khutsiev, in which the story of the friendship of a demobilized soldier and a small homeless boy forms the backdrop for examining the everyday reality of postwar Soviet urban life. *The Communist* (*Kommunist*-1957) by Yuli Raizman, is a typical example of a film embodying the new "pedagogical concept." In fact, later, its scenarist, Yevgeni Gabrilovich, became one of its foremost proponents. Academic in style, bathetic in tone, *The Communist* is a model of cinematic socialist realism of the post-Stalinist period. Yet it differs from earlier films made in this style, most significantly in the characterization of its hero: he is no longer a superhuman commander, but simply a man whose sincere belief in, and desire to fight and suffer for, the Soviet cause gives him a kind of tragic stature.

Chukhrai's *Ballad of a Soldier* (*Ballada o soldate*-1958)—which appears to have become a landmark—was a successful attempt to escape to the "atypical" poetic story of an ordinary person. A soldier on the front line receives a pass and travels to his native village to see his mother. He is held up en route by the interests and demands of others until he has no more time for his own affairs. *Ballad of a Soldier* is also a morality play, but its strength lies in its lack of bathos and its anonymous humanity. The truly poetic language of this film—once again in black and white—is sophisticatedly simple, conspicuously inconspicuous. Part of this is certainly to be attributed to the camera work of V. Nikolaev and Era Savelieva.

A visually outstanding film, and a film that might be called the "cameraman's film" of the Soviet postwar era, *The Letter That Wasn't Sent* (*Neotpravlennoe pismo*-1959), was brought to the screen by Urusevsky, who did the camerawork and also codirected with Kalatozov. The story of a group of geologists fleeing from a grassfire on the Siberian taiga is simply a pretext for the film's creators to assert the primacy of the visual element in film. In this sense, it was indisputably a significant motion picture, but it also is not surprising that it encountered a critical rebuff.

The Letter That Was Not Sent

Events were taking an interesting turn in the film industries of the Soviet republics as well. Twelve fiction films were made in Turkmenistan between 1955 and 1965; in Uzbekistan, 26; over 40 in Armenia; and over 30 in Azerbaidzhan. Georgia, however, was the most significant artistically. Chiaureli returned to Tbilisi after years of Stalinist fame and made, among others, *Otar's Widow* (*Otarova vdova*-1957) and *Story of a Girl* (*Povest ob odnoi devushke*-1960). T. Abuladze obtained here his first independent success with *Other People's Children* (*Chuzhie deti*-1958). A real surprise, however, was the veritable birth of Lithuanian cinema, which soon found its own style, based on national artistic and poetic traditions. The central figure of this cinema was the productive scenarist and director, Vitautas Zhalakevichius (b. 1930), who had called attention to himself with his poetically perceived feature debut, *Adam Wants to Be a Man* (*Adam khochet byt chelovekom*-1959), about the lives of Lithuanian laborers emigrating to South America in search of work. The Lithuanians won their first international success with a film about children in wartime, *Living Heroes* (*Zhiviye geroi*-1960), which was codirected by Zhalakevichius and A. Zhebryunas (b. 1931) and photographed by Jonas Gritsius.

The controversy surrounding the awarding of the Nobel Prize to Pasternak was the best proof that de-Stalinization was not going according to any preestablished plan but was advancing as a result of an internal struggle. Culture, and particularly literature, was one of the main battlefields. Of necessity, film lagged behind, although production figures kept increasing and new names kept turning up. They included that of Andrei Tarkovsky (b. 1932), a young graduate of vgik (All-Union State Cinematography Institute), who gained attention with his graduation film project entitled *Steamroller and Violin* (*Katok i skripka*-1960), done in collaboration with Andrei (Andron) Konchalovsky (Mikhalkov) (b. 1937). It told the story of a friendship between a little boy who plays the violin and a worker and of the influence they have on each other. Some others were Georgi Danelia (b. 1930) of Georgia, and Igor Talankin (b. 1927), who made their successful joint debut with the film *Seriozha* (1960), a tender study of the emotional life of a child. Talankin followed it with what remained probably his best film, *Entry* (*Vstupleniye*-1962). Both films were based on stories by the nonconformist writer, Vera Panova.

After more than 10 years, the unfinished second part of *Ivan the Terrible* appeared on the screen, but there was still a long way to go to the full rehabilitation of Eisenstein. M. Schweitzer reacted to the mass return of political prisoners from Stalin's concentration camps with an academistic two-part version of Tolstoy's *Resurrection* (1960-1961). Alov and Naumov attempted, with a fair degree of success, to depict the transition from war to peaceful coexistence in the film *Peace to Those Who Enter* (*Mir vkhodiashchemu*-1961). And before them, Segel had dealt with the end of the war in Germany in *The First Day of Peace* (*Perviy den mira*-1959). In 1961, Segel made *Farewell, Doves* (*Proshchaite, golubi*) in which he turned away from conventional story dramaturgy and focused his camera on undramatic daily life and its humorous poetic aspects. There was also the science-fiction film, *The Amphibious Man* (*Chelovek-amfibia*-1961), directed by A. Kazansky (b. 1910) and V. Chebotarev (b. 1907). Raizman spoke out against hypocritical attitudes toward the values of young people in the film *If This Is Love* (*A esli eto lyubov*-1961), at that time a rather important and controversial attempt to reassess some almost forgotten moral standards, such as the priority of the feelings over social conventions.

Contemporary Soviet literature continued to play its role in liberating film from the bonds of the past, pushing it to confront the present in an authentic way. The films *The Magic Ikon* (*Chudotvornaya*-1960) and *Trial* (*Sud*-1962) directed by Vladimir Skuybin (b. 1919) were based on Tendryakov's stories. Vladimir Basov took Galina Nikolayeva's novel, *Battle on the March*, as the basis for his film of the same name (*Bitva v puti*-1961), but he stressed the conventional aspects of the novel, which provoked quite a response, and underplayed its provocative observations about postwar Soviet society. V. Aksyonov's Salingeresque novel about an adolescent boy, *Ticket to the Sun*, controversial above all in its language, lost almost all its charm in A. Zarkhi's film version, *My Younger Brother* (*Moy mladshiy brat*-1962). Many film versions of the works of other leading contemporary authors—for example, Bondarev, Baklanov, Kazakov, Konetsky, Nagibin, Rekemchuk, Granin—also failed to measure up to the originals. On the other hand, E. Kazakevich fared quite well in the hands of director Anatol Efros, who filmed his story, *Two in the Steppe* (*Dvoye v stepi*-1962) in the studio at Novosibirsk, as did Chengis Aitmatov, whose *Heat* (*Znoy*-1962) was the directorial debut of Larissa Shepitko (b. 1938).

REASONS FOR OPTIMISM

The very best of these literary adaptations was the film made from V. Bogomolov's story, *Ivan's Childhood* (*Ivanovo detstvo*-1962), Andrei Tarkovsky's debut as an independent director. Its theme was war, which had become the essential theme for literature and film both in the Soviet Union and elsewhere in Eastern Europe during the post-Stalin period. Suddenly it was possible to use modern narration and—in undeclared opposition to the drabness of socialist realism—to present man in human dimensions and coping with actual conflicts. Tarkovsky went further along this route than anyone else. His Ivan, a lad who is deprived of his childhood by the war and whose young mind struggles desperately with the reality he encounters, is shaped as a film character by various techniques of modern art. The international success of this film, which blended realism, expressionism, and surrealism, could be credited in part to the work of the great cameraman, V. Yusov. Its warm reception abroad not only catapulted Tarkovsky into a position of leadership among young Soviet film-makers,

Ivan's Childhood

it also protected him for some time from the criticism of officials at home.

In 1961, two other films appeared that indicated Soviet film was finally catching up with Soviet literature and assuming an important role in the process that many hoped would lead the Soviet Union to democratic socialism. *Clear Sky* (*Chistoye nebo*), directed by Grigori Chukhrai, belongs, in both the spirit and the form of the original script by Daniil Khrabrovitsky, to the pedagogic series of the sixties. But the story of the hero, a pilot who becomes the victim of false accusations and Stalinist persecution, underwent, thanks to Chukhrai, several metamorphoses and eventually spoke with the same kind of voice as did a contemporary novella, Solzhenitsyn's *One Day in the Life of Ivan Denisovich*. True, *Clear Sky* was still too heavy-handed and message-oriented, but it nonetheless had an enormous impact in the Soviet Union. The fact that its director eventually won for it both official approval and support caused many to hope for even more.

Clear
Sky

Nine Days in a Year

Of even greater importance, from the point of view of the search for self, and aimed at a more restricted audience was the film *Nine Days in a Year* (*Devyat dnei odnogo goda*) by Mikhail Romm, who in the thirties directed two notable films on Lenin (from which, in 1956, Romm cut the footage about Stalin). Romm's film, based on a script by Khrabrovitsky, took a philosophical point of view of his protagonists, two scientists with entirely different temperaments who are rivals for the same woman and who reveal their dreams and doubts as they confront both success and death. Romm both accurately captured the mood of Soviet society and strove for a new, contemporary approach to its problems, problems that no longer could be solved with grandiose slogans and parrotted optimism.

And then there were two other successes of a different, more poetic nature, that of T. Abuladze, the film *Me, Grandma, Iliko and Illarion* (*Ya, babushka, Iliko i Illarion*-1962), cinematographically inspired by Georgian folklore, and Kalik's *Man Follows the Sun* (*Chelovek idet za solntsem*-1967), filmed in color in the Moldavian film studio. In the context of Soviet cinema Kalik's work was a truly revolutionary attempt to return to the inspiration of the avant-garde and its concept of film as visual art.

STALIN'S HEIRS

In the autumn of 1962, the magazine *Noviy Mir* printed Alexander Solzhenitsyn's novella, *One Day in the Life of Ivan Denisovich*. Almost simultaneously, V. Nekrasov published his report on his stay in the United States, entitled *Both Sides of the Ocean*. Preparations were in progress for the premiere performance of Shostakovich's Thirteenth Symphony, in

Man
Follows
the
Sun

which the composer used a quotation from Yevtushenko's poem "Babi Yar" about the massacre of the Jews in the Ukraine during the war. And it was the same Yevtushenko, in a poem called "Stalin's Heirs," published in October 1962, who voiced the warning:

> I appeal to our government
> With the request
> To double
> To triple
> The guard at this slab
> So that Stalin may not rise
> And with Stalin the past . . .
> As long as Stalin's heirs exist on earth
> It will seem to me
> That Stalin is still in the Mausoleum.

Stalin's heirs themselves launched a counterattack almost immediately. Their main spokesman was Stalin's last editor-in-chief of *Pravda*, Leonid Ilyichev. On December 1, 1962, Khrushchev—accompanied by other Soviet leaders—attended the exhibition "Thirty Years of Pictorial Art" in Moscow. This exhibition marked the first public showing of paintings by some so-called modernists, i.e., above all the delayed fauvists and expressionists of the Stalinist period. It became apparent once again that the heritage of the past weighed very heavy as Khrushchev spelled out the state policy:

We won't spend a kopeck on your art . . . Just give me a list of those who want to go abroad, to the so-called 'free world.' We'll give you foreign passports tomorrow and you can get out. Your prospects here are nil. What is hung here is simply anti-Soviet. It's amoral. . . . History can be our judge. For the time being, history has put us at the head of this state and we have to answer for everything that goes on in it. Therefore we are going to maintain a strict policy on art. . . . Gentlemen, we are declaring war on you.

Soviet culture and the Soviet people were given to understand the following: the new leadership wants to change its methods, but not the principles of the preceding policy. But, as Yevtushenko had already written in one of his earlier poems, the deadly silencing fear that had reigned in Russia since the purges of the late thirties had vanished. And so there ensued a struggle that lasted many years and did not end until the introduction of a new regimentation when the Soviet Union entered another political period.

Mikhail Romm characterized the new attacks in an address at a meeting of film and theatrical workers in the fall of 1962:

The magazine *Oktyabr* . . . published articles smearing all the progress achieved by Soviet films . . . inspired by the same persons who led the campaign of denunciation of "cosmopolites without fatherland." The articles began with a piece on the film *Peace to Those Who Enter*. Ten years ago, after such a denunciation, somebody would have been put in chains. Then came the attack on the films *The Letter That Wasn't Sent, If This Is Love,* and *Nine Days in a Year*. . . . For *Nine Days,* the hero was not positive enough. In *The Letter That Wasn't Sent,* a decadent pessimism is to be found. Raizman's heroes show moral deficiencies and amorality. . . .

The attacks had an immediate effect, and the production of the year 1963 was particularly drab, especially from the point of view of form. The most interesting films were traditional illustrations of literary works that tried, in one way or another, to face up to the past. A. Stolper filmed the first part of K. Simonov's novel, *The Living and the Dead* (*Zhiviye i myortviye*), about the catastrophe suffered by Soviet troops in the first days of the war. Kulidzhanov attempted to film *Blue Notebook* (*Sinnaya tetrad*), the last work of E. Kazakevich, who died in his prime. But what was revealing and effective in writing—the confrontation of Lenin's pre-revolutionary statements about Soviet power and democracy with the experiences of the reader—did not find an equivalent expression in the medium of film. The same fate befell Basov's version of *Silence* (*Tishina*) by Yuri Bondarev, which was one of the bolder literary views of the Stalinist period. And so, finally, certain positive entries can be made on the balance sheet—for the first independent film by Georgi Danelia, *I Walk About*

Silence

White
Caravan

Moscow (*Ya shagayu po Moskve*), a minor lyrical story of the day-to-day reality of the metropolis, and for *White Caravan* (*Byeliy Karavan*), an unconventional story about the life of Georgian shepherds, directed by Eldar Shengelaya (b. 1933) in collaboration with Tamaz Meliava.

On the other hand, the third joint film venture of Kalatozov and Urusevsky ended later in a strange dead end. It was *I Am Cuba* (*Ya Kuba*–1965), based on a script by Yevtushenko, a real catalogue or textbook of the formal possibilities of film photography, avoiding carefully any confrontation with reality.

MARLEN KHUTSIEV

In March 1963, the attack on culture culminated in a speech by Khrushchev that was so extreme that it was not published in the daily press of several Eastern European countries, something unheard of at that time. Film

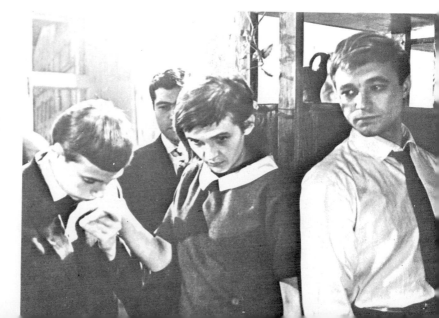

I'm
Twenty

became a principal target of attack, and particularly a film by one of the most talented representatives of the middle generation of film-makers, Marlen Khutsiev.

What had happened? Quite simply, in Khutsiev's film, *I'm Twenty*, known at the time under the working title of *Lenin's Guard* (*Zastava Ilycha*), the new supreme "Spectator" was confronted with an author's film—far more so than Romm's *Nine Days*—a film that presented an almost plotless flow of narration that showed the everyday life of three young people of Moscow seeking desperately and in vain for a moral ideal. The past of the fathers, who had an ideal to live and to die for, is mute, the present empty and often superficially eloquent. One of the key dialogues states what was to be the content of the conflict of the ensuing years: "What cowards you are. Don't you see that they want to wipe decent human beings from the face of the earth . . . And we are supposed to live, and to know that the man living next to us is a rascal, young, satiated, with honest eyes!"—"You say 'rascal'! And does that change anything? What can we do? The main thing is to stay honest yourself."—"This may not be the best point of view," says one of the friends, "but I've heard of worse."

Khutsiev in this film was consistent in his "ordinary" view of the world and thus succeeded in creating an authentic cinematic style. His portrait of the city and the inhabitants of Moscow was then unique in Soviet cinema.

Khrushchev attacked this unfinished work in a way that was reminiscent of the worst expressions of Zhdanovism. He explicitly objected to a scene where the hero asks his father, killed in the war, for advice. The dead father appears to the young boy: "I was younger than you are now, when I died. How can I give you any advice?" Khrushchev considered this scene an open attack on the wisdom of the fathers, a rebellion of the young against the older generation. A year and a half later, toward the end of 1964 (three months after Khrushchev's fall) Khutsiev's film, retitled *I'm Twenty* (*Mnye dvadsat let*), was shown in movie theaters, having been partly reshot, reedited by Gerasimov, and finally completed under extremely difficult conditions. The critics gave it some uneasy praise, while audiences passed it by without particular attention. Thus a film that should have established a new direction in Soviet cinema did not find any immediate followers. The coauthor of the script, one of the most gifted Soviet script-writers, Gennadi Shpalikov, killed himself 10 years later, when he saw no more hope for independent creative work.

THE END OF A PERIOD

What happened in the interim can be summarized very briefly. The situation relaxed somewhat, but all progress was stopped—as evidenced by the refusal to award Solzhenitsyn the Lenin Prize. Grigori Kozintsev followed *Don*

Hamlet

Quixote with *Hamlet* (1964), his best film since *Maxim* and a poignant statement on the intellectual's fate in a society corrupted by crime. Alexei Saltykov (b. 1934) made an extremely popular controversial film touching on the "personality cult" entitled *Chairman* (*Predsedatel*-1964), based on the story by Yuri Nagibin, a courageous and talented writer who played a significant role in Soviet film during this period. Probably the most "political" film of the period, *Chairman* was eventually backed personally by Khrushchev, whose fall followed shortly after. V. Ordynsky once again failed to find a cinematic equivalent for one of the best stories of the period, Vladimov's *Great Ore* (*Bolshaya ruda*-1964). On the other hand, the film version of V. Baklanov's unconventional and heroic war story, *This Palm of Land* (*Piad zemli*-1964), proved to be a successful debut for two young directors, Boris Yashin (b. 1932) and Andrei Smirnov (b. 1941). In Lithuania, Zhalakevichius continued successfully with another film that tried to come to terms with the past, *Chronicle of a Day* (*Khronika odnogo dnya*-1963). The actor Shukshin (1929-1974) filmed a comedy, *There Was a Lad* (*Zhivyot takoi paren*-1964), and his multifaceted personality immediately became the center of attention. But Elen Klimov's (b. 1935) *We Welcome You* (*Dobro pozhalovat*-1964), a highly satirical but cinematically rather conventional comedy about "educating" Soviet children in pioneer camps encountered sharp criticism.

We
Welcome
You

Three noteworthy films once again emerged from the studios of the Soviet republics. Boris Rytsarev (b. 1930), who had collaborated with Kalik, worked in Belorusfilm, one of the less stimulating of the Soviet Studios, to create an interesting work combining wartime memories with the contemporary experiences of its heroes, *Forty Minutes Till Dawn* (*Sorok minut do rastsveta*-1964). In his *Father of a Soldier* (*Otets soldata*-1964), Chkheidze confirmed his unusual ability to introduce a strange, almost grotesque tragicomedy into even the most pathetic of themes, an attribute characteristic of Georgian art.

Father of a Soldier

PARADZHANOV

Perhaps the most surprising event—the significance of which was not fully comprehended until some time later—was a film by Armenian-born director Sergei Paradzhanov, *Shadows of Forgotten Ancestors* (*Teni zabytykh predkov*-1964). Together with cameraman Yuri Ilyenko, Paradzhanov made a film poem inspired by the writings of M. Kotsyubinsky and by Western Ukrainian folklore. Paradzhanov was the first to indicate the degree to which folklore and local artistic tradition could once again become a source of visual wealth in Soviet national cinema. The spirit of Dovzhenko seemed to live again on the screen—though not through imitation. This spirit that had not even been resurrected by Solntseva's completion of yet another of his unrealized plans *The Enchanted Desna* (*Zacharovanaya Desna*-1964).

Shadows of Forgotten Ancestors

The Khrushchev era gradually opened the door to a new generation, a new insight and a new approach. As had happened in the past, however, the interest of the establishment and that of the artists seemed identical only on the surface. The political leadership was interested in finding better spokesmen for its policy, whereas the artists took the degree of freedom they were granted as an opportunity to speak for themselves and contrast their experience with the official version. The period that followed the setbacks of 1962 and 1963 inevitably became a period of direct confrontation. The first answer as to the direction things would take in the transitional period after the fall of Khrushchev (on October 16, 1964) came less than a year later: in September 1965, Andrei Sinyavsky and Yuli Daniel were arrested—the first writers to be jailed since the Twentieth Congress of the Soviet Communist Party.

THE SECOND GENERATION:
Czechoslovakia, 1956–1962

Late in April 1956, at the Second Congress of Czechoslovak Writers, the poet František Hrubín characterized the situation of Czech literature by using Mallarmé's metaphor of a swan frozen in ice. At the same time, the periodical of the Czechoslovak Writer's Union published a discussion by philosophers Karel Kosík and Ivan Sviták on the relationship between ideology and politics, exploding the basic canons of Stalinism. The literary press simultaneously published the most critical and the most nonconformist speeches presented at the Congress. Almost two years after comparable developments had occurred, not only in Hungary and Poland, but also in the Soviet Union, the thaw had commenced in Czechoslovakia as well. There was a reason for the delay. The mood among the intelligentsia in Czechoslovakia was similar to that elsewhere, intellectuals spoke of the same problems. But what was missing was a deep national resentment of the Russians; Czechoslovak communism was traditionally more Stalinist, and in addition the economic situation was far better there than elsewhere in Eastern Europe. Czechoslovakia had entered the postwar era indisputably richer, and thus the crises remained limited—for the present at least—to the cultural sphere.

INITIAL THAW

Before the films that would be the fruit of the changed situation appeared in Czechoslovakia, the political thaw was ending in Poland and the Hungarian revolution had been crushed. Paradoxically, the sole support of Czechoslovak film's subsequent effort to break open the door to Europe was the hesitant but still advancing thaw in the Soviet Union.

The films of the initial thaw were above all the work of the "second generation," the ones who shot their first features after 1945. To many of them Khrushchev's speech at the Twentieth Congress of the Soviet Communist Party was not a shock, but a confirmation of the rightness of the road on which they had embarked. They believed that the strength of a society comes from such public "self-criticism," and they started with great moral élan to try to eliminate "deformations," be they in public life or in art.

The leading figures of this brief period were Vojtěch Jasný, Ladislav Helge, Zbyněk Brynych, Ján Kadár, and Elmar Klos.

Jasný's *September Nights* (*Zářijové noci*–1956) was based on a play by Pavel Kohout, one of the most talented and influential of the young Stalinist poets who later played an exceptional role in the development of Czech culture and society. The film was the first open attack on functionary dogmatism, insensitivity, pettyness, and despotism; its target was, of all things, the army. As to form, Jasný avoided the crude realism of *The Clouds Will Roll Away* and cameraman Jaroslav Kučera was still only hesitantly examining the landscape beyond the limits of convention; but the film was a breakthrough in the thematic sphere.

Jasný's next film, *Dèsire* (*Touha*-1958) was the first real *auteur* film in Czech cinema. Jasný himself wrote the four-part screenplay for the film, in which four periods of human life are framed by the seasons of the year, and then surrendered himself to lyrical meditation through the lens of Kučera's camera. Basic human problems took the place of political or historical facts. Lyricism in the best Rovenský tradition replaced descriptive realism, and the contemporaneity of the third story for the first time demonstrated that bitter flavor of personal destiny, measured by the times, that gradually became characteristic not only for Jasný, but for Czechoslovak film in general.

Desire

As a young film enthusiast, Ladislav Helge (b. 1927) began by helping Jindřich Brichta build a unique film museum in Prague. Later, he worked as Krejčík's assistant and eventually made his debut, *School for Fathers* (*Škola otců*-1957). Helge, along with his permanent scriptwriter, author Ivan Kříž, was always a true socialist moralist. The hero of *School for Fathers,* a village teacher, wages a struggle against everyday practices in the name of proclaimed ideals—and loses. That was something entirely new, even as compared to *September Nights*. No longer a pacifying end, but rather an appeal to continue a struggle that does not end on the screen.

Helge's next film, *Great Solitude* (*Velká samota*-1959) was more concise in form and its attitude was tougher. It told a story of a young party enthusiast who brings a foundering cooperative farm to a degree of prosperity by using dictatorial methods, but in so doing loses the affection and the confidence of the people. By then, however, it was already 1959 and the thaw was ending. Helge had to redo the end at the last moment to give it a sort of false optimism, and an effort to award the film the critics' prize ended in scandal.

Great Solitude   A Local Romance

Zbyněk Brynych (b. 1927), who was to become much better known internationally than Helge, was not a graduate of the Prague Film Academy either, but rather had come up through the ranks of the film industry. His very first film, *A Local Romance* (*Žižkovská romance*-1957), brought him laurels abroad, and they kept coming in as the years passed. The heroes of his first effort bore a strong resemblance to the heroes of Hungary's best films of the fifties: their romance took place in the grey streets, among the dingy tenements of the Prague workers' suburbs. In fact, "dingy realism" was the term later used by official critics of the film. But it was just this sense of reality that became the heritage for the period that followed. Brynych tried somewhat to stay on this ground in his multi-part film, *Five out of a Million* (*Pět z miliónu*-1958), but in *Skid* (*Smyk*-1959), his next film, he adopted an eclectic style that concealed the old pattern.

WEISS, KREJČÍK AND THE OTHERS

Some members of the previous generation joined the new movement. After his attempt to speak out on racism and the gypsy question in *My Friend the Gypsy* (*Můj přítel Fabian*-1954), which was distorted by the work of the censors, Weiss turned to psychological realism and made one of his best—if not his very best—films, *Wolf Trap* (*Vlčí jáma*-1957). The film was an adaptation of a popular novel set in the twenties, and presented an accurate portrait of a provincial petit-bourgeois marital triangle. But at the same time, it indicated that Weiss had departed from the direct commitment and documentarism of his youth and had become a director of psychological films that were carried primarily by the performances of the actors.

Wolf Trap

Krejčík devoted the first half of the fifties to vain attempts to breathe life into the period films. Eventually, in 1959, he completed *Awakening* (*Probuzení*-1959), another in a series of films on disturbed youth, and a film badly damaged by the censors.

Miloš Makovec (b. 1919) first arrived at making feature films, via documentary film, at the time of the most profound schematism. As late as 1957, he made the film that was to remain identified with his name in Czech film, *Three Men Missing* (*Ztracenci*). It shows an entirely different kind of history than was depicted in Vávra's *Hussite Trilogy* or in the biographical films of the first half of the fifties. It told of one of the infamous wars of the mid-eighteenth century, which was part of Czech history only because it had been waged on Czech soil, and because the casualties were Czech recruits. These were represented by three nameless soldiers, malingerers, torn away from their army in an alien countryside, where they die to defend the lives of an unknown farm family. In a situation not of their own making in which they took on a responsibility that was not their own, the three found an opportunity to become men. The assistant director on this film was Věra Chytilová. But Makovec's ideas were not

Three
Men
Missing

central to Czech film development, and once again he found himself on the periphery of Czech cinema. His contemporary, Miroslav Hubáček, who had made a promising debut in 1950, tried his hand again with *The Plain Old Maid* (*Ošklivá slečna*-1959), but he found no official support at all.

The relaxation of ideological censorship did make possible a differentiation of genre in general production. Mysteries and spy stories appeared—the best of them was Karel Kachyňa's second independent film, *Smugglers of Death* (*Král Šumavy*-1959)—and there was even a successful comedy of the type René Clair did in Hollywood, *Out of Reach of the Devil* (*Kam čert nemůže*-1959), directed by Zdeněk Podskalský (b. 1923).

More interesting was Ivo Novák's (b. 1918) contemporary comedy, *Puppies* (*Štěňata*-1957). The story of a young couple and their in-laws violated all the canons of scriptwriting, based as it was entirely on finely drawn situations. The author of the script and the assistant director was Miloš Forman.

SLOVAKIA AFTER 1956

Slovak cinema also brought forth its first ripe fruit during that period: the film *Forty-four* (*Štyridsaťštyri*-1957), directed by Palo Bielik. With a strong feeling for detail and a sense of the tragic, Bielik used a real incident to create a powerful film about a suppressed revolt of Slovak soldiers during World War One.

In terms of production facilities, Slovak cinema had been on its own since early in the fifties, but most films—21 in all during the decade following 1947—were still made by Czech directors, for whom Slovakia was mainly a land of natural beauty and folklore. These aspects of Slovakia were also used as criteria for assessing the work of Slovak directors— c.g., Medved, Lettrich, Žáček. Efforts to measure up to these criteria weakened such better Slovak films as *Untilled Fields* (*Pole neorané*-1953), directed by Vlado Bahna (b. 1914). In time Kadár's work was also found lacking in folkloric character. It was not until a new generation, trained in the Prague Film Academy and imbued with an entirely Slovak vision, came to the fore that a beginning was finally made. It started with *Song of the Grey Dove* (*Pieseň o sivom holubovi*), directed in 1960 by Stanislav Barabáš (b. 1924) a tragic and lyric vision of war seen through children's eyes.

MAGIC LANTERN

Another success of this period was *Magic Lantern*. Born on the periphery of Czechoslovak cinema, its extraordinary success at the Brussels EXPO 58 reminded the world of the existence of Czechoslovak culture. Alfred Radok, the creator of *Magic Lantern*, joined the heritage of the Czech theatrical avant-garde with film, surrounded himself with a number of talented young people (e.g., Miloš Forman, Vladimír Svitáček, Jan Roháč), and in collaboration with that genius of stage design, Josef Svoboda, created a new type of film theater for which a great future was prophesied. But the second program of *Magic Lantern*—which was to transform a temporary exhibition into a permanent artistic institution—fell victim to the new "cold wave." Radok and his collaborators were forced out of *Magic Lantern*, and, after an unsuccessful attempt to make use of its principles for a hybrid version of Offenbach's *Tales of Hoffmann* under the direction of opera director Václav Kašlík, it became nothing but a tourist attraction.

THE CONFERENCE AT BANSKÁ BYSTRICA

The immediate pretext for the neo-Stalinist counteroffensive—sealed by a conference convened in Banská Bystrica in early 1959—was found in three films: *Three Wishes* (*Tři přání*-1958), *Hic sunt leones* (*Zde jsou lvi*-1958), and the medium-length *The End of the Soothsayer* (*Konec jasnovidce*-1958).

The creators of *Three Wishes,* Ján Kadár and Elmar Klos, made their first film together in 1952, beginning a noteworthy collaboration that lasted almost 20 years. That first film was called *Kidnapped (Únos),* and was on the surface a typical product of its time: a group of people unwilling to accept the post-1948 regime hijacks a Czechoslovak plane to Munich. The American intelligence service puts forward all possible effort to keep the rest of the passengers from returning home. But for the most part, they resist the temptation and remain true to their homeland and its new system. In spite of the predictability of the plot the film was interesting for its language and the low-key approach to a highly propagandistic topic, which differed significantly from cold-war esthetic conventions.

Klos and Kadár's next film was *Music from Mars (Hudba z Marsu–* 1955), in color, the first real attempt at a musical satirical comedy, which implied that the sources of evil are to be found all the way at the top; it encountered overt and pointed rejection. As a result, Kadár and Klos moved to a less controversial theme, and did *House at the Terminus (Dům na konečné).* In 1956, this film was primarily attractive for its poetic realism. It concerned itself with lives of ordinary people, the tenants of one appartment building, and avoided all ideology.

The second generation—and Kadár was indisputably a member of it— was a generation of moralists. Another member was playwright Vratislav Blažek, author of the successful stage play, *Three Wishes.* A young man, head of a family, unable to find an apartment in a Prague plagued by a housing shortage, does a kindness to an old man. It turns out that he is a sort of magic godfather, who promises to fulfill three wishes as a reward. The young man finds himself embarked on a meteoric career. But when his best friend is tossed out of his job for justly and openly criticizing evil doings, the old man can no longer be of any help. The three wishes have been exhausted. Of course, if the hero is willing to relinquish what he has gained through his three wishes, the old man would be willing to help. The question of what decision the hero will make is left open. The film of the same name, filmed by Kadár and Klos in 1958, showed what the stage version had concealed: the mechanism of social corruption, cowardice, and hypocrisy that the old man takes advantage of to fulfill the wishes. And so the concluding question in the film was different from the one posed

Three
Wishes

on the stage: if you truly begin to fight a situation that is destroying honest people, you have to count on losing the advantages that this situation brought to you. Are you really willing to do it? That was a crucial question in the period of the first reckoning around 1956. But it was also the period following the "events" in Poland and Hungary, when so many people wanted what they had said just yesterday to be forgotten as soon as possible. The Spectator understood the film, and reacted the only way he knew how; the film was banned, and did not get to movie screens until 1963. Its criticism was toothless by then, and its film language outdated.

Hic
Sunt
Leones

The film *Three Wishes* became the cornerstone of the case made against Czechoslovak cinema at the conference convened in February 1959 in Banská Bystrica in Slovakia. The second film to come under fire was *Hic sunt leones,* another work by Krška, with a script by the young writer Oldřich Daněk (b. 1927). After the rehabilitation of *Silvery Wind,* Krška felt that perhaps this was the end of his torture, and he made his own story into what was apparently his best film: a man is on an operating table, gravely wounded; a group of surgeons tries to bring the man back to life. The flashback shows that he is an exceptionally talented engineer who was being crushed by the wheels of the bureaucracy and in vain sought the help of those around him. In a condition of nervous collapse, he fell victim to an accident that brought him to the operating table. In its conclusion, the film declared: they are all doing what they can to save him, but who moved a finger to help him when it would have been so much easier? The wound inflicted at the Banská Bystrica conference, where the film was violently attacked, was one from which Krška never recovered as an artist. He went on teaching at the Film Academy, where his most faithful pupils included Jan Němec, he wrote scripts, he went on shooting until his last breath, but he never made another significant film.

Many believed that *The End of the Soothsayer* would be what Vladimír Svitáček (b. 1921) needed to demonstrate his talent. The short satiric feature seemed almost timid, the allegory comparatively conventional: the soothsayer's business prospered beautifully as long as he offered his services on a private basis; once it was incorporated in the system of state services, the institution began to fail. But at home, behind the door to his own apartment, the soothsayer offers a handful of the select his services as before. The film was so well-made, however, and the acting so excellent that its impact literally bowled the Spectator over. It was banned too, though released later in 1963, and Svitáček never directed another independent film.

Attacks were also made on Brynych's "falsely comprehended neo-realism," on Helge's "moral indignation," on Jasný's "formalism," and, in general, on "themes taken almost exclusively from private life." This new interruption of artistic development dealt a particularly heavy blow to the second postwar generation. But it only postponed the appearance of the third generation, and did not succeed in stopping it entirely.

The efforts of the second generation in this period brought back to film a personal viewpoint, a sense of the times, and a direct commitment. But it was just this reawakening that led to the most violent of conflicts with the establishment. When the axe fell on these efforts in 1959 in Banská Bystrica, new paths were sought.

INSPIRED BY THE WAR

The first postwar films in Eastern Europe sought their inspiration for the most part from wartime experiences and the Nazi occupation. Nor had this theme lost its power by the second half of the fifties, when it played an important role in the evolution of Polish, Soviet, and Yugoslav cinema. In addition, it gradually became a safe refuge in moments of repression for cinema as a whole as well as for individual film-makers. The distinctions in these stories were precise: good was white and ultimately victorious, evil was black and safely vanquished, and the audience's identification with the "good guys" was ensured. These war films resembled westerns, even in their abundance of action. But there was a third dimension of wartime subject matter, one that came to the forefront in the difficult period at the end of the fifties and in the early sixties. The occupation and the war were used as a package to smuggle in contemporary themes: films about the recent past became a disguise for contemporary commitments.

After Banská Bystrica, this path brought the greatest success in Czecho-slovakia. What ensued was an interim period of uncertainty and void, what had been permitted yesterday was banned. There was no going backward, either. At that point, Weiss made his internationally successful film, *Romeo, Juliet, and the Darkness,* shown in the United States under the title *Sweet Light in the Dark Window* (*Romeo, Julie a tma*-1959). The story of the Czech Anne Frank and her youthful Romeo was a condemnation of indifference toward force and terrorism.

No less successful was Krejčík's *A Higher Principle* (*Vyšší princip*-1960), about an old Latin professor who stands up in support of his students at the height of Nazi terrorism, embodying the heroic ideals of antiquity.

Vojtěch Jasný also did an unconventional job of the story of human solidarity, *I Survived Certain Death* (*Přežil jsem svou smrt*-1960), in which the hero, a prisoner in a concentration camp, sings *Ave Maria* at the moment of his execution—probably the first time in years the hymn had been sung in a film made in this part of the world.

Weiss's next film, *The Coward* (*Zbabělec*-1961), originated in the same spirit, as did Krejčík's *Midnight Mass* (*Pol'nočná omša*-1961) shot in Slovakia, and Helge's *White Clouds* (*Bílá oblaka*-1962). This series also includes Barabáš's *Song of the Grey Dove*—as mentioned earlier, the first significant effort of an independent Slovak cinematography—and *The Boxer and Death* (*Boxer a smrt*-1962) by another Slovak director, Peter

Death Is Called Engelchen

Solan (b. 1929), elaborating with an unconventionality and a surprising maturity on a conflict between two types of strength in a concentration camp.

Inspired by these films, Ján Kadár and Elmar Klos returned to work after two years of enforced silence, making their best film up until that time, *Death Is Called Engelchen* (*Smrt si říká Engelchen*-1963), based on the novel by Ladislav Mňačko. Here again war is also a pretext for a moral message with its roots in the present. The Polish and Yugoslav influence is clearly apparent. It is no longer a question of the "good guys" and the "bad guys" but of war itself, war as an evil, destroying moral values on all sides and scarring the victors as profoundly as the vanquished. The style also underwent a radical change, the camera freely altering both time and narration; documentary reconstruction, sheer lyricism and philosophical meditation coexisted side by side in a new unity of style.

Transport from Paradise (*Transport z ráje*-1962), directed by Zbyněk Brynych on the basis of short stories by Arnošt Lustig, also exemplified this discovery of style. Brynych, together with cameraman Jaroslav Čuřík, advanced from neorealistic rawness through lyricism to a sort of expressionistic documentarism. *Transport from Paradise* finally brought to the screen what Radok had intended in his *Distant Journey*: a reconstruction of one of the visits of the International Red Cross Commission to the Jewish ghettoes. After the departure of the commission, the Nazis call for a mass deportation to the gas chambers. For some this is a signal to revolt, and the cry "Never again like sheep!" sounds loud and clear from the screen as a message for the present and the future.

Transport from Paradise

VLÁČIL

In the past, the problem of film form and rhetoric had never been a social or political one in Eastern Europe. What made it become one was the campaign against the avant-garde, the canonization of socialist realism, and the Zhdanov line. Thus, one by one, every advance, every experiment, as well as any mere attempt to establish contact with native or European artistic tradition of the twentieth century, was considered to be an expression of opposition and rebellion—and in effect, really was. After the 1958 neo-Stalinist attack, the area of form became another refuge from which it was possible to wage war on the past. The major protagonist here was František Vláčil (b. 1924). After working for some years in animated film, Vláčil entered the army, where, during his tour of duty, he made two visually noteworthy short films, *Glass Clouds* (*Skleněná oblaka*-1958) and *Pursuit* (*Pronásledování*-1959). In 1960, he made his first feature film, *The White Dove* (*Bílá holubice*), about a sick boy who holds a dove captive. The entire story is concentrated on the small area inside and outside the window beside which the child lives. Vláčil's visual poem on freedom met with considerable international success, but its pioneering significance remained, for the most part, unrecognized.

The
White
Dove

Vláčil's next film confirmed the fact that his debut had been no exception. *The Devil's Trap* (*Ďáblova past*-1961), to some extent inspired in its style by Bergman's films, told the story of religious intolerance in Bohemia at the turn of the seventeenth and eighteenth centuries and anticipated the interest in history—which was not to remain limited to Vláčil—as another window to the present.

35 FICTION FILMS A YEAR

Comedy and mystery accounted for two other interesting films—Jasný's humorously ironic view of religious feeling in a Czech village, *Pilgrimage to the Virgin Mary* (*Procesí k panence*-1961), and the documentaristically treated spy film, *Department Five* (*Páté oddělení*), directed by Jindřich Polák (b. 1925).

Pilgrimage
to the
Virgin
Mary

The area of films for and about children also became a momentary refuge or a departure point for future talents. Karel Kachyňa began his collaboration with author Jan Procházka, which lasted for 10 years and produced several interesting results. The first of them was *Piebald* (*Trápení*-1961), a paraphrase of Lamorisse's *Crin Blanc,* striving to reply to the melancholy sorrow of the French model of lyricism, aiming at conciliation and harmony. Václav Gajer (b. 1923) called attention to himself more for the subject matter of his film *Rabbits in the Tall Grass* (*Králíci ve vysoké trávě*-1961) than for its form. It told of a youth forced to suicide by two conflicting educational influences, one Christian and one atheistic. In the final version of the film, tragedy had to give way to a more conciliatory ending. In his *Guilt of Vladimír Olmer* (*Vina Vladimíra Olmera*-1956)—as well as in his later films—Gajer inclined toward controversial themes, but he never developed them far enough, and there was always—even cinematically—a feeling of a promise not fulfilled.

In Slovakia, Štefan Uher (b. 1930), a graduate of the Prague Film Academy, made his debut with the unconventional children's film *Form 9A* (*My z deviatej A*-1961). He was soon to play an exemplary role in Czechoslovak cinema.

The second half of the fifties also witnessed the revival of the old glory of Czech cameramen. Aside from those of the middle generation—Rudolf

Stahl, the Slovak Karol Krška, Jaromír Holpuch, Rudolf Milič, Vladimír Novotný, and above all Josef Illík—new names began to appear, soon to become well known throughout Europe: Jan Čuřík, Jaroslav Kučera, and Jan Kališ were the first, later to be joined by Jan Němeček, Bedřich Baťka, Miroslav Ondříček and Slovaks Stanislav Szomolanyi and Igor Luther.

In the late fifties and early sixties most of these young men were still shooting school films at the Prague Film Academy where a new generation was completing its training. Their professors were the most experienced directors of the older generation, a luxury characteristic of the Eastern European film schools that no film school in the West could afford. But the slogan "Opportunity for Youth" sounded from the Soviet Union, and so one of their graduation projects, *A Loaf of Bread* (*Sousto*-1960), a short film by Jan Němec (b. 1936) was accepted for distribution. It was followed by *Hall of Lost Footsteps* (*Sál ztracených kroků*-1961) by Jaromil Jireš (b. 1935). The theme of the Jireš film was still a traditional one, filled with reminiscences of the Nazi occupation, but the language and the viewpoint were entirely new, reflecting the previously neglected sources of twentieth-century imagination. The new theme sounded louder with Věra Chytilová (b. 1929) and her graduation project *Ceiling* (*Strop*-1961).

A
Loaf
of
Bread

A SURPRISE: Bulgaria, 1956-1964

Up to 1956, it seemed that only Bulgaria and Romania would continue on the Stalinist path. Vulko Chervenkov succeeded Georgi Dimitrov, the almost legendary leader who died in 1950, only six months after Traicho Kostov, his fellow freedom fighter and the head of the native Communist antifascist resistance, was tried and executed as an alleged traitor. Chervenkov was determined to keep concessions to those who wanted to democratize society at a minimum. He had to abandon power in 1956, and Todor Zhivkov, younger and less tied to the past, came to the fore.

The year 1956 is connected with the first displays of opposition to ideological uniformity. More open-minded books appeared on the market, films already conceived were hurriedly readied for production, and the unified note of enthusiasm disappeared from literature, to be replaced by the dissonance of disillusionment, attempts at criticism, and reflections on the path that Bulgaria had taken. Emil Manov's novel, *An Unauthentic Case,* for example, criticized the system through its portrait of a Communist of long years' standing who, desperate over what he had witnessed, falls victim to alcoholism and ultimately to madness. And 1956 also saw the production of the story of a man of ruthless ambition who is elevated to the highest of jobs (Todor Genov's play *Fear*). Literature began to ask questions about the essence of the national character, questions never posed in Bulgaria, which—as already mentioned—had only existed as an independent state for a few decades. With the exploration of national authenticity, two trends began to come into focus in the intellectual field. The first, which saw Bulgarian civilization as a continuation of the traditions of Thrace—and hence not exclusively the fruit of Slavic elements—sought opportunities for an intellectual revival in a return to native roots. The second, and no less active current—whose adherents were the so-called "cosmopolits"—saw the main cause of Bulgaria's anemia in the isolation of its life from that of the rest of Europe. After the events in Poland and Hungary, both of these trends were condemned as being revisionist and repressed even before there was a chance for any real polarization or confrontation.

In 1957, Chervenkov was named Minister of Culture and Education and placed Todor Pavlov, the most rigid of Bulgaria's cultural dogmatics, in charge of liquidating everything that was even remotely reminiscent of the Hungarian, Polish, or Yugoslav cultural ferment. In April 1958, Zhivkov declared a return to a single esthetic model, and in a speech before the Union of Bulgarian Writers, he condemned "all spontaneous development

On a Small Island

in literature and art" as being "alien to our Party and our Marxism-Leninism." Eight members of the Writers' Union Presidium resigned, including Emil Manov, playwright Orlin Vasilev—the scriptwriter of the first films of the fifties—and poet Valeri Petrov, an outstanding figure of postwar Bulgarian literature.

ON A SMALL ISLAND

But because of the delay that is typical for cinema, the fruits of the thaw of 1956 only then began to appear in movie theaters. The first was *On a Small Island* (*Na malkya ostrov*-1957), written by Valeri Petrov, directed by Rangel Vulchanov, and photographed by Dimo Kolarov. Their film, based on the same ideological and artistic sources as the works of the "Polish school," introduced true poetry and passion into the provincialism of Bulgarian film, and above all freely employed the immense vocabulary of film language, much of which surpassed the discoveries of the latter "new wave." Vulchanov's film, a stylized poetic variation on a historical theme, was attacked as being a deviation from the party line, and was labeled pessimist, existentialist, Freudian, and so on. The story of the film takes place in 1925 on a deserted island in the Black Sea where several participants in the unsuccessful 1923 uprising are held prisoner. They plan their escape; they fail; four of those who organized the flight die, yet hope lives on, and the will to be free along with it. The theme was novel primarily in its romantically individualized approach to the characters, who were seen from many viewpoints, including an ironical one. For the first time, Kolarov's camera explored the rawness of reality without the artificiality of the studio, and the entire film—as opposed, for example, to *The Cranes Are Flying*—was informed with a noneclectic admiration for the great masters of world cinema.

Not surprisingly, Vulchanov was one of the few Bulgarian directors who had not studied in Moscow. He graduated from a vocational high school and the Theatrical Institute, worked as an assistant director for five years, and in 1956 was Sharaliev's second-unit director on *Two Victories.* After the critique of *Small Island,* he also was employed as a second-unit director in 1958 on *Stars* (*Zvezdi*), a coproduction between Bulgaria and East Germany that was directed by Konrad Wolf. It is difficult to say just what part Vulchanov had in the creation of this exceptional film, but the detailed portrayal of the background, above all the excellently perceived atmosphere of a small Bulgarian town, was recognizably his work.

In his next film, which was not made until 1960, he once again collaborated with Petrov and Kolarov. Entitled *The First Lesson* (*Purvi urok*), it told the story of the collapse of the friendship and love of two young people during the war, showing a sensitive perception of the details of two different social strata in the Bulgarian capital. It was once again a film of pure poetic and philosophical vision, and the actors were guided by a modern hand. The film did not have the originality of *Small Island,* but nonetheless it was quite clear that here was the first Bulgarian director of international caliber. Vulchanov, however, created only one more significant film, *Sunshine and Shadow* (*Sluntseto i syankata*-1962), an attempt at a modern expression of the emotional attachment of two young people whose love is being smashed against the wall that separates contemporary Europe into East and West. In this film, even more than in the two others, the plot retreated to the background, yielding its place to philosophical reflections and formal experimentation. *Sunshine and Shadow,* which was also written by Petrov, was accused of "abstract humanism." Petrov's next script, *Man with a Gate,* was rejected and Vulchanov started work on an autobiographical story, *The Unknown Soldier's Patent Leather Shoes* (*Lachenite obuvki na neznaynya voyn*),

Sunshine
and
Shadow

work that was to continue for a number of years. The story, however, was never filmed.

OTHER NEW DIRECTORS

The antifascist resistance movement as a major life experience was a theme that reappeared again and again in Bulgarian cinematography. In these films, the war was not seen as a national tragedy but rather as an initiation into life, as a test of adulthood, the premature discovery of the tragic aspects of life, but a discovery that always breathed the soft breath of hope. Centuries of Turkish rule, along with the philosophy of the Eastern Orthodox Church, had taught the Bulgarian people a conciliatory acceptance of life's reality, an attitude that has no room for romantic and individualistic rebellion.

Outstanding among the antifascist films was the work of Binka Zhelyazkova (b. 1923)—the first woman director in the Balkans—who in 1960 made *When We Were Young* (*A byakhme mladi*), based on a script by Khristo Ganev (b. 1924). Its story of unconsummated love, taking place against the setting of a war-torn city, is evidence of the power of the emotional and visual memories left by the war in the minds of this generation. They are transformed in *When We Were Young* into supremely dreamy, thought-provoking images, which Zhelyazkova composed in the style of modern Bulgarian pictorial art, deserting any plot line right at the start and concentrating on evoking an atmosphere saturated with the premonition of death. The emotional tension of the final prison scenes is unique in Bulgarian film. And yet, it did not get its strength from dramatic emphasis, but rather from a lyrical-poetic form, disarming in its spontaneity, immediacy, and overt subjectivity. Zhelyazkova was also criticized, but unlike Vulchanov, who kept trying to break through the official opposition, she was not heard from for the next six years.

When
We
Were
Young

In 1963, Ganev filmed a documentary about Algeria entitled *Holiday of Hope* (*Prasnik na nadezhdata*), a sensitive poetic essay on war and freedom, and then he too fell silent.

Not a single one of this generation's directors, all of whom had lost part of their youth to the war, found it possible to assert their talent and strength—not even Khristo Piskov (b. 1927), a graduate of the Moscow VGIK and Lev Arnshtam's assistant on the coproduction, *Lesson from History*. Piskov's *Poor Man's Street* (*Bednata ulitsa*-1960) and *There Is No Death* (*Smurt nyama*-1962) were the pinnacle of expressionistic and symbolic language—the so-called expressive realism—as the voice of modern Bulgarian film. While *Poor Man's Street* was the weakest of the young generation's antifascist films (reminiscent in plot of Vulchanov's *First Lesson*), *There Is No Death* was, in its day, one of the more important films from Eastern Europe. Based on Todor Monov's novel, it unfolds a story of work, love, and everyday heroism against the backdrop of work on a large construction project. It was the first time that Bulgarian film depicted workers made of flesh and blood, people full of doubts, anxieties, and weaknesses, who spend hours of solitude over a glass of cheap liquor, with few illusions about themselves or others. The picture of the workers' environment, which had until then been idealized without reservation, aroused even greater criticisms than Vulchanov's films. Piskov did not return to film work until 1966, when, in collaboration with his wife, Irina Aktasheva, he made a timid attempt at a nonconformist tale about young workers, *Monday Morning* (*Ponedelnik sutrin*).

In 1962, after Khrushchev's address opposing "formalism in art," Todor Zhivkov made a similar speech. He accused all artists, but especially the younger generation, of aping Western models, of decadence, and of pessimism. In spite of the naming of names, and in spite of numerous administrative measures, a segment of Bulgarian literature remained in a position of mild opposition. This group was headed by Emil Manov, whose novel *The Flight of Galatea* was attacked for its "decadent opinions," and whose play *Abel's Mistake* was criticized for "grave political failings."

Not a single one of Manov's more important works found its way to the motion picture screen. The best film to be made from one of his scripts was *Captive Squadron* (*Pleneno yato*-1962), which was also the best of director Ducho Mundrov's (b. 1920) work. In 1952, as a student in Moscow, Mundrov collaborated with Nikola Korabov (b. 1928) to make a documentary on the poet Nikola Vaptsarov. Upon his return home, Mundrov, once again with Korabov, filmed a classical social-realist story, *Men of Dimitrovgrad* (*Dimitrovgradtsi*-1956) and followed that in 1957 with an independent film, *Unit Commander* (*Komandirut na otryada*), a tale of the partisans. In *Captive Squadron*, Mundrov relinquished the schematic line and the conventional forms he had employed at the start of his career and rather than concentrating his attention on the plot, showed more concern for the psychological atmosphere of a cell where a group of political prisoners were spending the last days before their execution.

This stress on psychology and atmosphere was something new in Bulgarian cinema, which had traditionally been inspired by realism. Nonetheless, Mundrov's approach was typical for the generation of directors and scriptwriters that became prominent after 1956, and may be one of the reasons for the dissatisfaction aroused by their films. Bulgarian film historian and journalist Todor Andreykov wrote about the film *On a Small Island*: "The power of the esthetic explosion in the film was so immense that it delivered a serious blow to the equilibrium of many people, who, overcome by the daring of the work, looked to the canons of schematism to prove that there were grave faults in the film" (*Film*, August 1968, Warsaw). His words indisputably apply to other innovative films of the period, particularly to the work of the talented Lyubomir Sharlandzhiev (b. 1931), graduate of the Theatrical Institute and vGIK. In both his social-conscience film, *Chronicle of Sentiments* (*Khronika na chuvstvata*-1962), based on a story by Todor Monov, and in *Chain* (*Verigata*-1964), after a script by Wagenstein (scenarist for *Stars*), Sharlandzhiev arrived at a poetic way of depicting crisis situations that evolved from the necessity to make an existential choice. The hero of *Chain*, an antifascist fighter, undergoes various psychological crises when he is on the run, particularly a mistrust of people, until he finally overcomes the doubts within himself

Chain

and thus perhaps even saves his own life. In *Chronicle of Sentiments*, author Monov strove to reveal some of the contemporary conflicts inherent in individual relationships. The description of the environment—a large construction project—was a complementary element to the developing psychological crises and vice versa. In a sort of uninterrupted murmuring, voices had been audible even in Bulgaria, saying that socialism had not done away with despair or alienation. In spite of the fact that *Chronicle of Sentiments,* like all Bulgarian films, ended on an optimistic note, it suffered the same fate as Vulchanov's films.

After 1962, as a consequence of the constant political criticism, the first wave of autonomous Bulgarian film started to peter out; its creators gradually began to fall silent. An exemplary case in the campaign against the new trend was *An Incredible Tale* (*Neveroyatna istoria*-1962). This attempt at a satirical comedy—a rather tame attempt at that time—did not appear on the screens until 1964-1965. It took that long for a decision to be reached about the acceptability of the film's critique of hypocrisy, opportunism, etc. Based on a script by Radoi Ralin and directed by Vladimir Yanchev (b. 1930), it was the story of a newspaper article attacking a fictitious person, unleashing panic among important personages who identified with the attacked individual. The lead was played by Rangel Vulchanov, whose acting career—less successful than his career as a film director—began in 1951 with the role of a partisan in *Alarm.* Following the lead of *An Incredible Tale,* Vulchanov tried to adapt to the current trend of general film production with the mystery *The Inspector and the Night* (*Inspektorat i noshta*-1963), a well-made detective story about the psychology of an investigator. The script was the work of the gifted young writer Bogomil Raynov, but his intention of creating in the inspector a portrait of contemporary man could, under the circumstances of those times, remain only that—an intention, unfulfilled.

Early in the sixties, Bulgarian cinema, with fairly well-equipped studios and laboratories in Sofia, produced 10 fiction films and 100 to 150 short films annually. Fiction-film production expanded in the area of mysteries and comedies with an aim to regaining the interest of audiences, weary by now of socialist dramas and war stories. Most of them catered to popular taste and offered simple-minded entertainment, and all of them were

Tobacco

limited to the domestic market. The most successful were the mystery films, *The Gold Tooth* (*Zlatnyat zub*-1962) and *The Night of the Thirteenth* (*Noshta sreshtu 13*-1961), directed by the most prolific of Bulgaria's directors, Anton Marinovich, and Yanchev's comedies, *Favorite No. 13* (*Lyubimets no. 13*-1958) and *Be Happy, Annie* (*Badi shchastliva, Anni*-1964). The adaptation of Dimitur Dimov's novel, *Tobacco* (*Tiutun*-1962), made at considerable expense, was to have been a representative example of Bulgarian film work. The inventiveness of director Nikola Korabov, however, found room to assert itself in only a few scenes, where Vulo Radev's photography contributed hugely to their originality. Pictures of the social oppression in prewar Bulgaria and the subsequent partisan fighting was conveyed by Korabov in the tested style of socialist realist historical frescoes. In addition, he filled the film with model characters: the bestial policemen, the drunken capitalist, and the mustachioed foreign agent stood opposed to the golden-haired angelic young girl, the unbending strikers, and the ideal "positive hero." *Tobacco* won the Grand Prix at the official festival of Bulgarian cinema at Varna in 1963, while *There Is No Death* was listed as a marginal film.

RADEV

In 1964, cameraman Vulo Radev (b. 1934) made his directorial debut with *The Peach Thief* (*Kradetsut na praskovi*), a refined film that won a great deal of international recognition. A surprising variation on *Stars,* the story is especially notable for its nostalgic re-creation of the atmosphere of a small town during World War One. The characters, a Bulgarian officer, his wife, and a Serbian prisoner of war, constitute the classical romantic triangle. Radev's sympathy is on the side of the Serbian officer, an extraordinary attitude, given the context of Bulgarian relations with the Yugoslavs, in both the distant and the recent past.

The
Peach
Thief

As a chamber piece, the drama was made in the style of the then popular realistic psychological literature. Its reserved, restrained, and lyrical visual and spoken language was the film's most distinguishing quality.

Radev used the same style in his next film, *The King and the General* (*Tsar i general*-1966), a story of the conflict between King Boris III and General Zaymov, who tried at the beginning of World War Two to prevent both Bulgaria's alliance with Germany and its entry into the war against the Soviet Union. Although Radev broke a number of conventions in this film too, he was not able to candidly and thoroughly explore the film's historico-philosophical struggle. The time had not yet come for the public airing of such ideological conflicts.

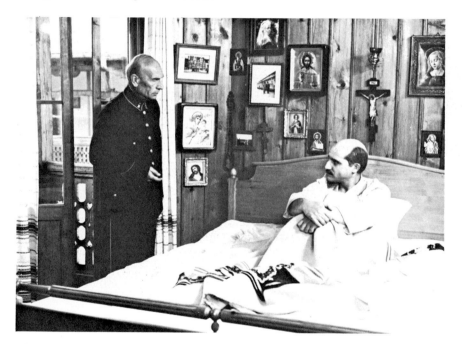

The King and the General

THE RIPENING:
Yugoslavia, 1955–1961

"REHABILITATION" OF YUGOSLAVIA

Khrushchev's trip to Belgrade, at the end of which he and Tito embraced at the airport on May 27, 1955, did not mean an end to conflicts between politics and culture. Milovan Djilas had no intention of remaining silent; his articles about Yugoslav socialism that were published in the American press, and the foreign edition of *The New Class,* his systematic sociological analysis of the Stalinist regimes, brought him a seven-year prison sentence in 1957. There were some who maintained that the hard line with respect to Yugoslavia's number-one revisionist was the price for reconciliation with Moscow. In any case, Tito set an important example for other Eastern European countries; his actions made it clear that the measure of autonomy tolerated within a communist country is directly proportional to the degree to which those in power can keep their own intelligentsia and their "revisionist" and liberal tendencies under control.

In 1958, however, a new deterioration of relations between Yugoslavia and the Soviet Union took place. The Yugoslav leadership could not and did not want to risk a conflict with the cultural intelligentsia, the majority of whom supported Tito's national version of a more liberal communism, and at the same time jealously guarded their autonomy, the greatest in all Eastern Europe. The dialectics of this situation gave birth to the cultural atmosphere that existed in Yugoslavia in the latter half of the fifties, a period referred to by some critics as "the best period in Yugoslav literature." The improvement in the Yugoslav international situation brought about a certain liberalization within the country. Esthetic controls over art practically vanished, and the duties of art were delimited more in negative terms; that is, what it should avoid in the way of topics, etc., and not what it should do. As a result, contemporary subjects which until then had been categorically postulated for all the arts, began to appear only sporadically in film; moreover, literature also turned to the past. In addition to this change in thematic emphasis, this period brought a decisive victory for the modern stylists over the traditionalists, "socialist estheticism" (Lukić) gaining the upper hand as a reply to socialist and so-called "national" realism. The development in cinema became a specific reflection of this situation.

THE CRUEL WAR

The seeds that Radoš Novaković, together with Ćosić and Bergström, had sown—and continued to sow, though with lesser success, in antifascist resistance films like *The Wind Dropped Before Dawn* (*Vetar je stao pred zoru*-1959)—started to bear fruit. The past began to acquire an increasingly human, and tragic, dimension. Wartime subjects thus gave birth to a new type of psychological realism, and along with it came a new style, represented by France Štiglic, Branko Bauer, Vladimir Pogačić, Stole Janković (b. 1926) and others. In 1956, in his native Slovenia, Štiglic filmed *Valley of Peace* (*Dolina miru*), a lyrical tale about deserted children who are rescued by a black American pilot who had been shot down. *The Ninth Circle* (*Deveti krug*-1960), set in Nazi-occupied Zagreb, was a successful version of the Anne Frank theme, which cropped up so often in European films of that period. Working again with Triglav Film in

The Ballad
of the
Trumpet
and the
Cloud

Ljubljana in 1961, Štiglic made *The Ballad of the Trumpet and the Cloud* (*Balada o trobenti in oblaku*), based on a novella by Slovenia's foremost writer, Cyril Kosmać. Filmed with keen poetic perception (Rudi Vavpotić was director of photography), it is a tragic story of a peasant who gives his life on Christmas Eve to rescue a group of partisans in the Slovenian mountains.

In 1956, in the Croatian Jadran Film, Branko Bauer made a film about the fate of the child of a dead resistance fighter, *Don't Turn Back, My Son* (*Ne okreć se, sine*). Most other important films of this genre were the work of Slovenian directors. Among them was *Five Minutes of Paradise* (*Pet minut raja*-1959), directed by Igor Pretnar. One of the most important Yugoslav films of that period and a work directly influenced by existentialism, it told the story of the legendary "Himmelfahrtskommandos," who were drafted by the Nazis from among prisoners of war to immobilize unexploded bombs. *Three Quarters of the Sun* (*Tri četrtine sonce*-1959), directed by J. Babić, with a script by Slovak writer L. Lahola, was about the

Don't Turn
Back,
My Son

Five
Minutes
of
Paradise

difficult homecoming of those who were united by the war and then separated by the peace again into various nationalities. *Kula* (1958), the story of a dog transformed by the war into a beast of prey, was the new success of Krešo Golik (b. 1922), following his earlier noteworthy achievement, the rural drama *The Girl and the Oak* (*Devojka i hrast*-1955).

A film worth mentioning is the debut of Serbian director Stole Janković, *Through Branches the Sky* (*Kroz granje nebo*-1958), an almost naturalistically faithful picture of the tragedies and the horrors of guerrilla warfare. Later, in 1963, Janković made the film *Radopolje,* "the village of black biers . . . damned at the foot of the mountains," a story about the attempt to resurrect a village that had been razed by the Nazis, the only survivors being women.

Also, Vladimir Pogačić, a native of Croatia active in Belgrade, made films about the struggle for national liberation: *Big and Small* (*Veliki i mali*-1956), a strong psychological drama of a man hiding in wartime Belgrade, seen through the eyes of a child. He did not achieve the same unity of theme and style in *Alone* (*Sam*-1959), another attempt to create a realistic portrait of the partisans by refusing to gloss over negative human behavior.

Big
and
Small

THE PRESENT AND NEOREALISM

But the same Vladimir Pogačić, with his composite film *Saturday Night* (*Subotom uveče*-1957), was eventually the first to successfully break through the chronic aversion to contemporary problematics. In the film's second, neorealistic episode *"Doc"* (*Doktor*), about a ruin of a man whose passion is boxing, he created one of the first truly successful portraits of his contemporaries. But Pogačić, who at that time became chief of the Belgrade film archive, found few equally skillful successors.

The most popular film on a contemporary theme in this period was *H-8* (1958), the directorial debut of a director of cinematography, Nikola

Saturday
Night
("Doc")

Tanhofer (b. 1926). Tanhofer based his film on a real-life event, a bus trip that ended in an accident, and made excellent use of his wealth of experience as a cameraman and editor. It seemed that the vicious circle of wartime dramas was finally broken. But the development of Yugoslav film took other paths, and Tanhofer was another who did not live up to the promise of his first film.

At that time, foreign directors were coming to Yugoslavia, not yet in search of cheap film locations, but rather to make pictures that they were unable to make at home. They included French director Claude Autant-Lara, who made a film on conscientious objectors, *Thou Shalt Not Kill* (*Tu ne tueras point*–1961), West German director Helmut Käutner, who directed the antifascist, antiwar piece, *The Last Bridge* (*Die Letzte Brücke*–1954), and Italian directors Giuseppe De Santis, who directed *A One-Year Trip* (*Cesta duga godinu dana*–1958) and Gillo Pontecorvo, who directed *The Great Blue Road* (*Veliki plavi put*–1958). Both Italian film-makers tried, with no great success, to prolong elsewhere the life of Italian neorealism. Not until 1959 did one of De Sica's assistants, Veljko Bulajić, make a Yugoslav neorealist film, *Train Without Timetable* (*Vlak bez voznog reda*),

Train
Without
Timetable

one of the best films of the period. With a genuine neorealistic feeling for postwar reality and its nameless heroes, Bulajić tells of the mass migration of peasants from the arid, underdeveloped land of Dalmatia to the more fertile areas in the north. Bulajić's other film, *City in Ferment* (*Uzavreli grad*-1961) was in part a reply, in the neorealistic tradition, to the socialist bathos of Živanović and Miloš Stefanović's film *Zenica*. Both films were about the construction of a foundry in Zenica and its influence on the feelings of the people who lived there. But none of them gave a true picture of the dimensions of the problems of industrialization, and Bulajić soon chose a path that took him far away from the most important current of Yugoslav cinematography—to costly spectaculars about the partisan heroism that enjoyed no small degree of box-office success: *Kozara* (1962) and *The Battle on the River Neretva* (*Bitka na Neretvi*-1969).

Kozara

ADVENTURE, LITERATURE, AND SATIRE

Žika Mitrović followed up the success of his *The Echelon of Doctor M* by specializing in adventure films such as *Miss Stone* (*Mis Ston*-1958), the story of an American lady missionary in the middle of the Macedonian uprising against the Turks.

Fedor Hanžeković continued in his film adaptations of works of literature, achieving his greatest success with the film version of the Slavko Kolar's

The
Owner
of One's
Own
Body

play, *The Owner of One's Own Body* (*Svoga tela gospodar*-1956), a rural drama about a peasant's son who is forced by his parents to marry the homely, lame daughter of a wealthy farmer because that is the only way they can get a cow to replace the one that died as a result of the son's negligence. An adaptation of Stevan Sremac's classical light comedy, *Father Čira and Father Spira* (*Pop Čira i pop Spira*-1957), was the debut of the first Yugoslav woman director, Soja Jovanović (b. 1922). She surpassed the box office success of this Avala Film production—the first feature in color to be filmed in Yugoslavia—with *Dr.*, a successful adaptation of the classic Serbian comedy by Branislav Nušić.

Four
Kilometers
per Hour

Montenegran Velimir Stojanović (1921-1959) specialized in satirical films. His *Cursed Money* (*Zle pare*-1956), a story of villagers who found a treasure hidden by the prewar Yugoslav government so that it would not be found by the Nazis, and *Four Kilometers per Hour* (*Četiri kilometra na sat*-1958), a clever picture of a small town in the period between the wars, seemed to be the beginning of an interesting career, abruptly broken off by Stojanović's premature death.

ZAGREB FILM

Beginning in 1952, when Jože Gale (b. 1913) made the children's film *Kekec* for the Slovenian Triglav Film, films for children, and mainly animated films, gained an international reputation for the Yugoslav film industry.

The development of children's and animated film production was one of the indisputable successes of the nationalized film industries of Eastern Europe in the fifties. Prestige projects heavily subsidized by the state—these kinds of films originally had no aspirations of direct contact with political and social realities, thus giving directors wide freedom to develop and realize highly individualized works. The production of animated films in Yugoslavia was concentrated in the specialized studio of Zagreb Film, which was developed in 1953 as a replacement for Duga Film. The history of Duga Film was closely linked with the name of Fadil Hadžić (b. 1922), a versatile talent who worked in many areas of Croatian cultural life. *The Assassination at Sarajevo* (*Sarajevski atentat*-1969) was one of his feature films.

The leading representatives of Zagreb Film's school of animated film were Montenegran cartoonist Dušan Vukotić and Croatian director Vatroslav Mimica, whose debut was the aforementioned fiction film, *Mr. Ikl's Anniversary*. The "socialist estheticism" popular in literature had almost free rein in animated film, achieving particularly outstanding results between 1958 and 1962. Vukotić created an original, almost abstract style for his tragicomical paradoxes about man's helplessness and limitations. He was the creator of a now-classical cycle of films of which the most outstanding were *Ersatz* (*Surogat*-1961), *Piccolo* (1960), *Cow on the Moon* (*Krava na mesjecu*-1959), and *Concerto for Submachine Gun* (*Koncert za mašinsku pušku*-1959). Mimica's *The Lonely Man* (*Samac*-1958), *At the Photographer's* (*Kod fotografa*-1958), *A Little Story* (*Mala kronika*-1962), *The Egg* (*Jaje*-1960), and *Happy Ending* (1958) are tart and poignant meditations on. a similar theme, anticipating the development of Yugoslav film in the forthcoming period. Vukotić, Mimica, and Vlado Kristl, another artist from Zagreb Film, later turned to fiction film (Kristl in West Germany). But Mimica was the only one to successfully assert his talent there.

Ersatz

CRISIS

In the second half of the fifties, Yugoslav feature fiction film production was stabilized at an average of 15 films annually. But at the end of the period, voices began to be heard for a radical increase in production, which many saw as a guarantee of artistic development, according to the motto "quantity guarantees quality." The application of this approach resulted in a sharp increase in the number of light commercial films, and in an overextension of economic possibilities, which subsequently threatened the financial foundations of some film studios. But the crisis in art and production that came about at the turn of the decade, had another side to it as well. The sudden increase in production did in fact bring a new generation into the studios, a generation which would lead Yugoslav film onto a new path, winning it world renown.

ON ITS OWN TWO FEET:
Romania, 1956–1963

Of all the countries in Eastern Europe, Romania was the only one, when Stalin died, lacking a broad enough foundation for a new regime to permit any kind of internal liberalization. Romanian Communism remained so much a matter of the Party, the military, and the police machinery—not to mention the presence of Soviet troops—that a self-contained effort of this sort was unthinkable. But, as opposed to the other Eastern European countries (with the exception of Yugoslavia, and to some degree the GDR), the Romanian Communists had in their party chief Gheorghe Gheorghiu-Dej a leader who had emerged from the earlier purges and trials (Pauker, Luca, Patrascanu) as the only true and recognized representative of political and state power. He was the sole author and executor of Romanian policy in this complex period, which began with the hurried reconciliation with Yugoslavia, and ended with the successful attempt to gain greater independence from the Soviet Union, Gheorghiu-Dej showed himself an heir to Romanian political traditions, and it is in the last years of his reign (he died in 1965) that we can find the roots of the policy that was to be firmly formulated in the next stage.

In all matters of policy, then, action was from the top down, and that included decisions about the degree of liberalization and freedom that culture and art would be given. In 1959, premier Chivu Stoica expressed the desire to develop cultural relations with France and Italy, as well as "the other nations of Europe and South America with whom we are linked by common cultural heritages, customs, and traditions." A temporary liberalization of the policy with respect to the various nationalities was initiated from above, and some of the writers, university professors, and others who had been silent for years reappeared on the scene. But this was followed immediately by an extensive purge among the Transylvanian intellectuals, who made no secret of their sympathy for the Hungarian revolution of 1956. The Jewish and German minorities paid the price for the first steps toward the nationalization of Romanian Communism. The purges ultimately were costly to Romania, weakening its overall cultural creativity. Not unlike the situation in Yugoslavia, but under a far more stringent ideological regime, the duties and tasks in the cultural sphere were delimited from the negative point of view, stating "don'ts" rather than "dos," facilitating the first attempts at reviving so-called "non-ideological" entertainment and the lighter genres.

DEBUTS AND THE FIRST POLEMICS

In 1957, the Romanian film industry was literally flooded with graduates of the IATC (Institute of Theater and Film Art). Romanian film directors could no longer be counted on the fingers of one hand, but the films themselves, as well as their evaluation by the authorities, were none too different from the ones that went before. The tight bonds of party orthodoxy and the fear of any experimentation tied the hands of even the more talented of the young directors. The new generation essentially continued on the path begun seven years earlier, and not a single nonconformist film is to be found among the works that it produced, nothing that might even remotely resemble works of the same period in, say, Bulgaria or Yugoslavia. The most interesting film of the period, *Life Will Not Forgive* (*Viaţa nu iartă*–1958), directed by Iulian Mihu and Manole Marcus, was based on the stories of the politically commit- ted writer, Alexandru Sahia. But the film's attempt to tell the story of a father and son—soldiers in two different wars, who could not withstand the test of their hours of decision—in a modern form encountered a wall of opposition. The debates it provoked, however, were beneficial: it was the first time that film was spoken of publicly as a specific art.

In addition to graduates of the IATC, film-makers entered the field by means of the theater. Liviu Ciulei (b. 1923), who was to dominate Romanian film for several years, just as Iliu had once dominated it in the past, was an actor and designer in the theater before he applied those skills in film. Soon he became the long-awaited "hope of Romanian film."

In *Eruption* (*Erupţia*–1957), he displayed a sense for visual composition and for the cinematic rendering of an epic tale, set against the pictorial background of the oil fields. A work site was also the center of Ciulei's attention in his next film, *The Danube Waves* (*Valurile Dunării*–1959). It was the dramatic story of a navigator in the war, whose task is to deliver munitions to the Nazis, but who instead turns his cargo over to the guerrillas, after surviving a number of dangers. Ciulei's work gives evidence of his eternal vacillation between screen and stage, and stage wins out in the end. After *Danube Waves,* Ciulei went back to stage direction for five years, achieving considerable recognition at home and abroad.

The
Danube
Waves

LESSONS FROM HISTORY

The most versatile of the graduates of the IATC was Mircea Drăgan (b. 1932), who eventually became one of the toughest partisans of the official line in the Romanian film industry. His broad range of subjects did not avoid the generally carefully neglected topic of antifascism. Joining forces with Mihai Iacob (b. 1933), he made his debut with a film on the resistance, *Beyond the Fir Trees* (*Dincolo de brazi*-1957), and in 1960, he adapted Titus Popovici's popular novel for the first Romanian wide-screen film, *Thirst* (*Setea*), once again evoking the past and its social injustices. This was the first show of Drăgan's interest in human destinies captured at moments of historical crisis. Gradually, Drăgan took over Ciulei's position, and in 1962, he started work on a film based on an authentic event, the great miners' strike in 1929 in the valley of the river Jiu, known as "Vale of Tears."

Lupeni 29

This film, *Lupeni 29* (1962) belongs in the category of social-conscience historical films that strove to counterbalance the traditional posterlike historical films in which the historical event was the mere pretext for the presentation of a romatic farce or an adventure story. Romanian historical films—or so it was stated in the articles and speeches of the period—were supposed to make the viewer think, and lead him to seek the roots of current problems in the past. Historical films were elevated to the category of "cultural deeds," and were expected to give lessons in patriotism; esthetic notions had to retreat, to make room for the didactic presentation of evidence. The management of Romanian Film approved a plan at that time to shoot a series of films to cover all epochs of Romanian history. They gradually became more and more spectacular, the lessons in patriotism frequently resembling out-and-out nationalism.

Stranger

Mihai Iacob, who, like Drăgan, became a professor at the IATC as soon as he graduated from there, filmed the biography of a famous Romanian opera singer, *Darclée* (1960), as an expansive historical fresco in the style of the worst schematic biographies. Iacob was always much more a professor than an artist (he made a number of instructional films for students). Rational consideration and a didactic distribution of subject matter prevail in all his films, for example, *Stranger* (*Străinul* 1963) about the friendship between two men who are separated by the social upheaval in their native land. The script for *Stranger* was the work of the author of the original novel, Titus Popovici, who also wrote the screenplays for a number of other Romanian films: *Mill of Good Luck, The Danube Waves, Thirst,* and *The Forest of the Hanged.*

The first widescreen costume spectacular from Romania was *Tudor* (1963), which won a number of prizes at home and abroad. Directed by Lucian Bratu (b. 1924), one of the few Romanian directors who had studied at VGIK in Moscow, and written by the novelist Mihnea Gheorghiu, *Tudor* cost the Romanian film industry a great deal in the way of material expenditure and was Bratu's only important film. It tells the story of the Romanian revolt against the Turks in 1821, and traces the personal history of Tudor, a leader of the revolt and a fascinating figure of Romanian

Tudor

history. Offered the throne upon his victorious entry into Bucharest, Tudor
refused it with the words, "Of what use to me is this coffin?" Later, he
fell victim to an intricate and treasonous conspiracy. But at the end of the
film we hear the cry, "We shall return, like the spring grass and blossoms,"
just one of the visionary images of national history that Romanian films
presented during the sixties.

The box-office success of costume films was immense. Of the 20 million
inhabitants of Romania at that time, 8.7 milion saw *Tudor.*

COMEDIES

The second preferred genre was comedy. In the second half of the fifties,
comedies once again took their old place in movie theaters, with all the
second-rate traditions of boulevard theater. For example, *Hello? Wrong
Number* (*Alo? aţi greşit numărul*-1958), directed by Andrei Călărasu, is the
story of two students—one an incorrigible Don Juan, the other a timid
youth—who are constantly being confused. *On My Responsibility* (*Pe
răspunderea mea*-1956), directed by Paul Călinescu, tells how the em-
ployees of a fashion enterprise teach a conceited designer, whose design is
in bad taste, a lesson in humility. After the critique of *Life Will Not
Forgive,* Manole Marcus also tried his hand at comedy, but with no great
success—*I Don't Want to Get Married* (*Nu vreau să mă însor*-1960).

ION POPESCU-GOPO

It was the small workshops that gave birth to the films that brought the
Romanian film industry its first truly extensive successes. The Bucharest
animated film studio, like Czechoslovakia's Prague and Gottwaldov
animated film studios, or Yugoslavia's Zagreb Film, was established as the
direct result of nationalization and the state's role as patron of the arts.

Sancta
Simplicitas

The animafilm studio began in the early fifties, and by the mid-sixties, it was producing 25 animated films a year, making Romania one of the world centers for cartoon film. Credit for this goes to the genius of Romanian animated film, Ion Popescu-Gopo, who created the pathetic figure of "The little man with the flower," and the films *A Short History* (*Scurtă istorie*-1957), *The Seven Arts* (*Sapte arte*-1958), *Homo Sapiens* (1960), *Hello, Hello!* (*Allo! Allo!*-1962), *Sancta Simplicitas* (1968), and others. With these films, he assured himself a place among the foremost masters in the genre of animated cartoons.

Ion Popescu-Gopo entered the field of fiction comedy and satire, too. But it was as if the wings of his world-renowned wit and poetry had grown heavy. Romanian fiction film had neither the tradition nor the experience for such poetic fantasies as Popescu-Gopo's *Stolen Bomb* (*S a furat o bombă*-1961), bearing an antiwar message, science-fiction comedy like *Steps to the Moon* (*Paşi spre lună*-1963), or experimental fairy tales like *The White Moor* (*Harap Alb*-1965). Things that were possible in the realm of pure artistic stylization, in the small workshop of animated film, remained just a fond wish within the clumsy machine-burdened world of fiction film.

THE FRENCH AND PANAIT ISTRATI

By the end of the fifties, Romanian film stood for the first time on its own two feet, and plans were being made to produce 20 feature-length fiction films, 52 news films, and 23 popular science films a year.

From 1957 on, there were always some foreign film-makers working at Romanian studios. The first was Louis Daquin, who filmed Panait Istrati's novel *Baragan Thistles* (*Ciulinii Bărăganului* 1957), the story of a child at the turn of the century who discovers the misery of the rural people, but at the same time experiences his first moments of happiness. It was the first

Codin

time that Romanian film had made a film based on the writings of one of its great émigrés. It was the first time that Istrati—and also, for example, poet Tristan Tzara—could be mentioned in Romania in more than a whisper. After Daquin, who unfortunately turned in only a mediocre film, capturing just the social aspect of the complex structures of Istrati's narrative, another French director, Henri Colpi, turned to the work of Istrati. Colpi had far more in his favor when he filmed *Codin* (1963), but he too remained only on the surface of Istrati's fantastic world, making of this mystical tale of the strange comradeship between a little boy and a village strong-man a Gorkian story, with a delicate lyrical tone.

The director had not yet appeared who could understand the profound relationships in Istrati's work between the characters and their surroundings and express those relationships in cinematic terms.

OPTIMISM IN MOURNING:
German Democratic Republic, 1956–1963

THE SUN SEEKERS

The posters were already displayed on the streets, the newspapers carried the date of the opening, finally, after a delay of two years, *The Sun Seekers* (*Die Sonnensucher* 1957) was to be shown on the screen. But that October day in 1959 was to mark just one more stage in the history of a film that had the most complex fate of all the films made in Eastern Europe. The morning that it was to have its premiere, newspapers printed an item announcing that the management of DEFA "decided, with the agreement of the film's creators, not to show the film, even though the respective authorities had released it for showing." The posters, with sunbeams illuminating the face of a young girl and the silhouette of a miner, were taken down, and the film's title vanished from all reference books and from biographies of director Konrad Wolf (b. 1925), who had emigrated to the Soviet Union before the war with his father, playwright Friedrich Wolf, and returned to his homeland with the Soviet army.

The Sun Seekers was one of the films shot in 1957 during the post-Stalinist thaw in the GDR, and the best of them at that, but it waited 15 years to be shown. The difficulty was not primarily the oppressive atmosphere in the area where uranium was being mined under Soviet supervision in the fifties, nor was it Wolf's sensitive neorealistically inspired depiction of the day-to-day life of the miners, their sorrows, and their isolation. Nor was the prime problem the characters of the heroes—human wrecks, uprooted by the war, who vegetated rather than lived, on the periphery of the new society. Nor was it the plot itself—the story of a young girl who is sent to the uranium mines as a punishment, and the man she later marries, a former member of Hitler's SS. And as for the optimistic ending—the man dies in a mining accident and the woman, thanks in part to a Soviet major, realizes where her place is—it evoked no objections at all. The reason *Sun Seekers* was not shown until 1972 had nothing to do with the film world, but it was typical of Ulbricht's GDR: at the time the film was to open on East German screens, the Soviet Union called for the banning of nuclear weapons.

A strange reason indeed for the GDR to become, in the eyes of the world, the country that did not have a parallel to *The House I Live In, A Glass of Beer,* or *Great Solitude.* Especially since all the other East German films of the post-Stalinist thaw were below the level of the *Sun Seekers.*

The final ban, however, served the purposes of many cultural functionaries of the GDR, who with alacrity and a heavy hand ended the "new
course" after the Polish and Hungarian events in the autumn of 1956. Wolf
was not one of their favorites, even though he did not suffer the fate of
some of his Bulgarian or Czech colleagues. It is true that films were being
banned in the GDR—more often than not, the axe fell on the script or even
on the story idea—but, contrary to the situation in other intellectual
spheres, film-makers were not persecuted. The country that had lost so
many directors, scriptwriters, and actors to emigration prior to 1956 did
not want to lose any more talented creators of an art form it needed badly.
Many of those who remained felt that they might get to have a shot at
something that other film industries could hardly promise: a share in the
development of their country's film industry and an opportunity to work
in a continuous way in the atmosphere of the "new course" which was at
that time still open to different interpretations. The overpopulated and
at that time totally uninteresting cinema in West Germany was hardly
attractive. So the only area of cultural endeavor in the GDR that did not
continue to lose artists and craftsmen to West Germany was film.

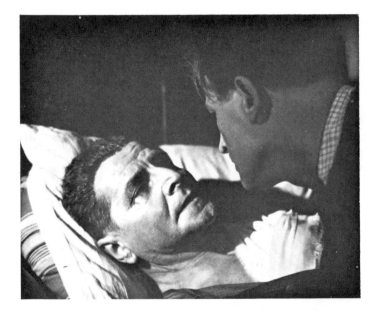

Recovery

Konrad Wolf, who in 1956 was one of the critics of Ulbricht's regime—
although he was also one of those who retained a faith in the possibility of its
democratic development—stayed at the top even after the affair surrounding
The Sun Seekers. Following an unsuccessful debut with the comedy *Once Is
More than Once* (*Einmal ist keinmal*-1953), Wolf had attracted attention
with the drama *Recovery* (*Genesung*-1955), which was—aside from *The Sun*

Seekers—the most noteworthy product of the so-called "human approach," the main expression of the new course. In it, human destinies, melodramatically presented, were equal in importance to political motivations. The hero of *Recovery* was a wartime dropout from medical school, who, after the war, was in conflict between admitting the successfully concealed fact that he had not completed his studies and his love for the wife of his incurably ill patient. As they did with the SS man Beier in *The Sun Seekers,* Wolf and his collaborators cleared him of all guilt, accusing instead the society that did not permit him to complete his studies. The basis for *Recovery* was an immensely popular radio play. In it, Karl-Georg Egel, scriptwriter of *The Solvay Dossier* and *Dangerous Load,* and Paul Wiens, who wrote the script for *Little and Great Happiness,* elaborated in part on the then extremely timely idea that "we must build socialism with the people that we've got," which, in the words of the establishment, was also the East German rationale for the integration of former Nazis.

Aside from Wolf's, the most successful films in the area of "the human approach," were those of Gerhard Klein (1920-1970) and those of Frank Beyer (b. 1932), who was a graduate of the Prague Film Academy. Klein's *Berlin Romance (Eine Berliner Romanze-*1956), a story of the love between a girl from the East and a boy from the West, and *Berlin, Schoenhauser Corner*

Berlin
Romance

*(Berlin, Ecke Schönhauser-*1957), based on the life of East German hooligans, both attacked West Berlin with the same propagandistic undertone as DEFA's other films. But what was new was that they also took into account the shady aspects of life in the East. Their form was also innovative, particularly that of *Berlin Romance,* which revealed the effort to capture ordinary details in real-life locations. Beyer's debut, *Two Mothers (Zwei Mütter-*1957), relinquished politics in the script phase, concentrating on the sentimental aspects

of the story of two women who accidentally exchanged babies during the war. The traditional German sentimentality characterized all the films with the "human approach," *The Sun Seekers* and *Recovery* not excepted. Maetzig's comedy, *Don't Forget My Traudel* (*Vergesst mir meine Traudel nicht*-1957) was a typical example of this style, recalling the old UFA films in the way it turned the story of a 16-year-old girl, a war orphan, and a young policeman from East Berlin who takes her in, into a tale of cheap sentimentality.

The ideological thaw was most obvious, as was true even before 1956, in the sphere of pure entertainment. For example, musicals such as *My Wife Makes Music* (*Meine Frau macht Music*-1957) set aside all ideology and picked up where the old German wartime musicals had left off. In spite of the fact that they were constantly the target of criticism, they remained a staple of DEFA's production.

In those years, the management of DEFA also returned to the concept of international cooperation, which had originated before 1949 but was never realized, and was very active in making contacts with the West. But neither Gérard Philipe with *The Adventures of Till Ulenspiegel* (*Die Abenteuer des Till Ulenspiegel*-1957), nor Jean-Paul Le Chanois with Hugo's *Les Misérables* (*Die Elenden*-1958), nor Raymond Rouleau with Arthur Miller's *The Crucible* (*Die Hexen von Salem*-1958), created a film that could be measured against Wolf's *Stars* (*Sterne*-1958). *Stars,* which was filmed in Bulgaria with a script by Angel Wagenstein and the directorial collaboration of Rangel Vulchanov,

Stars

was exceptional in its poetic, suggestive depiction of a small Bulgarian town in wartime, and its human portraits of the heroes: a Greek Jewish girl waiting to be transported to a death camp, and a German soldier, slowly and torturously arriving at the realization of the evil that he had been fighting for. The story of their love crystallizes out of a strong emotive atmosphere, and for the first time in East German film, feelings take precedence over the prejudices of the times. The exceptional photography was the work of Werner Bergmann, who was the head cameraman for all of Wolf's other films.

Wolf, together with Bergmann, reconstructed, in a nonschematic manner, the atmosphere of prewar Germany in *Lissy* (1957), the portrait of a working-class girl in the thirties who, after much hesitation and tragic experience, finally breaks up with her husband, a member of the Nazi SA guard.

Lissy

THE END OF THE "PRINCIPLE OF HOPE"

In the GDR, the thaw was brief. As early as autumn of 1956, the first attacks against all proponents of the new course began. A sharp campaign was waged above all against the Marxist philosopher Ernest Bloch—author of the criticized book *Principle of Hope* and one of the most significant figures in modern German philosophy, against Wolfgang Harich, and against physicist Robert Havemann. These men were among the first in the socialist states to consider the problems of individual subjectivity and to call for a detailed analysis of the "alienated structures of socialism." Havemann was eventually banned from the University and from his scientific research work, Harich was convicted on the basis of a false indictment and sentenced to 10 years in prison, and Bloch was forced into exile. A number of Bloch's supporters crossed over to West Germany, as did some leading literary figures. But the attack continued, shifting to members of the prewar German intelligentsia—particularly the group that had once surrounded Bertolt Brecht, people who originally had seen in the GDR an opportunity for the birth of a democratic German state, where their ideas of autonomous art could come to fruition.

In 1957 and 1958, all of East German culture was turned upside down. The huge number of actions taken and changes made show just how very deep the roots of the opposition movement were. It was not until this period that Ulbricht's regime achieved a sort of a "normalization," establishing an ideological line that was much more orthodox than those of the other Eastern European countries and that lasted into the early seventies. It was the end of the "principle of hope," which was the subject of so much conversation in 1956, and the beginning of an "optimism in mourning," as the tenor of the time was described by Bloch's talented pupil, Günter Zehm, who was sent to prison for four years.

Film-makers were not as severely reprimanded as people in other fields, and not only Wolf, but also Maetzig and Martin Hellberg went on working, even though they had in 1956 moderately criticized the status quo. In 1957, Maetzig made a poor propaganda film, *Castles and Cabins* (*Schlösser und Katen*), a picture-book image of an East German village between 1945 and 1956. For the anniversary of the Russian Revolution, he completed a "made-to-order" film, *Song of the Sailors* (*Das Lied der Matrosen*-1958), which was a clumsy and heavy-handed effort.

Hellberg continued to make adaptations of classical dramas and was repeatedly criticized for their ideological implications—for example, Calderon's *The Judge of Salamea* (*Richter von Zalamea*-1955), Lessing's *Emilia Galotti* (1957), Schiller's *Intrigue and Love* (*Kabale und Liebe*-1959)—but at the same time he returned to the superficially tendentious subject matter of his early films in such works as *Captains Do Not Leave the Ship* (*Kapitäne bleiben an Bord*-1958) and *Senta Goes Astray* (*Senta auf Abwegen*-1959). His work got worse and worse, and finally Hellberg, originally an actor, returned to the stage where he had begun his career in the thirties.

In Wolf's next two films, creative inventiveness—from both the director's and the cameraman's point of view—also found itself forced into a pre-established outline. Both *Men With Wings* (*Leute mit Flügeln*-1960), which developed in parallel the hero's reminiscences of the Spanish Civil War, the Nazi concentration camps, and images from the present, and the remake of *Professor Mamlock* (1961), filmed already in the Soviet Union in 1938, based on a play by Friedrich Wolf that showed the conflict between an apolitical Jewish scientist and the Hitler regime, were far below the level of *Stars* and *Lissy*.

Nor was Frank Beyer able to fully develop his abilities in DEFA's ideological mill. In 1960, he filmed *Five Shell Casings* (*Fünf Patronenhülsen*), a story of the Spanish Civil War that employed a somewhat theatrical style in tracing its theme through the lives of five people. A year later, in *Invincible Love* (*Königskinder*), he borrowed some techniques from German expressionism to evoke the atmosphere of prewar and wartime Germany, as reflected in the emotions and fates of his tragic lovers.

Invincible
Love

Heiner Carow (b. 1929) also used carefully the proven techniques of subjective narration and expressionist photography in making *They Called Him Amigo* (*Sie nannten ihn Amigo*-1958), a concentration camp story, and *Life Begins* (*Das Leben beginnt*-1959), a drama set in the divided city of Berlin.

DEFA balanced the heavy-handed ideological content of most of its fiction films by filming suspense films and comedies. They were truly simple-minded poorly crafted films, characterized mainly by stolid beer-hall humor. The smoothest of these were Günther Reisch's (b. 1927) comedies *Maibowle* (1959) and *New Year's Punch* (*Silvesterpunsch*-1960).

Slatan Dudow's (d. 1963) last film, *Love Confusion* (*Verwirrung der Liebe*-1959), was also a comedy. After his *Captain from Köln* (*Der Hauptmann von Köln*-1956), a satire on West German militarism in which an unemployed waiter takes the identity of his namesake, a former Nazi officer, Dudow made a stab at a "comedy of errors," above all striving to enrich the impoverished vocabulary of East German film by a return to the old gags. The film, which propagandized contemporary subject matter in a light, noncommittal tone, was an exception among DEFA productions and was an honorable conclusion to Dudow's career.

"SOCIALIST CONTEMPORARY FILM"

DEFA was the only national film industry in Eastern Europe that produced a preponderance of "socialist contemporary films" (sozialistischer Gegenwartsfilm): of the approximately 20 films that were released annually, about two-thirds belonged in this category. Reflecting their ties to the past, they bore such titles as, *Always Prepared* (*Zu jeder Stunde*-1960), a film on the life of border guards, *Step by Step* (*Schritt für Schritt*-1960), a film about life in the army, or *The Physician from Bothenow* (*Der Artzt von Bothenow*-1961).

Since the war, Germany has been a divided country. And Berlin, though inside the GDR, has been a divided city. Until 1961, however, the division of Berlin between East and West had only been economic. People living in one part of the city could work in the other and the city's public service systems—telephone, mass transit, water—served the entire municipal area. One consequence of this openness was a mass emigration of East Germans to West Germany via Berlin. Between 1952 and 1962, 2,269,769 people left the GDR, among them 38,467 intellectuals and artists. On the night of August 13, 1961, GDR authorities sealed the border between East and West Berlin and began to build a wall several yards high, a wall GDR officials dubbed the "Wall of Peace" (Friedenswall). Eventually the barrier was extended the full length of the border between East and West Germany, sometimes in the form of electrified barbed wire, sometimes in the form of concrete roadblocks. No matter what form it took, it was extremely difficult to cross. Several hundred people, in fact, died in the attempt, shot by guards who were ordered to fire without warning or by automatic shooting devices. With all common services of communication cut between East and West, the GDR was to all intents and purposes sealed off from the western part of the world. Only television remained as a link, and a very important one.

A few years after the frontier had been sealed, ideological controls in the arts relaxed a bit in the GDR. "Socialist contemporary films" began to show love stories, in harmony, of course, with the theory that the aims of society are inseparable from individual happiness. But all the same, behind the carefully structured personal conflicts, social problems occasionally still emerged. Finally, these socialist film romances became the only testimony to contemporary life in East Germany.

A forerunner of this category was created in 1960 by Maetzig in *September Love* (*Septemberliebe*), a story of a romantic triangle—later almost revered—in which a young scientist finds himself involved with two sisters: he wants to run away to West Berlin with the younger one, but ends up in the hands of the police, his intended having turned him in.

Socialist love stories were very successful with audiences, who could, if they chose, sift the emotional aspects from the political. Early in the sixties, these films comprised the more interesting part of the production of DEFA. Particularly successful were the films of the young director Frank Vogel

Julia Lives

(b. 1929) *And Your Love Too* (*Une deine Liebe auch*-1962), the story of a romantic triangle set during the time the Berlin Wall was being erected, and *Julia Lives* (*Julia lebt*-1963), criticized by the party press because it brought to the screen a nonschematic character, a young intellectual girl full of inner conflicts, and because her boyfriend, a border guard and a "positive hero," met a tragic death.

The subject of marital crisis was first touched upon in *Description of a Summer* (*Beschreibung eines Sommers*-1963), a weak rewrite of an interesting novel by Karl-Heinz Jakob, one of the first works of what was known as the GDR's "own literature," the beginnings of which date back to the time the wall was built in 1961. The love story of an engineer who is not a member of the Party and the wife of a party functionary became the GDR's first best-seller and a DEFA box-office triumph, even though the film eliminated almost all of Jakob's criticism of the moral hypocrisy of certain social strata.

Another novel of the new literature, *Divided Sky* by Christa Wolf, a woman writer—not related to the director—who was an important figure in the East German cultural world, was rewritten for the screen by Konrad Wolf. The film, also called *Divided Sky* (*Der geteilte Himmel*-1964), was the culmination of Wolf's earlier efforts to find a new narrative form. It follows the novel in form and plot, telling the story of two sweethearts who are separated by the border between the two Germanies. Using flashbacks, interwoven with images of the present, Wolf puts together fragments of the heroine's conversations, memories, and introspections. But the psychology of a divided country, the fundamental theme of the book, yielded its place of primacy on the screen to social argumentation.

Description of a Summer

Divided Sky

Egon Günther's (b. 1927) debut, *Lot's Wife* (*Lots Weib*-1964), aroused a great deal of interest as the first film about women's problems, attacking one of the bastions of socialist morality—marriage and the family. The heroine rejected the hypocrisy of a loveless family union, becoming a thief in order to force her highly placed husband to divorce her. In court she proclaimed her right to raise her children and her right to independence.

Lot's Wife

ARMY EPICS

Another important kind of film was the "army epic," the first of which
was made in the period of the new course by Kurt Jung-Alsen (b. 1915),
who was clever at filling "social" orders of all sorts. The film was *Betrayed
Until Judgment Day* (*Betrogen bis zum jüngsten Tag*-1957), based on
Franz Fühmann's successful novel, *Buddies*. What was characteristic of
the army epics, far more than of DEFA's other films, was their professionally
thought-through scripts and their characters, which were structured according to the models of contemporary ideology. They were designed primarily to
counterbalance the German concept of masculine friendship (Kameradschaft) as a relationship standing far above all else, and for the most part
were examples of the practiced pedagogical approach. Almost invariably,
the stories involved two or more army buddies, who, during some moment
in German history, find themselves faced with a critical choice. In Jung-
Alsen's *Those Over Forty Today* (*Die heute über vierzig sind*-1960), it was
the son of a worker and the son of a factory owner, childhood pals, who
find themselves on opposite sides of the barricades, both during the war

and after it, in their divided homeland. In *The Adventures of Werner Holt* (*Die Abenteuer des Werner Holts*-1965), directed by Joachim Kunert on the basis of Dieter Noll's best-seller, one of two close buddies finally rejects his friend's fanatical fascism, and after bitter experiences on the front line arrives at the realization of "social and personal truth."

The Adventures of Werner Holt

The most noteworthy of the films aimed at settling accounts with the past was *The Gleiwitz Case* (*Der Fall Gleiwitz*-1961), telling the true story of the phony attack on a German radio transmission post in 1939, which became Hitler's pretext for invading Poland. Director Gerhard Klein, together with Czech cameraman Jan Čuřík, sought inspiration (as did Beyer in *Invincible Love*) in a prewar symbolism that stressed the individualized portraits of the heroes.

THE THORNDIKES

The main, if not the sole, aim of East German cinema—that of educating the public—came across best in films about the past. Propagandistic art, as it developed in the GDR, was based on the convergence of the creative act—at every stage preorganized and controlled—with ideology. Its consistency, and above all its continuity, was unparalleled throughout Eastern Europe.

Annelie (b. 1925) and Andrew (b. 1909) Thorndike were masters in this field. Before the war, Thorndike was manager of the publicity department of UFA. From the first days of the GDR, he was one of its most active documentarists, making such films as *The Way Up* (*Der Weg nach oben*-1951), made for the first anniversary of the GDR; *Wilhelm Pieck, the Life of Our President* (*Wilhelm Pieck, das Leben unseres Präsidenten*-1952); *The German Story* (*Du und mancher Kamarad*-1956), the history of the first half of the twentieth century in Europe; *Operation Teutonic Sword* (*Unternehmen Teutonenschwert*-1958), about the alleged part that German espionage played in the assassination of Yugoslavia's King Alexander, tracing the history of Germany from the thirties to the postwar period. The Thorndikes worked primarily with archive materials, period documents, which they connected with acted scenes and updated commentaries. The culmination of their propagandistic art was *The Russian Miracle* (*Das russische Wunder*-1963), a two-part montage film capturing 50 years of the history of the Russian Empire and the Soviet Union. The question of the historical truthfulness of this film—or more precisely, of the degree to which historical fact was doctored—as well as the question of the artistic morality of its creators inspired the first debate on film between the GDR and Czechoslovakia, a debate that, in the years that followed, disclosed two profoundly opposing viewpoints on the meaning and the aims of film.

PART IV: The Possibilities of Art and the Art of the Possible

THE MIRACLE AND THE YOUNG
WAVE: Czechoslovakia after 1963

SUNSHINE IN A NET

"As long as I'm here, this anti-socialist art will not be distributed!" This statement was made in the spring of 1963 by Karol Bacílek, First Secretary of the Communist Party of Slovakia, and erstwhile Minister of State Security in the early fifties. In response to this statement, the Film Journalists' Club organized in Prague a special premiere showing of Štefan Uher's film, *Sunshine in a Net (Slnko v sieti*-1962). At just about the same time, a commission composed of political leaders, historians, and political scientists was meeting in Prague. The resolutions passed by this commission resulted in the rehabilitation of the so-called "Slovak nationalists," some of whom had been condemned to life imprisonment in the witch-hunt trials of the fifties. (One of these "nationalists," Gustav Husák, succeeded Dubček as First Secretary of the Communist Party after Soviet troops occupied Czechoslavakia in 1968.) Karol Bacílek soon vanished into political limbo, to be replaced by the unknown Alexander Dubček as the head of the Slovak Communist Party. That year only Czechoslovakia, among all the industrial countries in the world, showed a drop in national income. The total drop was 2.2 percent, industrial production dropping 0.7 percent (agricultural production fell 0.4 percent between 1961 and 1965), and productivity 1.4 percent. What had been the foundation of Czechoslovakia's political stability since 1956 was in an unprecedented shambles.

The history of *Sunshine in a Net* aptly illustrates the direct link between culture and politics in another land where the Spectator was simultaneously the wielder of absolute power and the embodiment of absolute authority. A shock to political power brought about a crisis of authority, and art—above all film—emerged from this crisis into open conflict with the established cultural policy.

Sunshine in a Net was entirely different from practically everything that preceded it. The script rejected the axioms about dramatic structure, turning instead to the inner life of its characters, the complex problems of their intercommunication—the hero's mother, for example, is blind, which forces her to perceive reality through the eyes of others. Uher acted with utter freedom, within the limits of the real world; he cast off all political opportunism and showed on the screen some of the aspects of the true face of economic reality. Stanislav Szomolanyi's camerawork went on to contribute an entirely new dimension of almost surreal lyricism.

Thus *Sunshine in a Net* became the symbol of the upsurge that at that time was ripening on all fronts. Almost simultaneously with the opening of *Sunshine in a Net,* a program of films directed by Věra Chytilová finally was

Sunshine in a Net

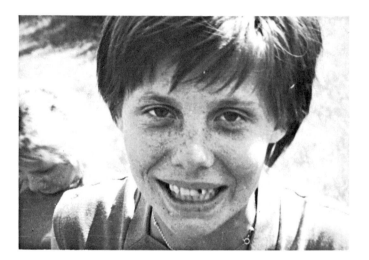

Bag
of
Fleas

distributed, after endless delays. The two medium-length films were shown under the title *There's a Bag of Fleas at the Ceiling* (*U stropu je pytel blech*–1962). In the style of cinéma vérité, and influenced by American underground films, the films were on one hand a personal contemplation of the lot of women—*The Ceiling*—a complete departure from past themes, and on the other hand, a sharply-honed, moralizing, sarcastic tract against the hypocrisy of educators in a girl's apprentice dormitory—*A Bag of Fleas* (*Pytel blech*). Shortly thereafter, Chytilová concluded work on her first feature film, *Something Different* (*O něčem jiném*–1963), one of the best films made in Czechoslovakia in the sixties. In it, she remained true to the cinéma vérité method, but she introduced a new philosophical note into Czech film by showing the parallelism of success and failure, the relativity of two totally dissimilar "women's destinies."

PRECEDING GENERATIONS

One thing that was characteristic of the exceptional upsurge in Czechoslovak film between 1963 and 1969 was the fact that although the youngest generation dominated the scene, the "Czechoslovak Film Miracle" was not only their affair. It was as if what three generations had striven to achieve— the prewar generation, the postwar generation, and the "second" generation of 1956—was suddenly coming to pass in this period. Film-makers of all generations were finally, for the first time, finding it possible to make films the way they wanted, the way they felt they should be made, and to arrive at some measure of self-realization.

Ján Kadár and Elmar Klos pushed directly into contemporary problems with *The Defendant* (*Obžalovaný*-1964). A classical "trial film," and social-conscience picture, but on a timely theme: three men stand before

The Defendant

a court of law, accused of economic crimes. It gradually becomes apparent, however, that it is the nonsensical state economic system that stands accused, accused of punishing people who display personal initiative, take risks, and achieve success in spite of the system. In the film's conclusion, the hero refuses the compromise offered by the court, preferring to return to prison, because that is the only way that he can even hope to see the true culprits finally brought to trial. It was the film audience that became the true judge, and in its open end, the film turns to the viewers as to a court of last resort. Following this film, their most political, Kodár and Klos finally won international acclaim. On the surface, their *The Shop on Main Street* (*Obchod na korze*-1965) appeared to be a story of the persecution of Jews in the

The Shop on Main Street

fascist Slovak state during World War Two. But in fact Kadár and Klos used this plot as a vehicle to express a more universal moral credo—their hatred of indifference and opportunism and of all oppression. Once again they reminded their audiences: "You all share the responsibility, no one can escape from himself."

It was a leading representative of the generation of 1956, Vojtěch Jasný, who declared in 1963 that Czechoslovak film-makers are aware of this responsibility, that they don't intend to keep silent any longer, and that from then on, they would call things by their right names. *Cassandra Cat* (*Až přijde kocour*–1963) was a modern fairy tale, one of the political morality

Cassandra Cat

films that became so typical in those years. Stylized to the extreme, almost a kind of film ballet, it was the story of a magic cat whose gaze made everyone show his true colors: it not only opened a Pandora's box of taboo subject matter, it also broke the lock on the chest that for so many years had confined visual fantasy. Following *Desire,* it was another pioneering feat, and it was no accident that Jasný was to conclude this era of film-making—after the unsuccessful international coproduction of *Pipes* (*Dýmky*-1966)—with one of the most significant films of 1968, *All My Countrymen* (*Všichni dobří rodáci*).

The dominant "young wave" succeeded, by means of its élan and its example, in inspiring many of the older film-makers who seemed already to have thrown in the towel. Such, for example, was the case of Otakar Vávra, teacher of many of the young people at the film academy, who in the mid-sixties emerged with two of his very best films, *Golden Rennet* (*Zlatá reneta*-1965), a portrait of intellectual cowardice in the early fifties, and *Romance for Trumpet* (*Romance pro křídlovku*-1966), about the drama of growing up in the Southern Bohemian countryside that Vávra had used as a setting in several earlier films. It was no coincidence that the author of the story on which each of these films was based was František Hrubín, the same poet who years earlier had reminded Czech writers of the metaphor of the swan frozen in the ice.

Romance
for
Trumpet

Jiří Weiss and Jiří Krejčík were other members of the previous generations to catch their second breath in this period. In his fairy-tale spectacular, *The Golden Fern* (*Zlaté kapradí*-1963), Weiss confirmed his somewhat cool mastery of film material. *Ninety in the Shade* (*Třicet jedna ve stínu*-1966), a psychological mystery aimed at the hypocrisy and immorality of society, made in coproduction with Great Britain, suffered as a result of the misalliance of Czech material and the ambitions of an international coproduction. *Murder Czech Style* (*Vražda po našem*-1967) took its place in the bitter moralizing context of the sixties. Through the story of a wool-gathering office worker, Weiss attempted to show Czech indecisiveness, pettiness, and opportunism in a mixture of the imaginary and the real. Krejčík was also successful in this area in *Wedding under Supervision* (*Svatba jako řemen*-1967), which tied in with the tradition of black and grotesque humor that strongly colored his prewar student days. One of his very best films, it was something of a screwball comedy, exposing the dullness of both the old and the new petty bourgeoisie and the representatives of law and order. Later the same year, he made a comedy based on a farce by Sean O'Casey *Boarding House for Bachelors* (*Penzión pro svobodné pány*-1967), noteworthy above all for the acting.

Wedding
Under
Supervision

THE YOUNG WAVE—JIREŠ

In 1963, Jaromil Jireš completed his first feature film, *The First Cry* (*Křik*), which, along with the films of Chytilová and Uher, definitively confirmed that something new was happening in Czech film-making. The young parents-to-be in the film walked onto the screen directly from the street, from the midst of an anonymous crowd that came to life before Kučera's camera, while the anti-hero of the film, dressed in the overalls of a TV repairman, entered the apartments of members of the socialist–realist establishment; his honesty and simplicity functioned as a kind of "truth mirror" making apparent their "new" values and attitudes. Although Jireš made a successful debut in the early sixties, the demands that he made of himself and his uncompromising examination of the present and of future possibilities created difficulties that kept him from realizing any more of his scripts until 1968. During the five-year interim, he made only a few excep-

The First Cry

tional short films, but his personality remained an integral part of everything that happened in those years in Czechoslovak film.

FORMAN, PASSER, PAPOUŠEK

Almost simultaneously, three names appeared in the mid-sixties that became inseparable in the audience's consciousness: Miloš Forman (b. 1932), Ivan Passer (b. 1933) and Jaroslav Papoušek (b. 1929). Forman made his independent debut with two medium-length films, *Competition* (*Konkurs*) and *If There Were No Music* (*Kdyby ty muziky nebyly*), shown jointly in 1964 under the title *Competition*. His style, which was evident from the beginning, was simple: focus the eye of the camera as closely as possible on human detail, and then put on the screen, in uncensored form, everything that turns up as a result of such a microscopic view. The result of this method, as it became obvious in Forman's later films, was unexpected: in addition to painstaking observations of individual people and their daily lives, another portrait appeared on the screen, a merciless portrait of the whole fabric of society, the like of which Czechoslovak film had never produced before. The whole offered to view an embarrassed, convulsive grimace, a countenance verging on the grotesque; but Forman laughed with gusto and with no condescension at what he saw, and the audience laughed with him, accepting him as one of themselves.

His first feature film, *Black Peter* (*Černý Petr*-1963), proved Forman's exceptional ability to see in detail, to capture the unrepeatable, small incidents of life, incidents chosen with uncanny insight as being socially representative. Both Passer and Papoušek collaborated on the film. In *Black Peter*, a young boy who is just starting out in life receives his first mission

Black Peter

on his new job: to be an informer, to spy on his fellow-citizens, to watch and to mistrust people. As a consequence, a gulf opens between the puzzled boy and his painfully smug father that at the film's end has become unbridge-able. We encounter the same abyss, the same lack of humanity, in the final sequence of the film that made Forman known throughout the world, *Loves of a Blonde* (*Lásky jedné plavovlásky*–1965). Here also, everything was predetermined from the outset. A small town has a shoe factory that employs hundreds of young women. The army is asked to provide the missing "male element," but instead of the promised garrison of young soldiers, the army stations a unit of middle-aged reservists there. The mixed-up situation made audiences laugh, but at the same time, it revealed the inhumanity of this "problem-solving" approach to emotional human needs. The rest of the film, including the relationship of a young blonde and a touring piano player,

Loves
of a
Blonde

was kept within the framework of the basic "problem," bringing *Loves of a Blonde* onto a plane that the film's creators had not imagined at the start. Miroslav Ondříček was Forman's cameraman.

Although Passer was considered by some to be Forman's double, his debut, the short *A Boring Afternoon* (*Fádní odpoledne*-1965)—based on a story by one of the key writers of the period, Bohumil Hrabal—introduced an entirely unique personality. Whereas Forman had a firm and irrepressible confidence in the belief that revelations alone are sufficient for the ends of satire and ridicule, Passer was a melancholy observer, whose laughter contained the mournful element of understanding. His masterful first feature film, *Intimate Lighting* (*Intimní osvětlení*-1965), was an almost plotless portrait of the tragicomic futility of the life of a provincial intellectual, who is confronted with the almost identical futility of his urban counterpart. This film immediately placed Passer in the ranks of Europe's foremost directors. It turned out, however, that he was not to make another film until six years later, when, as an émigré in the United States, he directed *Born to Win* (1971).

Intimate Lighting

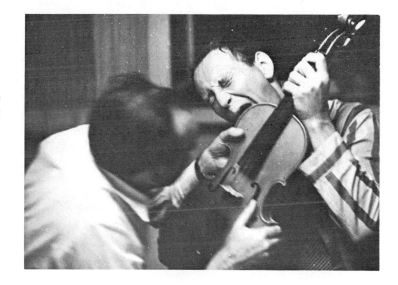

The third member of the trio, Papoušek, whose name always appeared among the credits of Passer's and Forman's films, did not make his independent debut until 1968, with *The Most Beautiful Age* (*Nejkrásnější věk*). Later, in 1969-1971, he made a series of films about the life of a lower middle-class Czech family, *Ecce Homo Homolka*, *Big Shot Homolka* (*Hogo fogo Homolka*), and *Homolka and the Purse* (*Homolka a tobolka*). His exceptional talent for observation turned out to be more literary than cinematic and under circumstances that had already changed, he did not have the success enjoyed by his two colleagues.

Forman, Passer, and Papoušek destroyed the old conventions of the scenario, striving for a reconstruction of reality not so much by a realistic plot as by means of the acute perception of details of situations and characters. They found in nonprofessional actors the ideal interpreters of the unique moments they brought to life on the screen. This "uniqueness" became the foundation of their esthetic credo.

NĚMEC, JURÁČEK, KRUMBACHOVÁ

Jan Němec and Pavel Juráček (b. 1935) also believed in this uniqueness, and in nonprofessional actors as its main interpreters. But for all that, their approach was almost diametrically opposed to that of the aforementioned trio. They did not use slice-of-life portrayals as their point of departure, but rather the whole, the philosophical fable, a metaphor for which they sought and found concrete forms of expression that frequently were not fleshed out with details until the shooting itself. This was true particularly of Němec and his scenarist and art director, Ester Krumbachová (b. 1923). Němec's feature debut, *Diamonds of the Night* (*Démanty noci*-1964), still had a realistic foundation—it was based on Arnošt Lustig's story of two Jewish boys who escaped from the Nazis as they were being taken to a concentration camp. But director Němec and cameraman Kučera transformed the story into an almost abstract vision of young people persecuted by a hostile world with which they strive in vain to establish contact—a world that is most tellingly represented by a group of impotent old men in a position of power, who in the end organize a hunt for the two helpless boys. Jan Němec went on to shoot one segment of the episodic film, *Pearls at the Bottom* (*Perličky na dně*-1965). Hrabal's short stories formed the basis for all the episodes of the film, which brought most of the leading members of the 'young wave' together. But it was *Report on the Party and the Guests* (*O slavnosti a hostech*-1966), that revealed Němec's full range of talents. Němec transformed a philosophical morality play about man's indifference to the fate of others, about his willingness to accept force and violence, and even to voluntarily become its tool, into a film metaphor, a series of human situations that are experienced before our eyes by "ordinary" people that most of us, the viewers, can identify with. This autoreflection—which was a common trait of the films of the "young wave," along with the effort to capture and demystify social realities—was drawn to its inevitable conclusion when all the "voluntary" participants in that odd, morbid party set out willingly, accompanied by a pack of dogs, to track down the only one of the "guests" who simply couldn't take it and fled the party. The fight to overcome the banning of the film became one of the lessons in the school of practical politics that was attended in those years by all Czechoslovak artists. The struggle ended in 1968, when, at least for the time being, the film was released for public screening. In the meantime, Němec made *Martyrs of Love* (*Mučedníci lásky*-1967), three surreal and comic dream

The Party and the Guests

stories about the unfulfilled amorous hopes of heroes who had been variously trodden on by destiny. No matter how obvious it was that this film represented a temporary digression from his fundamental concerns—no one imagined that it would be his last film until the mid-seventies—something to fill the gap until he could work with more significant material, *Martyrs of Love* was clear evidence of Němec's maturity, of his ability to give an intriguing shape and style to any film material.

THROUGH WOMEN'S EYES

Another cinematic milestone of Czech film in the sixties was shot from a script by Krumbachová, who also worked on the film as art director. It was *Daisies* (*Sedmikrásky*-1966), directed by Věra Chytilová, who—as did Forman after *Competition*—abandoned the method of cinéma vérité after *Something Different*. Chytilová, with Jaroslav Kučera at the camera, combined fragments of everyday reality with artistic and motion-picture recollections to create an artificial, stylized reality as a setting for her modern fable. The story deals with the inner void, with boredom, with the destructive impulse that these bring into being; it deals with the indifference of the world, and also with people whose indignation in a world of mass murder and silent inhumanity "is reserved for an overturned bowl of salad." When their real-life Czech counterparts were confronted with the finished work, it was almost a foregone conclusion that they would turn that indignation on *Daisies*. Mainly because the film spoke in a language that was almost totally incomprehensible to them—for, as they used to say in Prague, isn't "socialist realism" just a euphemism for "celebrating the Party and the Government in a language that even they can understand"?

Daisies

In 1970, Chytilová, Krumbachová, and Kučera—in a coproduction with Belgium—completed another of their philosophical visions of the contemporary world, an ambitious artistic parable about women in a man's world, *The Fruit of Paradise* (*Ovoce stromů rajských jíme*). A symphony of surrealist estheticism, not always molded into comprehensible form; a film for the next decade, as one American reviewer wrote.

The Fruit of Paradise   Josef Kilian

Ester Krumbachová made her first—and for a long time, her only—independent film, *The Murder of Dr. Lucifer* (*Vražda ing. Čerta*-1970), at the moment when it was all coming to an end. A sarcastic tract on the myth of maleness, it is practically the only really Brechtian film made in Czechoslovakia during the period. It achieves the necessary "distances," not through cinematic techniques but through acting and staging.

JURÁČEK

Josef Kilian (*Postava k podpírání*-1963), directed by Pavel Juráček and Jan Schmidt (b. 1934), was not banned like *Report on the Party and the Guests,* but its distribution within the country was limited. A Kafkaesque story that takes place in contemporary Czechoslovakia, it seems almost to foretell the position Franz Kafka was to have in his native land in the sixties. In the spring of 1963, at an international scholarly conference at Liblice, Kafka, long damned by the establishment, was officially rehabilitated. In the eyes of the world, Pavel Juráček, one of the most striking personalities of the period, remained the author of just this one film. His feature debut—a single film consisting of two thematically connected stories—*Every Young Man* (*Každý mladý muž*-1965), revealed with melancholy humor the alienation of young men in military uniform, and confirmed the existence of an extraordinary talent. But Juráček's major work was to be *Case for a Rookie Hangman* (*Případ pro začínajícího kata*-1969), inspired by Part III of Swift's *Gulliver's Travels.* Although the script was finished in the early sixties, the shooting was postponed under various pretexts for years, Juráček, in the meanwhile, helping other "young wave" directors with their scripts. He finally got to shoot his long-awaited film in 1968–1969, but it was completed only for the storage vaults of the post-Soviet occupation censors.

Case for
a Rookie
Hangman

The codirector of *Josef Kilian,* Jan Schmidt, also had to wait more than a year for the opening of his film *The End of August in the Hotel Ozone* (*Konec srpna v hotelu Ozón*-1966), which was written by Juráček. His picture of a world destroyed by atomic war, a world inhabited only by a surviving group of young women, was too depressing and too desolate for representatives of official optimism and leaders of the military. Whereupon the athletic, anti-intellectual Schmidt—director of a number of interesting short films on sports themes—tried, within the Czechoslovak context, to create something that was practically unknown there—a romantic action film. His two efforts in this area were *Lanfieri Colony* (*Kolonie Lanfieri*-1968), and the multi-episode film based on the short stories of V. Vančura, *Queen Dorothy's Bow* (*Luk královny Dorotky*-1970).

SCHORM

The greater the determination of Czech film-makers to do away with the old taboos, taking advantage of every opportunity that the crisis of the system and the ideology's gradual disintegration suddenly afforded them, the more they found bans, censorship, and the fight against them to be a part of their day-to-day existence. This was the atmosphere at the time of the feature-length debut of Evald Schorm (b. 1931)—who had emerged as the director of a number of fascinating philosophizing shorts. Schorm's *Courage for Everyday* (*Odvahu pro všední den*-1964) marked the birth of another directorial personality. It brought together the most varied sources of modern inspiration with traditional elements to create a truthful picture of the disillusionment of the postwar political generation. The script was by Antonín Máša (b. 1935)

Courage for Everyday

In his later films, Schorm remained one of the most controversial directors, an uncompromising moralist in the best sense of the word. In his *The Return of the Prodigal Son* (*Návrat ztraceného syna*-1966), he posed the question that was later to become a supremely important one, particularly in the Soviet Union—is it a sign of social or individual abnormality when the individual's inability to make a moral compromise is classified as madness? In *Saddled with Five Girls* (*Pět holek na krku*-1967), he re-created a novel for adolescent girls, transforming it into a study of human malice and at the same time pointing up the hypocrisy appearing among the "new class."

The Return
of the
Prodigal
Son

MÁŠA

Máša made his debut as the director of *Wandering* (*Bloudění*-1965), a sharply defined story of the conflict between generations projected against the backdrop of the post-Stalinist period. Shortly thereafter, in *Hotel for Strangers* (*Hotel pro cizince*-1966), he created, in an *art nouveau* style, a picture of an ivory-tower world that kills a poet who has come seeking sensitivity and truth. This metaphor was replaced by direct political reflection in his next film, *Looking Back* (*Ohlédnutí*-1968), an attempt at finally integrating the experiences of the last 25 years.

Máša's metaphor about the death of the poet seemed to take up the theme that was expressed earlier on the stage in Ivan Klíma's play, *The Castle*. The sixties in Czechoslovakia had become a period of renaissance for the legitimate theater, which found—for the first time since the Čapek brothers—true dramatists in Milan Kundera, Václav Havel, Josef Topol, Ivan Klíma, and others. The stage became an important platform for the intellectual destruction of myths and taboos, and at the same time a focus and a departure point for cultural ferment, dominated by the Prague

Theater Behind the Arch (Otomar Krejča), Theater on the Ballustrade
(Jan Grossman), Semafor Theater (Jiří Šlitr, Jiří Suchý), Drama Club, and
others.

Aside from the Soviet Union, Czechoslovakia was the only country in
which the belated de-Stalinization brought with it an exceptional flowering
of national literature, bringing to light such extraordinary talents as Fuks,
Hrabal, Kundera, Linhartová, Páral, Škvorecký, Vaculík, and, later,
Šotola and others. The symbiosis of theater, literature, art, and music with
film, in a tense period of anxiety and searching, and in the inspiring
uniqueness of the setting that was Prague, indisputably represented an
important stimulus to the development of film culture. In many ways it was
a repeat of what had happened in the thirties.

MENZEL

This atmosphere also nourished the distinctive and versatile talent of Jiří
Menzel (b. 1938)—actor, stage director, and film-maker. His film career
was closely linked with the name of Bohumil Hrabal, from the story *The
Death of Mr. Baltisberger* (Smrt pana Baltazara-1965), another of the
episodes in *Pearls at the Bottom,* through his to-date most successful film,
Closely Watched Trains (Ostře sledované vlaky-1966), to the banned *Larks
on a String* (Skřivánci na niti-1969). Hrabal's tragicomic everyday absurdity
found a congenial poet in Menzel, who viewed life with an attitude of artful
irony, and at the same time with an almost philosophical understanding
for the tragicomic non-heroes of his films. Menzel proved equally at home
making the film version of twentieth-century Czech classic by Vladislav
Vančura, the sagely ironic parable of illusion and reality, *Capricious
Summer* (Rozmarné léto-1967). On the other hand, the mystery comedies
of Josef Škvorecký, *Crime at the Girls' School* (Zločin v dívčí škole-1965),
and *Crime at the Nightclub* (Zločin v šantánu-1968), were too different in

Capricious Summer

style and too abstractly literary to provide Menzel enough specific human material for his compassionate irony.

KACHYŇA AND PROCHÁZKA

An entirely different link with literature brought about the successes and the failures of Vojtěch Jasný's former codirector, Karel Kachyňa. By a series of coincidences, Jan Procházka, a hearty, talented and exceptionally prolific writer, became a favorite of the political leadership for a number of years, and thus gained almost unlimited influence in Czechoslovak film. As time went on, Kachyňa became the sole director of Procházka's scripts, touching with increasing daring on painful and taboo subjects from the past 25 years. Between 1961 and 1970, the Kachyňa-Procházka team made 11 fiction films. The best of them, *Long Live the Republic* (*Ať žije republika-*1965), looks through the merciless, politically unbiased eyes of a child at a legend of national heroism at the time the country was being liberated from the fascist occupation. Procházka's position inspired and made

Long
Live
the
Republic

possible other controversial Kachyňa films, including another provocative view of the war, *Carriage to Vienna* (*Kočár do Vídně-*1966). This held true until the film *Night of the Bride* (*Noc nevěsty-*1967), which, in showing the period of the collectivization of agriculture in a most unflattering light, initiated the open conflict between Procházka and the political establishment. The last two films to emerge from this collaboration, *Funny Old Man* (*Směšný pán-*1969) about a victim of the persecution of the fifties, and *The Ear* (*Ucho-*1970), about powerful men's horror of the system that they themselves established, were eventually banned. Procházka became one of the targets of the persecution of intellectuals after 1968, and died of cancer in 1971.

BOČAN

Literary works also inspired another member of the young generation, Hynek Bočan (b. 1935), who displayed an exceptional sense of social irony and sarcasm in the films *No Laughing Matter* (*Nikdo se smát nebude*-1965), based on a story by Milan Kundera; *Private Hurricane* (*Soukromá vichřice*-1967), based on a novel by Páral; and *Honor and Glory* (*Čest a slava*-1969), based on a novel by Michal. Self-irony, a sense of atmosphere, and an intellectual approach to the subject matter were characteristic of Bočan's talent. Contrary to his contemporaries—Bočan inclined more toward traditional cinematic techniques and the use of professional actors.

No Laughing Matter

PRODUCTION GROUPS AND FITES

The reorganization of film production went the furthest in Czechoslovakia between 1963 and 1968, finally permitting film to exist as an art, and allowing the independent development of a plurality of heterogeneous talents and styles. In fact, this production concept became a prevalent notion throughout Eastern Europe, but its realization never quite came to be.

What follows applies in varying degrees to all the Eastern European film industries. The basic idea was that of small workshops with a stable state subsidy, the workshops increasingly acting as customers vis-à-vis the studios and the laboratories. The workshops, or production groups, each of which in Czechoslovakia produced on the average of five or six films annually, were headed by a producer-scenarist team, and they each had their own art council, while directors were free to work with various groups, depending on the circumstances surrounding the origin of the specific film. The centralized evaluation and approval of films was gradually limited as the production groups' autonomy increased until finally, in 1968, they were entirely independent. The idea was gradually accepted that the entire system of film distribution, including the import and export of motion pictures, should be governed by the cultural and artistic role of film, while television would gradually take over the role of the main source of popular entertainment. By 1968, the overall reorganization of film production and distribution was practically ready, having returned to the original concept of a nationalized cinematography that had been altered and realtered over the years.

The gradual success of this reorganization, as well as that of numerous specific films, generated constant friction and tests of strength between film-makers, on the one hand, supported by the majority of film critics, and on the other the still dominant, but shaken, state power, which simultaneously acted as the sole financier. The Union of Film and Television Artists (FITES) carried the banner of the film-makers in this conflict, becoming, as time went on, the first specialized labor organization in Czechoslovakia with the admitted aim of being a partner, and, when necessary, an opponent, to the state in establishing conditions for artistic film work. The key positions in the union in these years were occupied by film journalist Ludvík Pacovský and director Ladislav Helge. The latter, a leading representative of the generation of 1956, and one of the main targets of the 1958 neo-Stalinist counteroffensive, for several years sacrificed his own promising film career to the struggle to create the prerequisites for the film work of others. He did not make a single film between 1963 and 1968, but nonetheless he was the central figure of the Czech film industry. It was not until 1968 that he completed *Shame* (*Stud*), the portrait of a political functionary who is corrupted by power and ends his life as a total failure, the hero of *Great Solitude* 20 years later. From the political point of view *Shame* was one of the most outspoken works of the entire period. This film was unfortunately weakened by Helge's long absence from the director's chair.

BRYNYCH, DANĚK, VLÁČIL

In addition to Vojtěch Jasný, the contemporary of Helge's to achieve the greatest artistic success was Zyněk Brynych. In . . . *And the Fifth Rider Is Fear* (. . . *a pátý jezdec je strach*–1964), he used the stories of the inhabitants of an apartment house in Prague during the Nazi occupation as a framework for an expressionistic and entirely contemporary commentary on how man acts in a situation where police terrorism makes ordinary honesty and decency a matter of life and death. Brynych also considered the fundamental questions of political morality in his later film *I, Justice* (*Já, spravedlnost*-1968), a fantastic story of a group of people who want to make the punishment of Adolf Hitler a matter of their own vengeful concept of justice. Oldřich Daněk, the scriptwriter for *Hic Sunt Leones,* who made his debut as a director in 1960 with the officially irreproachable *Three Tons of Dust* (*Tři tuny prachu*), also turned to history—*The Nuremberg Campaign* (*Spanilá jízda*-1963)—to seek metaphors for the present. In 1967, Daněk made his best film, *The Royal Blunder* (*Královský omyl*), a fourteenth-century tale about the relativity of despotic power.

Historical material was by far the best medium for František Vláčil, who in 1967 completed his unique reconstruction of thirteenth-century Bohemia, *Markéta Lazarová,* based on the novel by V. Vančura. Supported by the photography of B. Baťka, he achieved an almost flawless recreation of a period that hovered between paganism and Christianity and filled it with authentic portraits of people from another civilization. But in the last stages, Vláčil unfortunately lost artistic control of the large amount of material, which ultimately lacked the disciplined structure and the orderliness of the poetic original. In this sphere, he was more successful in another historically based film, *The Valley of the Bees* (*Udolí včel*-1968). The conflict between paganism and Christianity, between two moralities, two civilizations, is once again the central theme. But the things that had made of *Markéta*

Marketa Lazarova

Lazarová a flawed great work of art, the immediate rawness and the poetic vision, were lacking in *The Valley of the Bees.*

GOOD ENTERTAINMENT

Searching for a new language, doing away with the traditional script and with studio sets—unless a high degree of stylization is needed—viewing film art as a persistent destroyer of myths and a seeker of the truth about man and society—those were the dominant characteristics of Czech film during the period known as "The Czechoslovak Film Miracle," dominated by the directors of the "young wave." The tradition of highly professional, good comedy, musical, mystery, thriller, and adventure story, that had developed over the years, specially in the United States, France, and Great Britain, was entirely lacking in Czechoslovakia and in Eastern Europe in general. From the very beginning, commercial production here was provincial by nature and was aimed exclusively at the least demanding audiences on the domestic market or in the neighboring countries. But under the pressure of an unusually high percentage of artistically ambitious films made by the Czechoslovak film industry, which by the mid-sixties was producing about 40 films a year, as much as 25 to 35 percent of which were beyond the framework of common commercial production, the quality of the so-called entertainment genres also went up.

In 1964, the first successful Czechoslovak musical was shown. Called *The Hop Pickers* (*Starci na chmelu*), and directed by Ladislav Rychman (b. 1922), its central motif was the confrontation of middle-aged hypocrisy with the honesty of youth. Director Zdeněk Podskalský came up with a "ghost story," the politically daring satirical comedy *White Lady* (*Bílá paní*-1965), based on a story by Karel Michal. Another specialist in the comedy genre, Oldřich Lipský (b. 1924), achieved great success with his intelligent but uneven parody of westerns, *Lemonade Joe* (*Limonádový Joe*-1964). Václav Vorlíček (b. 1930) achieved a good response internationally with his spoof of the comic strips, *Who Wants to Kill Jessie?* (*Kdo chce zabít Jessii?*-1966).

A turn for the better as far as quality is concerned was also taken by the mystery and adventure film genres. There were detective stories by Petr Schulhoff (b. 1922)—for example, *The Murderer Hides His Face* (*Vrah skrývá tvář*-1966)—and a mystery with political motivations filmed by Štěpán Skalský (1925)—*The Pathway Through the Deep Forest* (*Cesta hlubokým lesem*-1964), which revealed the background of one of the most infamous secret police "frame-ups" of the early fifties—as well as the exceptional *Sign of Cancer* (*Ve znamení raka*-1966), directed by Slovak director Juraj Herz, who was working in Prague. In 1968, Herz made an interesting political horror film, *The Cremator* (*Spalovač mrtvol*), the story of a "small" man who is transformed by ideology into a mass murderer.

The traditionally important area of films for children and young people was graced with a number of film-makers that raised the overall standards of that genre, including Josef Pinkava, Milan Vošmik, Ludmila Plívová, Jiří Hanibal, and above all, Milan Hobl (b. 1935), who directed *Do You Keep a Lion at Home?* (*Máte doma lva?*-1963).

In the area of animated films Jiří Trnka added his voice to those of the fiction-film directors with a powerful metaphor about the fate of the artist in a totalitarian society, *The Hand* (*Ruka*-1966). Karel Zeman continued in his efforts to combine animation with live actors, particularly in *War of the Fools* (*Bláznova kronika*-1964), but he never could rise to the poetical immediacy of his first great successes.

War of the Fools

SLOVAKIA IN THE SIXTIES

After the success of *Sunshine in a Net,* Slovak film did not keep up with Prague. Only Uher fulfilled the hopes he had raised, creating in *The Organ* (*Organ*-1965), a baroque metaphor about life and art against the backdrop of Slovak fascism during World War Two. Uher's less successful attempt to make a screen version of one of the authentic works of Slovak surrealism, Dominik Tatarka's novel, *The Miraculous Virgin* (*Panna zázračnica*-1966) is typical of the efforts to find a source for a genuine modern Slovak style.

With his by then usual scriptwriter, Alfonz Bednár, Uher had unearthed it in *Three Daughters* (*Tri dcéry*-1968), a Learian ballad about an old peasant who had put his daughters in a convent in order to avoid having to provide dowries for them, and then, dispossessed as a result of collectivization, sought help from them after the convents had been disbanded. The poetically realistic metaphor once again gave way to the surreal metaphor in *Genius* (*Génius*-1969), which shows the Devil weeping over the fate of Man—Devil and Man have traded places. To maintain their ancient role, the devils set out to convert man to love and goodness so that he might once again be accessible to corruption.

Genius

Uher's peers, Peter Solan, Eduard Grečner, Martin Hollý (b. 1931), and the somewhat older Stanislav Barabáš, formed the vanguard of Slovak film of this period. The older generation of directors (Bielik, Bahna, Andrej Lettrich, Jozef Medveď, Ján Lacko, and others) was capable of ensuring the industrial running of the Koliba studios in Bratislava, but was unsuccessful in wrenching themselves away from provincial standards. But even among the younger generation, many failed to find the means to achieve a radical modernization of language and style: Eduard Grečner did not succeed in *Nylon Moon* (*Nylonový mesiac*-1965); Solan vainly sought his own approach to portraying the psychological makeup of his contemporaries in *Before Tonight Is Over* (*Kým sa skončí táto noc*-1966), as did Barabáš, who strove for a new existencial dimension in his *Knell for the Barefooted* (*Zvony pre bosych*-1965). Solan, in *The Case of Barnabáš Kos* (*Prípad Barnabáš Kos*-1964), and Barabáš, in *Tango for a Bear* (*Tango pre medveda*-1966) certainly did not find a compatible genre in political satire. Then, in 1967 they began to make original films for television. *A Gentle Creature* (*Něžná*-1967) meant the beginning of Barabáš's international career as an interpreter of the work of Dostoyevsky. As for Solan, he directed a penetrating view of the fifties, the medium-length *And Behave Yourself* (*A sekat dobrotu*-1968). Martin Hollý too achieved his greatest success in Leonid Andreyev's ballad *Seven Hanged Men* (*Sedm oběšených*-1968), also originally intended for TV.

The Case of Barnabáš Kos

JAKUBISKO, HANÁK, HAVETTA

But an entirely new note sounded when Juraj Jakubisko (b. 1938), a graduate of the Film Academy in Prague, who as a cameraman shot a promising graduation project in *Waiting for Godot* (*Čekání na Godota*-1965), finished his first feature film, *Crucial Years* (*Kristove roky*-1967). This film signaled not only the birth of an exceptional talent, but also the birth of a Slovak style, with roots in different, more natural, and wilder soil than the style of the Czech young wave. *Crucial Years* is still for the most

Crucial Years

Deserters and Nomads

part an urban film, the story of a painter who, at the age of 33, enters his "age of reason," and finally comprehends that life is compounded of "love, foolishness, and death." What he had only implied in his debut, Jakubisko stated openly in his next film. *Deserters and Nomads* (*Zbehovia a pútníci-*

1968), a wild ballad about war and killing, that deals with "death and obscenity." It is a passionate protest, an eruption of metaphors flowing directly from the imaginative world of surrealism and from authentic Eastern European folklore, still pure and uncommercialized, literally swimming in blood and violence. In this film, Jakubisko discovered a compatible cameraman in Igor Luther and indicated that the focus of seeking and finding a new cinematic language for the forthcoming era of Czechoslovak film might be shifting to Bratislava. Shortly thereafter, two others made debuts as fiction-film directors, the documentarist Dušan Hanák, and the former graphic artist Elo Havetta (d. 1975). Their appearance confirmed the originality of the contribution of the new generation from Slovakia. In his film *322* (1968), Hanák presented a parallel between the cancer that eats away at the guts of the film's hero and the cancer that destroys human relations and the social tissue. Havetta, on the other hand, in his *Party in the Botanical Garden* (*Slávnosť v botanickej zahrade*-1969) proclaimed an anarchist joy in an unwarped, undistorted life, a protest against pettiness. It was a film full of surreal images that drew their inspiration from the rural life of the Slovakian hill country.

Party in the Botanical Garden

IMAGES OF "CONCRETE TOTALITY"

It took only five years (1963–1968) for Czech and Slovak film artists to lead the Czechoslovak film industry to one of the leading positions in Europe. The young generation, just entering upon the scene in those years, was dominant, but—as mentioned before—in essence the achievement resulted from the efforts of all generations, which up until then had been repeatedly frustrated and constrained by political and administrative forces. Thus, in the second half of the sixties, Czechoslovakia had a number of film directors of European renown, united in their opposition to those who would either restrict their originality or fetter them with endless delays in production or distribution. Together with all of Czechoslovak culture, with scholars of the humanities, with the economists, the best of the journalists, and, in the final stages, with the contribution of some members of the political establishment, Czechoslovak film played a significant role in laying the cultural and social groundwork for what was to become known as "the Prague Spring of 1968." But it was not until 1968, when all censorship had been withdrawn and production groups had attained full autonomy that the Czechoslovak films would cease to be just partial analyses and trial balloons and would create a portrait of what philosopher Karl Kosík referred to as the "concrete totality" of the Stalinist world. These films included Forman's *Firemen's Ball* (*Hoří, má panenko!*), which was completed in 1967 and was an extended Gogolian metaphor about stupidity, dullness, and incapacity. In it, its authors brought to the extreme their method of using the concrete reality of detail—in this case the world of the provincial functionaries of a fire brigade—to reveal the truth behind it, the truth about the social system as a whole. The film opened in movie theaters on December 15, 1967, at the moment when a political crisis was coming to a head—the crisis that was to bring Alexander Dubček and his reform Communism to power in the first week of January, 1968.

Firemen's Ball

Other films in this unique series of "total" views of the previous period did not enter production until later in 1968—even though the scripts had long since been ready for shooting—and they were not completed until the armed intervention of the Warsaw Pact troops in August 1968 brought an end to the period that had permitted them to come into being. Thus, paradoxically, 1969 became the year in which the efforts of the years past came to fruition, and simultaneously the year in which they were frustrated. Jaromil Jireš completed the brutally realistic *Joke* (*Žert*), based on the novel by Milan Kundera, in which a man who had been among the revolutionary youth of the postwar period comes to bitter terms with events of those days

Joke

and of his young adulthood. In *The End of a Priest* (*Konec faráře*), Evald Schorm used the script by J. Škvorecký to view under a magnifying glass a grotesque world distorted by ideologies that also hide the real human beings behind them. In his lyrically melancholy *All My Countrymen,* Vojtěch Jasný erected a mournful and nostalgic monument to the wasted lives of his friends from a Moravian village, who after the war worked with him for a "better life." And finally, in Slovakia, Juraj Jakubisko made his third film, *Birds, Orphans, and Fools* (*Vtáčkovia, siroty a blázni*), a desperate scream of protest against the brutal absurdity of the world, declaring: "When soldiers invade your country and steal your house and your language, if you build yourself a house in your soul, you will be happy." The hero of the film—just to be on the safe side—commits threefold suicide.

"NORMALIZATION"

The so-called normalization of Czechoslovakia following 1969 also meant an end to the Czechoslovak film miracle. The General Manager of Czecho-

Birds, Orphans and Fools

slovak Film was arrested; Radok, Kadár, Weiss, Jasný, Barabáš, Forman, Passer, Luter, and others went abroad, later joined by Němec, while other leading directors of the sixties were fired by Czechoslovak Film. Only Jaromil Jireš was to shoot two of his long-prepared scripts. One of them was *Valerie and the Week of Wonders* (*Valerie a týden divů*-1969), an excellent poetic vampire film based on a story full of childhood fantasies by the Czech surrealist poet of the twenties, Vítězslav Nezval. The other was *And Give My Love to the Swallows* (*A pozdravujte vlaštovky*-1971), a lyrical, stylized story based on the diaries of a 17-year-old girl who was executed during the Nazi occupation.

It was with far less success that Juraj Herz escaped into the unreal world of art nouveau and made *Kerosene Lamps* (*Petrolejové lampy*-1971) and *Morgiana* (1972), while Karel Kachyňa returned to films for youth with *Jumping the Puddles Again* (*Už zase skáču přes kaluže*-1971), and *Destination Heaven* (*Vlak do stanice nebe*-1973). And the censors' vaults swallowed up not only such finished films as Jiří Menzel's *Larks on a String*, Pavel Juráček's *Case for a Rookie Hangman*, Evald Schorm's *The Seventh Day, the Eighth Night* (*Sedmý den, osmá noc*) and *Dogs and People* (*Psi a lidé*), which he codirected with Vojtěch Jasný, Karel Kachyňa's *The Ear*, Hynek Bočan's *Reformatory* (*Pasťák*), and others—all works by experienced directors—but also films that marked the debuts of other directors, including the fourth and youngest generation of film-makers to work under the nationalized film industry. Of particular note among these films was *Dull Sunday* (*Nudná neděle*) by Drahomíra Vihanová (b. 1930), Ivan Renč's (b. 1937) *Prison Guard* (*Hlídač*), and Václav Matějka's (b. 1937) *Nakedness* (*Nahota*). Karel Vachek (b. 1931), one of the most incisive new talents

Valerie and the Week of Wonders

Jumping the Puddles Again

of the late sixties, director of a shattering documentary about the degeneration of folklore entitled *Moravian Hellas* (*Moravská Hellas*) and the feature-length documentary about the "Czechoslovak Spring," *Elective Affinities* (*Spříznění volbou*–1968), was unable to complete his first fiction film.

At the beginning of the seventies, Czechoslovak fiction-film production dropped to half that of the immediately preceding period. Except for the aforementioned films, these were for the most part mediocre and sub-mediocre films, made by second- and third-rate directors. Otakar Vávra, however, reappeared at this time, attempting, at the end of his long career, to revive the "publicistic" and "artistic documentary" genres of the Stalin years in *The Days of Treason* (*Dny zrady*-1972), about the Munich crisis in 1938, and *Sokolovo* (1975), devoted to the deeds of the Czechoslovak army unit on the Soviet front in World War Two. And Zbyněk Brynych soon became the showcase director of this period, bringing to the screen conformist scripts in every conceivable genres, e.g. the love story *What Is the Color of Love?* (*Jakou barvu má láska*-1973) or the film on prison life *The Night of Orange Bonfires* (*Noc oranžových ohňů*-1975).

In Slovakia in 1973, Juraj Jakubisko was permitted to shoot *Construction of the Century* (*Stavba storočia*), a documentary about the building of a gas pipeline across Czechoslovakia for delivering natural gas from the Soviet Union to West Germany. Štefan Uher filmed an amusing view of the war as seen through the eyes of children in *If I Had a Gun* (*Keby som mal pušku*-1971), and shortly thereafter made a film version of the balladic folk tale, *The Maple and Juliana* (*Javor a Juliana*-1973). Elo Havetta, in his second and last film, *Lilies of the Field* (*Lalie polné*-1973), confirmed the promise of his debut. Nonetheless, the overall tendency in Slovakia was also to revert to the conservative approach of the period prior to 1962.

And so, a prophecy was fulfilled, the one made by Soviet critic V. Bolshakov in the spring of 1968 in *Komsomolskaya Pravda*: "I believe," he wrote, "that the period of the development of Czechoslovak film, as represented by the Formans, the Menzels, the Němecs, and their kind, will, all things notwithstanding, not last long."

In 1973, a list of banned films was issued in Prague that contained practically all the best films of the sixties. The list concluded with an enumeration of films BANNED FOREVER: *Firemen's Ball, End of a Priest, A Report on the Party and the Guests, All My Countrymen.*

FAR FROM MOSFILM:
The Soviet Union After 1963

As early as the mid-fifties, critic and author Andrei Sinyavsky wrote in the conclusion of his essay "On Socialist Realism":

After the death of Stalin, we entered upon a period of destruction and reevaluation. It is a slow and inconsistent process, it lacks perspective, and the inertia of both past and future lie heavy on it. . . . Maybe [a new God] will have to be supplemented by other stakes of the Inquisition, by further 'personality cults,' and by new terrestrial labors, so that after many centuries, a new Purpose will rise above the world. . . . And meanwhile, our art is marking time between an insufficient realism and an insufficient classicism. Since the loss it suffered, it is no longer able to fly toward the ideal and to sing the praises of our life in a sincere and elevated style, presenting what should be as what is. In our works of glorification resound ever more openly the notes of baseness and hypocrisy. . . . But is the dream of the old, good, and honest 'realism' the only heresy to which Russian literature is susceptible? Is it possible that all we wish is to return to the naturalist school and the critical tendency? Let us hope that this is not so and that our need for truth will not interfere with the work of thought and imagination.

Having lost our faith. . . . we don't know where to go; but, realizing that there is nothing to be done about it, we start to think, to set riddles, to make assumptions. May we thus invent something marvelous? Perhaps; but it will no longer be socialist realism.

When Andrei Sinyavsky was imprisoned for this and other texts, it was the end of the epoch of slow "destruction and reevaluation." In its letter to the founding congress of the Union of Film Workers of the Soviet Union in October 1965, the Central Committee of the Soviet Communist Party expressed other ideas: "It is the direct duty of film workers to take part with their work in the constant growth of the political and economic activity of the working people. . . . Creative workers are expected to maintain a special ideological stability, a clarity of creative ideas. We must constantly see to the ideological level of works of art, and their ability to speak to the broadest of popular masses."

The tension between these two texts characterizes the period in Soviet culture after the ouster of Khrushchev. On one hand, there was pressure from the artists, who were unwilling to relinquish the place they had worked so hard to gain. Refusing to believe in the permanence of the turnabout, they looked to the language of fables, allegories, and parables as a means for continuing the fight they had begun. On the other hand, government leaders called for the regimentation of culture and the intelligentsia, for the liquidation of "foreign influences," although this call was muted for a time by surviving vestiges of "liberalism." It was not entirely clear how the policy of the forthcoming period would look, nor who would be its true representative. Tactical fighting was still being waged over these issues, including film scripts that had overstepped the bounds of the previous period and would subsequently be bound to new inquisitorial stakes.

This period of uncertainty and indecision—which saw the creation and noncreation, the banning and unbanning, the approval, disapproval, and reapproval of a number of interesting scripts and films, and even a few promising debuts—ended in 1969. After the occupation and "normalization" of Czechoslovakia, the campaign against the liberal Soviet culture and intelligentsia that had placed great hope in the "Prague Spring," revealed eloquently some of the Soviet Union's motives for the intervention.

Indeed, it was a welcome relief to the conservative establishments in countries such as the GDR and Bulgaria, dependent as they were on the Soviet Union, for it strengthened their position and self-confidence and resulted in a certain "controlled détente" in the sphere of culture. But the Soviet Union, as the center of power, was especially concerned with making the cultural intelligentsia forget the role it had played in the previous period, and relinquish the desire for independent action and autonomous work. The period of hesitation ended and a new time of firm decisions began. This change in the political and social climate explains many new aspects of Soviet culture after 1964: the break both in the work of individual artists and in general production, the flight away from contemporary problems, and an unstated return to the "theory of lack of conflicts," resulting both in the blandness of Russian artistic works and the tragic artistic failures of figures such as G. Chukhrai, who were symbolic of times past.

Andrei Rublev

ANDREI RUBLEV

In the mid-sixties, the creator of *Ivan's Childhood,* Andrei Tarkovsky, together with Andrei Konchalovsky, found a hero who seemed to personify all the important themes of their own time: Andrei Rublev. This monk, who in the early fifteenth century had brought the Russian school of icon painting to its peak, appeared to them to embody the struggle between Russian backwardness, barbarism, and Asiaticism, and the effort to confront all this with an ideal. He embodied as well the faith that "Sooner or later, someone always appears in Russia who will stand up and speak the truth." In a land flooded with blood and violence, he was a proponent of brotherly love, beauty, and goodness; for him art served the ideal, but was not subservient to the powerful. After all the horrors he had witnessed, horrors that had forced him to give up his painting for a long time, he once again found faith in his mission by merging with the creative force of the ordinary man, who was disdained and unseen by the powerful. *Andrei Rublev* (1965)—in which Tarkovsky and cameraman Vadim Yusov combined the inspirations of Eisenstein with a modern cinematic view of history as the real present—went from the studio directly to the "stake," via a memorable showing for the Moscow cultural community in the old Dom Kino (House of Film), surrounded by mounted police. The film was shelved and after numerous editing suggestions by the censors—which Tarkovsky for years stubbornly refused to accept—it was released in France in 1969. But it had

A Mirror

to wait another three years for even a limited distribution in the Soviet Union, and a broader distribution abroad, where it often underwent further corrective surgery. When finally shown, the crippled film almost entirely missed its mark with the Soviet audiences, as was the case earlier with Khutsiev's *I'm Twenty,* but nonetheless, was far superior to any other film of its day. It was a reminder of the talent and the possibilities that were born in the period of de-Stalinization and that were repressed in the following period, before they had a chance to fully develop.

It took Andrei Tarkovsky another five years to complete his next film, the metaphoric science-fiction film about future space flights, *Solaris* (1971). The long years of fighting for *Rublev* had all but broken his wings, and his effort to consider the present through "a fantasy art, working from hypotheses rather than aims" did not get off the ground.

But all of Takovsky's talent, assuring him, together with Sergei Paradjanov, a leading position among Soviet film artists, was evident again in his next film, *A Mirror* (*Zerkalo*-1974). A finely woven cinematic tapestry of childhood reminiscences, with the director's mother as the central figure, Tarkovsky's "Amarcord" very much displeased the authorities, primarily for its language, which was labelled "incomprehensible." But with some delay the film was given a limited release in summer 1975.

KONCHALOVSKY

The story of the scenarist of *Andrei Rublev* is, in a somewhat different way, also typical of the times. Andrei Konchalovsky made his first independent film in 1965, *The First Teacher* (*Perviy uchitel*), which revealed in a poetic and naïve style the postrevolutionary conflict between the values of a young enthusiastic teacher and the ancient traditions of the Kirghiz mountains. The film was greeted with enthusiasm abroad, but in the Soviet Union, some felt that it was too unorthodox in its view of the period. Right after he completed the script for *Rublev,* Konchalovsky made another film, *Asya's Happiness* (*Asino schastie*-1966). As in *First Teacher,* the plot itself—a crippled village girl, Asya, refuses the conventional solution of her fate as an unmarried mother—was only a pretext for showing a particular environment and real human characters. This time, however, Konchalovsky did not restrain his anger at what he saw and filled the screen with a hitherto unfilmed and unexpected reality. The effect was electrifying; the official response predictable. The film was damned and banned, and this time there was no appeal. As a consequence, Konchalovsky, the heir to one of the more noteworthy traditions of Russian painting, turned to the classics. He directed a color version of Turgenev's *Nest of Gentry* (*Dvoryanskoye gnezdo*-1969), an extremely effective visual work, and then made *Uncle Vanya* (*Dyadya Vanya*-1970), easily the best film version of the Chekhov play. The sorrow, the nostalgia and the hopelessness of the Russian intelligentsia had found a true poet even in Soviet film.

Nest
of
Gentry

But unlike Tarkovsky, Konchalovsky didn't go on battering his head against the wall. He wrote some scripts for the regional studios and eventually made *In Love* (*Vlyublonnye*-1974), a visually attractive and adroit story of two separated and happily reconciled "typically Soviet" lovers, a true model of well-polished conformism for the seventies.

Uncle Vanya

THE DAMNED FILMS

It was Alov and Naumov who brought the cruelty of a grotesque depiction of reality to Soviet film for the first time since the twenties. Their film version of Dostoyevsky's *A Disgraceful Affair* (*Skverniy anekdot*-1965) took one's breath away with its disgust at the monstrous world of the oppressed and the debased, the world of bureaucratic despotism and human obsequiousness and sycophancy, a world filled with the degradation and dehumanization of man. After the death of Stalin, Dostoyevsky was once again an acceptable literary figure, and he became a means for self-analysis for many people who had been the leading lights of Stalinist cinematography, for example, I. Pyriev. But no one, either before or after them, went as far as Alov and Naumov. The result: another important film that fell victim to the censors.

Following this experience, Alov and Naumov turned to the history of the Revolution, basing their film on the work of the long-banned M. A. Bulgakov. *The Flight* (*Beg*), a two-part epic, was not completed until 1970. There are many strong sections in the first part, which is a veritable triumph of photography in its poetic depiction of historical action, especially the movements of soldiers and crowds—almost as if it were holding a silent debate with the officious monumentality of the films by Ozerov and Bondarchuk. The second part is seriously weakened by a naïve descriptiveness, a vain effort to give an air of probability to a sometimes unsuccessfully stylized narration that traces the destinies of Russian émigrés in Turkey and France.

The
Flight

The ranks of the "damned" cannot help but include Mikhail Kalik. After the success of *Man Follows the Sun,* Kalik made *Goodbye Boys* (*Do svidanya, malchiki*), which was completed in 1966. Based on a popular book for young readers, the film presented an ironical picture of the manner in which its empty, superficial "young heroes" were raised and educated. Only after much hesitation was the film released in the Soviet Union, and even then it received only limited distribution. It was never shown abroad. In the years that followed, Kalik made *To Love* (*Lyubit*-1968), and early in the seventies, he emigrated from the Soviet Union.

These are only a few examples of how the Soviet leadership responded in the mid-sixties to efforts to make personal films. Most of these efforts had been conceived in the preceding period and carried over into this one. It was a time that lacked the inner vitality of the "Khrushchev era," but which was still full of hope, a period during which it still seemed worthwhile to try. But most of the efforts never got as far as the studio, not to mention the projection rooms. One outstanding example is the script of *The Law* by Leonid Zorin, Alov, and Naumov. A story about people returning from Stalinist concentration camps, it was approved, but never filmed.

HISTORY—MONUMENTAL AND ORDINARY

Official support was given, however, to monumental films, which, with the expenditure of immense amounts of money, brought the Russian classics or incidents from Soviet history to the screen in a manner in line with the official standards of taste. Foremost among these films are the four-part *War and Peace* (*Voyna i mir*—1965-1967), and *Waterloo* (1970) by Sergei Bondarchuk, both based on Tolstoy, and the five-part history of the Soviet role in World War Two, *Liberation* (*Osvobozhdenie*—1967-1971) by Yuri

War and Peace

Ozerov. Bondarchuk sought his inspiration in the familiar type of super-production, for which he had at his disposal far more money and facilities than either Cecil B. DeMille or King Vidor. *Liberation's* overall structure was based on interweaving three kinds of sequences: meetings of officers and politicians at staff headquarters, episodes of individual encounters that give a human touch, and gigantic battle scenes. In this respect, *Liberation* was reminiscent of the films of the "artistic documentary" period. Now, however, Stalin was only one of the leaders, and Chiaurelian stylization gave way to Petrov's dry description of the Battle of Stalingrad. As a whole, if measured by its models and ambitions, *War and Peace* could stand on its own merits, but *Liberation* was entirely sterile. When Sergei Bondarchuk turned out another superproduction, *They Fought for the Country* (*Oni srazhalis za rodinu*-1975)—a pathetic film based on M. Sholokhov's novel about a group of ordinary soldiers in the first days of the war—some inter-

Lenin in Poland

The Sixth of July

preted it as an indirect polemic against a return to the taste and values of the original Spectator, as represented by *Liberation*.

Other Soviet historical films that should be mentioned here include Mark Donskoy's lyrical and bathetic films about Lenin's mother, *Heart of a Mother* (*Serdse materi*-1966), and *A Mother's Devotion* (*Vernost materi*-1967), which he later followed with a portrait of Lenin's wife, *Nadezhda* (1973). Also in this category is Yutkevich's attempt to take Lenin down from his pedestal, *Lenin in Poland* (*Lenin v Polshe*-1965), Yosif Heifitz's *Salud, Maria* (*Salyut, Maria*-1970), Yuli Karasik's *Sixth of July* (*Shestoye yulia*-1968) and the unsuccessful international coproduction, inspired by the polar expedition of General Nobile, *The Red Tent* (*Krasnaya palatka*-1969), Mikhail Kalatozov's last film. *Tchaikovsky* (1970) was another international coproduction (Warner Brothers), directed by Igor Talankin. A few years before, Talankin had made *Daytime Stars* (*Dnevnye zvezdy*-1968), based on the writings of Olga Bergoltz and dedicated to Leningrad and to its inhabitants during the time of the Stalinist purges and the wartime siege. Stanislav Rostotski tried later for a more individualistic and poetic view of the period in a two-part film, *And the Mornings Here Are Quiet* (. . . *a zori zdes tikhie*-1972), but the director's attitude towards this melancholy literary story of a woman's unit on the Soviet front turned it into a socialist-realist disaster.

Better suited to Rostotski's directing style was the film that was to be his greatest success—largely due to Georgi Polonsky's script. It was a socially critical story of the moral problems of a Soviet secondary school, *Until Monday* (*Dozhivem do ponedelnika*-1968). This film represented the end of the period of hesitation, and such cinematic social criticism did not appear again in the years that followed.

Motifs from Soviet history clearly carried one of the new talents of this period to the fore, Gleb Panfilov (b. 1933), who made his belated debut

No Path Through the Flames

with *No Path Through the Flames* (*V ogne broda nyet*-1968). In this film, "there aren't the schematic 'Whites' and the idealized 'Reds,' but the people, put into motion and split in two as if by lightning, and from it emerges the inexhaustible talent of the Russian, personified in the nurse, a self-taught painter" (E. Yevtushenko). Perhaps there is no better example in Russian cinema of a film born of the immense inspiration of *Rublev,* of a film that indicates the path that could have been taken. Its author, however, did not win international acclaim until his next, more polished film, *The Beginning* (*Nachalo*-1970). The story of a young heroine who finds in the film role of Joan of Arc an odd parallel to her efforts to find an authentic approach to her own life contained the theme that inspired Panfilov's next project—a vain attempt to film the story of the real Joan of Arc.

The
Beginning

A special place among Soviet films on war and films about contemporary history is set aside for Mikhail Romm's *Ordinary Fascism* (*Obyknovennyi fashism*-1965). Using documentary material from German film archives, Romm finally put his philosophical testament on the screen. The old director, who three years earlier, in front of his students, had rejected most of his own previous films, insisted on personally reading the commentary, an artist's personal testimony about the world he lives in. The film was intended as the first part of Romm's comment on the "personality cult" and was aimed at showing that fascism is not simply terrorism and war, but day-to-day indoctrination, propaganda, parades, the complete manipulation of man in order to reduce him to a puppet in the hands of a totalitarian state. Until his death in 1972, Romm remained faithful to his conviction that he could never again return to fiction films.

FILM VERSIONS OF THE CLASSICS

Adaptations of the classics were not limited to Tolstoy, Turgenev, or Chekhov. Few other adaptations, however, were successful. Zarchi did not do well with his film version of *Anna Karenina* (1967). *Bela* (1966), directed by Rostotski and based on the novel of M. Lermontov, did not turn out any better. More interesting was *The Brothers Karamazov* (*Bratya Karamazovi-*1968), completed by the two leading actors, Mikhail Ulyanov and Kirill Lavrov after the death of director Ivan Pyriev in the middle of the shooting. The new version of *Crime and Punishment* (*Prestupleniye i nakazaniye-*1969) in the smooth and cool direction and interpretation of Lev Kulidzhanov, and Vengerov's version of Tolstoy's *Living Corpse* (*Zhivoy trup-*1969) were interesting only because of the acting. And Andrei Batalov's *The Gambler* (*Igrok-*1972), based on the Dostoyevsky novella, did not even come close to the artistic success of *The Overcoat*.

One aspect of the reworking of Soviet classics in film is the attention devoted to two well-known Soviet humorists of the thirties, Ilf and Petrov. Moisei Schweitzer made a film version of their *Golden Calf* (*Zolotoy telenok-*1969), and *The Twelve Chairs* (*Dvenadsat stulev-*1971) won new plaudits for Leonid Gaydai (b. 1921), already a popular director of film comedies.

The only truly autonomous film to be realized from adaptations of literary classics in this period, was Grigori Kozintsev's last film, *King Lear* (*Korol Lir-*1970). In it, Kozintsev once again used the master cameraman of black-and-white film, the Lithuanian Jonas Gritsius, as well as the raw, brutal, and stylized historicism that had given birth to *Ivan the Terrible* and *Andrei Rublev*. As a result he created a film that was noteworthy in its style, content, and acting performances, a controversial work of film art that turned Shakespeare's parable to face the present. King Lear represents the pinnacle of Kozintsev's exceptional trilogy of reflections about post-Stalinist Russia, which began with the portrait of an honorable man fighting in vain against the cynicism that surrounds him (*Don Quixote*), and continued with the tragedy of an intellectual who seeks the truth, and for whom the entire land is an enormous prison (*Hamlet*).

PEDAGOGIC REALISM

Thus it was not only Soviet literature that seemed to turn to the Soviet present, or to the years immediately following Stalin's death. But neither of these periods were the sources of personal films, as attempted by Khutsiev and others. Efforts to replace film pedagogics and socialist realism by individual testimony met with failure. Of course, that did not mean a complete return to the former type of film. The new pedagogical realism was more complex, not only more demanding from a technical point of view, but less static and less reminiscent of poster art, and not as schematic in

King Lear

its plot structure and in the dimensions of its characters. The most interesting and temperamental among the creators of this type of film was the director of *Chairman,* Alexei Saltykov, who was particularly adept at creating strong dramatic scenes in cinematic terms. He made four films in rapid succession: *Women's Rule* (*Babye tsarstvo*-1967) about the fate of rural Soviet women under the Nazi occupation; *Director* (*Direktor*-1969), a portrait of the working-class director of the first Soviet automobile factory, marked by the events that accompanied the shooting of the film (the death of the leading actor); *Government* (*Sibiryachka*-1971), whose central character was a Communist village woman; and finally, *There Is No Returning* (*Vozvrata nyet*-1973), which is set on the Don River during and after the war and takes place over a 20-year period. But growing pressures progressively weakened his bite, and his talent fell victim to the strictures of the post-1968 period. Veteran director Gerasimov did not lag behind Saltykov in the number of films or in ambitions, although the artistic result remained on the mediocre side. Gerasimov used his own scripts to shoot *Journalist* (*Zhurnalist*-1967), *By the Lake* (*U ozera*-1969), and *To Love Man* (*Lyubit cheloveka*-1972), broad contemporary epics made in a style that was the epitome of the socialist realism and conformism of the period. In 1974, he turned to the excellent dramatic author, V. Volodin, for the script of his *Daughters and Mothers* (*Materi i docheri*), clearly taking a strong critical stand against the Soviet "new class." Cinematically, however, the film was as conformist and uninteresting as those that preceded it. Y. Raizman's *Your Contemporary* (*Tvoy sovremennik*-1967), based on Gabrilovich's script, which contained a critique of bureaucracy within the Soviet context, followed the life of the son of the hero of *Communist,* and was filmed in the same style.

Another poorly made film of a similar type is *The Taming of Fire* (*Okroshcheniye ognia*-1971), which was rather successful in the Soviet Union. Its director, Daniil Khrabrovitsky (b. 1923)—who wrote the scripts for *Clear Sky* and *Nine Days of One Year*—made his debut in 1965 with *Roll-Call* (*Pereklichka*), an attempt to argue with Khutsiev's view of the conflict between the generations. In *The Taming of Fire,* Khrabrovitsky tried to create an epic about the development of Soviet rocket technology.

Daughters
and
Mothers

KHUTSIEV AND TODOROVSKY

But what happened to those who had been on the very threshold of an entirely new approach to the present, the ones whose rocket could truly carry Soviet cinema to new heights? Marlen Khutsiev did not give up, and his *July Rain* (*Yulskiy dozhd*-1965) once again criticized the generation that was in its thirties—their smugness, their callousness, and their cynicism—

concluding with a rare view of the generation gap between fathers and sons. It was an apt continuation of *I'm Twenty*, which was distributed almost simultaneously. "I stress what is not stated directly, what can be read between the lines," said Khutsiev at the time. And that was why *It Was in the Month of May (Byl mesiats mai)*, his next film, and once again a superior one—it was made for television where Khutsiev found a new home—was not made until 1970, why it was set in Germany in May 1945, and why it was followed by a documentary about the Paris Commune, *The Red Banner of Paris (Aloe znamya Paryzha)*.

Khutsiev's cameraman, Pavel Todorovsky (b. 1925), had a worse fate. In 1965, he achieved international acclaim with his debut, *Fidelity (Viernost)*, based on a story by B. Okudzhava about young people in 1940. But his next film, a strange, somewhat Bergmanesque attempt at an urban romance, *The Enigmatic Indian (Fokusnik-1968)* fell victim, in these years of crisis, to the censor's blue pencil.

URBAN AND RURAL WORLDS

In the middle of the sixties, a number of clearly formulated cinematic attempts were made to show the difficulties of human communication within the structure of modern urban life, which did not stabilize in the Soviet

Fidelity

Union until the sixties. The most interesting of these efforts was the film of Larissa Shepitko, *Wings (Krilya-1966)*, in which she created an interesting portrait of a famous woman pilot unable to spend the rest of her life living on her past reputation and experiencing all the difficulties of establishing new relations with her surroundings. Even more ambitious was Shepitko's almost Antonionian portrait of a successful man in his

Wings

thirties who, in a desperate effort to recover his own identity, flees from the city to the distant natural surroundings of Siberia. Entitled *You and I* (*Ty i ya*–1971), and filmed in color, the film was mainly significant in its endeavor to move away from a strict descriptive realism to a more interpretive approach. The times were not favorable to this type of thinking however, nor to a search for style. The medium-length fiction film, *The Homeland of Electricity* (*Rodina electrichestva*), based on the novel by Andrei Platonov, was another interesting effort by Shepitko, but it was shelved in 1968 (see Chukhrai).

Unlike Shepitko, Vassili Shukshin turned to the rural world. He was one of the most talented among those artists who were struggling persistently to hang on to the present. He had the courage and strength to show on the screen the real Soviet *muzhik* and his inner world, not just his dressed-up image. Soviet audiences were grateful for these bits of truthful life, and Shukshin's *Your Son and Brother* (*Vash syn i brat*–1966), as well as the episode film *Strange People* (*Strannye lyudi*–1971), became great successes. A writer and actor as well as a director, Shukshin was usually involved in all aspects of any film he directed. He achieved his greatest success with *The Red Snowball Bush* (*Kalina krasnaya*–1973), a tragic and highly unusual tale of an ex-convict and the Soviet underworld that conveyed the notion that modern urban life is a corrupting source of evil and that men can rebuild their morality only by returning to their roots in the ethically pure countryside. His strongest talent, however, was in the literary field, a bias that naturally influenced his cinematic vision.

Another director of films centering on urban life was the former cameraman, Mark Ozepyan (b. 1937), who made his directorial debut with *Three Days of Victor Chernyshev* (*Tri dnya Viktora Chernysheva*–1968). Working from a "non-pedagogical" script by Yevgeni Grigoriev, Ozepyan drew upon his experience as a cameraman to give an unusual slant to the story of a young Soviet worker and his day-to-day life. In a way, the film was an indirect off-shoot of Khutsiev's style; it met with an extremely divided response.

The difficulty of finding a personal approach to present-day Soviet life was not the only problem facing Soviet cinema. The middle and the younger generations bore the weighty burden of the realistic convention, as canonized by VGIK. (This was true even though the governmental Committee for Cinematography established a new two-year film school of "Advanced Courses for Scriptwriters and Directors," primarily for those who had already achieved a measure of craftsmanship in other fields, such as writing, painting, and acting.) The convention of descriptive realism, which was occasionally shaken off on the pretext of the need to stylize the past, had long bound film-makers to a certain view of the present. It was this convention that in the end destroyed any interesting attempts to break through the vicious circle of the same old reworking of the same old themes. This is true of the over-praised independent debut of Andrei Smirnov—who earlier had codirected *This Palm of Land*—*The Byelorussian Station* (*Byelorusskiy vokzal*-1970), an interesting Khutsievian story of the empty lives of wartime heroes; and is even more true of another debut, Nikolai Gubenko's (b. 1941) *A Soldier Came From the Front* (*Prishel soldat s frontu*-1971). It also applies to *Monologue* (*Monolog*-1973) by Yevgeni Averbakh, the still more conventional work by Nikolai Moskalenko (b. 1926)—*Russian Field* (*Russkoye pole*-1970) and *The Young Ones* (*Molodye*-1971)—and to a number of other films.

Certainly more successful cinematographically, and more original too, was the work of Smirnov's former collaborator Boris Yashin in a film of original perception and immediacy, *Autumn Wedding* (*Ossennye svadby*-1968).

Among the directors who made their debuts in the sixties but remained overshadowed by the above-named film-makers was Pavel Lubimov (b. 1938), whose films, for the most part, featured female central characters. His most important work was *The Women* (*Zhenshchini*-1966), a story about a moral conflict between a conservative "old Bolshevik" mother and

The Bielo-
russian
Station

Virineya

her son and daughter-in-law. He later made, with less success, *The New Girl* (*Novenkaya*-1969) and *A Day Ahead* (*Vperedi den*-1970). But foremost was Alexander Mitta (b. 1933), the director of *My Friend Kolka* (*Drug moy Kolka*-1961), who first found a refuge in making films for or about young people and made a well-deserved name for himself by the film he made with one of the most talented and nonconformist of Soviet playwrights, Alexander Volodin. The film, entitled *Open the Door When the Bell Rings* (*Zvoniat, otkroyte dver*-1966), was another sharp moral commentary on the generation gap, and, like all such commentaries in Eastern Europe, had political aspects as well. *Shine, Shine, My Star* (*Gori, gori moya zvezda*-1971), a poetic and tragic comedy about an artist in the Revolution, achieves an unusual degree of freedom from the realistic narrative convention. The last of these directors worth mentioning is Vladimir Fetin (b. 1936), whose *Virineya* (1969) was in part a "rehabilitation" of the once famous revolutionary novel by Lydia Seifullina that was blacklisted during the Stalinist purges.

Mikhail Bogin (b. 1936) was the lyricist among the directors who began in the mid-sixties, winning international laurels with his medium-length *The Two* (*Dvoe*-1965), a story of a young musician and a deaf-mute girl. But in his later films—*Zosya* (1967) and *About Love* (*O lyubvi*-1971)—Bogin had difficulty finding again that strange, intimate, poetic melody that he had created in *The Two*. In 1975 he joined the ranks of the émigrés.

Of the famous names of the Khrushchev period, the most tragic artistic victims of the last decade were Yakov Segel and, of course, Grigori Chukhrai. In 1965, Chukhrai made a touching, profoundly Russian—though cinematically deceptive—contemporary fairy tale, *There Was an Old Man and an Old Woman* (*Zhili byli starik so starukhoy*), about an old couple who prefer their good-natured son-in-law to their own daughter. Later on, Chukhrai, who had become the symbol of the previous period, devoted his time mainly to leading his "experimental studio," in which he tried in vain to keep alive at least some of the hopes of the past few years. The studio was closed—to reopen as a small production group—after it produced *The Beginning of An Unknown Era* (*Nachalo nevedomogo veka*), a three-episode film directed by Smirnov, Shepitko, and Gabay that was intended for the fiftieth anniversary of the October Revolution in 1967. Once finished, it was immediately shelved. Unable to make films of his own liking, and failing even in an attempt to promote what he himself called "commercial films," he followed the example of Romm—but without his success—by endeavoring to confront past with present in a documentary montage film, *The Memory* (*Pamyat*-1972). After that, he turned to literature, attempting to make films from the works of Alexis Tolstoy and Pushkin.

OTHER GENRES

The vicious circle of descriptive realism remained unbroken even by the genres of comedy, adventure, and suspense. Elem Klimov's attempt at a satire in the film *Welcome* had but one follower, *Adventures of a Dentist* (*Pokhozhdeniya zubnogo vracha*-1967). Later on, Klimov filmed a popular half-acted, half-documentary film about the history of sports, *Sport, Sport, Sport* (1971), probably his greatest success. In 1975 he directed *Agony* (*Agoniya*), a film about Rasputin, depicting an isolated ruling class unable to prevent a disaster. The film has a Brechtian approach mixing true and false documentary, in black and white, with fiction in color. It was immediately shelved as "useless."

In spite of the limitations, however, Eldar Ryazanov brought to Soviet film an almost inconceivable degree of self-irony, and succeeded in guiding his lunatic heroes to the verge of tragi-comedy. His most successful film was *Beware the Car* (*Beregis avtomobiliya*-1966), the tale of a philanthropic car thief. Another success in the genre of ironic comedy has to be credited to Genrikh Gabay (b. 1923) and his portrait of an irresolute, hesitating, "Oblomovian" antihero *Lebedev Against Lebedev* (*Lebedev protiv Lebedeva*-1966). In the early seventies Gabay followed Kalik into emigration.

Among the suspense films that aroused some positive response was a somewhat clumsy effort at an espionage film in the so-called "documentary style," *Dead Season* (*Mertviy sezon*-1968), directed by Savva Kulish and inspired by the story of Rudoph Abel, the Soviet master spy in the United States. In 1972, Kulish made another film in a similar style, *The Committee of Nineteen* (*Komitet devyatnadsati*) about the danger of bacteriological and chemical warfare.

In the adventure-film genre, director Vladimir Motyl made several unusual films. In 1967 he directed a film version of the fairy tale by popular Soviet author and singer Bulat Okudzhava, *Mourning for a Knight* (*Zhenia, Zheniechka i katusha*), about a young romantic on the battlefront. But

Motyl's greatest success was an adventure film, *White Sun of the Desert* (*Beloye solntse pustyni*-1969) the first Russian film in which the subject of civil war (in this case, in Central Asia) was only a pretext for the creation of a commercial "western," which adopted to the last detail the style of Italian copies of the American original.

Film-makers frequently found more breathing space when making films on children's topics than when making films on contemporary adult life. Among the more interesting films made for young viewers were the internationally popular *I Loved You* (*Ya vas lyubil*-1967) by Ilya Frez (b. 1909) and *Oh, That Nastia* (*Okh, uzh eta Nastia*-1972) by Georgi Pobedonostsev (b. 1910).

In this less closely controlled area of film-making analogous to animated film-making in Czechoslovakia, Yugoslavia, or Romania during the fifties, the actor and director Roland Bykov (b. 1930) grew to become a significant artistic personality in the Soviet cinema. His *Careful, a Turtle!* (*Vnimanie, cherepakha!*-1970) and *Telegram* (*Telegramma*-1973), which are, in fact, adult films about youngsters, brought him much deserved international recognition.

FAR FROM MOSFILM

By the end of the fifties and the beginning of the sixties, Soviet cinema had received inspiration for revival from all quarters. But calm maintenance of the status quo, without controversy or debates, and no searches or discoveries, became the guidelines for the tough regime after 1968. The use of literature, once an important source of inspiration, was also sharply curtailed. And what literature there was that still retained its autonomy, even at the cost of being ostracized and persecuted, was separated from film by a high wall of unspoken policy. For example, there never was any serious effort to film any of the works of Solzhenitsyn that were published in the Soviet Union. The battles that had been fought in the cultural arena not long before quickly became political conflicts; the battleground became the courtrooms; and defeat meant years spent in concentration camps, prisons, and psychiatric clinics.

But film as an art had become too mature, even if it was too close to the state to be held up in comparison to the best works of the literature of the sixties. It had acquired technology, language, experience, and popularity, and so it sought its own ways, attracted its own new impulses. It gradually found material in the national ethnic uniqueness of the non-Russian nations of the Soviet Union, their folklore, legends, history, literature, and art. These brought refreshment and enrichment to the language of film, and on more than one occasion led it out of the vicious circle of the socialist realist convention. It was no longer a question of establishing a cinema industry in backward regions, with master film-makers and beginning directors arriving in a flourish to shoot unforgettable documentaries against exotic backdrops and then return to Moscow. A true autonomous film culture emerged, so autonomous and natural, so fresh and real that it aroused trepidation.

It was not only the focus of interest in Soviet cinema that was shifting from Moscow to the republics; inevitably, all those political and social impulses that had sprung up early in the sixties and were being crushed at the center found their fertile soil in the republics as well. Witch hunts for "nationalist" heresy again became a part of the political scene, and early in the seventies, Moscow reinstated the practice of the centralized approval of film scripts, which had been rescinded in the late fifties.

Films produced in the non-Russian republics of the Soviet Union have always, as a rule, been dubbed into Russian when shown outside the producing republic and exported abroad. Attempts originating in the republics and abroad to change this practice have generally met with failure. Thus, the foreign viewer, and even the Soviet audience, can in most cases only see the nonauthentic version of these films, and generally only knows the Russian translation of their titles.

White Bird
with a
Black Spot

THE UKRAINE

When the world stared astonished at the wild cavalcade of colors, the unrestrained natural beauty, and the noncommercial folklore in Paradzhanov's *Shadows of the Forgotten Ancestors,* it could not help but ask the name of the director of photography. "The surrealist from Zaporozhye"—that was the nickname foreign critics thought up for Yuri Ilyenko (b. 1936)—soon found himself in the director's chair. He confirmed the fact that the lyrical genius of the Ukraine and the film heritage of Dovzhenko were still alive and well. In 1967, Ilyenko made his first independent film, *On the Eve of Ivan Kupala Day* (*Noch nakanune Ivana Kupaly*), based on Gogol's story of the same name, with his brother Vadim at the camera. Vadim had already been Segel's cameraman on *Farewell, Doves.* The poetic Chagallesque imagery that characterized Ilyenko's first film alternated in his second film with a brutal, bloody, and occasionally surreal vision of the events at Bukovina in the years during and immediately after the war. Entitled *White Bird with a Black Spot* (*Belaya ptitsa s chernoy otmetinoy*-1971), it was visually one of the most exceptional Soviet films of the period. But its interpretation of the complicated events was rather conformist, following the official line. A year later, in coproduction with Yugoslavia, Ilyenko made the costly *In Spite of Everything* (*Naperekor vsemu*-1972), inspired by the life of an eighteenth-century Montenegran national hero, Petar Negosh, and reflecting the characteristics of the Paradzhanov school.

In 1968, Sergei Paradzhanov returned to Armenia to continue his efforts to break the convention of narrative film by speaking a purely pictorial language, unheard of in Soviet cinema since the liquidation of the avantgarde. Based on the story of Armenian poet Sarutin Saydyan, the film *Color of the Pomegranate* (*Sayat Nova*; also known as *Tsvet granata*-1968) was accused of formalism and other sins, and met the same fate as *Rublev.*

Color of the Pomegranate

Reedited by S. Yutkevich, it was released in 1971 in the Soviet Union but received only limited distribution. Paradzhanov, to many the greatest living Soviet film-maker, started a number of projects during the next few years, but most of them were turned down, among them, the shooting scripts of Lermontov's *The Demon* and Kotsyubinsky's *Intermezzo*. Early in 1974, after having addressed to the Central Administration in Moscow a passionate pamphlet about the situation of Soviet cinema in general and his own in particular, Paradzhanov was arrested on fabricated charges unrelated to film-making and sentenced to six years in jail.

Leonid Osyka also sought his inspiration in the nature, legends, and folklore of the Ukraine, making *Stone Cross* (*Kamenniy krest*), based on the Ukrainian classic by Ivan Franko, in 1968, and in 1971 confirming his abilities with *Zakhar Berkut*, a historical legend that elaborated on the Ukrainian elements mentioned earlier.

Among other notable Ukrainian directors were the experienced Viktor Ivchenko (b. 1912), who filmed an interesting adaptation of A. Tolstoy's short story about an innocent victim of the civil war, *Viper* (*Gadiuka*-1966) and Artur Woytecki (b. 1928), who directed *Because of Spleen* (*Skuki radi*-1968) and *The Bell* (*Tronka*-1970).

MOLDAVIA

In the neighboring Moldavian Republic, a similar development matured in the sixties. Kalik emerged from the Moldavian studio to launch his short but significant career in Soviet film and Vadim Derbenev (b. 1934), who manned the camera for most of Kalik's films, first made *Journey Into April* (*Puteshestviye v aprel*-1963), and then, two years later, directed *The Last Month of Autumn* (*Posledniy mesiats oseni*), a mature, lyrical film about the yearnings, dreams, and disappointments of old age, but above all a poem about Derbenev's native land and its people.

The Last
Month
of
Autumn

Victor Gazjiu (b. 1938), another of Kalik's collaborators, having written the script for *Man Follows the Sun,* made his independent debut with *Ten Winters, One Summer (Desyat zim odno leto*-1969), followed by *Time Bomb Explosion (Vzryv zamedenogo deistvya*-1971), and *The Last Haiduk (Posledniy haiduk*-1973).

But the most exceptional figure in Moldavian film in the late sixties was Emil Lotyanu (b. 1936). After his directorial debut, *Wait For Us at Dawn (Zhdite nas na rassvete*-1963), he made an almost ethnographic film about the life of herdsmen in the mountains of Moldavia, inspired by Pushkin, *The Red Glades (Krasnye Polyany*-1966). This initial success was followed by *The Leutary (Leutary*-1972), a film conceived as a musical poem and dedicated to the Moldavian itinerant musicians called the Leutary.

The Leutary

LITHUANIA

Perhaps the most surprising emergence of a national cinema occurred in Lithuania. It was based primarily on an artistically mature and strongly nationalistic film tradition. Lithuania's first feature-length films, *Lithuanian Little Soldier* and *Onite and Ionelis,* had been made in 1930-1931, but the international renown of such Lithuanian cameramen as A. Rachunas and of acting teacher I. Vaichkus goes back many years. Nurtured by this tradition, a galaxy of talented cameramen and a number of films with

Nobody
Wanted
to Die

unconventional subject matter appeared in the sixties. Vitautas Zhalakevichius remained the leading figure. In 1966, he made the successful *Nobody Wanted to Die* (*Nikto nye chotiel umirat*), in which the situation at the time of the Soviet annexation of Lithuania—interpreted in the official way—provided a backdrop for an action film that was inspired by the best elements of the American western. His television film, *The Whole Truth About Columbus* (*Vsya pravda o Kolumbe*-1971), set in Latin America after Columbus' death, is a Brechtian, Dürrenmattian view of the birth of historical myths. Zhalakevichius returned to Latin America for the theme of his feature film *The Sweet Word "Freedom"* (*Eto sludkoye slovo-svoboda* -1972), but the attempt to give life to the standard Soviet view of a Latin American urban guerilla, ended in artistic failure.

Arunas Jebrunas (b. 1931) succeeded with two studies, rather exceptional both artistically and psychologically, of the world of an adolescent girl, *The Girl and the Echo* (*Devushka i ekho*-1965) and *The Beautiful Girl* (*Gruzhuole*-1969). Algirdas Araminas (b. 1937), who came from the ranks of Lithuania's foremost cameramen—which included among others, Gritsius, Motskus, Pechiura, and Tomaszcwicz—was also attracted by the world of maturing youth. In both *Nightingale*, one of the episodes from the composite film *Living Heroes*, and in *Find Me* (*Naydi menya*-1968), another multi-episode film, he looks at the adult world through the eyes of children. *When I Was Young* (*Kogda byl malenkim*-1969) is a story of first love and disillusionment seen from an almost surreal vantage point. *A Little Confession* (*Malenkaya ispoved*-1972), an indirect sequel to *When I Was Young*, is an effort at a drama about growing up.

The motifs of disillusionment, sorrow, melancholy, and insecurity are in a way the mark of Lithuanian cinema of those years. This is true of Raymondas Vabalas (b. 1937), who, after making several films focusing primarily on the past—e.g., *Stairs to the Sky* (*Lesnitsa v nebo*-1966)—directed *July—the Start of Summer* (*Yul nachalo leta*-1969), which was filled with these emotions. It is the story of a young actress seeking in vain for her place in life. In 1972, Vabalas concluded his two-episode film, *Stone on a Stone* (*Kamen na kamen*-1971), the central theme of which explored many aspects of violence and power.

In 1970, another Lithuanian film talent, Almantas Grikiavicius, made his independent film debut with *Ave Vita* (*Da budet zhizn*), based on an old script by Zhalakevichius. A series of contemplations on the past and the present, the film did not live up to the promise of Grikiavicius's earlier film, *Feelings* (*Chuvstva*), made in collaboration with Algirdas Dausa in 1968. *Feelings* was an attempt at a panoramic view of Lithuanian social questions—the German occupation, the Soviet occupation, the camps in Siberia, the return of camp prisoners, etc.—through the prism of ruined lives. The symbol of the twin brothers, whose father was also a twin, as was his father, became, through the eye of Tomaszewicz's camera a metaphor for the split destiny of the Lithuanian people, the like of which was indeed rare in Soviet cinema in the sixties.

GEORGIA

Original and independent film talents had always thrived in Georgia, perhaps more than anywhere else in the Soviet Union. One of them, Georgi Danelia, who was working in Moscow, followed his initial successes with a satire that aroused the disfavor of the government, *The Thirty-Three* (*Tridsat tretiy*-1965), the story of a Soviet citizen who grows a thirty-third tooth. This satire was aimed at the process by which the media manufacture heroes for reasons having little to do with their value as human beings. It met the predictable fate, being banned upon its completion.

After this experience, Danelia returned to Tbilisi and attempted to translate some humorous world literature into the language of film humor. Hence the origin of the amusing and very Georgian *Cheer Up!* (*Ne goryui*-1969), based on Claude Tellier's *My Uncle Benjamin,* followed by a new version of Mark Twain's *Adventures of Huckleberry Finn* entitled *Hopelessly Lost* (*Sovsem propavshyi*-1973), which was filmed in Moscow and thereby lost any Georgian or American originality it might have had.

After the success of *The Father of a Soldier,* Revaz Chkheidze made the mediocre *The Young Came Too* (*Nu i molodezh poshla*-1969), and then

Hopelessly
Lost

Pirosmani

directed *Seedlings* (*Sazhentsy*-1973), a rather sentimental story of an old man and his grandson travelling the countryside, looking for the progeny of an exceptional fruit tree. The motif of returning, the significance of traditions, the mistrust of success, all these themes kept reappearing in Soviet films with increasing frequency.

Tengiz Abuladze also had his turn and, in collaboration with Alexander Kveselava, made the romantic *The Appeal* (*Molba*-1968), the film version of a poem by Georgian poet Vazha Pshavela. Inspired by the experiments of Paradzhanov, Ilyenko, and others, *The Appeal* called attention to a new cameraman, A. Antipenko. But Abuladze was much less successful when he used Dagestan folklore in the action comedy *A Necklace for My Love* (*Ozherelye dlya moyey lyubimoy*-1971).

At that time, Chkheidze and Abuladze had already become "classics," and a new generation took its place behind them. Georgi (b. 1937) and Eldar (b. 1933) Shengelaya were the sons of a film director of the older generation, Nikolai Shengelaya. Georgi made his debut in 1967 with a historical film about the eighteenth-century Georgian folk hero, Matsy Khvitia, *He Did Not Want to Kill* (*On ubiyat ne khotyel*), but his unconventional documentary *Allaverdoba* (1967) was far more significant. It seemed to be a distant echo of Kalatozov's *Salt for Svanetia*. No less controversial was *Pirosmani,* his second feature film, completed in 1971, which was inspired by the life and work of the Georgian primitive painter, Pirosmani, who had already been the subject of a Shengelaya short. This beautiful film about the tragic life of another artist—based on his perception of reality—reaffirmed the importance of the national element and its autonomous artistic perception in the contemporary cinema of the Soviet republics. Shengelaya's film musical about the inhabitants of an old district in Tbilisi, *Melodies of an Old Quarter* (*Melodii Veriyskogo kvartala*–1973), revealed the same characteristics.

Eldar Shengelaya, the director of *Love, Dagger and Treason* (*Neobyk-novennaya vystavka*–1969), remained overshadowed by his brother's work, and has not yet surpassed his own feature debut, *White Caravan*. His charming, typically Georgian crazy tale *Odd People* (*Chudaki*–1974), did, however, win him some international renown.

Internationally, the best-known of the young directors was Otar Yoseliani (b. 1934), another of the "damned" directors of Soviet film. A pupil of Dovzhenko, he made a revealing debut with *Stories about Things* (*Aprel*–1961), a fairy-tale fantasy about things that destroy relationships between people. The film was attacked by the censors, and for several years Yoseliani worked as a laborer and a sailor. He did not return to film work until 1964, with the documentary *Cast Iron* (*Chugun*). In 1967, he finished another feature, *When Leaves Fall* (*Listopad*), which once again gained him some notoriety. A modern, humorous story about a boy who enters an adult world characterized by general apathy, petty fraud, and hypocrisy, it became the object of sharp criticism. In the export version, the film was deformed and muted by means of the customary Russian-language dubbing.

When
Leaves
Fall

In 1970, Yoseliani completed his third film, *There Lived a Singing Blackbird* (*Zhil pevchiy drozd*), about another Georgian youth, his day-to-day life, his encounters with people, and his tragic, unnoticed death. There was still less plot, less intrigue, less scenaristic and cinematic convention in this extraordinary film about a man who considers his relations to other people more important than anything else in his life, than in the already unorthodox and very Georgian *When Leaves Fall*. No wonder that the raw humorous realism and the melancholy of this film offended the censors; it was a long time before it was allowed into Soviet movie theaters.

Another strong talent from Georgia was Mikhail Kobakhidze (b. 1939), the creator of fiction shorts—for example, *The Wedding* (*Svadba*-1964), *The Umbrella* (*Zontik*-1967), and *The Musicians*.

All those, and others, confirmed that the strength of Georgian film is in its concrete detailed view of real human beings and in its irony, humor, and poetic vision, through which its best film-makers have frequently shaken off the conventions prevailing in Soviet cinema.

ARMENIA

Armenian film production tried to take the same path, as is evident from the film *Hello, It's Me* (*Alo, eto ya*-1965), directed by Frunze Dovlatian (b. 1927). An even more interesting film, *Triangle* (*Treugolnik*-1967), the first film of importance directed by Genrikh Malian, connected several in-dependent film episodes through use of locale and narration. And there is of course the unequalled Paradzhanov's *Sayat Nova,* and the popular action films of Edmund Kheosayan, all of which were made in Moscow.

THE ASIAN REPUBLICS

An event of note in the sixties was the appearance of a new generation of film-makers in the Asian Soviet republics, often replacing film conventions with original individual approaches and native story-telling traditions. The first successes of this period were still the work of Russian directors. So following in the steps of Larissa Shepitko, another woman director, Irina Poplavskaya made *Djamila* (1971) in the Kirghiz studio, based on a novella by one of the best contemporary Soviet writers, Chengiz Aitmatov, who in the coming years became the driving force behind Kirghiz film-making. Poplavskaya's next film, *Me, Tan-Shan* (*Ya Tan-Shan*-1973), was inspired by an Aitmatov short story, and his novel, *Farewell Gulsary,* supplied the material for the controversial directorial debut of cameraman Sergei Urusevsky (1908-1975), *The Trotter's Gait* (*Beg inokhodtsa*-1968). (Uru-sevsky completed his second and last film, *Sing Your Song, Poet* (*Poy pyesnyu, poet*-1973), which dealt with the life of Sergei Yesenin, in Moscow.) But in 1966, Bolotbek Shamshiev (b. 1941), who acted in Shepitko's *Heat,* earned a degree of success with his short film *Manashi,* to which he added *The Herdsman* (*Tshaban*) in 1967. In 1969, in the Kirghiz studio, he made his first feature-length film, *The Gunshot in the Mountain Pass* (*Vystrel na perevale*).

Tolomush Okeyev (b. 1934) also began with Shepitko, and also first called attention to himself with a short film, *These Are Horses* (1965). His somewhat sentimental films, *The Sky of Our Childhood* (*Nebo nashego detstva*-1967) and *The Heritage* (*Muras*-1971) are paeans to a rapidly disappearing world. In 1972, he completed *Bow to the Fire* (*Poklonis ognyu*), dealing in a rather unusual way with the period of collectivization. His greatest success was *The Savage One* (*Lyutiy*-1974), a romantic story of a boy's friendship with a wolf, where the revolutionary period serves only as a background for a strong affirmation of native style and vision.

Tenderness

The Uzbek studio's first voice was that of Eliör Ishmukhamedov (b. 1942), in whose multi-episode film *Tenderness* (*Nezhnost*-1966) we find the kind of capacity for a concrete detailed vision avoiding clichés and generalities that we encountered with some Georgian film-makers. This is enhanced by the camerawork of Dilshat Fatkhullin, whose somewhat melancholy sensitivity imaginatively captured what is uniquely Uzbek. The result was already something that could be identified as an Uzbek cinema.

The episodic structure facilitated Ishmukhamedov's debut, but he confirmed what he promised in his first film by the maturity of his second, *In Love* (*Zalubentsy*-1969). Ishmukhamedov's scriptwriter, Odelsha Agishev, and his cameraman, Fatkhullin, also joined forces with director Ali Khamrayev to produce *White, White Storks* (*Belye, belye aisti*-1967), the story of a married woman who deserts her husband for her lover—an extremely controversial theme for Uzbek society.

A new name was that of Ravil Batyrov, who won considerable acclaim for *We'll Be Waiting for You, Lad* (*Zhdyom tebya, paren*-1972), which was written by Konchalovsky.

In Bulat Mansurov (b. 1937), Turkmenfilm found a director who accepted the challenge of creating a tradition, which he successfully did with *Quenching the Thirst* (*Utolenie zhazhdy*-1967), and, particularly, *Takyr the Slave Girl* (*Rabinya*-1969), based on a story by Andrei Platonov. His cameraman, Khodjakuli Narliev (b. 1937), directed *Daughter-in-Law* (*Nevestka*-1972), about a woman who lost her husband in the war, revealing a strong cinematic feeling for local settings. He remained faithful to his interest in female destiny in *When a Woman Saddles a Horse* (*Kogda zhenshchina osedlayet konya*-1973). A Turkmen director of the older generation, Alti Karliev (b. 1909), directed several features, the best of which is the historical film in color, *Makhtumkuli* (1968).

Daughter
in
Law

Kazakhfilm also has its native director, Abdulla Karsakbayev (b. 1940), who made his name with his debut about the vicissitudes in the life of a little boy, *My Name is Kozha* (*Menya zvut Kozhu*-1964), and later made *Journey into Childhood* (*Puteshestvie v detstvo*-1970). And Azerbaidzhan also found its cinematic voice, represented by the brothers, Rustan (scriptwriter) and Maksud Ibragimbekov (director), who displayed their talents in *Blood Revenge.*

EARLY IN THE SEVENTIES

Early in the seventies, a total of about 130 feature fiction films (plus 70 more fiction films for television) were produced annually in all the republics of the Soviet Union, 77 of them in color and 67 of them in cinemascope. Thirteen to fourteen million customers passed through the box offices daily. The 39 film studios employed 300,000 people, over 3,000 of them creative workers. This army of people for the most part turned out films that were undistinguished for their thematic material or artistic qualities. Moreover the management of all the studios was vigilantly on the lookout for anything that was in any way original, experimental, or even slightly unconventional. The hopes and inspirations of the late fifties and the sixties had vanished, and after another Resolution of the Central Committee of the Soviet Communist Party in 1972, "On Measures for the Further Development of Soviet Cinematography," the new chief, F. T. Yermash summarized the tasks for the future:

There are too many grey, formless works in which contemporary and historical themes are worked in a superficial manner, not finding any reflection of a fundamental social change taking place in Soviet society. . . . There are few films about the working class, and the ones that appear are frequently shallow in the manner in which they depict the Soviet people. Persistent thematic planning will enable the creation of films which will center on the positive hero of our time—man, for whom the struggle for the embodiment of the Communist ideal becomes the personal aim of his existence. . . . films like *The Chairman, Nine Days of One Year, Your Contemporary, To Love Man, The Taming of Fire.* . . .

In effect, this was a new authoritative confirmation of the "pedagogic line," complete with the citation of examples that illustrate almost nothing of the best that Soviet cinema produced in the past decade. This new "line" was best represented in 1974 by *The Bonus* (*Premiya*), directed by Sergei Mikaelian (b. 1923), which dramatized in a rather theatrical style, the official party criticism of a well-publicized case of mismanagement.

Nonetheless, the immense growth of production and technology, the emergence of a new generation of film artists, the tenacious search for new paths and possibilities in the republics, the hampered but inevitable contact with international modern film-making, the rising level of film craft and film language—all these factors militated against giving up hope. In the first half of the seventies, Soviet film artists, having all the necessary prerequisites for once again surprising the world, waited to see if they would get a chance to do so.

NOTE: Films produced in the Soviet national republics, using the languages of those republics, are dubbed into Russian for export, and are given titles in Russian. Thus many original titles (and personal names) were not available to us. For practical reasons we reluctantly followed the Soviet practice, but we hope it will soon be discontinued.—*M.L.* and *A.J.L.*

METEORS OR STARS:
Bulgaria after 1964

In the late sixties, after an extended period of cultural dormancy, the first signs of a less authoritarian cultural policy began to appear in Bulgaria. An editorial published January 18, 1968, in *Literaturen Front* called on official critics to stop treating artists the way "governesses treat mentally retarded children." But neither Vulchanov, Zhelyazkova, Ganev, nor Piskov—all truly members of a "lost generation"—could wipe out the 10 wasted years. And by then, there was a new generation vying for the positions of leadership. In 1967, Zhelyazkova's second film, *The Attached Balloon* (*Prevurzanyat balon*-1966) did not even appear in the festival of Bulgarian films in Varna—which gave its award to Radev's inferior espionage film, *Night Without End* (*Nay dulgata nosht*-1966)—nor was it shown in the course of any of the Bulgarian Film Weeks that were being held at that time in many countries. Yet, this film shares with *Iconostasis* (*Iconostassut*-1968) the position of the most interesting Bulgarian film of the late sixties, both of them better than the widely praised *Side Track* (*Malko otklonenie*-1967).

Zhelyazkova's *Balloon,* with a far from orthodox view of the war, pointedly attempted to demystify national heroism, giving it an exceptional significance in a national film industry that built its foundations on antifascist subject matter. Not to mention the fact that it was also the first brutal, and hence quite unfamiliar, treatment of the question of a Bulgarian "national character." The film was based on a novella by Yordan Radichkov, who holds a unique position in Bulgarian literature for his avoidance of sentimentality and bathos, his rich, imaginative vocabulary, and his black humor and surrealist visions. *The Balloon* is a vision too—a fairy-tale vision, a metaphor, revealing the depth of moral degeneration that results from a totalitarian regime. During World War Two a military balloon drifts to earth near a remote rural village in Bulgaria. To the villagers the balloon means dozens of yards of silk for shirts. They organize an expedition to recover it, but they are not alone. The gendarmes are out looking for a woman partisan whose capture will bring them a large reward. When the gendarmes threaten villagers with punishment for stealing military property, they not only turn over the girl, but on the gendarmes' orders shoot her, and in the end, beat each other up with sticks. This curious, tragic, satiric tale was developed by Zhelyazkova through the use of unique local color, once again confirming her mastery of the visual aspects of film narration.

Zhelyazkova's next film, for which she wrote the script herself, did not appear until six years later. Entitled *The Last Word* (*Poslednata duma*-

Night
Without
End

The
Last
Word

1972), it was the story of six women in a death cell, each of whom is connected with the antifascist resistance, and each of whom can save her life by betraying the rest. But after all the years and after such a long silence, the struggle against fascism was no longer the "great" theme for Zhelyazkova. Her film is primarily an anthology of "quotations" from the masters of world cinematography. Many things are exaggerated, however, and on the whole, the film is cool and rational.

Vulchanov was unable to wait like Zhelyazkova. He made whatever films he could, and soon found himself on the periphery of the film world. His *Inspector and the Night* met with no great success, nor did his *The Wolverine* (*Vulchitsa*-1965). In the latter, he tried to depict social problems and their effect on the spiritual attitudes of young people. In the person of the heroine, called Wolverine, he wanted to indict today's world and its dogmas, but he was unable to avoid the pitfalls of schematism and stereotyping. He oversimplifies life in a reformatory and the relationships of Wolverine and her friends to their surroundings, but worst of all he tacks on a falsely optimistic ending, when, after failing in an attempt to escape, Wolverine finally finds a person she can trust—the director of the reformatory.

In 1967, Vulchanov and his cameraman, Kolarov, set out on an ocean voyage with the Bulgarian merchant fleet. In the film that he edited down from all the material shot during the trip, *Between Two Coasts* (*Mezhdu dva bryaga*-1967), we can once again discern the lyrical tones evident in his early films. Between the pictures of the paradoxes of contemporary civilization, there are flashes of the perception of a film poet. But although the situation in Bulgaria was less strict by then, Vulchanov continued to have difficulties. His script for *The Unknown Soldier's Patent Leather Shoes,* stirred up aprehension among the administrators of the Bulgarian film industry. Then Czechoslovakia of 1968 offered a helping hand, and Vulchanov went there that spring. But by early 1969, when he was completing *Aesop,* he was working in a country occupied by the Soviet Army. He conceived the biography of the legendary author of fables as a generalized story of a freedom-loving man and poet, entrapped by powerful men who feel threatened by his democratic thinking, and finally betrayed even by the woman he loved. Although *Aesop* is an interesting film for its atmosphere and for the idea behind it, its style is conventional and it lacks the formal originality of Vulchanov's earlier works. Vulchanov also filmed a psychological drama in Czechoslovakia, *Chance* (*Šance*-1970). The latter, filmed from Vulchanov's own script, is a contemplation of life and death that is presented in a poetic form, real-life locations alternating with dreams and reminiscences. Structurally, it is the story of the man behind the mask, who, after his conscience comes to life, leaps to his death from a window.

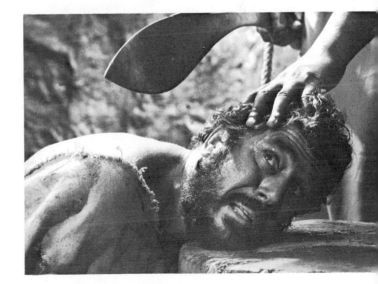

Aesop

In 1971, a new manager was appointed for the Bulgarian film industry. Zhelyazkova and Piskov were once again permitted to work and Vulchanov was named Honored Artist of the Bulgarian People's Republic. Nonetheless, instead of shooting *The Unknown Soldier's Patent Leather Shoes,* he made the musical comedy *Escape to Ropotamo* (*Byagstvo v Ropotamo*-1973).

As for others who created the first authentic works of Bulgarian film, they met with a similar fate. After an interruption of six years, Khristo Piskov and Irina Aktasheva made an autobiographical evocation of revolutionary youth in *Like a Song* (*Kato pesen*-1972), bathetic in its reminder of the disillusionment that followed. *Like a Song*—like *Poor Man's Street*— is a story of young love against the backdrop of historical events. But it lacks both the intimate tenderness of Piskov's first film and its freshness of expression.

Like a Song   Knight Without Armor

CHRONICLES OF SENTIMENTS

In the comebacks after 1970, the names of Khristo Ganev and Valeri Petrov were conspicuous by their absence. They were expelled from the Union of Writers and the Communist Party in 1971 for refusing to condemn Alexander Solzhenitsyn. Petrov's last film script was the scenario for *Man With the Gate.* Borislav Sharaliev directed the film, after Vulchanov was refused permission to work with Petrov. Sharaliev was among the better Bulgarian directors, most of whom had completed their professional education in Prague, Moscow, or Łódź, but whose selection as candidates for the respective film schools was not always made on the basis of talent—which was not true only of Bulgaria. Sharaliev had always been an honest artisan, and his best work unquestionably was the film version of *Man With the Gate*, which was eventually given the title *Knight Without Armor* (*Ritsar bez bronya*-1965). It was a view of social ills through the eyes of a small boy, a depiction of the discrepancies between truth and lies, words and deeds. Later on, Sharaliev remained true to this moralistic tone, which was generally in keeping with Bulgarian traditions. In 1970, he achieved a great box-office success with his film about student life, *So Long, Friends* (*Sbogom, pryatelya*), which criticized outdated pedagogical methods. A year later, his *Indispensable Sinner* (*Neobkhodimyat greshnik*-1971) stimulated widespread discussion on how much trust could be placed in the younger generation.

Knight Without Armor was the first of an important group of films that dealt with the ethics of emotional relationships. The conformist wing of this group is represented by Lyubomir Sharlandzhiev, who at one time initiated discussions on the topic of emotional crisis with his films *There Is No Death* and *Chronicle of Sentiments*. His later films also strove to examine what goes on inside people, and to discover more than a superficial glance can reveal. But to an increasing degree, authenticity in these films gave way to superficiality, which, through stilted cinematic forms, tried unsuccessfully to be modern. In *Crack-Up* (*Karambol*-1966), Sharlandzhiev showed the spiritual crisis of a newspaperman who had to resort to fraud to put across a beneficial project. In *Prosecuting Attorney* (*Prokurorut*-1968), he explored the dilemma of a man who is supposed to sign a warrant for the arrest of a friend he knows to be innocent. In *The Odor of Almonds* (*S duh na bademi*-1967), based on a scenario by the most experienced Bulgarian scriptwriter, Pavel Vezhinov, he presented the love story of three couples, two nonequilateral marital triangles. In later films, such as *The Best Man I Know* (*Naydobriyat chovek, kotogo poznavam*-1973), Sharlandzhiev resorted to sheer moralizing.

The film that did the most systematic job of analyzing an emotional and social crisis was *Side Track*, one of the few Bulgarian motion pictures that did not suffer from a lack of professionality. A love story colored by occasional tones of irony uncommon in Bulgaria, this chamber film possessed a rare elegance. *Side Track* owed much to Antonioni, particularly its languid narrative form, but it was, nonetheless, original in its attitude toward the generation that was raised by the fifties to a uniformity of thought and to intolerance. The main plot takes place in the period of Stalinism that was characterized by frequent meetings and so-called voluntary work brigades, a time when romantic relationships were condemned, classified as relics of the past. The hero and heroine of *Side Track* attempt to create their own version of love, a sort of trial marriage, but the attempt fails. Many years later, they meet again, both of them successful,

Side Track

established specialists, but as for a return, for the rediscovery of lost emotions, it is too late. They are left with a balance sheet showing what was accomplished and what was not, and with thoughts about true and false values.

A young poet, Blaga Dimitrova, wrote the script for *Side Track,* basing it on one of her own short stories. The film was then jointly directed by the experienced stage director Grisha Ostrovski (b. 1918) and by Todor Stoyanov (b. 1930), the cameraman for *Poor Men's Street, Peach Thief, Chronicle of Sentiments,* and others. *Side Track* remained an exception in their careers. Later joint efforts included an adventure comedy, *Five from Moby Dick* (*Petimata ot Moby Dick*-1969), and a multi-episode film on the central motif of marital crisis, *Men on Business Trips* (*Muzhe v komandirovka*-1970), but they were not successful, nor were films that they directed independently.

Metodi Andonov (1932-1974), following the lead of *Side Track,* made a refined adaptation of Raynov's novel, *Journeys into Emptiness,* another of the many period pieces dealing with Stalinism. The film entitled *White Chamber* (*Byalata staya*-1968) was a balance sheet of bitterness, injustice, and wasted life: the hero dies at the moment when his life's work, a book, is finally approved for publication. Andonov, an associate professor at the Theatrical Institute, asserted himself as quickly in film as he had done earlier on the stage. His *Goat Horn* (*Kozyat rog*-1971), a classical story of outlaws, revenge, and blood, an epic drama set during the period of the

Goat
Horn

Turkish occupation, joins *Side Track* as evidence that Bulgarian cinema had achieved a professional level of craftsmanship.

White Chamber nonetheless only skimmed the surface of the complex problems treated most openly in the early seventies in Poland. The same was true for Lyudmil Staykov, (b. 1937), who, in his debut, *Affection* (*Obich*– 1972), treated the story of a young girl's conflict with her parents' generation as a popular theme that was intended to throw light on far broader problems. Staykov made use of his former experience with stage and television, but once again it was the imaginative photography that captured the viewers' interest. There was no comparison, however, between this film and the first films of Vulchanov's generation.

ICONOSTASIS

A work that could stand comparison with the latter was concerned with entirely different thematic material, and appeared literally like a bolt from the blue, like a sudden revelation. It was Todor Dinov's (b. 1919) and Khristo Khristov's (b. 1926) *Iconostasis,* one of the high points of European cinema of the late sixties. In a way a parallel to *Andrei Rublev,* with a

Iconostasis

similar historical perspective and some of the same key motifs, it resounded also with the echoes of Vulchanov's *Aesop*. Social superiors twist and destroy an artist who values freedom above all else. The things that could not be expressed candidly in films about the complex problems of the present, could be expressed by Dinov and Khristov in a story set in nineteenth-century rural Bulgaria, where a work of art is coming to life in the midst of apathy, hatred, backwardness, and prejudice. The beauty of an iconostasis (an altar decorated with icons in the Eastern Orthodox Church), created by Rafe the woodcarver from his own imagination and dreams, remains vital and valid long after those who wanted to destroy it have been fogotten and turned to dust. Inspired by the broad range of Bulgarian folk art, *Iconostasis,* filmed in black and white, is a work with a beautiful multidimensional structure, a work full of intimations and silences, with a vague, merely outlined plot and a wealth of fantasy, unfolding in grandly conceived cinemascope.

Miracle? Coincidence? An unretrievable moment? Perhaps. But there is no question that it came to be because of the efforts of four artists. There was the novel by one of the most incisive Bulgarian storytellers, Dimitur Talev; there was the photography of the experienced cameraman, Anastas Tasev; there was the broadly based artistry of cofounder of the Bulgarian animated film Dinov; and there was the theatrical experience of his co-director, Khristov. After *Iconostasis*, Dinov shot a historical super-production based on a novel by Haytov, *The Dragon* (1974), combining fiction film with animation. Khristov, for his part, made a two-part spectacular about the life of Georgi Dimitrov, *Hammer or Anvil (Nakovalna ili chuk*–1972), followed by the stunning *The Last Summer (Posledno liato*– 1973). His film was mutilated by the censors, who added a "prologue," but like *Iconostasis,* a large part of its strength lay in its use of a daring dramatic metaphor and in a loose narrative structure that blended dreams, memories, and reality. An adaptation of one of Radishkov's works, it told the story of a peasant who violently refuses to be integrated into the modern urban world. It had reverberations that went beyond the first-level meaning of the theme. The same was true of Khristov's next film, *A Tree Without Roots (Durvo bez koren*–1974), which dealt with the generation gap and offered another bitter accounting of the past. Its script was written by Haytov.

Although even after 1965, many films dealt with antifascist themes, these topics, particularly as presented in the works of the older generation, became increasingly dull, unless they were used as a mere pretext for other thematic concerns. In 1966, Nikola Korabov filmed *Permission to Marry (Vula)*, about a marriage that took place in a prison cell shortly before the groom's execution by the fascists. In *Black Angels (Chernite angeli*–1970), Vulo Radev, who was relying more and more on second-rate material, made a rather awkward attempt at psychological portraits of young antifascist fighters.

The Last Summer

On the other hand, Zako Kheskiya (b. 1926) fared better with his well-handled war stories *The Eighth* (*Osmiyat*-1969), *Three Reservists* (*Tri v reserva*-1971), and his two-part *Dawn Over the Drava* (*Zarevo nad Drava*-1972), which was the first Bulgarian war picture to be made as a super-spectacle, a kind of production usually reserved for the heroic epics of past centuries. The most ostentatious displays of the technical capabilities of Bulgarian cinema were to be found in *Shibil* (1968), a bathetic eulogy to a legendary Bulgarian outlaw in the time of Turkish rule that was directed by veteran director Zakhari Zhandov, and in *Prince* (*Knyazut*-1969), which recalled the Russo-Bulgarian alliance in the fight against the Tartars, and was directed by Peter Vasilev (b. 1918).

25TH ANNIVERSARY OF BULGARIAN FILM

In 1969, Bulgarian cinema celebrated the first quarter century of its existence, a period that boasted impressive results. Since 1944, it had made a total of 130 fiction films and over 2,000 documentaries.

Like Yugoslavia—and, in Western Europe, Spain—Bulgaria had begun at that time to welcome producers from the capitalist countries in search of inexpensive Bulgarian technical services, and to rent them the beauties of the countryside for locations. Bulgaria entered into 15 coproductions prior to 1969 that made use of Bulgarian locations, cheap extras, and auxiliary technical manpower. For instance, Austrian director Georg Marischka made a Bulgarian-German-Italian-Spanish-Peruvian coproduction in Bulgaria, *The Last Will of the Incas* (*Zavetut na Inkata*-1966); Liliana Cavani filmed the biography of *Galileo Galilei* (1967); and Carlo

Lizzani made *Gramigna's Mistress* (*Lyubovnitsata na Gramigna*-1968), based on a story by Giovanni Verga.

Traditionally in Bulgarian cinema, coproductions with the Soviet Union had long provided Bulgarian artists and technicians with a chance to learn the fundamentals of film-making. The most ambitious of these coproductions in the latter part of the sixties was a story about one of Lenin's coworkers on a pre-Revolution journal, the Bulgarian, Zagubanski. Entitled *The First Courier* (*Purvyat kurier*-1968), it was directed by Vladimir Yanchev.

A new approach to history, based—as was the case in Poland and Hungary—on evoking an overall atmosphere of oppression and violence, started to prevail in the early seventies in the films of the younger generation, which also tended to do away with moralizing. These new films were surprising in their sense of visual composition, inspired by the sharply contrasting darks and lights of Bulgarian landscapes, and in the degree to which they learned lessons from modern film. Bathetic dialogue and stilted scripts seemed to disappear. Most of the best films continued to be adaptations of works of literature, and there were fewer attempts in Bulgaria than in the other socialist countries to make films *d'auteur*. But the adaptations looked more and more to the work of new, still unestablished writers—Nikola Haytov, for example. These was also a continuation of the close interconnection between film and the stage: at a time when there was no film school in Bulgaria, many film directors came from the Theatrical Institute, alternating stage and screen direction.

In 1970, 10 years after they had been set up in Hungary and 15 years after they had been set up in Poland, three production groups were established in Bulgaria, breaking up the central film administration for the first time.

DYULGEROV, STOYANOV

One of the first products of the reorganized cinema industry was the medium-length *Examination* (*Izpit*-1971), directed by Georgi Dyulgerov (b. 1943), a graduate of vGIK at Moscow. This nineteenth-century story of a young apprentice who must pass an examination to become a master cooper, was made with a keen sensitivity for dramatic detail, which enabled Dyulgerov to develop a minor story into a fine cinematic poem of courage and heroism.

The poetic, almost surrealistic evocation of atmosphere full of flashbacks and visions, and a plot that unfolds in a peripheral way, is characteristic of Dyulgerov's first full-length feature film, the very successful *There Came the Day* (*Doyde denyat*-1973). It tells the stories of members of a partisan unit as seen through the eyes of a 19-year-old youth. On liberation day, he finds himself in command of his friends, his enemies, and those who took no sides. He fails, however, to find the answers to a number of questions, above all to the one that the young director posed through him to his fellow-citizens: "How can you answer others when you are unable to answer yourself?"

Metaphoric vision, going from the concrete, oftentimes poetic and surrealistic, detail to a general statement, was appearing in films with increasing frequency. In 1974, Ivan Nichev (b. 1940) shot as his first feature film *Memory* (*Spomen*), in which the maturing of a young musician is traced out against the backdrop of the period of uncertainty between war and peace. Another member of the young generation to call attention to himself in this sphere was Georgi Stoyanov (b. 1939), a graduate of the IDHEC in Paris. The best story in his multi-episode film, *The Painlevé Case* (*Sluchayat Painlevé*-1968), is the third, a satire about a military officer and his rooster that re-creates with excellent perception the idiotic atmosphere of military life. Mordant irony and a caricatured exaggeration also give bite to his next film, *Birds and Greyhounds* (*Ptitsi i khrutki*-1969), which combines poetic metaphor with powerful visual images. The world of the dogs—policemen, judges, hangmen—intermingles with the world of the birds—students, victims, freedom-loving people. In its ironic expression and abstract transfiguration we find the essence of Stoyanov's—and also Němec's, Jancsó's, and Zhelyazkova's—theme of the unavoidability of violence in oppressive societies.

Fantasy and imagination, as well as good craftsmanship, characterized Stoyanov's first science fiction film, and the first in Bulgaria, *Third From the Sun* (*Tret sled sluntseto*-1972), with a script by Vezhinov. In 1973, Eduard Zakhariev (b. 1938) made the subtle, melancholy, ironical comedy, *Hare Census* (*Prebroyavane na divite zaytsi*). His film about the human passion of judging, pigeon-holing, and classifying was outstanding for its atmosphere of contemporary allusions and intimations that gave color to its allegorical plot.

Bulgarian film did not have—nor could it have, in view of the newness of the Bulgarian state and the nonexistence of a bourgeois Bulgarian culture—a unified thematic line like Polish, Hungarian, or Czechoslovak films have had. A glance at its development shows a certain degree of randomness and heterogeneousness; in the midst of the mediocre, and often less than mediocre, something extraordinary would crop up now and again, but the artist responsible for it rarely remained at the top.

It is at these extraordinary moments during the history of Bulgarian film-making that we can observe the crystallization of a culture that is surprisingly talented in the area of cinema. But in spite of the material conditions created by the nationalization of the film industry, the provincial attitudes and values of the overall cultural atmosphere, which became the object of new debates in the early seventies, kept giving renewed support to the convention of schematism and the mechanism of auto-censorship, hampering the continuous development of the most able talents. Only a change of this situation can light the sky of Bulgarian cinema with stars of greater permanence than an occasional meteor.

FILM AND REASONS OF STATE:
Romania after 1963

Dumitru Radu Popescu, writer, playwright, and scriptwriter, author of one of the first Romanian political problem plays, *Cat Out of the Bag,* the plot of which centers on the return of a political prisoner long thought dead, wrote in mid-1970:

The success to date of Romanian film rests mainly on the fact that it has created and trained a nucleus of actors, artists, scriptwriters, directors, cameramen, etc. The ones who asserted themselves the most strongly were the directors, who represent a true cinematically specific force today. Evidence of their talent, however, is not to be found in entire films, but rather in sections and sequences. With the exception of perhaps Ciulei in *Forest of the Hanged,* Victor Iliu, or Pintilie, our directors have for the most part been working below the level of their capabilities. There is no disputing that we have many talented people, but the films do not fulfill our expectations, or our demands. They are hybrid films, placing a variety of heterogeneous images on the film strip. They do not bear a visual testimony, nor are they the materialization of an idea. Instead, they remain a fog that we try to stuff full of too many things at once, and what happens is that all of them remain suspended, and there is no force to connect them and give them meaning and credibility (*Cinéma,* April 1970, Bucharest).

It would be difficult to describe more accurately the artistic situation in Romanian film 20 years after its inception. Clearly it had all the material prerequisites, but it nonetheless lagged behind the development of the other Eastern European film industries. The situation did begin to improve around 1965 when Romania produced 18 fiction films. The form remained conventional, as did the credibility of the argumentation, but the level of craftsmanship rose, and the thematic assortment became more varied.

It was no coincidence that, in this period, Romanian film turned to the past. During the sixties the leadership of the Romanian state succeeded—by means of adroit and systematic diplomacy and with a sensitivity for what is feasible—in getting Romania out of the Soviet embrace and into an international position that was perhaps the most independent of all the countries in Eastern Europe except Yugoslavia's. After the withdrawal of Soviet troops and the liquidation of the Soviet-Romanian corporations (SOVROM) late in the fifties, Romania took a successful stand in opposition to the integration of the Eastern European economies in the Council for Mutual Economic Assistance, and thus salvaged a large degree of economic independence and sovereignty in connection with her own wealth of raw materials.

The Soviet Union's share in Romanian foreign trade—and thus also the measure of Romanian dependence on the Soviet Union—dropped by one half in the sixties. Romania was no less successful later in opposing the integration of the armies within the Warsaw Pact. Not only did an expansion of economic and political relations with the West follow, but Romania remained the only Warsaw Pact country to maintain friendly relations with China. These relations were to become one of the cornerstones of the success of Romania's policies.

From the beginning of the sixties on, there was an overall emphasis not only on the distant past, but also on the national aspect of contemporary Romanian history, on the "Romanisation of Romanian Communism." Native historians were called upon to revise past views on the history of Romania's liberation from fascism, emphasizing the native resistance movement, the role of Romanian military units in the defeat of fascism, and at the same time pointing out Romania's own traditions in the struggle for socialism. All this had a profound influence on Romanian film, which was given, among other things, the task of helping to erase the complex that resulted from the role that Romania had played in World War Two on the side of Nazi Germany.

In 1963, the Maxim Gorky Institute, the main center for the dissemination of Russian culture, was closed and Russian was dropped as a compulsory second language in Romanian schools, being given equal status with all other languages. At the same time, a campaign was launched for the reintegration of some other "great Romanians" active in other countries. Brancusi's "Infinite Column" was used on a poster celebrating the Romanian national holiday, Ionesco's *The Rhinoceros* was placed on theater repertoires. Of course, Romania was no Yugoslavia. This entire emancipation process was surrounded by ideological orthodoxy, and the whole cultural liberalization was carefully manipulated from above. The cultural intelligentsia that supported the policy of national emancipation, as carried out by the leaders of the Party and the state, generally accepted the rigid ideological discipline for "reasons of state." The type of large open conflict between intellectuals and the establishment that existed elsewhere in Eastern Europe was nonexistent in Romania.

THE DACIANS, THE HAIDUKS, AND OTHERS

The sixties were also a period when well-known film-makers from the West came to Romania, a period that saw the production in Romanian studios of films like *The Struggle for Rome, Tom Sawyer, Mayerlink,* etc. Generally, the Romanian side was represented by Sergiu Nicolaescu (b. 1930), who had worked in film first as an engineer, then as a cameraman, a scriptwriter, a director of short films, and finally as a specialist in super-productions of all sorts. His most significant films were *The Dacians* (*Dacii*-1966) and *Michael the Brave* (*Mihai Viteazul*-1971), both coproductions made with Western firms. *The Dacians* tells of a victory of the Dacians over the Romans in the first century B.C. (The gradual blending of the Dacian and the Roman peoples formed the beginnings of the Romanian nation.) *Michael the Brave* is set in the sixteenth century, when Prince Michael

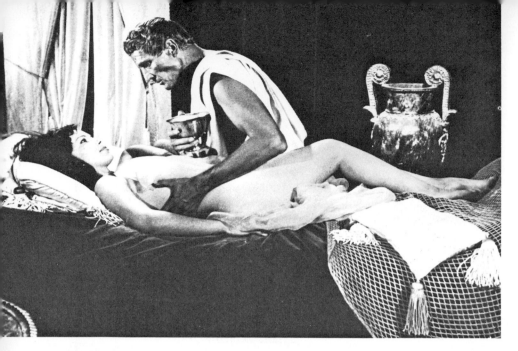

The Dacians

fought for the unity of the Romanian land, which was divided at that time into three kingdoms. He was assassinated in 1601. Nicolaescu's other films, all produced with the aid of foreign capital, technology, and directorial help, included *Adventures in Ontario* (*Aventuri în Ontario*-1968); *The Last of the Mohicans* (*Ultimul Mohican*-1968); and *The Deerslayer* (*Vînătorul de cerbi*-1969).

The pathos of *The Dacians* and *Michael the Brave* was so moving for the Romanian audience and the films' naïveté so sincere that their success became something of a sociological phenomenon. Even the critics were indulgent, primarily because they felt that these films would inspire the masses of film-goers to stop and think about problems of national independence and pride.

The Dacians was followed by an entire series of swashbuckling cloak-and-sword romances, the most popular of which was *The Haiduks* (*Haiducii* -1965) and its five sequels, *The Revenge of the Haiduks* (*Răzbunarea haiducilor*-1968), *The Haiduks of Captain Anghel* (*Haiducii lui Şaptecai*-1970), etc. The Haiduks were outlaws, the Robin Hoods of the Carpathian

The
Revenge
of the
Haiduks

mountains. The films were directed—though weakly—by Dinu Cocea (b. 1929); the scripts, however, were skillfully written works by the well-known writer, Eugene Barbu. These films are filled with musketeers, dressed in the tight-fitting leggings of Romanian peasants, who take from the rich and give to the poor, strike terror in the hearts of tyrants, and are welcomed as heroes by lovely maidens, until they finally withdraw to the forests and hills, leaving behind an abundance of legends and women's tears, and the saying, "Let come what will, as long as we live on."

FOREST OF THE HANGED

The mid-sixties gave birth to a number of dramas in which history, or better said, a given historical moment, was the framework for an individual tragedy. The individual did not succumb to the superior strength of the attackers—such as the Haiduks—but rather to the power of oppressive regimes. The conflict was born of the individual's refusal to accept his historical fate. One of these, a sequel to *Lupeni 29*, was *Golgotha* (*Golgota*-1967), directed by Drăgan. It was the story of the six widows of workers killed in the 1929 strike on the Jiu River. Two other noteworthy films of this type were also produced. One was *Blazing Winter* (*Răscoala*-1965), based on the novel by Liviu Rebreanu, an important Romanian novel of the period between the wars. It tells the story of the peasant uprising in 1907, in which 11,000 people were killed. Director Mircea Mureşan (b. 1928) had already demonstrated his interest in individual destinies at moments of historical crisis in his first medium-length film, *Your Share of the Responsibility* (*Partea de ta vină*-1962). In the figure of the leader of the 1907 revolt, he created an opponent of the historical system who "simply cannot go on." The hero of the second film in this category, *Forest of the*

(Left) Blazing Winter

(Below) Your Share of the Responsibility

Hanged (*Pădurea spînzuraţilor*–1964), directed by Ciulei, was similar. During World War One, he refuses to fight his fellow citizens, and pays with his life for wanting to write his own version of history. *Blazing Winter* and *Forest of the Hanged* were the first international successes of Romanian fiction film.

A NEW FACE FOR OLD TOPICS

Films referring back to recent or distant history were for the most part simply a series of scenes illustrating heroism: the heroism of Communists in the resistance movement, the heroism of Romanian soldiers in the fight against fascism, the heroism of the working class, which was led to victory by the Romanian Communist Party. Many of these living tableaux were outdated by the time the films had their premiere showings. Others differed from similar films of earlier years, as they used to say in Romania, simply in the fact that instead of resolving problems to the beat of a military march they did it to the beat of the cha-cha-cha. Among these films were *The District of Gaiety* (*Cartierul veseliei*–1964), directed by Marcus; *Sky Without Bars* (*Cerul n-are gratii*–1962) directed by Francisc Munteanu (b. 1924); and *Tunnel* (*Tunelul*–1966), a Romanian-Soviet coproduction directed by Munteanu. But as antifascism and the resistance movement became the dominant thematic current, an opportunity was created for a certain differentiation of style. For example, in *White Trial* (*Procesul alb*–1965) Mihu and Barbu tried to present the struggle against fascism in the form of a chamber piece.

White
Trial

By the middle of the sixties, Romanian film had enough directors, but it still lacked the director-writer teams and director-cameraman teams who can be so important for smooth artistic development. At that time about

15 fiction films, 25 animated cartoons, 76 newsreels, and 150 documentaries were produced each year. There were so many directors, however, that only a few of them were able to work regularly. At the time when elsewhere in Eastern Europe film-makers were focusing their attention on how the events since 1940 had formed national character or on life in a socialist society, Romanian film was using the present merely as a backdrop for stereotyped primitive comedies and mysteries.

It was not until the latter half of the sixties that a nonschematic perception of the world and the new society led to the introduction of contemporary topics and attitudes, although the bounds of political and esthetic conventions still were closely followed. Films were still made about new construction programs, but the construction plans did not fall into place quite as smoothly as building blocks; the party secretary relinquished the halo of the angel of salvation; and enthusiasm on the job did not always lead to medals; as a matter of fact, it frequently brought with it conflicts on the job and in personal life. An example of this new kind of film is *Underground* (*Subteranul*-1967), directed by Virgil Calotescu (b. 1928), originally a documentarist who made his debut in fiction film in 1965 with *White Ward* (*Camera alba*), a film on a similar theme. The young people portrayed in these films had lost much of their enthusiasm, and often did not know how to go on, as in Andrei Blaier's (b. 1933) *The Mornings of a Sensible Youth* (*Diminețile unui băiat cuminte*-1966).

Films about emotional crises and family dramas began to appear—e.g., *Meanders* (*Meandre*-1966), directed by Mircea Săucan (b. 1928). Women started to demand true equality, even though it frequently meant solitude and misunderstanding, as in *Gioconda Without That Smile* (*Gioconda fără surîs*-1967), directed by woman director Malvina Urșianu (b. 1927). The village was no longer divided between the good guys and the bad guys, failures could not be attributed solely to the evil kulaks, and Romanian peasants once again found that fate brought them their loves, their revenges, and their passionate devotion to the soil—e.g., *Virgo* (*Zodia fecioarei*-1966), directed by Marcus.

LUCIAN PINTILIE AND RECONSTRUCTION

But what was still lacking was an individual viewpoint, a creative person who would speak out in his own fashion, stating his own opinion. And then Lucian Pintilie (b. 1933) arrived on the scene. He found his first inspiration for authentic expression in wartime subject matter; it seemed that Romanian film finally had a director of international status. His *Sunday at Six* (*Duminică la ora 6*-1965), which was skilfully shot by the young cameraman, Sergiu Huzum, told the story of the resistance according to the rules of intimate conflict—vaguely reminiscent of Resnais' "films of memory." It was characterized by pathos but completely lacked the usual clichés. The period and the characters, artfully developed by scriptwriter Ion Mihăileanu,

are honestly analyzed by a team of film-makers who wanted to state everything in all lucidity.

The best film to emerge from Romania during the sixties, indeed one of the pinnacles of European cinema during that decade, was Pintilie's *Reconstruction (Reconstituirea*-1969). Pintilie came to film from the theater, where he successfully produced Shaw, Frisch, Dürrenmatt, and, of course, Caragiale. *Reconstruction* is admirably structured on the basis of the unity of place, time, and plot. The director has called it a tragedy, but it might be better described as tragic confusion strongly colored by elements of black humor in the tradition of Gogol and Swift. It is the story of collective irresponsibility, an allegory about cowardice and indifference reminiscent of the work of Czech director Evald Schorm and others, an allegory absolutely uncompromising in its moral criticism. A tavern with a terrace stands by a river in a musty countryside. The camera shows the surroundings from various viewpoints, and then, in long static shots and slow panoramatic sweeps, focuses with equal disinterest on the characters. It remains disinterested throughout. Two students had caused a row in the tavern, wounding a waiter. Now they are supposed to reconstruct the incident before an investigating judge, and also before a film camera. The judge is a dullard, perspiring, drinking, obviously not in the least interested. The students' professor understands it all, but in the end he also falls into drunken apathy. The local constable is anxious to please with a feverish obsequiousness, as is the servile waiter and the cameraman, who is supposed to be shooting an educational film about the boys' bad example. The youths finally accept the conditions of their judges, who keep encouraging them to be more "realistic." They reconstruct the scene of the fracas and the fist-fight, egged on by the organizers, and in the process one of the students is killed. An indifferent, frustrated, noisy crowd—which, invisible, provides the sound background for the film's action—emerges from a nearby soccer stadium. While passing the second youth, weeping over the dead body of his friend, the crowd becomes clearly aggressive and hostile, scorning the boy and accusing

Recon-
struction

him of drunkenness. On the other hand, the same people are only too happy to push the judge's car out of the mud, in a sort of visual apotheosis of power, law, and order.

Reconstruction, which evoked passionate arguments, was not released until a year after its completion. "The subject is atypical of real life in Romania, and the film shows evidence of Western influences." That summarizes the decision of official critics. In 1972, Pintilie made a comeback and staged Gogol's *Inspector General* at the Bulandra Theater in Bucharest. Its manager, Liviu Ciulei, gave him a completely free hand, but after only a few performances, the production, which had become an artistic event, was closed down. The main complaint: "The play was staged as if it were a contemporary story." Ciulei was dismissed as the theater's manager and Pintilie went to work abroad.

Nicolae Breban (b. 1934) also emerged as a strong personality, though not so strong as Pintilie. A successful author, Breban had written the script for *A Woman for One Season* (*O femeie pentru un anotimp*–1969), which centered on the emotional crisis of a young physician. This film, a big box-office success and referred to as the Romanian *A Man and a Woman,*

A Woman
for
One Season

had been directed by Breban's contemporary, Gheorghe Vitanidis (b. 1929), one of the most adroit craftsmen among the new directors. In 1971, Breban evoked critical controversy with his directorial debut, *Sick Animals* (*Animale bolnave*). Made in an original style, though marked with all the awkwardness of a first effort, the film was a psychological analysis of character and of the ethical aspects of society within the framework of an investigation of three mysterious murders.

A CLASH

The triumph of Lucian Pintilie was part of a current that was new in Romanian postwar culture, and one that apparently was a harbinger of the future. In the second half of the sixties, a third generation appeared on the film scene in Romania that was to do the job done elsewhere by the previous generation, the job of demanding from the system the trust that they would not misuse the freedom they were asking for, and the credit for supporting Romanian socialism. Thus emerged the surprising poetry of the late sixties, followed by drama, prose, and art, and along with them, Pintilie's *Reconstruction*. It seemed for a moment that there would be a breakthrough as there had been in Yugoslavia, Hungary, Czechoslovakia, and Poland. But the blow came in the spring of 1971, in the form of a special meeting of party activists in the field of ideology, and more particularly in the form of a speech delivered at that meeting by the First Secretary of the Romanian Communist Party, Nicolae Ceaucescu, a speech that was severely critical of the intelligentsia and creative artists and aroused an unexpectedly strong wave of dissent. The party's hard line—apparently motivated by fears of an adverse reaction from the Soviet Union to increased freedoms in the sphere of culture, but undoubtedly also by Ceaucescu's own overt anti-intellectualism and his genuine admiration for some of the policies of People's China—had to be revised later the same year. Early in the seventies, the first symptoms of a revised relationship between Romanian politics and Romanian culture began to be apparent. Socialist realism of a Romanian kind was still encouraged by the authorities, but the tough stand with regard to the content of art was accompanied by a certain degree of increased tolerance toward experimentation in the area of form. And at the same time, the officially proclaimed campaign against corruption brought about the first Romanian "political" film.

ATTEMPTS AT NEW FORMS AND AT POLITICS

What had Romanian cinema become in the early seventies? On one hand, there were directors like Drăgan or Nicolaescu filming such craftsmanlike comedies and mysteries for the domestic market as the mystery series *The Brigade Steps In* (*Brigad diverse in alerte*-1970-1972), *With Clean Hands* (*Cu mîinile curate*-1972), and *The Last Cartridge* (*Ultimul cartus*-1973).

There were also people like Elisabeta Bostan (b. 1931), who continued working in specialized fields—in Bostan's case, films for children: *Veronica* (1972) and *Return of Veronica* (*Veronica se întoarce*-1973). On the other hand, there were the scattered attempts of the few directors who tried to find some kind of artistic liberty in the strictly delimited field of "allowed" subjects. Urșianu strove to capture new psychological undertones of familiar themes, for example, *Party* (*Serata*-1971), a symbolic gathering on the anniversary of the antifascist uprising in 1944, or *Transient Loves* (*Trecătoarele iubiri*-1974), a simplified picture of the problems of contemporary women. Muresan shot two undistinguished films on antifascist themes—*Siege* (*Asediul*-1971) and *Barrier* (*Bariera*-1972). Two new interesting directors emerged, both graduates of the Bucharest Film and Theater Academy: Dan Pița (b. 1938) and Mircea Veroiu (b. 1941), whose first film *Stone Wedding* (*Nuntă de piatră*-1973) brought them into the category of young film-makers seeking a way out into the world by means of an, at times, eclectic estheticism.

Another example of a film that strove for a renaissance of content by means of a renaissance of form was *The Canary and the Storm* (*Canarul*

Stone Wedding

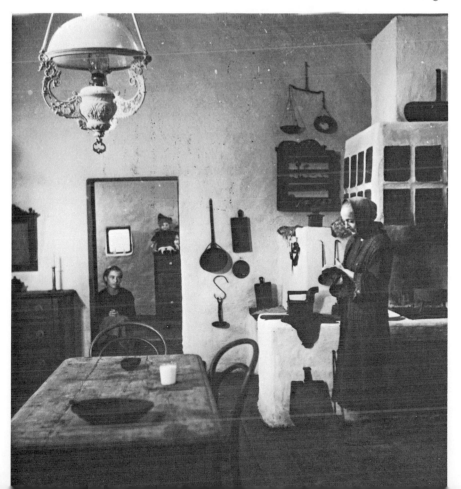

și viscolul-1970). The director, Marcus, however, selected shots primarily for their visual effects on the viewer, thus interfering with the integrity of the narration and the appeal of the story itself, that of a young boy who tries to make contact with the resistance movement but perishes in a snowstorm. Two years later, Marcus was entrusted with a political task: to film parts of the biography of Romania's leader N. Ceaucescu. *The Power and the Truth* (*Puterea si adevărul*-1972) told the story of regional political functionaries and gave the director and his scriptwriter Titus Popovici an opportunity to reveal some of the power structure of the new society.

Artists who emerged in the early seventies in literature (Paul Goma, Dumitru Tsepeneag, etc.), as well as in other fields, were given the choice of either cutting themselves down to the size of what surrounded them or seeing their work mutilated. In the field of film, a good example was Radu Gabrea (b. 1937). He attracted international attention with his first film, *Too Small for Such a Big War* (*Prea mic pentru un război atît de mare*-1970), the visual language of which was clearly drawn from the same folkloristic sources that inspired his Bulgarian (Dyulgerov, Khristov), Soviet (Paradjanov), and Slovak (Jakubisko) contemporaries. Continuing along these lines, his third film, *Beyond the Sands* (*Dincolo de nisipuri*-1973), followed the story of its anarchist hero through several decades of Romanian modern history in a way that clearly made it the most important Romanian film of the first half of the seventies. But the film displeased the authorities: the hero had to be made a Communist, the film got a cheap political ending, and Gabrea left Romania.

In the first half of the seventies, the Romanian film industry decentralized its production. The production of fiction films was split into five groups, which made a total of 25 films annually. In addition, the Buftea Studios were completed and the number of movie theaters and movie-goers greatly increased. The flow of foreign producers and directors to the film city in Bucharest grew stronger, even though the best coproduction to be made in Romania remained René Clair's 1965 film, *Fêtes galantes,* with Gheorghe Vitanidis representing Romania on the film's crew.

After a quarter of a century, Romanian film had not only material resources but also the artistic ones to begin to form its own variant on the schools, waves and currents that had characterized the film industries of its neighbors during the sixties.

BEYOND THE WALL: German Democratic Republic after 1964

On January 23, 1966, the East German daily, *Neues Deutschland,* published a letter from Walter Ulbricht to Kurt Maetzig, criticizing his film, *The Rabbit Is Me (Das Kaninchen bin ich*-1965). Although other Communist Party or government heads had set cultural policy, it was highly unusual for such a figure to concern himself so specifically with film. The letter, which filled an entire page, said in part:

Our writers and artists have absolute freedom to create anything that benefits our state and society. But any demand for a freedom the results of which would be aimed against our state, our Party, should be contrary to their morality. . . . The standpoint of progressive film artists is all the more worthy of respect, the more consistently they laud the first German state of workers and farmers, supporting their approval with talented socialist works of art, arousing profound, noble, and fertile thoughts in the viewers. . . . In order for similar works to originate in all branches of our socialist culture, writers and artists must unite around the Party, they must fight hard and unceasingly against ideological diversion, against the poison of scepticism and the negation of heroism and great emotions. Thus: freedom to all that benefits our state, but no freedom to ideological conspiracy with the enemies of socialism, no freedom for the sullying of our state!"

RABBIT FILMS

Ulbricht's letter followed the Eleventh Plenary Session of the Central Committee of the SED, which once again—this time very firmly—had stood up in opposition to deviations from the party's ideological orthodoxy. A new critique was presented of Robert Havemann, who had been thrown out of the Humboldt University in Berlin. The pretext for the attack was his article "Argument for a New German CP," which was published in the West German newsweekly *Spiegel.* Furthermore, popular poet and songwriter Wolf Biermann, accused of "ultra-leftist deviation," was prohibited from all publication, as was writer Stefan Heym, who had returned to the GDR from his wartime exile in the United States, and now found himself being pilloried as a result of his demand for autonomous artistic development.

In cinema, the attack was concentrated on one hand on the quarterly, *Film-wissenschaftliche Mitteilungen,* a publication of the East Berlin Film Institute. In its poll on the state of East German cinema, sentiments were voiced that had echoes in other Eastern European countries—primarily in Czechoslovakia—voices that called for a more liberal cultural policy. On the other hand, the Plenary Session criticized a number of new films that ostensibly "sullied the first German state of workers and farmers." None of them found its way into the movie theaters, and all that was left of DEFA's 1965-1966 production was a pile of rubble.

The "rabbit films" as they were aptly referred to, were not great works of art, and their criticisms of some social phenomena were in fact quite tame. But they did seek new forms and state unpleasant facts. They were intended to be "films for adults," as Maetzig declared, films that would lead DEFA's production out of the "vicious circle of conventions" and "fictitious ideas of reality." Their model was Czechoslovak cinema, their German forerunners were the "socialist romances" of the early sixties. The rabbit films differed from the romances in their more active emphasis on socialist contexts. And, what is more important, they were all the work of representative East German artists. Maetzig's *The Rabbit Is Me* was an adaptation of a novel—never published in the GDR—by one of the stars of "the GDR's own literature," Manfred Bieler, who left for Czechoslovakia after the Eleventh Plenary Session, and, in 1968, moved to West Germany. The heroine of the film is a girl who is kept by political circumstances from completing her studies, but the main plot focuses on the character of a young lawyer and his opportunistic career in jurisprudence.

Günther Stahnke, originally a film journalist and then a television and opera director, also made a first feature film that was concerned with social justice. The film, *Spring Needs Time (Der Frühling braucht Zeit)* was reminiscent in subject matter to Czechoslovakia's *Defendant,* directed by Klos and Kadár: an engineer tries to improve work methods, finds himself at odds with the plant management, and under the management's pressure, is arrested and tried. The coauthor of the script was Konrad Schwalbe, head of the Film Academy.

Just Don't Think I'm Crying (Denk bloss nicht, ich heule) was described by the SED's chief ideologist Kurt Hager as being "in keeping with the theory about the alienation of the individual in socialist society, disclosing the influence of Franz Kafka." This film about a student expelled from school and forced to work in an agricultural cooperative was made by the same writer-director team that created *Julia Lives,* director Frank Vogel and scriptwriters Manfred Freitag and Joachim Nestler.

Another film to appear on the index of the banned was Egon Günther's new film, *When You Grow Up, Dear Adam (Wenn du gross bist, lieber Adam)*—something of a parallel to Czechoslovakia's *Cassandra Cat,* directed by Jasný—in which the light of a little boy's lamp discloses hypocrites and frauds.

Two debuts that were awaited with great interest also did not find their way to movie screens. One was *Miss Butterfly (Fräulein Schmetterling),* written by Christa Wolf and directed by Kurt Barthel, former assistant director fo K. Wolf. The second was *Karla,* based on a script by one of the outstanding young talents in East German theater, Ulrich Plenzdorf, and directed by Herrmann Zschoche. *Miss Butterfly* was the first East German film to use the method of cinéma vérité, referred to by East German ideologists as an expression of "unscientific bourgeois objectivism." Both *Miss Butterfly* and *Karla* dealt with the life of young people and their conflicts

with the life around them, conflicts more emotional than political. "I've lived here all my life," says the young hero of *Just Don't Think I'm Crying,* "and here, there is socialism. How is it that I'm not one, too?"

After three days, Frank Beyer's *Track of Stones (Spur der Steine)* was withdrawn from the movie theater where it had opened, in spite of the fact that it had been presented on the occasion of the twentieth anniversary of the founding of the SED, and in spite of the fact that—as compared to its literary source—its cutting edge had been considerably dulled. The novel of the same title by Erik Neutsch became a best-seller primarily because it removed the myths surrounding so-called "heroes of socialist labor." One of the things that Beyer's film did was to smooth out the character of the party secretary who, in the novel, emerges as a careerist and a hypocrite. Even after this change, the film was still accused of "distorting the image of our socialist reality, the struggle of our working class, its great Party, and the devoted efforts of its members" (*Neues Deutschland,* July 6, 1966).

Together with the other rabbit films, it followed *Sun Seekers* into the censor's vaults. Frank Beyer turned to TV production and tried to start a new career. In 1975, his *Jacob the Liar (Jakob der Lügner)* brought him again into the spotlight. Because of its subject (a poetic tale of life in a Jewish ghetto during the Nazi era) the film was turned down by the Moscow festival and eventually became the first East German entry ever to compete at the West Berlin International Film Festival.

WESTERNS

Not much was left, then, of the DEFA production of 1965–1966, and the years that followed did not bring about any improvement. There was the undistinguished film about Karl Liebknecht *As Long As I Live (Solange Leben in mir ist*-1965), directed by Günther Reisch; there was the sensitive story for youngsters by Heiner Carow, *The Trip to Sundevit* (*Die Reise nach Sundevit*-1966); there was Ralf Kirsten's successful comedy, *Follow Me, Mob!* (*Mir nach Canaillen!*-1966); and then there were westerns, which came in a flood after the first one, the simple-minded *Sons of the Great Bear* (*Die Söhne der grossen Bärin*-1965), directed by the Czech director Josef Mach. The sequels were *Clue of the Falcon* (*Spur des Falken*-1968), *White Wolves* (*Weisse Wölfe*-1969), *Fatal Error* (*Tödlicher Irrtum*-1969), *Oscoela* (1971), and many others.

Clue
of the
Falcon

Even more than had been the case in the past, cheap entertainment, most of it imported from West Germany, took over the film screens. The best works of other Eastern European directors were as systematically concealed from GDR viewers as were the rabbit films. In 1965, Maetzig, as well as Beyer and Vogel, admitted responsibility for all the errors of their rabbit films. But Maetzig also wrote, almost 20 years after the GDR had initiated a systematic educational effort vis-à-vis the film viewer: "The development of our film-goer's taste disturbs and frightens me. I don't mean only his reaction to westerns, but also his aversion to all serious subjects, typical of the large majority of our audience. I say quite openly that the relationship

Farewell

I Was
Nineteen

between the audience and ourselves is abnormal" (*Filmspiegel,* East Berlin, October 4, 1967).

After the experiences of 1966, it was a long time before anyone dared even approach contemporary subject matter; the only place that the present appeared, even as a backdrop, was in mysteries or musical comedies. Egon Günther wrote a script based on Johannes Becher's autobiographical novel in a form that was reminiscent of *The Kaiser's Lackey,* and from it made the film *Farewell* (*Abschied*-1968), a broad picture of imperial Germany against which was placed the revolt of a young boy—the son of a "good family"—against his environment, himself, the people he likes, and the people he dislikes. Joachim Kunert adapted Anna Seghers' novel, *The Dead Stay Young* (*Die Toten bleiben jung*-1967), which takes place at the end of World War One, and, for the anniversary of the Russian Revolution, Maetzig made *The Flag at Krivoy Rog* (*Die Fahne von Krivoy Rog*-1967), which was another of Maetzig's portrayals of workers' struggles.

Only Konrad Wolf made one of his best films in that period, the story of a young German who returns to Germany with the Red Army at the end of World War Two, after years in exile. *I Was Nineteen* (*Ich war neunzehn*-1967) is an autobiographical testimony, filmed with a feeling for the atmosphere of a vanquished land and for the psychology of the German youth who arrives there side by side with the victors. Wolf's next film, which also used historical events for its source material, was the realization of Wolf's long-standing intention to film a parable of the artist's destiny within society. His *Goya* (1970), which was given a maximum of technical and financial support by the two coproducing countries—the Soviet Union and the GDR—aimed at a synthesis of three values that DEFA films had until then been in vain trying to achieve: artistic quality, recognition abroad, and box-office success. It turned out to be rather academic and missed what Wolf personally had long been trying to put on film: a philosophical expression of the artist's "bitter road in search of knowledge," in the words of the subtitle of the novel by Lion Feuchtwanger on which the film was based.

DOCUMENTARY REALISM

The first attempts to somehow revive the films called "socialist romances" were very timid, and an optimistic note continued to dominate them from the opening to the closing scenes. But something did change beginning in 1968. Finally even the GDR permitted experimentation in the area of form and relinquished some of its puritanism. (In 1965, proponents of this old puritanism had created a huge flap surrounding the cover photo on the weekly *Filmspiegel* [No. 23], showing the half-undressed heroine of Czechoslovak director Miloš Forman's film, *Loves of a Blonde.*) In 1969, the most representative films produced by DEFA were *Dr. Med. Sommer II,* directed by Lothar Warneke (b. 1936); *In the Field of Tension (Im Spannungsfeld),* directed by Siegfried Kuhn (b. 1936); and *Network (Netzwerk),* directed by Ralf Kirsten. All of them were based on the method of documentary realism as formulated by L. Warneke in his graduation paper at the Babelsberg Film Academy entitled "Documentary Fiction Film" (1964). A kind of belated and incomplete attempt at combining cinéma vérité and neorealism, documentary realism attempted to capture at least a slice of life, by seeking inspiration in the unembellished work environment. These "socialist human portraits," which also include Frank Vogel's *Seventh Year (Das siebente Jahr*–1968), were above all stories of people caught at moments of individual crisis while in their work environments, the process of labor being understood as the catalyst of all their personal conflicts.

Seventh
Year

FILM UNDER ERICH HONECKER

In 1971, when the danger of ideological infection from Czechoslovakia had been definitely wiped out, and Erich Honecker had replaced Walter Ulbricht, DEFA's production was able to return to socialist romances and to depict more than just emotional crises and personal problems.

At that time, the focus of ideological policy, which determined every detail as well as the principal propagandistic aims of "socialist contemporary films," shifted its attention even more in the direction of television, which was above all concerned with the task of competing with West German television, easily received on East German sets. Thus film-makers had a bit more breathing space for carrying out challenging work. Nonetheless, the Babelsberg studios did not turn out anything that could be distinguished from its old tried-and-true products. New East German films were the sometimes more, sometimes less standardized products of a heavy-handed enterprise that had at least technically fallen in step with world development and improved the surface appearance of its creations. The precisely pigeon-holed organization—patterned after the old UFA—eliminated all possibility of a truly spontaneous expression of creative force, sudden élan, imagination, or a desire for experimentation. Since the beginning of the fifties, DEFA did not release a single film that was not the result of carefully supervised preparations and precise ideological dosages; not a single "artistic miracle" took place, no "revelation," no "pinnacles" of the sort that we witnessed in every other country in Eastern Europe. Thus the Wolf-Vulchanov *Stars* remained the most independent and individualistic DEFA film.

East Germany's cinematic 'miracle," which had been talked about prematurely in Western Europe in the early seventies, was just as doubtful a miracle as the GDR's even more frequently cited economic miracle. What was miraculous was that East German films that had relinquished the "fictitious images of reality" for the first time found their way to international festivals, although they certainly were no more profound than the unfortunate rabbit films; in fact, they were made in their image, though using, of course, all the technical facilities available to modern film craftsmen.

If any creative "miracle" took place at all, it was in the theater. In 1972, Ulrich Plenzdorf, one of the creators of the rabbit films, wrote an adroit drama entitled *The New Suffering of Young W.,* whose 17-year-old hero repeated with all emphasis the reflective question of the hero of *Just Don't Think I'm Crying* ("I've lived here all my life, and here, there is socialism. How is it that I'm not one, too?") After making a catastrophic balance sheet of his confused life, he electrocutes himself—"370 volts doesn't hurt a bit, folks." It was indeed a small miracle that Plenzdorf's drama was allowed to play to full houses, not just in East but in West Germany also. It was a miracle that books by East German authors (unpublished in the GDR) could be published in West Germany, with no penalty to their authors; that Christa Wolf was able to publish her nostalgic autobiographical meditations *The Quest for Christa T.* ; that the East German Egon Günther shot the first coproduction between the two Germanies, the rather academic transcription of Thomas Mann's novel *Lotte in Weimar* (1975) with the West German actress Lili Palmer in the leading role and Jutta Hoffmann, East German star number one, as a supporting character; that Konrad Wolf in his *Naked*

Man in the Playing Field (*Der nackte Mann auf dem Sportplatz*-1974) was able, without matching the achievement of *I Was Nineteen,* to express his faith that one day a more tolerant attitude toward the integrity of art and the artist's conscience would develop in the GDR; and that, after 15 years, the *Sun Seekers* was shown on television, and later in the movie theaters.

The Naked Man in the   The Third One
Playing Field

In 1973, when night after night on an East Berlin stage an actor declaimed: "This is the dullest country in the world!" in the play *Kippers* by Volker Braun, the country in question being the GDR, several new DEFA films were being shown with enormous success in movie houses. They did not include Günther Reisch's new Liebknechtian film *In Spite of It All* (*Trotz alledem*-1971), nor his film on Lenin, *On the Way to Lenin* (*Unterwegs zu Lenin*-1970); nor any of the fancy coproductions with the countries of Eastern Europe—for example, the science-fiction film *Icaros Signals* (*Ikaros Signale, Ein Weltraumabenteuer*-1970). They did, however, include, most especially, *The Third One* (*Der Dritte*-1971), in which Egon Günther once again treated a feminist issue, which he first approached 10 years earlier in *Lot's Weib,* and also *The Legend of Paul and Paula* (*Die Legende von Paul und Paula*-1972). Both films have as their focal point young, independent women who carry the burden of providing for and caring for their children; one, two, three men pass through their lives, and with them, solitude and lack of understanding. Whereas *The Third One* concentrated on the heroine's conflicts with the superficial surroundings embodied by the characters of husbands and lovers, Ulrich Plenzdorf centered the script of his *Legend of Paul and Paula*, directed by Heiner Carow, on the social differences between a young couple (a salesgirl and a ministerial official), using Paul's stale marriage as a pretext to describe the spiritual void of a "socialist consumer society."

Legend
of Paul
and
Paula

These new visions of the still canonized East German reality were the sole miracle of DEFA's production in the early seventies. To the above-mentioned films, should be added the sentimental love story, *Time of the Storks* (*Zeit der Störche*–1970), directed by Siegfried Kühn; L. Werneke's new films on the lives of young scientists, *It Is an Old Story* (*Es ist eine alte*

Geschichte-1972) and *Life with Uwe* (*Leben mit Uwe*-1973); and the last film of Gerhard Klein, who died unexpectedly in 1970, a mystery with the well-presented atmosphere of postwar Berlin, *The Zernik Affair* (*Leichensache Zernik*-1970).

WHY, YOU HAVEN'T CHANGED A BIT!

This limited miracle was not a prelude to a real change. Soon, the conventional narrative prevailed and attempts to modernize the language stopped at the brink of real innovation. Costly biographies in the old UFA style continued to be the backbone of production. Franz Vogel, for example, filmed the life of seventeenth-century astronomer Johannes Kepler in *Clean Up the Light of Common Sense* (*Putzt das Licht der Vernunft*-1975). Bernard Stephan (b. 1943), whose debut, *Too Skinny for Love?* (*Für die Liebe noch zu mager?*-1973), was rather successful with teenage audiences, centered on the childhood of the Communist leader Ernst Thaelmann in *My Childhood* (*Aus meiner Kindheit*-1975). More interesting was Günther Reisch's portrait of a romantic revolutionary *Wolz* (1975), but Reisch unfortunately was unable to refrain from preaching about the predominance of Communism over anarchism.

In the field of pure entertainment, Horst Bonnet continued another long-adopted UFA tradition, the one of lavish operettas, by filming Offenbach's *Orfeus in the Underworld* (*Orpheus in der Unterwelt*-1975). More serious classics also remained highly rated. Siegfried Kühn attempted to bring to the screen Goethe's masterpiece *Elective Affinities* (*Wahlverwandtschaften*-1975). This ambitious attempt at a modern "verbal" film failed, however, for it was unable to overcome the traditional bias for an academic approach to a classical subject. Kühn's greatest success up to then remained the satirical comedy, *The Second Life of Friedrich Wilhelm Georg Platow* (*Das zweite Leben des Friedrich Wilhelm Georg Platow*-1973). Kühn, together with the scriptwriter Helmut Baierl, employed tongue-in-cheek irony to tell the story of an old railway worker who takes his son's place at his qualification test, and who, as the advertising for the film says, "contrary to all his life experience, at the age of 57, discovers life." The film program used as its motto a quotation from Brecht's *Story of Mr. K.*: "A man who hadn't seen Mr. K. for a long time, greeted him with the words, 'Why, you haven't changed a bit.' 'Oh!' said Mr. K. and turned pale."

SILENCE AND CRY:
Poland after 1963

In the middle of the sixties, the Polish film industry appeared to be on the periphery of Eastern European film. The title of Janusz Morgenstern's (b. 1922) film *Then Comes Silence* (*Potom nastąpi cisza*-1966) was almost too precise a description of the atmosphere under the normalization of the Gomulka regime. The "Polish school" was rejected for expressing negativistic tendencies, but there was nothing to take its place.

Once again Andrzej Wajda ruffled the calm surface. His *Ashes* (*Popioly*-1965) passionately posed almost forgotten questions: What are we like? What is our destiny? What is the meaning of history? After the attack on his *Innocent Sorcerers* and the hostility aroused by *Samson,* Wajda had worked for foreign companies for four years. In 1962, he filmed an undistinguished episode for the French film *L'amour à vingt ans* and in 1967, in Yugoslavia, he directed *The Siberian Lady Macbeth* (*Sibirska ledi Magbet*), on a theme of the nineteenth-century Russian novelist, N. S. Leskov. But the precise, almost naturalistic narration of life in the Russian provinces was alien to Wajda, and at the point where he concentrated, as usual, on the introspection of his leading character, he ran head on into the stone wall of Russian realities.

In *Ashes,* he involved himself once again with the encounter between man and history. Inspired by the splendid neoromantic novel written in 1904 by Stefan Zeromski, Wajda elaborated on the novel's Byronian motifs and allowed them to crystallize into what had become the stable character of his films: the freedom fighter who is left disillusioned and sceptical by his struggle, but seems to retain his nobility. In addition, there is the tragic role played by Polish patriots in the Napoleonic wars, who, while fighting for their own freedom, ended up suppressing the freedom of others. The philosophy of *Ashes* aroused profound disapproval, and Wajda once more found himself the target of attacks. As a result, he made his next film, *Gates of Paradise* (*Bramy raju*-1967), based on Andrzejewski's novel about the children's crusades, in Yugoslavia.

Ashes had been a major production within its genre, considerable footage being taken up by battle scenes, but the apocalyptic sequence of the capture of Saragossa by the Poles who fought for Napoleon is among the best Wajda ever filmed.

To make such costume spectaculars demanded a great deal of preparation, which meant, of course, that a director was often tied up with one film for several years and could in this way put off dealing with contemporary topics. Between 1962 and 1968, for example, Jerzy Kawalerowicz made only one film, an adaptation of Boleslaw Prus's novel *Pharaoh* (*Faraon*-1966), a story of the fictional Egyptian ruler Ramses XIII. A pictorial monumentalism, a stylized theoretical interpretation, and a rich epic plot were the foundation of a work that was meant to illustrate the inner conflict of absolute power, and thus be an exotic replication of the current situation in Poland. But the various facets of the film somehow drowned each other out, and the end result, worthy of respect though it was, was not very convincing.

Wojciech Has was much more successful with *Manuscript Found in Saragossa* (*Rękopis znaleziony w Saragossie*-1965), which, together with *Farewells,* was his best work. *Manuscript,* a collection of fantastical tales by Count Potocki dating back to 1815, inspired by the Decameron and Arabian Nights, captivated Has as an opportunity to extend *ad absurdum* his favorite form, the projection of the present into the past and vice versa, and to merge the real and the surreal. The adventures of a Spanish captain, beginning with the battle for Saragossa, gave Has an opportunity to develop his visual imagination in a surrealistic vein, colored with a sceptical philosophy. Has's next adaptation of a national classic—*The Doll* (*Lalka*-1968)—was incredibly shallow. Only the bare narrative structure of Prus's novel about the nineteenth-century Polish middle class appeared on the screen, and only conventional means were used to express it.

The Doll

In the period of "silence," literary classics were the main source of themes for Polish films. Gomulka's regime was almost pathologically afraid of anything new, anything that was not approved, not tried-and-tested, and anything that might, as had happened 10 years earlier, inspire thoughts of rebellion. It did not take long for Poland to lose several of its foremost cultural personalities. This second wave of emigration, in the late sixties, saw the departure of playwright Slawomir Mrożek, critic Jan Kott, philosopher Leszek Kolakowski, and others. One of the pioneers of Polish cinema, Aleksander Ford, also left.

Ford's last film in Poland, *The First Day of Freedom* (*Pierwszy dzień wolności*-1964), interpreted one aspect of the wartime situation—the relationship between victors and vanquished. The play by Leon Kruczkowski, who in his later work strove not too successfully to join socialist realism with a Sartrian dramaturgy, rests on the ambiguity of the characters, and hence of the subject. The family of a German physician living in a small town is just as right in its demands for honor and justice as are the five Polish soldiers, brought by the war into the town and confronted with the ethics of guilt and forgiveness. Ford's film leaned heavily on careful direction and the dramatic value of the script, but the strength of the subject remained in the dialogues.

The other members of Ford's generation—Jakubowska, Zarzycki, Bohdziewicz—did not influence the further development of Polish film either. In the countries surrounding Poland, the sixties in the film industries were years of youth, years of debuts, commitment, and experiment. In Poland, this new wave was delayed, and at the outset had only one representative—Jerzy Skolimowski.

SKOLIMOWSKI

Originally a poet and a student of ethnography, Skolimowski wrote a film scenario in 1961 about the cynical and yet genuine young generation, *Innocent Sorcerers,* and worked on the script for *Knife in the Water,* directed by his older colleague from the Film Academy, Roman Polański. The leitmotif of what was to be Skolimowski's later work was already apparent here: the impulsive revolt against those who have put down roots. Skolimowski made his first film in the course of his studies, *Identification Marks: None* (*Rysopis*-1964), a record of the last day of an expelled student before he goes into the armed forces. In it, Skolimowski assimilated the

Identification
Marks:
None

contributions of the French new wave, cinéma vérité, and the new American underground films, joining them with the experiences of a child of the Polish soil. The theme of *Identification Marks: None*—a probing of the attitudes, myths, and mentality of various generations of Poles—also enters into two of his other films, *Walkover* (1965) and *Barrier* (*Bariera*-1966), the trio forming a sort of loose trilogy. Skolimowski also wrote the scripts for all three. The pretentiously nihilistic negation advocated by the heroes, their hatred for a stable existence, and their argument with the national mythology are in essence aspects of a romantic rebellion and an effort to classify Polish complexes. In *Identification Marks: None,* the hero had to come to grips with the fact that others make his decisions for him; in *Walkover,* he became bellicose, rejecting everything that the previous generations had created; in *Barrier,* he deserted his home and school, but he did not find anything to take their place, and ultimately began to imitate what he had repudiated. What is characteristic of Skolimowski's films is the visually abbreviated stylization, the symbolism of objects and characters, and the condensation of dialogues. Although in *Identification Marks: None,* the innovative style is also the result of the modest means at the director's disposal, in his later films, the style becomes even more baroque, in order to serve the purpose of more complicated social metaphors.

Skolimowski is profoundly marked by the experience of Stalinism and by his own hatred for dogma. That is why he is fascinated by any and all rebellion, and that is why he carries his rebellion all the way into the sixties, when, in his opinion, Stalinism still existed in Poland. His sharpest attack on the ideology of intolerance was in his fifth film, *Hands Up* (*Ręce do góry*-1967), which was never shown publicly and which is not listed in Polish filmographies. Once again, this time in the form of a parable, we find a picture of a society enclosed in a vicious circle, a circle of action and attitudes to which it has condemned itself. No one here is guiltless: neither the ones who force the others to live with their hands up, nor the ones who obey and put their hands up. In Skolimowski's symbolic vision, Poland is shown as a land full of trains that are carrying all the generations of Poles, linked by their collective tragedy, to an unknown destination. After completing *Hands Up,* Skolimowski went abroad for a number of years. He made his first non-Polish film, *Le Départ,* in Belgium in 1966.

THE END OF THE "POLISH SCHOOL"

One who was close to Skolimowski in his effort to elucidate some of the complexes of the "former fighters," was Tadeusz Konwicki. From the nostalgia and the melodrama of his earlier work, Konwicki advanced to the tragic irony of *Salto* (1965). Polish critics welcomed *Salto* with enthusiasm as the first systematic demystification of the Polish character and the Polish wartime legend, even though the tragic undertone that resounds in *Salto* seems to indicate rather the opposite. Konwicki brings his hero to a small town and lets him pretend that he used to live there during the German occupation. But perhaps he is telling the truth; nothing is certain, neither his name nor his world. The inhabitants of the town at first accept him as a prophet, but in the end, they reject him. *Salto* is full of the symbols and relics dear to the "Polish school," particularly in the long metaphoric sequence in which the unknown man teaches the others to dance the traditional Polish dance, the salto.

Has's *Ciphers* (*Szyfry*-1966), which also tried to come to terms with the "Polish school," is virtually a parade of wartime survivors whose memories and psychological deviations flash across the screen against a background of all the national symbols: white horses, wandering mercenaries, willows, battlefields, ruins of churches, red carnations, pale brides, and on and on.

But was it possible to do away with the "Polish school" when it was the most autonomous expression of Polish cinema that had yet appeared, when the orders to do so came from above, and when a large number of the current productions were floundering in conformist mediocrity? The films of Skolimowski, Konwicki, Wajda, and, later, those of other directors as well, bespoke the very opposite. They proved that the "Polish school" drew on the national philosophy and character, that at the time that Polish cinema first found an autonomous expression, it was just stating what had been and would continue to be the leitmotif of Polish literature.

Polish film production was then dominated by directors like Passendorfer, who based his *Scenes of Battle* (*Barwy walki*-1965) on the memoirs of Minister of Interior Mieczyslaw Moczar; the Petelskis, the husband-and-wife team known for carrying out official orders, as in the anticlerical *Wooden Rosary* (*Drewniany różaniec*-1965); or Rybkowski, who in the sixties began to prepare an adaptation of Reymont's great epic, *Peasants* (*Chlopy*-1973).

For a number of years, Jerzy Hoffman devoted himself to making films of the many-volumed popular historical novels of Henryk Sienkiewicz, *Pan Wolodyjowski* (1971) and *The Deluge* (*Potop*-1974). Różewicz turned away from the subjects that connected him with the work of his brother; in the second part of the sixties his most interesting film was *Westerplatte* (1967), a shallowly told history of the German attack on Poland in 1939. Kawalerowicz did not achieve success at home with *Game* (*Gra*-1969) nor abroad with *Maddalena* (1970). Among the best productions of those years was the psychological comedy, *Jowita* (1967), which, together with another film about the uncertainty of human relations, *Kill That Love* (*Trzeba zabić tę miłość*-1971), was the most original of the skillful and prolific director, Janusz Morgenstern.

TWO DEBUTS

In 1967, hopes were aroused by the debut of Janusz Majewski (b. 1931), *The Subtenant* (*Sublokator*), which has been compared to the comedy, *Eve Wants to Sleep*. Majewski, at that time the director of some 10 short films,

The
Subtenant

edged toward absurdity while trying to show as much as possible of everyday life—in the case of *The Subtenant* by using a story of three women in conflict over one man. The day-to-day existence that emerges is a life full of the past, which the director graces with an ironic smile, but he also shows that there is nothing to replace it.

Another director to make his debut in these years was Henryk Kluba (b. 1931), whose two best films were made in close collaboration with author W. T. Dymny. For years an assistant director, in 1967 he made a film about the life of laborers working on a dam, *The Thin One and the Others* (*Chudy i inni*), one of the few Polish films to concern itself with contemporary problems. Although the plot is typical of those used in socialist optimistic novels, the film deviates from the book by including a nonconformist depiction of the social process, going beyond the superficial plot line to explore the ways in which new production relationships are formed in the as yet only theoretically described socialist regime. In addition, Kluba stylized reality, part of the time structuring the narration like a ballad, and part of the time like a comic allegory, thereby further developing the baroque tendencies of the "Polish school."

The Thin One
and the Others

In *The Sun Rises Once a Day* (*Słońce wschodzi raz na dzień*-1968), Kluba was the first—and outside of Yugoslavia, the only one—to point out the discrepancy between the idea of the workers' direct ownership of their means of production and ownership by the bureaucratic state. Using as his tool a symbolic stylization that in moments of crisis relies exclusively on images from nature, he introduces the precise atmosphere of an unmistakable historical moment: the first stage of the building of a socialist state. The villagers build a sawmill, they build it all by themselves and finally they have something that belongs to them, they raise production and fulfill the planned quotas. When the order comes to turn over the work of their hands to the anonymous "state," they refuse, and they defend their rights, their concept of an authentic socialism, with weapons. Not until after the film was banned did Kluba add a more conciliatory ending to the story, but even so, *The Sun Rises Once a Day* was not put into distribution until five years later, and then only on a limited basis. It took years for the director to reemerge.

1968-1971 DUAL CRISIS

The year 1968 was one of the worst years for the Polish film industry. While Czechoslovakia was trying to put an end to the vestiges of the Stalinist dictatorship, the Gomulka and Moczar regime braked all attempts toward evolution, and, with the help of the secret police, maintained the status quo. March saw the arrest of student leaders who demonstrated their solidarity with Czechoslovakia and called for academic freedom. Censorship became stiffer, a passionate antisemitic movement rocked the land, and Jewish intellectuals once again fled into exile. Jerzy Toeplitz, the best Polish film historian, was removed from the post of chief of the Film Academy at Łódź; both Aleksander Ford and Jerzy Bossak—once head of the production unit for Polish documentary films, which under his leadership had achieved a position among the best in Europe—lost their positions as heads of production units.

In 1968, less than 20 fiction films were produced, and most of those were adaptations of well-known and approved literary works. The stagnation was the lull before the storm. As soon as the Czechoslovak reform movement, and along with it a source of possible contagion, was liquidated by means of military intervention, Gomulka relaxed police surveillance and tried to achieve economic reform without making any political concessions. This provoked a social explosion, accompanied, and almost anticipated, by a number of Polish films.

After demonstrations in 1971 in the ports of Northern Poland had been brutally supressed, Wladyslaw Gomulka was forced to step down, to be replaced by a representative of the party's technocratic wing, Edward Gierek. Secretary of justice and head of state security, General Moczar, left the public scene along with Gomulka.

Taste of the Black Earth

As usual, film took advantage of the half-opened door; within a short time a number of noteworthy films emerged, testifying to the hidden reserves of vitality in the Polish film world.

Kazimierz Kutz, a native of Silesia like the new political chief Gierek, was one director who got his chance. And he took full advantage of it, making two exceptional films about the national and social struggle of Polish miners in Silesia after World War One. The first of these films, *Taste of the Black Earth* (*Sól ziemi ciarnej*–1970), is an untraditional view of a struggle for national liberation that is filmed in a surrealist style as a folk celebration, a bloody carnival, and a folk ballad set against the back-drop of real events. The second film, *Pearl in the Crown* (*Perla v koronie*–1971) is a composition in violent contrasts of light and darkness. The darkness, captured in various shades of gray and in black, consists of expressionistic, almost unreal scenes shot at the bottom of a mine shaft, where the heroes of *Taste of the Black Earth,* 14 years later, during the depression years, are on strike. The light consists mainly of the whiteness of bodies or the walls of the room in which a ceremony is taking place, the family ritual of those happy hours that a miner spends in daylight, among his loved ones.

NEW BLACK SERIES

Early in 1972, production groups were reorganized and given considerably more authority with respect to the central administration. The six groups in existence until then (headed by Kawalerowicz, Wajda, Petelski, Różewicz,

Scibor-Rlski, and Passendorfer) were joined by a seventh, headed by
Kazimierz Kutz, which was aimed primarily at working with young
directors. It also included some young documentarists, among them,
Grzegorz Królikiewicz (b. 1939) and Tomasz Zygadlo (b. 1947). As in 1955,
the first evidence of the rejuvenation of Polish film appeared in the area
of documentary film (Krzysztof Gradowski, Antoni Krauze, Ewa Kruk).
Soon there was talk of a new black series.

The first to call attention to himself in fiction film was Marek Piwowski
(b. 1935). His documentary, *To Be Sixteen* (*Szesnaście mieć lat*-1969), a
series of conversations with young people who are unable to find their places
in society, was reminiscent, after a fashion, of Hoffman and Skórzewski's
1955 film, *Attention Hooligans.* Piwowski followed in the same line with his
fiction debut, *Cruise* (*Rejs* 1970), a bitter satire on some of the collective
manias of the socialist regime. Another outstanding fiction film was the
debut of Antoni Krauze (b. 1940), *God's Finger* (*Palec Boży*-1973), a
symbolic story of a young man who wants desperately to be an actor, but
finds his only chance and opportunity in a mental institution, where psychodrama makes life into a stage. In 1975, a similar theme was taken up by
Krzysztof Kieslowski (b. 1947) in *Personal* (*Personel*), which put into
question the moral pressures young people liave to face in an ailing society.

The portrait of Poland that emerged in the films of the early seventies
could hardly have been more sombre. There was an evident continuity of
ideas with the films of 1956, and even though the style was enriched by the
contributions of the sixties, in some cases it nonetheless retained traces of
expressionism and symbolism. A typical example of this trend was Królikiewicz's debut, *Through and Through* (*Na wylot*-1973), a portrait of a
desperate couple who, lacking inner values, commit a murder, and at the
trial passionately plea for their own death sentences. The three planes of
the story, reality, fantasy, and the subconscious, are borne along together by
the naturalism of the inner degeneration of people living lives of apathy
and deterioration. Only at the very end of the film do we glimpse a subtitle
telling us that the story took place in 1933.

Through
and
Through

The first film of Andrzej Żulawski (b. 1940), for years Wajda's assistant director, also takes place in the past. *Third Part of a Night* (*Trzecia częś nocy*-1971) is set during the occupation, and yet it leaves the impression that it is set in the present. Żulawski, like Królikiewicz, used expressionism and a wealth of naturalistic detail, stressing the overall atmosphere rather than the plot. His world, where the instinct of self-preservation makes man give his very blood to the lice, has all the attributes of the absurd, as it is known in the Polish literature of Gombrowicz, Bruno Schulz, Mrożek, and Witkiewicz. The story ends with madness and death. Żulawski's next film was another denial of all hope: *Devil* (*Diabel*-1971), using costumes from the eighteenth century (the time of the last Polish king) to evoke a feeling of negation and violence that was aroused in people by contemporary political events.

A Third of a Night

The work of directors who made their debuts early in the seventies has several common traits. They are as a rule films made from original ideas, films that turn away from the influence of literature. They are emotive films, atmospheric, and hence antischematic. They are contemplative films, concerned with the basic questions of existence. The most frequent object of this intense concern is death, accepted as the logical outgrowth of tragic lives. *Salvation* (*Oçalenie*-1972) by Edward Żebrowski (b. 1935), in contemplating the essence of death, confronts a successful, arrogant man with the ultimate experience and ordeal. In *Challenge* (*Wezwanie*-1970), Wojciech Solarz (b. 1934) contemplates the illness and death of an artist who cannot—or perhaps will not—live with other people. Solarz, who made his debut in 1960 with *Pier (Molo)*, also worked on the script for Witold Lesczyński's (b. 1933) *The Days of Matthew (Żyvot Mateusza*-1968), in which a new motif was introduced into the films of the new generation—man's escape to nature. *The Days of Matthew* developed a different lyrical note in Polish cinema by contrasting the hero's death to the life of nature.

ZANUSSI

The most potent figure among the directors that followed the generation of Skolimowski and Polański was Krzysztof Zanussi (b. 1939). Zanussi differs from his peers in his ambition to seek meaningful values in the contemporary world and to find some order in the problems of the present. He weaves into the plots of his films all the expected doubts, his figures alternately arousing favor and disfavor. Zanussi, originally a student of physics, affirms a basic deterministic view of man, but at the same time, he asks if we can free ourselves from it. He moves from a rationalistic analysis and a logical structure to a penetrating moral unrest. The plots of his films are built around the events surrounding an encounter, culminating at the moment

Family Life

when a choice must be made. In *Structure of Crystals* (*Struktura kryształu*–1969), two former university students meet, one of them a winner of international fame, the other an inhabitant of an isolated village. In *Family Life* (*Życie rodzinne*-1971), the hero's encounter with his family is transformed into his confrontation with the world to which he used to belong, and thus into a recapitulation of his existence, for which he is seeking a concrete dimension. In the television film, *Behind the Wall* (*Za ścianą*–1971), the conflict arises from the encounter of a successful chemist with an uncertain and unhappy woman, developing into a study of human life against a background of trivial banality. Zanussi's microscopic analyses primarily investigate both sides of success and failure, while leaving all consequences open.

The philosophical and autobiographic tendencies of Zanussi's work culminated in *Illumination* (*Iluminacja*-1972), in which his effort to create reflection-based anti-films was apparent as well. In this context we can also note the development of form, from the striking use of montage apparent in Zanussi's first medium-length fiction film, *The Death of the Monk* (*Śmierć prowincjala*-1966), and the partial improvisation in *Structure of Crystals*, to a fluid dramatic structure, adhering strictly to the evolution of the plot, the disposition of dialogue, and the functionality of the visual images. For *Illumination*, the story of a physicist who is unhinged by a confrontation with the mystery of man, Zanussi found his form in the joining of documentary, dramatic, and literary techniques. In *Balance* (*Bilans kwartalny*-1974), Zanussi created a striking portrait of a contemporary woman caught in the dragnet of traditional morality on one side and the attempt at emancipation of her frustrated potentials on the other. Thus he further extended his probing of moral ambiguity.

Illumination

KONWICKI AND HAS AGAIN

In *How Far It Is and Yet How Near* (*Jak daleko stąd, jak blisko*-1971), Tadeusz Konwicki created probably the most profound of all the films

How Far It Is
and Yet
How Near

striving to deal with the past. Here more than elsewhere we can see the connection between Konwicki's film work and his writing, particularly the novel *Ascension,* triumphally received in 1967 in spite of obstacles presented by the censors. His new film was also banned at the outset, undoubtedly for the note of pure desperation that resounds in it as strongly as it did in *Ascension.* In this film, Konwicki finally succeeded in doing what he had been striving for since the beginning: to be as creative with images as he had been with words. The thoughts of a person who is balancing accounts in his life give rise to images of what was, what is, and what might have been. The melange of characters and observations creates a broad panorama of contemporary Poland—haunted by the past, by the years of WW II—that ends with a statement on the vanity of life. Of all the films produced in Eastern Europe, this film of Konwicki's is the most complete expression of the sensation that despair does indeed exist in the socialist lands.

Has was less successful in taking advantage of the new trend. In 1972, he made a film version of a novel by Bruno Schulz, *Sanitarium Under the Hourglass* (*Sanatorium pod Klepsydrą*). Schulz (1892-1942), the great Polish master of the absurd, and the translator of the works of Franz Kafka, was for years one of the proscribed authors in socialist Poland, and one of the unappreciated writers in world literature. Has captured only a fraction of the oppressive atmosphere of Schulz's best work, for the most part burdening this exceptionally expensive film with scenes that are weighed down with symbols and dialogues.

WAJDA

In these years of searching, debuts, and new names, Andrzej Wajda dominated Polish cinema perhaps more than ever before. After no great success abroad, and various work for television, Wajda filmed his artistic confession in *Everything For Sale* (*Wszystko na sprzedaż*-1969). On a secondary plane, this film told the story of actor Zbygniew Cybulski, who died in an accident in 1967. It is a film about a film, a film about a friend who died a tragic accidental death, about a marriage that went on the rocks, and a love that was never fulfilled, about death and oblivion. It is Wajda's attempt to decipher his own consciousness, and the first film that he wrote himself. Although Wajda does not have the ability to be as brutal in self-analyses as Fellini, *Everything for Sale,* more a transition from Wajda's creative crisis in the sixties to the upsurge that was to follow, remains an important achievement. Not so another transitional film, *Hunting the Flies* (*Polowanie na muchy*-1969). Wajda had been drawn to a film with a female as its central character, if only because the hero in Polish literature and film is almost always a young man. The motif of a woman as a destructive element resounds to the fullest here, and gives a belated explanation of some of the female figures in Wajda's earlier films. But one wonders, from the final product, whether Wajda was really interested in his subject, and whether he felt comfortable in the field of satirical comedy, this being his first try at it.

It was not until *Landscape After the Battle* (*Krajobraz po bitwie*-1970) that Wajda created another of his great films, another of his tales about a victory that is in effect defeat, and about people who have no choice. He took a story by one of the most talented of Poland's postwar writers, Tadeusz Borowski, and made it into an epic study of Poland's destiny. The landscape of the film's title is situated somewhere in Germany during the last months of the war; it is peopled by former prisoners, soldiers, deserters, and desperadoes who are hesitant about crossing the line to freedom. It is as if they sensed that even beyond that line, there is no hope for them. The work of Borowski—who survived a Nazi concentration camp and a POW camp, and who committed suicide at the age of 30—is evidently autobiographical, full of concrete observations and concrete characters. Wajda remained close to the realistic level of the plot line, expanded its contemplative and symbolic aspects, and achieved the masterful blending of these three narrative plans through the story of an unhappy love. The result was an evocative drama that integrated the monumental style of *Ashes,* and the historical existential psychology of *Ashes and Diamonds,* with a scrupulous attention to realistic detail.

During the same year, Wajda also made *Birch Wood* (*Brzezina*-1970), a classical romantic tale of love and death, pictorially inspired by Polish painting at the turn of the nineteenth century. From the point of view of style, *Birch Wood* approaches crystal purity. It is a poetic study on several themes of love, borne by a graduated individualism and by the contrast between the flowering of nature and the waning of life. Although it is based on one of the best stories of Jaroslaw Iwaskiewicz, its dramatic structure goes back to the work of Stanislaw Wyspiański, the founder of modern Polish theater.

At that time, Wajda was working on the greatest challenge of his film career, *Wedding* (*Wesele*-1972), an adaptation of the play of the same title written by Wyspiański, (1869-1907). The play is among the best-known in Polish literature, and numerous quotations from it have become catchwords. In addition to putting characters on the stage, *Wedding* also gives fleshly form to their ideas as they crystallize in the minds of guests at a wedding party. They reflect all the ancient dreams and yearnings of the Polish land, above all their vain dream of independence. The music, which does not stop for a moment, and which culminates with the melodies and rhythms of the salto, helps to create an atmosphere of rare charm, and determines the editing structure of the film. The plot develops in an unbridled flow of characters, sets, colors, and costumes, the blending of which gives the impression of duration and depth. The characters and their fantasies represent a variety of social strata, traditions, opinions, and viewpoints. Skepticism, naïveté, sincerity, and falsehood merge when one of the characters imagines that a figure from Polish legend calls on him to stand up to the oppressors of Poland. At that point, the wedding guests are ready to follow him, but the villager that they send as the first of their number gets lost and finds himself between a Russian and an Austrian soldier. Poland, divided among the great powers, becomes the central character of the closing scenes of *Wedding,* which peak in a feeling of supreme expectation of a great, unnamed event. But all that comes is the dawn, and in the first light of the sun, the wedding guests appear as people with no will of their own, people who find moments of greatness only in their dreams.

After *Wedding,* Wajda, in 1975, made a super-production on the brutal growth of capitalism in Poland at the end of the nineteenth century, a brilliant film version of Wladyslaw Reymont's (Nobel Prize winner for 1924) classic epic, *Land of Promise* (*Ziemia obiecana*). To the criticism that he has once again dealt with a subject from the past, Wajda replied: "I find it

Land of Promise

difficult to find a key to approach political subjects right now. The reason for this is not directly political, but the country is in such a state of flux that it is difficult to define its condition and to find the right kind of terms to deal with contemporary themes" (Festival Bulletin, Cannes, May 1975). Compared with the symbolic imagery and "Polishness" which made *Wedding* so difficult for foreign viewers, *Land of Promise* proved that Wajda, being also a born storyteller, could successfully deal with a film aimed at large—and possibly international—audiences.

Only 30 years after it began, the Polish cinema thus confirmed that even in this field it can challenge those film industries with much longer traditions.

THE POSSIBILITIES OF ART AND THE ART OF THE POSSIBLE: Hungary after 1963

In Hungary, or at least in Hungarian culture, film nowadays plays the role of the avant-garde. If nothing gets in the way of its development, as happened to so many schools that were brutally crushed, it will remain one of the most important manifestations of our epoch, and will continue to surround us with exciting discoveries.

György Lukács, FILMKULTURA, 1969, Budapest

The new ascent of Hungarian cinematography, the third since the end of the war, followed what was also the third thaw in Hungarian culture, which began late in 1959 and bore first fruits two years later. The ensuing policy, which was intended to normalize life in a country that had been rocked by a revolution—and was even more shaken by its brutal suppression—eventually gave Hungary an exceptional position in Eastern Europe. Within the limits of the neo-Stalinist establishment, János Kádár strove, if necessary through compromise, for a reconciliation among all the factions of the nation, for a sort of a postrevolutionary adjustment. With Khrushchev's approval and support, he inverted the Stalinist threat of "who isn't with us is against us," to form the conciliatory slogan "who isn't against us is with us." Then, through Deputy Minister of Culture György Aczél, he heralded a principle entirely unheard of in Eastern Europe at that time: it called for the publication even "of works that are not socialist in their conception, but that possess artistic merit."

The economic situation had improved considerably as compared to the period before 1956, above all in terms of the availability of consumer goods, thanks to a large degree to Soviet aid; discrimination against non-Communists was tempered, as was the preferment of so-called "working-class cadres"—politically reliable party members, who were often placed in jobs for which they simply did not have the qualifications. Kádár, whose regime represented a marked improvement over that of Rákosi, also strove for a reconciliation with the intelligentsia, which had paid a bitter tax in the period immediately following the revolution. Déry, Háy, Zelk, and others were released from prison in the partial amnesty of 1960. (A general amnesty followed two years later.) A "realistic approach to reality" started to be called for by the people, including a segment of the intelligentsia—particularly the older generation—and along with this approach, the idea of profiting from the status quo as much as possible in all spheres of life.

DIALOGUE

The official version of the events in 1956—referred to as "the counter-revolution"—and of what preceded and followed them, and above all a rationale for Kádár's policies, was put on film in 1963 by János Herskó (b. 1926). *Dialogue* (*Párbeszéd*), filmed according to Herskó's own script, was the story of a classical marital triangle, this time composed of three devoted party members: the woman has to choose between her husband, who has spent his whole life fighting in the communist ranks and remained stalwart even during and after his unjust imprisonment, and her lover, a poet, who after 1954 joins the critics of the establishment and leaves defeated. This mediocre film was the first of several ultimately more successful attempts by Hungarian film-makers (Fábri, Kósa) to restore the unity of the past and the present, to bridge the rupture of 1956. Herskó's next film *Hello Vera* (*Szevasz Vera*-1967), a story of the adolescence of a young girl, was better received. In 1970, Herskó—head of the Film Academy since 1960, and in charge of his own production group—made his last film in Hungary, the bitterly satirical comedy *Requiem Hungarian Style* (*N. N. halál angyala*). Upon completing it, he emigrated to Western Europe, the only Hungarian film-maker active in the sixties to do so.

Hungarian cinema was very slow to revive. In 1965, Mihály Szemes (b. 1920), then head of one of the production groups, but a not-too-successful director—e.g., *New Gilgamesh* (*Uj Gilgames*-1963) about a man dying of cancer—spoke out: "The counterrevolution was a nasty business, but the truth is that we have not succeeded in rising to the former artistic level. Not a single important script turned up in the last seven years, and so there hasn't even been any reason for controversies" (*Film a doba,* No. 6, 1965, Prague).

A year later, Sándor Papp, chief of Hungarian Film, added, "The events of the fall of 1956 have still not been historically assimilated, nor have they been digested, nor healed. A consolidation was achieved in our land in 1962, but of course this was only in the sense that a general recognition of the acceptability of the new regime was arrived at, but no quiescence" (*Film a doba,* No. 10, 1966, Prague).

CONFESSIONS OF CHILDREN OF THE CENTURY

The seven empty years of Hungarian cinema came to an end with films like *Current* (*Sodrásban*-1963), *The Age of Daydreaming* (*Álmodozások kora*-1964), *Difficult People* (*Nehéz emberek*-1964), *Grimace* (*Gyerekbetegségek* -1965), *Green Years* (*Zöldár*-1965), and *Ten Thousand Suns* (*Tízezer nap*-1965). The new poetical approach of these films was founded on the thoughts and emotions of the up-and-coming generation: it was no longer just a matter of coming to rationalistic grips with fateful events like the war and the resultant historical transformations, but also of grasping, on an

Current

individual basis, the emotions of the day. The training of the young artists
was greatly influenced by the cinematic methods and discoveries that had
been spreading across all of Europe since the end of the fifties, as well as
by local conditions and traditions—and by the lack of traditions. The
absorption of these influences was facilitated by the establishment of
autonomous production groups at the beginning of the sixties. Another
important influence was the overall ideological atmosphere in convalescing
Hungary, which not only permitted but demanded a subjective approach.
This generation's beginnings can be characterized as the "confessions of
the children of the century," confessions of people who, in spite of their
youth, could remember the war, Rákosi's terrorism, and the happenings
of 1956. The first films to be shot in the Béla Balázs studio showed their
creators to be proponents of a subjective, unrestrained form, and demonstrated the ardor with which they sought new and rejected old canons,
canons that until recently had been considered sacrosanct.

In his first two films, István Gaál (b. 1933) investigated the vital
experiences of his own generation through an almost indeterminate jumble
of emotion-filled images. Gaál, who studied at the Centro Sperimentale in
Rome for two years after graduating from the Budapest Film Academy,
started his career with *Current,* essentially a film monologue on the subject
of how we live, the lyrical confession of a generation, its metaphor expand-
ing beyond the factual boundaries of the story. In the cinematically inventive
first half of the film, the camera follows a group of carefree, frivolous young
people on a midsummer excursion in the Hungarian countryside. One of
them is drowned in a swift-flowing river. Tragedy has disrupted their
lives, nothing will ever be the same, life gains another dimension, which

the film's heroes seek to investigate in the second, less successful, half of the picture. Gaál's next film, *Green Years,* is cinematically weaker and consists of a generational confession within the framework of social reality. The basis of the story is the autobiographical retrospection of a country boy who comes to study in Budapest in the fifties, and strives desperately to retain his integrity amid the wilfullness of the times.

The
Age of
Day-
dreaming

Similar emotional experiences were characteristic as well of the films of István Szabó (b. 1938), Herskó's assistant director on *Dialogue.* The heroes of his debut, *The Age of Daydreaming,* are his contemporaries, seeking an identity for their generation in the world formed by their parents. In *Father (Apa-*1966), Szabó's lyrical, almost diary-like efforts rose to the level of a critical encounter with the past (the subtitle of the film is "The Diary of a Faith"). In the story of the difficult adolescence of a youth whose defense mechanism consists of idealizing the memory of his dead father, Szabó tried to disrupt the traditional form by confronting the world of his own ideas with various versions of reality.

From the very outset, Ferenc Kósa (b. 1937) differed from his contemporaries in his analytical approach to his own subjective creed. His *Ten Thousand Suns* is a strong drama that skilfully draws on the best traditions of Hungarian populism—which is rich in balladry and folklore, and relies on beauty of expression as the only defense against poverty—and at the same time is a lyrical appraisal of, and a farewell to, the centuries-old credos of rural Hungary. The story focuses on a farmer who had spent the years before the war in poverty, a man whose life is rooted in the soil. In the period of the mandatory collectivization of agriculture, he refuses to enter the co-operative farm and is arrested. Kósa relates this man's individual story

against a backdrop of the general story of his entire village over a period of 30 years (or 10,000 days), from before the war, through the year 1956, to the sixties. The peasant returns from jail, and both he and his wife—who waited for him during his years of imprisonment—are too weary to believe that there could be a better life. To their son, their life seems like a distant, strange past. After two years of arguments Kósa finally agreed to make some requested cuts, primarily involving the events in 1956, and *Ten Thousand Suns* was approved for distribution.

Folkloric elements and symbols of rural Hungary, which were fast becoming a cliché in some Hungarian films, lost their inviolability in Pál Zsolnay's (b. 1928) third film, *The Sack* (*Hogy szaladnak a fák*-1966), in which an old theme and old characters rose to new dimensions. Marked by a light sentimentality, this story of a return to the place of one's childhood was above all a testimony to Zsolnay's ability to introduce broader themes by means of details precisely perceived.

The man behind the camera of the majority of films of the young generation was Sándor Sára (b. 1933), whose unrestrained photography contributed greatly to the original impressionist styles of *Current* and *Father,* and also played a significant role in the visual composition of *Ten Thousand Suns.* Sára was also the cameraman for *Grimace,* the debut of ·Ferenc Kardos (b. 1937) and János Rózsa (b. 1937). A poetic film of lyrical irony consisting of small episodes, its charm lay not only in the attractiveness of the montage and the delightful child actors, but also in the bitter malice

with which the directors attacked the world of adults. In 1963 Sára directed the then famous short, *Gypsies* (*Cigányok*-1963), with Gaál at the camera. A daring glance at a social group not fitting the preconceived patterns of a society that was unable to deal with people who were "different," *Gypsies* pictorial power recalled the films of István Szöts.

Gypsies

THE GENERATION OF 1956

The generation that had been a motivating force in the period between 1954–1957 underwent its artistic renaissance in parallel with the ascent of the younger generation, and was in essence an expression of the selfsame need to analyze some fundamental existential problems. Only in their work, the subjectivity of youth was replaced by an objective moralistic approach, typical of all artists who had been making films in Eastern Europe around 1956. Two new themes made their way to the forefront in the sixties: how to live with the established power and the nature of the individual's responsibility, particularly vis-à-vis the theoretical, anonymous responsibility of the masses. Two of the best films to be made by members of this generation, Fábri's *Twenty Hours* (*Húsz óra*-1964) and Kovács's *Cold Days* (*Hideg napok*-1966) sought their inspiration (as did the best films by Hungary's younger film-makers, for example, Kósa) in Hungarian history, with its vicious circles of violence, repression, and resignation.

In *Twenty Hours,* which was based on Ferenc Sánta's novelistic reportage of the events of 1956, Fábri strove to fuse a journalistic approach with a traditional dramatic structure, and to depict, in the stratified narrative framework, how critical events shape the lives of a wide variety of people. But Fábri and Sánta did not share Kósa's youthful ruthlessness, nor did they possess his negative bias or his fresh vision. The first cinematic attempt to show rural Hungary between 1945 and 1956, this motion picture was so scrutinized through the process of censorship that a great deal had to be read between the lines. Ultimately, it turned out that the complex structure of the narration itself called attention to what was left unsaid.

András Kovács, the literary advisor of the fiction-film studio since 1950 and the chief of its script department between 1951 and 1957, made his independent debut in 1960, after having been assistant director on a number of films. But his drama of the soil, *Summer Rain* (*Zápor*), was singularly undistinguished, as were his next two films. After a study trip to Paris, he made *Difficult People,* one of the first films to signal the end of the empty period in Hungarian cinema. Conceived in the style of cinéma vérité, it presented a slice of the present in the form of interviews with "difficult people" (in this case, inventors and discoverers) who refuse to give up when faced with bureaucracy, disinterest, and apathy. They were of the same. breed as Makk's *Fanatics,* but in Kovács's presentation they appear to have gained in authenticity. It was the first time in years that a Hungarian film expressed ideas and attitudes about cowardice and hypocrisy, tearing down the painted curtains before which rosy csardas princesses had for decades been performing their divertive dances. But the film was given a limited distribution and Kovács's attempt to continue in this direction failed—his *Collective Dwellings* (*Stalagház*–1965) was never released. (Nor was Jancsó's short about Hungarian village Jews, *A Village in Tókay.*)

The best film of Kovács's career was *Cold Days,* based on a novel and script by Tibor Cseres. It is a calm, matter-of-fact, and seemingly un-emotional analysis of the preparations for, and the carrying out of, a 1942 massacre in which Hungarian soldiers slaughtered over 3,000 Serbian and Hungarian nationals in Novi Sad, a town in the ethnically mixed region of what used to be called the Bánát. (This region is known today as Vojvodina, and is a part of Yugoslavia.) These soldiers carried out the slaughter without hesitation, simply because they were ordered to. Kovács sought answers to the question of how an ordinary person can become a mass murderer, and in so doing made a straightforward criminal accusation against Hungarian fascism. *Cold Days* was also a film about the man-in-the-street's responsibility for the atrocities he commits, for his share of the guilt, and

Cold
Days

Love

ultimately for his own tragedy. But *Cold Days* is just as much a drama of people in extreme situations, of which there has been no shortage in recent decades in the lands that are inaccurately embraced by the term "Eastern Europe." With the admirable camerawork of Ferenc Szécsényi, *Cold Days* went far beyond the simple retelling of an actual event. It asked questions of Kovács's contemporaries as well.

The directors who had been instrumental in shaping Hungarian film prior to 1956, although they continued to work, did not make any significant mark in the sixties. In 1968, Fábri did a coproduction with the United States, an adaptation of Ferenc Molnár's novel, *The Boys of Paul Street* (*A Pál utcai fiuk*), and a year later, *The Tóth Family* (*Isten hozta, örnagy úr*), a black comedy about the genesis of blind obedience and terrorism.

Máriássy made mostly comedies and satires—for example, *Fig-Leaf* (*Fügefalevél*-1966)—but in 1969, in collaboration with Judit Máriássy and cameraman Illés, he attempted to elucidate the origins of Hungarian fascism, primarily its antisemitic and nationalistic nature, in the film *Imposters* (*Imposztorok*).

Even in the early sixties, Károly Makk kept on seeking controversial themes, but the uneven form and narrative structure that had marred his *Fanatics,* as well as the impossibility of calling things by their right names, thwarted one attempt after another—for example, *Paradise Lost* (*Elveszett paradicsom*-1962), and *Last But One* (*Az utolsó elötti ember*-1963). After 1965, Makk began work on plans for *Love* (*Szerelem*), but like many another controversial film, its production was delayed until 1969-1970. This motion picture, Makk's best, was based on two stories by Tibor Déry that dealt with the period of Rákosi's terrorism, when people "disappeared," to reappear only rarely. *Love* is the story of a political prisoner's wife and sick mother, both of whom await his return, the mother being sustained by the delusion that her son is pursuing a successful career abroad. But it is also, of course, far more than that, for Makk succeeds in capturing the atmosphere of uncertainty and fear in which friendship, faith, and fidelity somehow collapse and turn into the exact opposites. The role of the mother is played by Ferenc Molnár's widow, Lily Darvas, who had lived in the United States since the thirties.

Like so many similar projects, Makk's film was ultimately weakened by the fact that it appeared on the screen five or six years after it was conceived. Makk's search for a new style resulted in *Catsplay* (*Macskajáték*-1974), an elaborate cinematic exploration of the lost world of an old woman that was based on a successful play by István Örkény (the author of *The Tóth Family*).

JANCSÓ

To many, it seemed as if all the themes, questions, obsessions, and anxieties that haunted Hungarian film artists were fused in the oeuvre of Miklós Jancsó. They were anticipated as far back as in *My Way Home* (*Igy jöttem*-1964), an exceptional depiction of Hungary in the last days of World War Two, when a young soldier of the defeated Hungarian army is taken prisoner by Soviet forces and enters into a strange friendship with his young, exhausted, and wounded Russian guard. After the guard dies, the Hungarian puts on the Soviet uniform as protection and as a result is beaten as a traitor by a group of refugees. But Jancsó's themes were not fully

My
Way
Home

developed until *The Round-up* (*Szegénylegények*-1965). In collaboration with Gyula Hernádi, the author of several collections of short stories who became Jancsó's scenaristic alter-ego, and with his director of photography, Tamás Somló, Jancsó turned his back on his beginnings to lay the ground-work for a style that he continued to develop in his later films. At the very beginning of all of Jancsó's films, the basic conflict situation is firmly established, releasing a chain of action and reaction. It seems, however, that neither the director, nor for that matter any one else, knows the real causes. The viewer always sees the consequences, the resultant vectors of forces that criss-cross in a sort of perpetual motion, with cause and effect, good and evil, victors and vanquished as interchangeable entities. Time seems to come to a halt, past resembles present, and both suggest a similar, or an identical, future. All political systems, all historical epochs, can be accommodated in this cinematic ballet of violence and oppression, evolved from the tension between the "beauty" of artistic stylization and the "ugliness" of testimony. But Jancsó is above all interested in the history of his homeland, "the lake of death," the destiny of his nation, "mournful and cursed"—as Hungary and Hungarians were labelled by Jancsó's favorite poet, Endre Ady. The metaphoric contents of Jancsó's images are strictly rationalistic, just as his depiction of the workings of nameless power is logically specific—the more absolute the power is, Jancsó seems to say, the more absolutely it corrupts—seeking its strength and ultimately finding its weakness in the powerlessness of the oppressed. Jancsó's language is aphoristic; within its rigorous system of symbols, each shot utters something universal: the nakedness of victims—their helplessness; a red rose—revolt and hope: a uniform—force, violence, etc.

The Red and the White

In *The Round-up*, we find ourselves taken back to a period 20 years after the Kossuth revolution of 1848, which was crushed with the aid of the Russian army. Clusters of former revolutionaries and peasant rebels were scattered through the land, some of them still fighting, others simply killing and robbing. Hunted and hounded no matter where they went, they won for themselves the epithet "the hopeless ones"—which is also the approximate translation of the Hungarian title of the film—and became the heroes of folk legends and songs. Jancsó destroyed their aura of heroism, challenged the theory of the purity of the poor—a theory that in his day was almost sacred—and did away with the romantic "outlaw" myths that had been an inseparable part of Hungarian cinema. The characters representing violence in *The Round-up*, as in other Jancsó films, are usually faceless. Men in uniforms are intentionally unidentifiable behind their billowing black capes. Since we know nothing about them, they could at any moment be replaced by anyone else. They come from nowhere; we do not know who gives them their orders; they disappear, and others reappear in their places, others who destroy their victims with an identical precision. The same anonymity rules on the other side, the faces of the pursued, the oppressed, are hidden by black hoods. The degradation, brutality, and alienation that are the consequences of violence take place on an anonymous, general plane, on both sides.

Jancsó's efforts to avoid psychologizing and interiority appears in an even purer form in *The Red and the White* (*Csillagosok, katonák*-1967), which deals with a detachment of Hungarian "Reds" in Russia in 1918 during the civil war, when power kept shifting from the "Reds" to the "Whites" and back. With this film the form used by Jancsó has become even more concise: long shots and the tracking shots alternate with close-ups and shots that appear to be static—for the most part of figures filmed in deep focus against an unchanging, indifferent, and lyrically "beautiful" landscape. This dance of death, in which the "Reds" happen to speak in Hungarian and the "Whites" in Russian, a Hungarian-Soviet coproduction, was never distributed in the Soviet Union.

Silence and Cry (*Csend és kiáltás*-1968), for which János Kende was the cameraman, deals with the theme of oppression within the four walls of one family's world, a world that gradually falls apart with the fear that is born of violence and terror. This time the story is set in the period after the Hungarian revolution was crushed in 1919, when constables and soldiers were hunting down everyone suspicious. One of the pursued finds refuge with a farm family, thereby transforming their lives into a frightening cycle of suffering, treachery, and animal craving for survival.

In *The Confrontation* (*Fényes szelek*-1968), Jancsó brought to a logical conclusion his *idée maîtresse*, affirming that power can only be used for its own ends, to maintain itself, not for the sake of anything else, and certainly not for the sake of freedom. At the same time, the stylization of Jancsó's stories came to a peak with the perfectly rhythmical movement of the camera, in phase with the motion of the characters. More than any of his previous films, *The Confrontation* is conceived as a ballet in which individual gestures have a precise political significance. The visual symbology of the images is linked with the aural symbology of the soundtrack; the dialogue,

Confrontation

Winter
Wind

or better said, the monologue, is made up of quotations and period songs. In 1947, a group of Hungarian Communist youngsters "confront" those who do not share their "faith"; more than anything else, such a confrontation means hatred, intolerance, and the quest for power. But parallel conflicts arise within the revolutionary group itself, until finally liquidations within their own ranks are ordered from above. In *The Confrontation,* the revolution is shown for the first time devouring its own children, consuming the ones incapable of escaping the vicious circle of violence.

Winter Wind (Sirokkó-1969) continued Jancsó's extreme, increasingly austere stylization. In this case, the moral deterioration takes place in the thirties, within a group of Croatian nationalists who were being trained on the Hungarian-Yugoslav border to assassinate King Alexander of Yugoslavia. Here once again, another reality emerged, in parallel with the reality of the story itself, to make another metaphorical point about the basic methods of a totalitarian society. Relationships between individuals are characterized by aggressiveness—threats, blackmail, denunciation—with no room left for trust. And again, the one who is to be liquidated could as easily be a fake hero as a fake traitor.

In 1970-1971, Jancsó made four films, two in Hungary and two in Italy. In *Agnus Dei* (*Égi bárány*-1970), he once again returned to 1919, but, as opposed to *Silence and Cry*, where several characters are still fighting for survival, this time the victims of terrorism allow themselves to be slaughtered—and perhaps even welcome it. And again the one that wields the power is a mysterious figure: no one knows anything about him, where he came from, where he is going, including his last victim, a fanatical priest, the first bearer of terrorism. He carries out his executions seemingly without violence, by means of a sort of music. It becomes clear that the masses are ready for him; they prostrate themselves at his feet. This time the system of symbols is taken over from the Catholic liturgy and ritual.

Upon completing *Agnus Dei*, Jancsó went to Italy, where he made *The Pacifist* (*La Pacifista*-1971), in which a pacifist newspaperwoman looks helplessly on as a leftist politician is murdered by rightist anarchists, and the feature-length TV film, *Technology and Ritual* (*La tecnica e il rito*-1971), reducing the legend of Attila the Hun, "the hammer of the world," to its bare bones, a naked journey along the road to power. With *Red Psalm* (*Még kér a nép*-1971) Jancsó created a stratified structure with an even further-reaching conception than ever before. Even though the essence is once again a death dance, this time based on real events from the 1890's and accompanied by quotations from revolutionary classics, songs, and slogans (the original title is taken from Petőfi's poem, "For the moment, the People Still Demand . . ."), the subject is the tragedy of revolutions. The first explosion of violence engenders the joy and the spontaneous enthusiasm of the people, who seem to be ignorant of the armed force that surrounds them. For the first time, Jancsó does not place an equal sign between the two sides of his equation, for the first time, his concluding metaphor speaks of hope and the immortality of the ideals of freedom. No doubt, memories of Berlin in 1953, of Budapest in 1956, and of Prague in 1968 brought on the extremely negative official attacks in Czechoslovakia, the GDR, and the Soviet Union, where the film was not shown. In contrast there was a favorable response in Gierek's Poland.

After the less successful *Rome Needs Another Caesar* (*Roma rivuole cesare*-1973) shot for Italian television, Jancsó continued his choreographic meditations on a single theme in Hungary with *Elektreia* (*Szerelmem, Elektra*-1975). Once again, those who prevail in the name of justice, Elektra and Orestes, are corrupted by their victory. At the end a red helicopter appears, symbolizing some new revolutionary hope and perspective.

It was thanks to years of uninterrupted work on his unique and originally conceived films—he made eight features in Hungary in as many years—that

Jancsó was able to develop a strong, distinctive film style. In a sense, he therefore became a symbol of what many founders of Eastern Europe's nationalized film industries had hoped the new production structure would bring about—strong creative personalities who would be able to develop their art the same way a writer, a poet, a painter or a composer could.

STABILIZATION

Hungary's four production groups for fiction film gradually increased their production from 15 to 20 films a year in the late sixties, which, in addition to being a decent level of general production, included a comparatively large number of high-quality films—about five annually. Not all of them were great works of art, nor did many of them introduce significant formal innovations. For the most part, however, they were interesting commentaries on the contemporary state of Hungarian society. Although the relationship between the artist and the establishment was far from ideal, it was indisputably more productive than in the other countries of Eastern Europe—with the exception of the brief intermezzo in Czechoslovakia. Kádár's vigilance, applied mainly to relations with the Soviet Union, was exercised through a combination of strict controls, with an extensive system of safety valves to avert any explosions. Thus the situation in the cultural sphere began to resemble situations in Hungary's past. As was the case earlier in Yugoslavia, the prevailing tendency was to put negative limits on freedom, suggesting what was forbidden rather than defining what was allowed or obligatory. Thus in Hungary the possibilities of art increasingly became the art of the possible.

In contrast to many other socialist states, the film industry in Hungary in the sixties and early seventies was not deprived of a constant influx of new film-makers, who spread out into the film world after obtaining a good background of basic knowledge at the Béla Balázs studio. The studio also supplied these young artists with the material aid they needed for their first independent work.

WOMEN DIRECTORS

In 1968 and 1969, three women directors made their debuts in Hungarian fiction film. Outstanding among them was Márta Mészáros (b. 1931), a director of short films since 1960, who in such films as *Blow Ball* (*Bóbita*-1964), displayed an intense desire to speak of human relationships as they are experienced at moments of crisis. One aspect of her work was inspired by the fine arts, for example, *The Town of Painters* (*A festök városa*-1964), and *Colors of Vasarhely* (*Vásárhelyi szinek*-1961), in which Mészáros, the daughter of one of the most significant Hungarian sculptors, for the first time in her 30 years discovers the beauty of her homeland. László Mészáros had emigrated with his family in 1936 to the Soviet Union, where he and his wife perished in one of Stalin's concentration camps. Márta Mészáros returned to her homeland as a 15-year-old, and was sent back to the Soviet Union in the fifties to study at VGIK. After 1956, she spent three years in Romania.

Her childhood and her youth among strangers and her long road to find her own personal truth kept reappearing in Mészáros's films; and it was always female characters who were bearers of restlessness and social anxiety: an isolated worker seeking her mother in *Girl* (*Eltávozott nap*-1968), which was her fiction-film debut; a widow, whose husband and the father of her children, a famous economist, dies a tragic death in *Binding Sentiments* (*Holdudvar*-1968). Mészáros's films disclose more than the bitter consequences of centuries of female inequality, which weighed heaviest in contemporary Hungary on the women of the lower social strata; they also show additional aspects of life in Hungary not revealed with the same frankness in the works of other Hungarian directors: on one hand, the existence of a number of young people who live in profound alienation from socialist society, experiencing a deep-seated existential anxiety, and on the other hand, class differences that emerged in the newly stratified Hungarian

Binding
Sentiments

society. In *Riddance* (*Szabad lélegzet*-1973), Mészáros tells of the love of two young people, a girl from a factory and the son of an established member of the "new bourgeoisie," whose life style and opinions differ little, if at all, from those of the prewar middle class. When the parents give the son his choice between the girl or his family's backing, the youth chooses the easy way. *Adoption* (*Örökbefogadás*-1975), another picture of personal individual dilemmas seen as a product of societal circumstances, focused on the solitary struggle of women striving for real emancipation. This time Mészáros concentrated her broad subject matter into an admirably coherent form, and as a result produced her first masterpiece.

Another woman director, Judit Elek (b. 1937), is significant for her profound philosophical contemplation of the cycle of life, expressed in the form of cinéma vérité. After two documentaries showing man in his social contexts—which appeared almost simultaneously with the publication of her novel, *Awakening,* in 1964—she made a medium-length fiction film, *How Long Does Man Matter? (Meddig el az ember*-1967), a meditation on life's end (an old worker retires) and its beginnings (a young apprentice comes to the factory).

The Lady from Constantinople

Elek's first feature film, *The Lady from Constantinople (Sziget a száraz-földön*-1969), was based on the cyclical nature of life, with an old lady, a widow, trying in vain to accommodate herself to a world that is entirely different from the world that once was "hers." With an extraordinary sensitivity to the decor, the atmosphere, the very fragrance of long-lost years, Elek reconstructed the old lady's world, casting on it the spell of days gone by, days brought to life by an old piano, an old-style phonograph, the ceremony of pouring coffee, and long-forgotten memories. In her subsequent films, *Hungarian Village (Istenmezején*-1974) and *A Simple Story (Egyszerü történet*-1975), while continuing to develop the style of her beginnings, Elek attained a high degree of artistic maturity. She worked with nonprofessional actors, using a cinéma vérité style and interviewing her characters herself. These politically engaged films were based on an elaborate system of montage, and drew their essential energy from their rhythmic visual structure. The films deal with the life situation of two young girls in a contemporary Hungarian mining village—revealing two types of behavior, two attitudes, and two aspects of the same reality. All Elek's films bear witness to one important fact: the new social base has left people with the same old prejudices, generational conflicts, existential questions—and the same feelings of frustration and loneliness.

Livia Gyarmathy (b. 1932) was another woman director who applied the method of cinéma vérité to contemporary Hungary. In her medium-length documentary, *Message* (*Üzenet*-1967), inspired by sociological research, she concerned herself with the welfare system in Hungary. Originally a chemical engineer, Gyarmathy had worked several years in a factory, and in her first feature, *Do You Know Sunday—Monday?* (*Ismeri a szandi mandit?*-1968), she chose a large production enterprise as the setting for a story in a comic vein, two women caught in the squirrel-cage of work at the plant. But she could not handle the ironical style she selected for herself, a weakness that was also evident in the script that she wrote in 1971 for her husband, Géza Böszörményi (b. 1924). Entitled *Birdies* (*Madárkák*), it was a weakly structured comedy about two village girls running away to the city. Gyarmathy's and Böszörményi's best film was *Stop the Music* (*Álljon meg a menet*-1973), an ironic observation of blue-collar workers, shot in a kind of "Formanesque" style, but lacking its bite.

GAÁL AND SZABÓ

Thanks to the relative lack of tension mentioned earlier, creative personalities developed rather smoothly in Hungarian film in the sixties, and as a result the characteristic traits of their work remained more stable and permanent. This included their refusal to make a fetish of the precisely prepared script and its approved ideological content, an object of unwarranted respect in the fifties. Another characteristic element was the effort to achieve as broad a range as possible of human testimony. As opposed to the work of the young Poles of this period, Hungarian directors made films with a more broadly based realistic perspective. This effort was in part the result of the endeavor—felt, in many cases, to be an obligation—to treat as profoundly as possible themes about their own people, separated from the world not only by language, but by a history that is less a part of the Eastern European—and hence, strongly Slavic—context than is that of its neighbors. ("The smaller the nation, the longer its anthem," Endre Ady once said.)

In this period, Gaál and Szabó joined Jancsó in the front rank of Hungarian film directors. The confrontation of the rural lifestyle with the rapid changes of an increasingly urban civilization and the skilled use of the visual beauty of the Hungarian landscape, filmed to express a certain gloominess, remained the basic characteristics of Gaál's work. *The Christen-*

ing (*Keresztelö*-1967) and *Dead Landscape* (*Holt vidék*-1971) were built on the conflict between two attitudes toward life, and hence on two sorts of yearnings. In the first film, an elder son, a successful sculptor and a classic example of the new middle class, pays a visit to his family in his native village. The second shows the disintegration of a marriage: the couple lives in a village that is being gradually deserted by its inhabitants, a process that is undermining their relationship, emptying their surroundings, not just of people, but of the essence of life, and drawing them toward an ambiguous and tragic end.

Gaál's most interesting film of that period was *Falcons* (*Magasiskola*-1970), the only motion picture that Gaál did not make from a script of his own. Based on a story by Miklós Meszöly, whose work expresses the existential anxiety and the alienation of modern man, it was Gaál's most abstract film. The process of training falcons to be obedient birds of prey is transformed into a visually conceived parable about a terrorized society. Through stylization, Gaál turned the birds into threatening symbols, viewed with fear by the villagers, and he imbued their trainer with a charge of violence and brutality the like of which had hardly been seen outside of Jancsó's films.

Falcons

Szabó's *Love Film* (*Szerelmes film*-1970) was a failure. It recalled another reality—the emigration after 1956, and the moments of truth and decision that went with it. The basic plot once again was a chronicle of the memories of a young man, the overly wise lad of *Age of Daydreaming* and *Father*. Within the heavy-handed framework of the problem's didactic presentation,

25 Fireman's Street

which remained a part of Hungarian life even into the late sixties, Szabó's heroes, a pair of lovers separated by the year 1956, were simply not believable.

In the incomparably more successful *25 Fireman's Street* (*Tüzoltó utca 25*-1973), Szabó, with Sára at the camera again, returned to the illusive essence of his work, filming a story about the dreams and memories of the inhabitants of an old house in postwar Budapest.

THROWN STONES

Sára was more than just the cameraman for a number of Hungarian films after 1963, he was also one of the motive forces of the film renaissance of the period. He himself directed a series of exceptional short films, and in 1968, made one of the best films of the time, *The Upthrown Stone*

The Upthrown
Stone

(*Feldobott kö*), with Kósa as coauthor of the script. In the spirit of the poem by Ady ("The stone you throw returns to earth / always returns, your faithful child, / small land of mine") was a passionate indictment of the recent past and an equally passionate declaration of love for the Hungarian land. In an autobiographical story that takes place in the early fifties, Sára captures the apprentice years of a young boy who was hindered by political events from gaining a higher education. He uses faces rather than dialogue to depict a country divided by mistrust into hostile camps, but united by a common hatred of foreigners, be it the Greek emigrant or a group of gypsies whose primitive frankness ultimately reflects the views of Sára himself. It was not until 1974 that Sára directed another feature, an amusing allegory of totalitarianism, *Pheasant Tomorrow*.

A number of films contained critiques of Stalinism and post-Stalinist thinking, either through contemporary stories or by the indirect means of historical subjects. Zsolt Kézdi-Kovács (b. 1936) made his debut in 1970, having spent years as Jancsó's assistant after graduating from the Film Academy. In *Temperate Zone* (*Mérsékelt égöy*-1970), Kézdi-Kovács created a chamber piece for three characters, something comparatively uncommon in new Hungarian film. The three: an aging physician who is incapable of freeing himself from a Stalinist past; his wife; and his pupil, who was formerly the wife's lover. Within the bounds of a classical structure, a drama with a broad social background unfolds, in which the doctor's passion for hunting, which was originally reserved for the aristocracy, is only part of a metaphor about the new establishment.

After the rejection of his next script, on a similar theme, Kézdi-Kovács made *Romanticism* (*Romantika*-1972), a story set in the seventeenth century. Its most notable quality is the effectively presented "civilized" atmosphere of life in a century that in fact was only superficially civilized: a young nobleman rejects the privileges of his time and flees to the forest, where he lives naked and alone, wild and free.

Imre Gyöngyössy (b. 1930), after writing scripts for *Green Years, Ten Thousand Suns,* the Czechoslovak film, *Adrift,* and others, made his directorial debut with a stylized treatment of a 1919 legend, *Palm Sunday* (*Viragvasarnap*-1967). *Palm Sunday* presented the tragic demise of the Hungarian Republic of Councils as the legend of the cricifixion of Christ, demonstrating the director's almost Pasolini-like need to complement Marxism with Christianity and vice versa. Gyöngyössy's next film, also done on a surreal plane, was *Legend about the Death and Ressurrection of Two Young Men* (*Meztelen vágy*-1972), a tale filled with an abundance of symbols and myths, in which a passionate explosion of intolerance provokes a group of gypsies to lynch one of their own band along with his white friend.

Ferenc Kardos's *Petöfi 73* (1973) must also be seen as more than a stylized living-theater reconstruction of Hungary's 1848 revolution. The heroes of that revolt—portrayed by young people dressed in the jeans and T-shirts of today—are shown by Kardos mouthing quotations from period speeches

Photography

Petőfi 73

Temperate Zone

about freedom and the need to fight the enemy, an enemy that at that time was not only Austria, but her ally Russia. Kardos, who spent years trying to get approval for scripts that overstepped the bounds of the unwritten agreement between artists and political leadership—his best film in that period was the satirical comedy *Mad Night* (*Egy őrült éjszaka*-1969)—showed himself in *Petőfi 73* to be an excellent director of mass scenes, but the film was not entirely successful, for it was politically impossible to bring this collective psychodrama to its logical conclusion. János Rózsa, who had shared Kardos's debut in 1965, continued the approach used in *Grimace,* though with less success, in *Charmers* (*Bűbájosok*-1969). In 1974, he achieved his greatest success with *Dreaming Youth* (*Álmodó ifjúság*), a poetic version of Béla Balázs's autobiographic novel.

Pál Zolnay's *Photography* (*Fotográfia*-1972) is an example of a sociological approach inspired by a visual imagination. Photographed by another extraordinary Hungarian cameraman, Elemer Ragalyi, this film is an original multilevelled composition, made in the cinéma vérité style of the seventies. The examination of several individual rural lives grows into a poetic enquiry into life, the nostalgia of old age, hatreds and bitterness, and covert dramas.

HUSZÁRIK

An extreme measure of stylization characteristic of one current of Hungarian film-making that draws heavily upon the native roots of estheticism in the fine arts, culminated in the work of Zoltán Huszárik (b. 1931). An eminent graphic artist and painter, Huszárik uses film as an extension of his art work, but at the same time he succeeds in touching on some very profound aspects of the Hungarian tradition. In 1965, he made his internationally renowned short, *Elegy* (*Elégia*), a pictorial composition on the theme of life and death, inspired by the life cycle of one of the oldest symbols in Hungary—horses. The attention aroused by his fiction debut was no less

Elegy

intense, for in making *Sindbad* (*Szinbád*-1971), he revived the hero of the stories of symbolist writer Gyula Krúdy, whose main theme is "life is not worth discussing." A series of visions—composed in refined colors—of habits and manners, flow against the backdrop of the Hungarian capital and the "nests of gentry" at the turn of the century, a social world overflowing with gallantry, refinement, and nonchalant elegance. Through this faded world, which represents a real part of the Hungarian national tradition and lifestyle, walks Sindbad, lover of women and good food, a Hungarian Don Juan, a Proustian hero, a Gargantua, whose love of women and fidelity to the traditions of true gourmandise is more important than life itself, which he measures rather in terms of beauty than in terms of time. The man who, with his camera, painted these surrealist visions and recollections was once again Sára. Huszárik's work stands alone in Hungarian cinema, the expression of the unique personality of its director.

MORALISTS

The fin-de-siècle modern style also inspired Pál Sándor (b. 1939) in *Love Emilia* (*Szeressétek odor Emíliát*-1969), which takes place in a boarding school for girls from aristocratic families, and is conceived above all as a collection of pretty pictures from pretty surroundings. Sándor's debut had been *Clowns on the Wall* (*Bohóc a falon*-1967), about contemporary youngsters, their conflicts with their parents, their petty revolts, and their first loves, and had been full of stylistic ostentation and borrowings from the European new wave. Sándor's third film, *Sarah, My Dear* (*Sárika, drágám*-1971) based on the same subject matter, firmly followed the moralistic current that had always been strong in Eastern Europe. In it, the nonchalance and the indecisiveness of young people is placed in apposition to the commitment of older people. Sándor's most successful film was the ironic *The Old Time Soccer* (*Régi idök focija*-1974), looking at the life and dreams of a small doomed man—a Jew in the thirties, once more against the backdrop of the Hungarian national passion, soccer.

Pál Gábor (b. 1932) is one of the leading moralists of Hungarian film. Originally a teacher, he used his socially critical topics not only to ask questions, but to seek their pedagogical answers as well. Thus, he made *Forbidden Ground* (*Tiltott terület*-1968), about the conflicts that explode at the moment of a castrophe, a fire in a factory; later *Horizon* (*Horizont*-1971) and *Journey with Jacob* (*Utazás Jakabbal*-1972), both stories about young men wandering through Hungary in a quest for "something else."

WHAT IS REVOLUTIONARY?

But what happened to that "most important art" that was to have mobilized the masses, educated "the new man," and helped to resolve the problems of building a new society? What is revolutionary in a society where the revolution is in power? Those were the questions posed by some Hungarian directors in the seventies.

Kovács sought the answer by elaborating on the theme of his *Difficult People*. Both his *Walls* (*Falak*-1967) and *Relay Race* (*Staféta*-1970) are indisputably films of the category referred to in all the countries of Eastern Europe as "films from the present." These films of Kovács's turned on

Walls

people within a bureaucratic and corrupt system who destroy or deform the talents and characters of others. But as soon as he departed from the method of cinéma vérité, the immediacy of Kovács's "difficult people" vanished from the screen, to be replaced by literary figures. In his next film, Kovács returned to the source of his greatest success—*Cold Days*—the past seen as the source of metaphors for the present. *Fallow Land* (*A magyar ugaron*-1972) takes place directly after the revolution was suppressed in 1919, in a period that gave birth to a strange symbology in Hungarian film. Its primary theme is man's adaptability, his willingness to forget today what he believed and worshipped yesterday. Kovács's deepest metaphor about the inner crisis of his generation was *Blindfold* (*Bekötött szemmel*-1974), a film about a priest at the end of World War Two who is confronted with the contradiction between an unquestioning faith and the demands of his religion and real facts. When his superiors manipulate him into giving false testimony, he suffers a profound shock and breaks down. Also Gyula Maár's (b. 1934) first full-length feature, *At the End of the Road* (*Vegül*-1974) belongs in this thematically related group. Maár, another of the Hungarian moralists, originally a teacher and film critic, tells of one day in the life of an old-time communist, one of the core members of the Party, at this moment an old retired man, bitter, frustrated, full of unanswered questions. The film closes with his long, painful weeping.

At the End
of the Road

Péter Bacsó (b. 1928) made his debut in 1963, after having completed numerous scripts and having spent years teaching scriptwriting at the Film Academy. Although he remained true to classical narrative structure, with a precisely detailed script at the basis of his work, in his fifth film he found his own approach. His *Outbreak* (*Kitörés*-1970)—whose co-scriptwriter, György Konrad, also wrote and attracted international attention with his brutal novella, *Case Worker*—as well as his *Present Indicative* (*Jelenidö*-1971) and *The Last Chance* (*Harmadik nekifutás*-1973) are all films about official heroes of the official Hungary, the working class. In Bacsó's films, however, they are tragic heroes, trying to remain "revolutionaries in the land of a victorious revolution," but succumbing in the fight against slipshod attitudes, greed, and the new class stratification. In 1969 Bacsó's *Witness* (*Tanú*), a political tragicomedy whose hero is a witness for the prosecution in the political trials of the fifties, was banned.

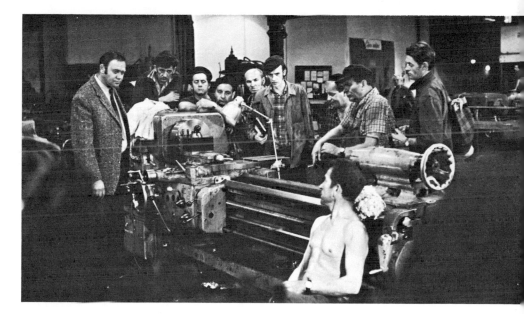

Present Indicative

Another banned film of this period was the debut of Dezsö Magyár (b. 1944), a former assistant to Kovács. The film was *The Agitators* (*Agitatorok*-1969), a kind of philosophical discussion on the 1919 revolution. There is an echo of the questions raised about Hungarian society by some Marxist sociologists in the late sixties, by a group of philosophers who were pupils of Lukács, and finally by leaders of radical youth, who showed traces of the Maoism and the other theories espoused by the student left of Western Europe. Paradoxically, these three groups were the victims of the only political persecutions launched in Hungary in the early seventies. But

Magyar was still able to make a short feature, *Punitive Expedition* (*Buntetö-expedició*-1970), before he left the country.

In the early seventies, the Hungarian film industry, distinguishing itself from the rest of Eastern Europe by the generally high quality of its productions, was about to receive another injection of new blood from the Béla Balázs Studio. Gyula Gazdag (b. 1947) was the first to attract attention, provoking a small storm with his *Whistling Cobblestone* (*A sípoló macskakö* -1971). It told the story of a group of youngsters in a vacation camp who are confronted for the first time with some socialist facts of life—for example, central planning, double standards, and work for the "private" and for the "collective." The cobblestone was thrown clumsily but with considerable force, and had to wait several years to reach international audiences. Another graduate from the Film and Drama Academy, István Dárday (b. 1940), used his feature debut, *Holiday in Britain* (*Jutalomutazás* -1974), to attack the blind obedience and moral hypocrisy of society. An unpretentious satirical comedy, it told the story of a village boy whose upcoming vacation trip is discussed and planned by the whole community, his parents included, without any effort being made to determine his own wishes.

One of the most valid answers to the question about the "new revolutionaries" was offered by Ferenc Kósa, who had made only two features since his debut in 1961. The hero of his *Judgment* (*Itélet*-1970), a broadly based historical allegory, was György Dózsa, who was elected to lead the crusade against the Turks early in the sixteenth century and transformed it into the greatest peasant rebellion of his time. In speaking of the film, he said:

"I wanted to put my own problems on the screen. Being a revolutionary today is no easier than it was 500 years ago. . . . The day of national revolutions is past, a revolution cannot win out if it limits itself to a single country. Dózsa succeeded in uniting serfs of a variety of nationalities under his banner. Nations must join forces in the struggle for revolution, otherwise history will always be full of tragic national revolutions, crushed by the alliance of neighboring reactionary forces. We do not have to go far in search of examples." (*Image et son,* Paris, 1971.)

The theme resembled those of Jancsó, but neither Kósa's nor Sára's camera found a style that would give the reconstruction of historical events the dimensions of a poetic metaphor and protect it from the hazards of an international super-production. They did not succeed until they made their next film, *Beyond Time* (*Nincs idö*-1973), in which baroque visions of a prison atmosphere blend together to tell the story of the origin and suppression of a political prisoners' revolt in the early twenties. The liberal, paternalistic, and, within the bounds of possibility, humanistic director of the prison must finally give way to a proponent of strict law and order. He leaves with a feeling of profound injustice, never completely understanding why people rebel in the most pleasant and most humane prison in the world.

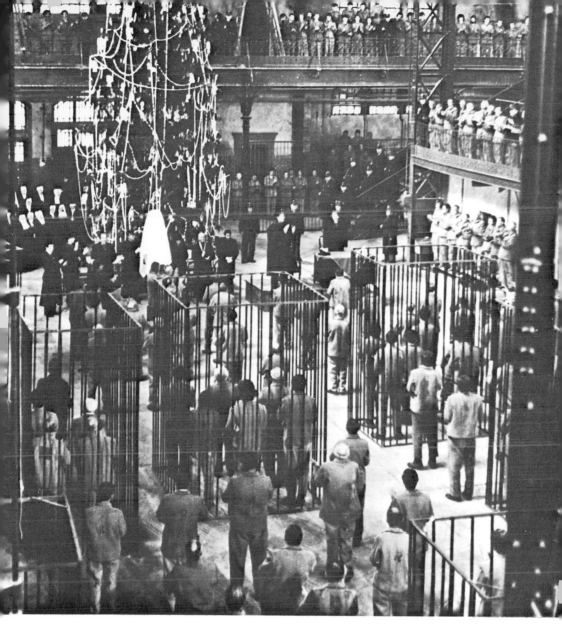

Beyond Time

"NEW FILM":
Yugoslavia After 1961

In 1961, a total of 32 feature films were produced in Yugoslavia, more than in any previous year, but also more than in the years that followed. This production peak was the result of a liberalization of cultural policy and a weakening of control over the film companies, which in turn led to a decrease in the number of ideologically "safe" films on one hand, and an increase in the production of entertainment films on the other. Thus the basic prerequisites for the birth of autonomous film art and of socially critical films were created.

The sudden surge of production brought the first members of the new generation into the studios. Where did they come from, and where did they find their inspiration? As opposed to the other Eastern European countries, Yugoslavia did not have a centrally organized film industry that could assign work to the new directors who came into the industry studios from film schools, or were recruited from the ranks of assistant directors. Moreover, the more democratic structure of Yugoslav society was far more conducive to the growth of original talents among documentary film-makers and in the ranks of amateurs than was the case elsewhere in Eastern Europe.

Documentary film in Eastern Europe of the fifties even lagged behind fiction film, because it had to surrender, a priori, one of its basic esthetic prerequisites: a direct, ideologically unwarped, view of reality. Any exceptions, like Poland's "black series," were soon suppressed. Yugoslavia's looser guidelines and its less stringent censorship of "reality" facilitated the origin of an interesting documentary school there in the fifties, dominated by directors Žika Čukulić, Velimir Stojanović, Milenko Štrpac, Rudolf Sremec, Stjepan Zaninović, Matjaž Klopčič, Krsta Škanata, Puriša Djordjević, Ante Babaja, Vladan Slijepčević, Aleksandar Petrović, Bata Čengić, Jože Pogačnik, Branko Gapo, Branislav Bastać. Later, another generation followed: Mako Sajko, Jože Bevc, Krsto Papić, Vlatko Gilić, Nikola Babić, and others. So that when feature-film production suddenly jumped in volume, many of the directors came from the documentary studios.

Another source for such directors was the amateur film clubs. The greater openness of Yugoslav society again was the source of their development and of the role they were to play in the evolution of Yugoslav film. In an open letter from Yugoslav film-makers, published in July 1966, we read:

The basic principle of the amateur film movement . . . is connected with the conviction that youngsters in the higher grades of secondary schools should learn to express themselves with film as they once learned to walk and talk, as they learn to read and write in school, and as they acquire the fundamental principles of mathematics and the natural sciences. Every person, every child must have the right to express himself by means of film. In order to establish a truly creative atmosphere, the disjunction of the process of film production and distribution must be overcome, and the fences separating movie theaters and the noncommercial film network, and the lines between professional and amateur film must be done away with . . . (*Film a doba* No. 2, 1967).

Since the beginning of the sixties, film amateurs had their own festival in Zagreb—the soul of which was director Mihovil Pansini—which over the years gradually became not only a review of esthetic experiments but also an important sounding board for social consciousness—e.g., the theme of the festival in 1970: "Sexuality as an Effort to Achieve a New Humanism." From the ranks of the amateurs came such fiction-film directors as Živojin Pavlović, Dušan Makavajev, Dragoslav Lazić, Kokan Rakonjac, Želimir Žilnik, Lordan Zafranović, Boštjan Hladnik, and others.

Some film critics and theoreticians—who, in Yugoslavia, as in Czechoslovakia, Hungary, and Poland, played an important role in fostering the imminent "Golden Age" of film—eventually also tried their hands at making films: Vlada Petrić—his most interesting film was *Time of Love* (*Vreme ljubavi*-1966)—Ante Peterlić, and Matjaž Klopčić, among others.

IN THE REPUBLICS

Another thing that came about in the early sixties was the more definitive delimitation of the character of the national film industries of Yugoslavia. Serbian film had the greatest number of film artists—Janković and Novaković of the older generation; then Petrović, Makavejev, Djordjević, Pavlović and Popović; and later in the generation of the late sixties and early seventies, Žilnik, Lazić, Kadijević, Mihić, and Kozomara. Emotionality and spontaneity dominated the works of these and other Serbian filmmakers, as did an original sense of poetry and a veristic approach to reality. The Serbian film-makers included the Vojvodina group in Novi Sad, Žilnik, for example.

Croatian film, showing the penetrating influence of animated film and of the experimental works of such amateurs as Vladimir Petek, was inclined to experimentation and stylization, both of which were based on the high visual level of Croatian culture and, as opposed to the Belgrade School, moved "not from life to ideas, but from idea to life" (S. Novaković). The veterans here include Hanžeković, Bulajić, and Bauer; the younger directors, Babaja, Berković, Vrdoljak; and the Dalmatian directors, Pansini, Mimica, and the younger Ivanda and Peterlić.

Slovenian film, founded primarily by Štiglic, who overshadowed other talented film-makers like Pretnar and Babić, was the source of important esthetic inspiration for Yugoslav film. The generation of the sixties—Hladnik, Pogačnik, and Klopčić—opened the door to a new sensitivity that changed Slovenian film lyricism into a tool of pure film thought and a romantic approach to life.

Bosnian film was one of the smaller film industries to establish a unique position for itself within the context of Yugoslav film. It gave birth to such original film artists as Čengić and Drašković. In addition, the studio for documentary film at Sarajevo had a reputation for being the most daring and the most committed.

INTIMATE FILM AND THE CONTEMPORARY SCENE

Two debuts were noteworthy among the flood of films in 1961: *Two (Dvoje)*, directed by Aleksandar Petrović (b. 1929), and *Dancing in the Rain (Ples v dežju)*, directed by Boštjan Hladnik (b. 1924). Both films responded in their own way to the *nouvelle vague,* and in addition Hladnik clearly attempted to employ some of the esthetics of silent film. Both films showed a lack of concern for the "social" and "pedagogic" line, breaking the ground for both a thematic revolution ("Intimate film and modern film were synonymous for us, in the beginning," said Aleksandar Petrović) and a revolution in the sphere of film language (Hladnik attempted an imaginative depiction of the stream of consciousness). Both of these films on romantic relationships—they could also be labelled "anti-optimistic manifestos"— were dominated by the concept of love as a type of tragic life experience.

Dancing in the Rain

At the same time, a definite turn toward the present was apparent. In 1960, Fedor Škubonja (b. 1926) completed his medium-length film *The Lost Pencil* (*Izgubljena olovka*), an extremely authentic and detailed re-creation of the atmosphere and mood in a village school. Branko Bauer filmed his *Superfluous* (*Prekobrojna*) in 1962, as a view of the naïve and candid élan of the construction job programs for young people, as seen from the perspective of 15 years. He went on a year later to treat conflicts within the workers' administration and the party organization of a factory in *Face to Face* (*Licom u lice*), violating the most rigorously enforced taboo with respect to contemporary subject matter. The traditional form of the film enabled it to reach a broad public, and to elicit an extensive political response as well.

Face
to
Face

Other newcomers were mainly concerned with seeking a new film vocabulary: Ante Babaja (b. 1927) in an expressive stylization of the fairy tale, *The Emperor's New Clothes* (*Carevo novo ruho*-1961), and Živojin Pavlović (b. 1933), Kokan Rakonjac (1935-1969), and Marko Babac with a veristic, almost naturalistic approach to wartime reality in the multi-episode film, *Raindrops, Waters, Warriors* (*Kapi, vode, ratnici*-1962).

This was also a period of the best and most meaningful Yugoslav co-productions. In 1962, Armand Gatti filmed *The Fence* (*L'Enclos*) in Yugoslavia, and a year later, Wolfgang Staudte came to make his *Gentlemen's Party* (*Herrenpartie*).

CONFLICTS

Guardians of the purity of ideology let themselves be heard almost at once. Petrović and Hladnik were criticized, the criticisms becoming even more vociferous with the release of their next films, Petrović's *Days* (*Dani*-1963), a melancholy meditation on the emptiness of a young woman's life, and Hladnik's *Sand Castle* (*Peščeni grad*-1962), an extremely metaphoric and stylized psychological study of three young people trying to escape from life into a world of illusions. Neither film was accepted for official showing at the national festival at Pula, and the new tendencies were sharply attacked in 1963 by leaders of the Communist Party. Another target of the attack was Miča Popović (b. 1923), a well-known Belgrade painter who made his debut in film with the complex portrait of a Yugoslav collaborator with the Nazis, *Man from the Oak Wood* (*Covek iz hrastove šume*-1963), twice banned and eventually reedited; and yet another was Živojin Pavlović, for his feature debut, *The Return* (*Povratak*-1963), depicting the vain efforts of a former convict to find his place in a society that refuses to help him. The release of this film was delayed until 1965.

The decision of the district court in Sarajevo banned the showing of *The City* (*Grad*), another multi-episode film by Pavlović, Rakonjac, and Babac, "because it could have a negative influence on the public, above all on young people." Aleksandar Petrović spoke out about this film at the Pula film festival that year: "As a result of a lack of comprehension and understanding, one of the best films Yugoslavia has produced was tossed into the wastebasket."

But by now, in Yugoslavia as in, for example, Czechoslovakia, the reaction to such prohibitions or to critical attacks on film-makers (like the one made by Velko Vlahović, chairman of the ideological commission of the Central Committee of Yugoslavia's Communist Party, in December 1963) could only be the opposite of the one intended. They aroused violent discussions, obliging film-makers and critics to formulate, step by step, a concrete program and specific aims for film work.

SECOND REVOLUTION

These conflicts were part and parcel of the struggle over the future political development inside Yugoslavia that was taking place among the political leadership of the country. The result was the so-called "Second Yugoslav Revolution," which brought with it an expansion of social and economic democracy. One victim of this expansion, in 1966, was Yugoslavia's "number 2" man, Aleksandar Ranković, chief of the secret police. Another decentralization of the economy took place; the rights of the republics were fortified. The Party was reformed, as was the state constitution. But it was not simply a matter of resolving conflicts in the sphere of established power, for the revolt of Belgrade students in 1968 clearly indicated that the young generation was demanding its share in the creation of the society.

In film, this process was ultimately reflected in the strengthening of creative autonomy, and, contrary to the other Eastern European countries, in the gradual legalization of new forms of film production, enabling independent groups of film-makers to obtain means to make films outside the framework of existing film enterprises. This measure, however, not only expanded the radius of action for new talents, but also gave far greater opportunities to less talented people, who proceeded to speculate on the low level of audience taste.

"NOVI FILM"

Such is the backdrop of the history of what is known as "New Film" (Novi film), the greatest success so far achieved by the young film industry of Yugoslavia. It was a period of personal films, films that claimed the right to subjective interpretations of the lives of individuals and society, the right to "open metaphors," leaving room for viewers to think and feel for themselves.

In 1964, Kokan Rakonjac made his first independent feature with a "negative hero," *Traitor* (*Izdajnik*), followed shortly by a second, *Horn* (*Klakson*-1965), about the vain attempts of a group of city-dwellers to overcome solitude and alienation. In 1969, just before his sudden death, he made the film, *Pent-Up*(*Zazidani*), a visually arresting, dynamically edited film about prison life with definite political overtones.

In 1964, Vladan Slijepčević (b. 1930) made his debut with *The Real State of Affairs* (*Pravo stanje stvari*), an interesting analysis of marital infidelity that showed the deep influence of documentary film. But his greatest success was *Protegé* (*Stičenik*-1966), a realistic exposition of corruption within bureaucratic institutions.

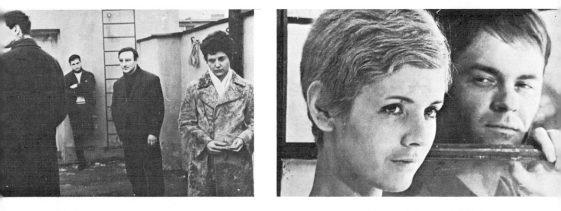

Traitor   The Real State of Affairs

Ante Babaja, who had returned to work in documentary film, made his best fiction film, *The Birch Tree* (*Breza*-1967), a picturesque love tragedy of a peasant girl that was visually inspired by Croatian folk painting.

Reflecting the inspiration by form that was characteristic of film-makers from Zagreb, scriptwriter Zvonimir Berković (b. 1928) wrote the script for his directorial debut, *Rondo* (1966), a tale of a romantic triangle, as a

The Birch Tree

Prometheus from
Vishevica
Island

literary and cinematic variation on a rondo by Mozart. He made his next
independent film, *Journey to the Site of the Accident* (*Putovanje na mjesto
nesreče*) five years later.

MIMICA

Vatroslav Mimica, one of the founding fathers of the Zagreb school of
animated film, returned to fiction film with *Prometheus from Vishevica
Island* (*Prometej sa otoka Viševice*-1964), a successful man's retrospective
view of the locale of his wartime heroism that was infused with melancholy,
sorrow, and disillusionment. The film was a landmark for two reasons.
First, because this was the war as described by a member of a generation
that had spent its youth in the mountains, rifles in hand, the generation
that gave its best years to the building of a new life and had already begun
to look back and balance accounts—not without bitterness and melancholy.
Second, Mimica was the first Yugoslav film-maker to blend plot and
narration into a single unit—the form giving birth to the story, and vice
versa. In so doing, Mimica showed the influence of the Zagreb animation
studio where he had worked, and where a new generation emerged with
Bourek, Dragić, Stalter, Vunak, Zaninović, and others. An ordinary
journalist's daydreams, breaking the monotonous rhythm of his days, are
the main style-forming element of Mimica's best film, *Monday or Tuesday*
(*Pondeljak ili utorak*-1966). Not only the atmosphere, but the very plot of
the terror that descends on a Dalmatian town in *Kaia, I'll Kill You* (*Kaja,
ubit ču te*-1967) grows out of the stylization of visual elements, the brown
parched walls of buildings, the narrow streets, and the black shirts of the
local fascists. The Chekhovian *Event* (*Dogadaj*-1969) consists of innumerable minute, almost ritualistic, details that gradually link together to tell
the tragic story of an old man and his grandson who are attacked by robbers

Monday or Tuesday

on the way to market; the old man is killed, and, in the course of the dispute as to whether the child should be killed as well, the brigands kill one another. The plot and the cinematic form are always so closely linked, that it is as if the tragedy in all of Mimica's films was simply the derailment of an esthetic structure created by the camera. *Nourishee* (*Hranjenik*-1971) is also a philosophical metaphor, in which the concentration camp, created by various shades of yellow, green, and black, is rather a picture of a world in which helpless people, left to their own devices, try over and over again to achieve a bit of freedom.

DJORDJEVIĆ

The poetry of Puriša Djordjević is different, more literary, in many ways imbued by the sources of surrealist associations, but the departure point

Morning

of the retrospective view of the partisan war and the postwar period is the same. The nucleus of Djordjević's work is the tetralogy, *Girl* (*Devojka*-1965), *Dream* (*San*-1966), *Morning* (*Jutro*-1967), and *Noon* (*Podne*-1968), beginning with a tragic wartime tale, followed by a poetic meditation about partisan warfare, a somber study of a peacetime dawn, and a reflection, in the full light of noon, on the break with Moscow. Except for the last section, in which Djordjević was no longer able to subjugate the color material to his poetics, the entire cycle is unified in style, and succeeds at a difficult task: capturing the same material—for example, the tragic reality of partisan warfare—by means of the most pictorial, the most dreamy of metaphors and also in a direct, almost documentary approach while maintaining a single style. It is as if the same questions were being asked that were posed all over Yugoslavia in those years: are free people able to sing about freedom the same way they did when they were dreaming about it during the war? And are they able to live in freedom? In his next film, *Cross Country* (1969), Djordjević changed topics, but he did not give up his vocabulary in the multilateral, almost grotesque story of a vain attempt to use athletics to tame a body that yearns for physical love. His return to wartime subject matter in *The Cyclists* (*Biciklisti*-1970) was very much influenced by the absurd-comedy poetics of the youngest generation. In 1975 Djordjević made a comeback to the forefront of the, at that time, already rather dull scene of Yugoslav film with *Pavle Pavlović*. His witty nonconformist depiction of corruption within the Yugoslav economic system—obviously following too closely Tito's attack on the same corruption— was labelled as "ridiculing the system of self-government" and prohibited from competing in the Yugoslav film festival at Pula.

PETROVIĆ

Throughout the entire period, Aleksandar Petrović remained one of the central figures of "New Film." Not only by his films, but also by his dynamic personality, which was intensely apparent in his activity as a journalist, as chairman of the Union of Film Workers, Chief of the Belgrade film studio, Professor of the Film School, and primarily as a film director. *Three* (*Tri*-1965), a multi-episode film based on the stories of Antonij Isaković, was a mature work about three encounters with death, leaving an open question at the end: to kill or to forgive? Some critics consider this film to be the director's best, but Petrović's greatest public success at home and abroad was his next film, *I Even Met Happy Gypsies* (*Skupljači perja*-1967), in which he strove intentionally for the most straightforward narrative form, supported by devastatingly real pictorial material, but at the same time drew many a metaphor for contemporary life and the contemporary world from the naïve tragedy of the lot of the Vojvodina gypsies. Since the borderline between life and fantasy, between reality and its grotesque projection in the world of imagination, attracted Petrović more and more, it is no

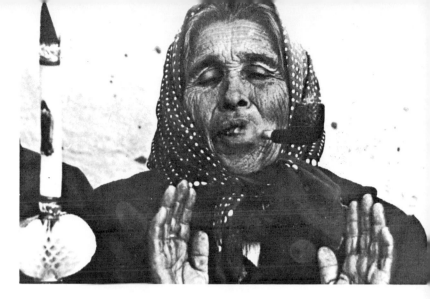

coincidence that he found the inspiration for his next two films in the work
of two writers who were penetratingly aware of just these dimensions of life
and the world: F. M. Dostoyevsky and Mikhail Bulgakov, each representing
a different epoch in Russian history. In *It Rains in My Village* (*Biče skoro
propast sveta*-1969), Petrović was inspired by motifs from Dostoyevsky's
Possessed, from a contemporary news story, and from the Soviet occupation
of Czechoslovakia. Against the backdrop of a gypsy choir singing about the
end of the world, he used the style of naïve art to present a testimony about
the omnipresence of evil, backwardness, and cynicism. The final form of the
film, however, remained too "open," as was the case with his most
ambitious film, *The Master and Margarita* (*Majstor i Margarita*-1972).
In the latter, an ambitious effort to put on film Bulgakov's multifaceted
novel, without limiting the fantastic and grotesque elements of Bulgakov's
metaphors by the realism of the reconstruction of Moscow in the twenties,
was uneven in quality. Under difficult conditions Petrović simply did not
always find a style that would provide a cinematic equivalent to the style
of the novel.

PAVLOVIC

Živojin Pavlović, a short-story writer and novelist, and a successful amateur
film artist, was from his very entry on the scene both the focus and the
instigator of conflicts that accompanied the birth and the successful advance
of 'New Film." His style is a poetic naturalism; his goal is to debunk all
myths about reality; and his "heroes" are generally people from Dostoyevsky's Yugoslavia. "How is it," he asks, "that one Russian, Lev Nikolaevich
(Tolstoy), seems to speak to us from the unreal world of fairy tales, while
another, Fedor (Dostoyevsky), fascinates us more and more with his truth?"
Dostoyevsky was Pavlović's source for his second feature film, *The Double*
(*Sovražnik*-1965); but immediately thereafter, with collaboration on the
script by two well-known journalists, Mihić and Kozomara, he turned to
current themes and portraits of Yugoslav social reality, *The Awakening of*

The Awakening
of the Rat

BUĐENJE PACOVA

the Rat (Budjenje pacova-1966), an evocative record of contemporary
existence in the slums of Belgrade, and When I Am Pale and Dead (Kad
budem mrtav i beo-1967), about the human "by-products" of industrialization. The Ambush (Zaseda), filmed in 1969, was a bitter view of the
period immediately following the war, "when Stalin was God." The hero
of the film is first a participant in a senseless killing in the name of the
revolution, and then is killed himself, in the name of the same cause. This
was totally Pavlović's film, as was Red Husks (Rdeče klasje-1971), a
reconstruction of the early postwar period and the failure of collectivization,
with some new poetic overtones made possible by Pavlović's first use of
color. In 1974 he went to Slovenia to shoot The Flight of a Dead Bird (Let
mrtve ptice), a melancholy tale of a village at the moment it is experiencing
the destruction of patriarchal norms of life under the pressure of contemporary ethics.

Of the directors that can be considered as founding fathers of "New
Film," only Boštjan Hladnik did not entirely live up to what he seemed to
promise at the outset. After the attack on Sand Castle, he made two films in
West Germany, Erotikon (1963) and Mai Britt (1964). The estheticism of
his subsequent films, made back at Viba Film in Slovenia, aged rapidly,
and the comic detective fantasies The Shout of the Sun (Sončni krik-1968),
Masquerade (Maškarada-1971) and When the Lion Comes (Ko pride
lev-1972) could not be salvaged from a similar fate, even by an emphasized
eroticism.

MAKAVEJEV

Dušan Makavejev (b. 1932) was the most original figure of "New Film."
When he made his first feature film in 1965, Man Is Not a Bird (Čovek nije
tica), he had to his credit several successful documentaries—e.g., Parade,
an ironic comment on a May Day manifestation—and a number of

Man Is Not a Bird

experimental avant-garde films, all of which reflected his background as
an amateur and as a student at the Film Academy. His ironic documentaristic vision was apparent in his feature debut, but the antipsychological
structure of the film was entirely new, even—as eventually became apparent—outside the context of Yugoslav cinema. For Makavejev, social reality
was nothing but a backdrop against which he unfolded the theme of an
erotic relationship between an engineer who is a party member and a young
hairdresser, who fulfills the sole function of a "sexual object." Makavejev
took this story as an opportunity to make some sophisticated and ironic
comments on Yugoslav society and its taboos—a commentary he continued
in subsequent films. *An Affair of the Heart or The Tragedy of the Switchboard Operator* (*Ljubavni slučaj ili tragedija službenice PTT*-1967) was tied
to social reality only by a thin thread. The center of the story is an erotic
relationship that ends up consuming both the man and the woman in the

An Affair of
the Heart or
The Tragedy
of a
Switchboard
Operator

middle of a cool, indifferent world. But Makavejev was not Pavlović; he did not accuse or condemn, he simply made a statement, and played with his subject and characters sadly and with virtuosity. *Innocence Unprotected* (*Nevinost bez zaštite*-1968) was above all a game, apparently lacking any deeper meaning, the triumph of the artist as *homo ludens*. A collage of Yugoslavia's first sound film with Nazi newsreels and 1968 discussions, it is a tour de force that suddenly emerged as an ironic ideological statement. In this sense, *Innocence Unprotected* was also a harbinger of Makavejev's provocative film, *W. R.—Mysteries of the Organism* (*W. R.—Misterije organizma*-1971). Here the surrealistic collage was composed of a grotesque evocation of Wilhelm Reich's theory of orgasm ("even the human orgasm can become a part of society, with all its systems, controls, viewpoints, and confusion"), an erotic criticism of the revolution ("Free love was where the October Revolution failed!"), and Stalinism, as seen from the same standpoint ("Stalin is a terribly pornographic figure"). In its visualization of sexual symbols and in its disclosure of the degeneration of the October Revolution, the film went further than any other film in Eastern Europe, and was an indisputable triumph of Makavejev's art. It was not shown in Yugoslavia, though. Makavejev's next cruel and bitter parable about the contemporary world, based on the esthetics of ugliness and repulsiveness, *Sweet Movie* (1974), had to be made abroad.

W. R.— Mysteries of the Organism

THIRD GENERATION

Along with Makavejev, a third generation of Yugoslav postwar film-makers came to the fore. While the generation of Mimica, Petrović, Pavlović, Djordjević and the others looked back on its own past, the new generation regarded the war and the laying of the foundation for Yugoslav socialism as ancient history. For them, it was a period that the members of the third generation were cast into, one for which they were not responsible, a period that they treated as disrespectfully as any new generation treats the history of its fathers.

The new generation passed through the door that had been opened by the founders of "New Film" into a period that saw the overall blossoming of Yugoslav democracy and culture—for literature, the theater, and the fine arts did not lag far behind the advances in cinema. But the student revolt, the Soviet occupation of Czechoslovakia, economic problems, and the tension generated among the various nationalities by the initiation of the new policies gradually fortified the position of the critics of cultural radicalism. No sooner had the jury at the national film festival at Pula distributed its awards in 1969, than the central daily of the Yugoslav Communist Party, *Borba,* published an eight-page article entitled "The Black Wave in Our Film" and the storm clouds began to gather. One of the targets of the criticism was Želimir Žilnik's (b. 1942) debut, *Early Works* (*Rani radovi*-1969), a Godardian reflection and at the same time a radical political pamphlet, resounding with the echoes of student unrest and, fiercely and provocatively, but with a feeling for grotesque self-irony, asking questions about the relationship between the principles that were preached and social

Early Works

practice. Gordan Mihić (b. 1938) and Ljubiša Kozomara (b. 1935), both
known until then primarily as scriptwriters, made their debut as directors
with *A Tale* (*Bajka*-1969), which was a matter-of-fact description, free of
all ideology or poetization, of "the world around us" in its most somber
aspects. The story, which seemed at first glance to be a detective story,
showed the almost grotesquely tuned destruction of the heroes. Its original
title, *Crows,* seems, in fact, more appropriate. This team of directors, who
showed themselves in this film to be mature artists, went on in 1972 to make
Bug Killer (*Bubasinter*).

The film of the Sarajevan documentarist Bata Čengić (b. 1931), *The Role
of My Family in the World Revolution* (*Uloga moje porodice u svetskoj
revoluciji*-1971)—based on a book and play by one of the most important
writers of this period, Boro Ćosić—was far more ideological. A satirical
pastiche of the frenetic period following the liberation, it was strongly
influenced by the cabaret style of the original play and by the work of
Godard, but also contained an abundance of local wit and humor. Čengić
had already demonstrated nonconformism in his debut, *Little Soldiers*
(*Mali vojnici*-1968), a story about the chauvinism that is the heir to war—a
little German boy, a war orphan, turns up at an institution for Yugoslav
war orphans. But Čengić's greatest success was *The Life of a Shock Worker*
(*Slike iz života udarnika*-1972), another return to the period immediately
following the war and to the naïve enthusiasm of its protagonists, who
gradually find themselves on the periphery of social reality. The film
succeeded in firmly combining a melancholy sympathy for the film's hero
with a sense of social irony and the grotesque.

The Role of My Family in the World Revolution

(Left) Life of
a Shock Worker

(Above) Funeral
Feast

In Slovenia, Matjaž Klopčić followed Štiglić's lyricism and Hladnik's sense of stylistic experimentation with his own original narrative style, which emerged not only from his genuine sense of form, but also from his familiarity with, and his love for, his native Ljubljana. The poetically perceived city is the true hero of his films, which are set both in the present—*A Nonexistent Story* (*Zgodba ki je ni*-1966) and particularly *On Wings of Paper* (*Na papirnatih avionih*-1967)—and in the past—his film about wartime youth, *Funeral Feast* (*Sedmina*-1968), also known as *Greetings to Maria* (*Pozdravi Mariju*). Klopčić finally turned away from Ljubljana in his abstract anti-ideological metaphor about the contemporary world, *Oxygen* (1971). In 1973 he directed a visually rich screen version of Ivan Tevčar's Slovenian classic, *Autumn Flowers* (*Cvetje v jeseni*) and in 1975 an estheticizing symbolic metaphor about the world as a brothel—but without the grip of a Genet—*Fear* (*Strah*). His compatriot, Rajko Rangl, was also rather successful with his first directorial effort, *Dead Ship* (*Mrtva ladja*-1972).

There were many noteworthy debuts in this period. In his film *Horoscope* (*Horoskop*-1969) Čengić's fellow Bosnian, Boro Drašković (b. 1937), painted a suggestive picture of the emptiness of idle life in a story of a group of young people who pass day after day in a small-town railroad station. The vitality of the characters inevitably leads to gratuitous violence. Drašković's second feature, *Knockout* (*Nokaut*-1971), designed to follow Makavejev's concept of a "truly international picture," was a visually attractive formalist experiment.

The debut of Zagreb director Branko Ivanda (b. 1941), greatly influenced by the Czech school, was *Gravitation* (*Gravitacija*-1968), a true-to-life

picture of his contemporaries, not just in Yugoslavia, but throughout
Eastern Europe. Lacking ideals, lacking any great degree of ambition,
adaptable, adjusting to the situation at hand, the young people Ivanda
portrayed in this film were fully in keeping with the film's ironical subtitle,
"The fantastic youth of bank clerk Boris Horvat."

Another Croatian to make his debut was former film critic Ante Peterlić,
who directed *Random Life* (*Slučajni život*-1972). But the really important
newcomer to Jadran Film in Zagreb was one of Yugoslavia's foremost
documentarists, Krsto Papić (b. 1933). His third feature film, *Handcuffs*
(*Lisice*-1970), a hardy peasant drama dealing with party bickerings during
the early forties, reconstructed in the actual locations, is one of the most
noteworthy features of the early seventies and received justified international
acclaim. Papić was successful in maintaining his new position among
Yugoslav film directors with his next film, *A Village Performance of Hamlet*
(*Hamlet u Mrduši Donjoj*-1973), a farcical spoof of an amateur theatrical
production in a Croatian village that develops into a strong drama about
the abuse of power.

Handcuffs

In Belgrade, it was above all Petrović's pupil at the Film Academy,
Miloš Radivojević (b. 1939) who followed the formal efforts of Mimica and
Berković with the film *Bats in the Belfry* (*Bube u glavi*-1970), a story about
how difficult it is to identify with contemporary society. The tragic heroes of

this film are a young couple who find themselves patients at a psychiatric clinic. In *Film Without Words* (*Film bez reči*-1972), as well as in *Testament* (1975), Radivojević elaborated even further on his style and his theme, relying heavily on the expressive mobile talent of a single actor. Zdravko Randić (b. 1925) filmed his Serbian Carmen, *Traces of a Brunette* (*Tragovi crne devojky*-1972) according to a script by Ž. Pavlović.

No review of the Golden Age of Yugoslav film would be complete without a mention of such directors of photography as Tomislav Pinter, Aleksandar Petković, Milorad Jakšić-Fando, Frano Vodopivec, Mihajlo Popović, Branko Perak, and Janez Kališnik; and in the younger generation, Karpo Ašimović-Godina, Ognjen Miličević, Ivica Rajković, and others. Without these cinematographers "New Film" would never have come into being.

THE OTHER SIDE OF THE STORY

We must of course not forget that "New Film" existed in parallel with, and surrounded by, the rest of Yugoslav film production, primarily heroic war films and films based on literature. An example of these films that should not be omitted is *Moaning Mountain* (*Lelejska gora*-1968), a forceful adaptation of an important war novel by Montenegran writer S. Mihalić that was directed by his compatriot, Zdravko Velimirović (b. 1934), a documentarist who made his debut in 1965 as codirector of a mediocre Yugoslav-Soviet political coproduction, *Mines Removed* (*Provereno, min niet*).

Also characteristic of this period was a wave of commercialization, typical of a large portion of the production in those years, amounting to between 25 and 30 fiction features annually. At the same time, Yugoslav studios and locations became very popular with film-makers from abroad. International coproductions of all varieties were made in Yugoslavia, which the individual Yugoslav film enterprises hoped (often mistakenly) would make up for the box-office failures of some local productions. Between 1957 and 1973, 110 such features were shot in Yugoslavia. Finally, the new organization of film production, and above all the distribution of federal subsidies (most of which went to Serbian cinema) evoked complaints, disputes, and controversies among the studios of the various republics, reflecting the overall political situation in the country and setting a pattern for the immediate future.

NEW FILM AND YUGOSLAV SOCIALISM

"New Film" was a genuine, authentic product of the "second revolution." It was the art of democratic socialism, an art that has no duties and obligations, but rather the freedom to be a conscience—often an unavoidably sombre one—of the land, the nation, the society, and the individuals that comprise it. It was more than the expression of Milovan Djilas's idea that "the obligation of man in our day is to accept the imperfection of society as a reality, but simultaneously to understand that humanism, humanist dreams and ideas are essential if society is to be constantly reformed, improved, and pushed forward. . . . At the instant a Utopian rises to power, he becomes a dogmatic, and, in the name of his scientism and his idealism, he can very easily bring misfortune on his people." (*The Unperfect Society*) The works of "New Film" were often an echo of the ideas of people who—like the philosophers of Belgrade and Zagreb associated with the magazine *Praxis*—maintained that creative Marxism, as opposed to Stalinist positivism, must be a constant source of criticism of socialist society. The creators of "New Film" numbered themselves, for the most part, among those who opposed democratic self-government to bureaucratic statism, who advocated praxis as the criterion and critique of ideology; they stormed against Marxist-Leninist determinism, which replaces the Providence of the Christians with social laws; they posed pressing questions as to the causes of man's alienation in a society that was supposed to have eliminated its causes. And all that in a country that was not only a state composed of a number of nationalities, but a land that stood with one foot in the middle of the twentieth century, and the other far back in the nineteenth.

As a result of the democratization of the system that took place in the second half of the sixties, conflicts surfaced that had been concealed by the prior, more closed and centralized one. The disputes between the more advanced and the more backward sections of the country were soon referred to as nationalistic, which gave many people a welcome opportunity to "repair the course," and to take revenge for 1966. The attack, led at first against the so-called Croatian nationalists, turned into a broad campaign in 1972, with purges, arrests, and even trials aimed against the liberal wing of the Yugoslav Communist Party, intellectuals, representatives of the radical students, etc.

Downstream
the Sun

Sutjeska

COUNTEROFFENSIVE

This counteroffensive of the "center-of-the-road" probably hit film harder than any other sphere of culture. Makavejev and Pavlović were expelled from the Party and Petrović had to leave his position at the Film Academy; Miča Popović was vociferously attacked; work was stopped on a number of films; production dropped to a bare 15 features in 1973; and the heroic partisan themes came to the forefront once again, along with the more conservative, tradition-oriented directors. These included Fedor Škubonja, who made an interesting film in 1969, *Downstream the Sun* (*S tokom sonca*), bringing shocking social facts onto the screen against the backdrop of a conflict in an isolated mountain village. One of these directors was Croatian Antun Vrdoljak (b. 1931), whose most successful films were *When the Bells Start Ringing* (*Kad čuješ zvona*-1969) and the war film, *A Pine Tree Grows in the Mountains* (*U gori raste zelen bor*-1971). Another film-maker was Serbian Djordje Kadijević (b. 1933), director of the films *Expedition* (*Trek*-1968), about a farmer's travels across Yugoslavia during World War Two, *The Colonel's Wife* (*Pukovnikovica*-1972), an ironic genre portrait from the period of the debacle of the Austrian army during World War One, and above all *The Feast* (*Praznik*-1967), a strong picture of a massacre of a Yugoslav village that is the result of the political rivalry of Nationalist and Communist Partisan forces during World War Two. The younger ones include Dragovan Jovanović, who made *Girl From the Mountains* (*Devojka sa planine*-1972); Branimir Toni Janković (b. 1934), who directed *The Stars Are the Eyes of the Warriors* (*Zvezde su oči ratnika*-1971), about the destiny of a group of children and old people during the Nazi occupation, *A Day Longer Than a Year* (*Dan duži od godine*-1972), inspired by the earthquake at Banja Luka in 1969, and *The Bloody Fairy Tale* (*Krvava bajka*-1969), a cinematic poem inspired by a tragic episode from World War Two, when the Nazis killed 120 children from a Sunday school in the Serbian town of Kragujevac; Macedonian Branko Ivanov-Gapo (b. 1931), the director of *World Without War* (*Svet bez rata*-1972) and *The Shot* (*Pucanj*-1973); and others. Long sought-for funds to finish another patriotic super-production, *Sutjeska,* suddenly were available; the film was directed by Stipe Delić, with Richard Burton in the role of Tito. The future of the young generation and of all film-makers considered to be a part of the "New Film" was extremely uncertain; some of its members sought opportunities to continue their work abroad.

The Twentieth National Film Festival in Pula in the summer of 1973—dominated by *Sutjeska*—was a faithful reflection of the crisis that had developed. In Yugoslavia, however, as opposed to the other Eastern European countries, the struggle for the future of what "New Film" had achieved, and for freedom of culture and art in the broader sense of the word, to some extent took the form, as it had in the past, of a public confrontation between opposing opinions and concepts. As the future course of Yugoslavia was being worked out in these debates, so also was the destiny of a national film culture that had taken important and original place in the Europe of the sixties.

APPENDIX

Because the question of Socialist Realism, and the proper definition of it, is a complex one, and this book refers to it constantly, some quotations may help the reader to understand better the different aspects of the problem.

Our literature is imbued with enthusiasm and the spirit of heroic deeds. It is optimistic, but not optimistic in accordance with any "inward," animal instinct. It is optimistic in essence, because it is the literature of the rising class, of the proletariat, the only progressive and advanced class. Our Soviet literature is strong by virtue of the fact that it is serving a new cause—the cause of socialist construction.

Comrade Stalin has called our writers engineers of human souls. What does it mean? What duties does the title confer upon you?

In the first place, it means knowing life so as to be able to depict it truthfully in works of art, not to depict it in a dead, scholastic way, not simply as "objective reality," but to depict reality in its revolutionary development.

In addition to this, the truthfulness and historical concreteness of the artistic portrayal should be combined with the ideological remolding and education of the laboring people in the spirit of socialism. This method in *belles lettres* and literary criticism is what we call the method of socialist realism.[1]

A. A. ZHDANOV
at the First Congress of Soviet Writers, 1934

The difference between socialist realism and the old realism consists, among other things, of the fact that the contradiction between philosophy and artistic method in socialist realism will be less characteristic, since the subjective hopes and interests of the proletariat do not contradict the objective laws of historical development . . .[2]

A. FADEYEV
"Socialist Realism," 1932

. . . Socialist realism wages a struggle against "vestiges of the past" and their corrupting influences, and also tries to uproot these influences. But its major task is to evoke a socialist, revolutionary understanding and comprehension of the world. . . . In general, we ought as often as possible to draw writers' attention to the following: the predictions of scientific socialism are being more and more widely and deeply brought about by the

[1] *Problems of Soviet Literature* (International Publishers, New York).

[2] *Socialist Realism in Literature and Art* (Progress Publishers, Moscow, 1971, pp. 65-66).

activity of the Party; the fundamental strength of these predictions lies in their scientific foundation. The socialist world is being built and the bourgeois world is crumbling just as Marxist reasoning foresaw.

Hence a completely legitimate conclusion may be drawn: an artist whose imagination is properly directed, who relies on a broad knowledge of reality and an intuitive wish to give his material the most perfect possible form, and who supplements his data with what is possible and desirable, is also able to "foresee"; in other words, socialist realist art has the right to exaggerate, to "fill out." "Intuitive" should not be understood as meaning something ahead of knowledge, something "prophetic." It provides the missing links and details to experimental searches when they have been started as hypotheses or images . . .[3]   MAXIM GORKY

in a letter to A. S. Shcherbakov, February 19, 1935

. . . Socialist realism differs sharply from bourgeois realism. The whole point is that socialist realism is itself active. It not only gets to know the world but strives to reshape it. It is for the sake of this reshaping that it gets to know the world, which is why all its pictures bear a peculiar stamp that is immediately felt. Socialist realism knows that Nature and society are dialectical and are constantly developing through contradictions, and it feels first and foremost this pulse, this passage of time. Moreover, it is purposeful: it knows what is good and what is evil and notes which forces hinder movement and which facilitate its tense straining toward the great goal. This illuminates each artistic image in a new way, both from within and from without. Hence, socialist realism has its own themes, for it considers important precisely what has a more or less direct bearing on the main process of our life, the struggle for a complete transformation of life on socialist lines . . .

. . . I might be asked whether that is not a form of romanticism. If your realists do not simply describe their environment as it actually is but introduce a subjective element, isn't that a tendency towards romanticism? Yes, it is. Gorky was right when he repeated several times that literature must be above reality, and that the very knowledge of reality was necessary in order to overcome it; he was right when he called such a militant and laborious overcoming of reality in its literary reflection romanticism.

Our romanticism, however, is a part of socialist realism. To a certain extent socialist realism is unthinkable without an element of romanticism. In this lies its difference from detached recording. It is realism plus enthusiasm, realism plus a militant mood. When this enthusiasm and militant mood predominate, when, for example, we introduce hyperbole or caricature for satirical purposes, or when we describe the future that we cannot yet know, or when we round off a type that has not yet crystallized

---

[3] *Socialist Realism in Literature and Art* (Progress Publishers, Moscow, 1971), pp. 53–54.

in reality and paint him in the stature toward which we aspire, we are, of course, giving emphasis to the romantic element . . .[4]

ANATOLY LUNACHARSKY,
"On Socialist Realism," 1933

. . . Soviet art must be "realistic."

Realism can be—and has been—a highly critical and progressive form of art: confronting reality "as it is" with its ideological and idealized representations, realism upholds the truth against concealment and falsification. In this sense, realism shows the ideal of human freedom in its actual negation and betrayal and thus preserves the transcendence without which art itself is cancelled. In contrast, Soviet realism conforms to the pattern of a repressive state. The conscious and controlled implementation of state policies through the medium of literature, music, painting, and so forth, is by itself not incompatible with art (examples could be cited from Greek art to Bert Brecht). However, Soviet realism goes beyond the artistic implementation of political norms by accepting the established social reality as the final framework for the artistic content, transcending it neither in style nor in substance. . . . The future is said to be nonantagonistic to the present; repression will gradually and through obedient effort engender freedom and happiness—no catastrophe separates history from prehistory, the negation from its negation. But it is precisely the catastrophic element inherent between man's essence and his existence that has been the center toward which art has gravitated since its secession from ritual. The artistic images have preserved the determinate negation of the established reality—ultimate freedom. When Soviet esthetics attack the notion of the "insurmountable antagonism" between essence and existence" as the theoretical principle of "formalism," it thereby attacks the principle of art itself . . . Soviet esthetics insists on art while outlawing the transcendence of art. It wants art that is not art and it gets what it asks for.

. . . The works of the great "bourgeois" antirealists and "formalists" are far deeper committed to the idea of freedom than is socialist and Soviet realism. The irreality of their art expresses the irreality of their freedom: art is as transcendental as its object. The Soviet state by administrative decree prohibits the transcendence of art; it thus eliminates even the ideological reflex of freedom in an unfree society. Soviet realistic art, complying with the decree, becomes an instrument of social control in the last still nonconformist dimension of human existence. Cut off from its historical base, socialized without a socialist reality, art reverts to its ancient prehistorical function: it assumes magical character. Thus, it becomes a decisive element in the pragmatic rationality of behaviorism. . . .

Within the general framework of the political controls over art, a wide range of policy modifications is possible. Relaxation and tightening, alter-

---

[4] Ibid, pp. 56–58.

ation of artistic standards and styles, depend on the internal and international constellations. Naturally, with the transition from terroristic to normal modes of societal regimentation, the claim for more artistic freedom will be heard and perhaps fulfilled. The rigidity of "Soviet realism" may well be loosened; realism and romanticism, in any case, have ceased to be opposites, and even "formalistic" and "abstract" elements may still become reconcilable with conformist enjoyment. In its societal function, art shares the growing impotence of individual autonomy and cognition.[5]

HERBERT MARCUSE,
Soviet Marxism, 1958

. . . the realist mode of writing is a combination of the formal signs of literature and of the no less formal signs of realism, so that no mode of writing was more artificial than that which set out to give the most accurate description of Nature. . . . there is, in the Naturalist esthetic, a convention of the real, just as there is a fabrication in its writing. . . . The writing of Realism is far from neutral; it is on the contrary loaded with the most spectacular signs of fabrication.

Between a proletariat excluded from all culture and an intelligentsia that has already begun to question literature itself, the average public produced by primary and secondary schools, roughly speaking, the middle class, will therefore find in the realistic-artistic mode of writing—which is that of a good proportion of commercial novels—the image *par excellence* of a literature which has all the striking and intelligible signs of its identity. In this case the function of the writer is not so much to create a work as to supply a literature that can be seen from afar.

This lower-middle-class mode of writing has been taken up by communist writers because, for the time being, the artistic norms of the proletariat cannot be different from those of the *petite bourgeoisie* (a fact that indeed agrees with their doctrine), and because the very dogma of socialist realism necessarily entails the adoption of a conventional mode of writing, to which is assigned the task of signifying in a conspicuous way a content that is powerless to impose itself without a form to identify it. Thus is understood the paradox whereby the communist mode of writing makes multiple use of the grossest signs of literature, and far from breaking with a form that is after all typically bourgeois—or that was such in the past—at least goes on assuming without reservation the formal preoccupation of the *petit-bourgeois* art of writing (which is moreover accredited with the communist public, thanks to the essays done in primary school). . . .

Perhaps there is, in this well-behaved writing of revolutionaries, a powerlessness to create forthwith a free writing. Perhaps also only bourgeois writers feel that bourgeois writing is compromised: the disintegration of literary language was a phenomenon that owed its existence to consciousness,

[5] Herbert Marcuse, *Soviet Marxism* (Vintage-Random House, 1961), pp. 113–120.

not to revolution. And certainly it is a fact that Stalinist ideology imposes its terroristic approach on all problematics, even and above all revolutionary problematics: bourgeois writing is thought to be, all in all, not dangerous enough to be put on trial. This is why communist writers are the only ones who go on imperturbably keeping alive a bourgeois writing that bourgeois writers have themselves condemned long ago—since the day when they felt it was endangered by the impostures of their own ideology, namely, the day when Marxism used it to justify itself.

. . . The closed character of the form (in Marxist writing) does not derive from rhetorical amplification or from grandiloquence in delivery, but from a lexicon as specialized and as functional as a technical vocabulary; even metaphors are here severly codified. French revolutionary writing always proclaimed a right founded on bloodshed or moral justification, whereas from the very start Marxist writing is presented as the language of knowledge. Here, writing is univocal, because it is meant to maintain the cohesion of a Nature; it is the lexical identity of this writing which allows it to impose a stability in its explanations and a permanence in its method; it is only in the light of its whole linguistic system that Marxism is perceived in all its political implications. Marxist writing is as much given to understatement as revolutionary writing is to grandiloquence, since each word is no longer anything but a narrow reference to the set of principles that tacitly underlie it. . . .

Being linked to action, Marxist writing has rapidly become, in fact, a language expressing value judgments. This character, already visible in Marx, whose writing, however, remains in general explanatory, has come to pervade writing completely in the era of triumphant Stalinism. Certain outwardly similar notions, for which a neutral vocabulary would not seek a dual designation, are evaluatively parted from each other, so that each element gravitates towards a different noun: for instance, "cosmopolitanism" is the negative of "internationalism" (already in Marx). In the Stalinist world, in which definition—that is to say the separation between Good and Evil—becomes the sole content of all language, there are no more words without values attached to them, so that finally the function of writing is to cut out one stage of a process: there is no longer a lapse of time between naming and judging, and the closed character of language is perfected, since in the last analysis language itself is a value that is used to explain another value . . .[6]

ROLAND BARTHES,
Le degré zéro de l'écriture, 1953

[6] Roland Barthes, *Writing: Degree Zero* (Beacon Press, 1968), pp. 67-73, 22-27.

SELECTED BIBLIOGRAPHY

GENERAL BIBLIOGRAPHY

Carr, H. L. The History of the Russian Revolution (Pelican-Penguin Books, London, 1966).
Fejtö, François. History of the People's Democracies (Praeger, New York, 1971).
Lichtenstein, George. Europe in the Twentieth Century (Praeger, New York, 1972).
Medvedev, Roy. Let History Judge (Knopf, New York, 1971).
Seton Watson, Hugh. Eastern Europe Between the Wars, 1918-1941 (Archon Books, Hemden, 1961).

GENERAL FILM BIBLIOGRAPHY

A Concise History of the Cinema (Ed. by P. Cowie; A. S. Barnes and Co., New York, 1971).
Gregor and Patalas, Geschichte des modernen Films (Sigbert Mohn Verlag, Gütersloh, 1965).
Hibbins, Nina. Eastern Europe (A. S. Barnes and Co., New York, 1969).
The International Encyclopedia of Film (Gen. editor Roger Manvell; Crown Publishers, New York, 1972).
Plazewski, Jerzy. Filmová řeč (Orbis, Prague, 1967).
Whyte, A. New Cinema in Eastern Europe (Dutton, New York, 1971).

Periodicals

Bianco e nero (Rome).
Cahiers du cinéma (Paris).
Cinéma (Paris).
Écran (Paris).

Film a doba (Prague).
Kino (Prague).
Sight and Sound (London).

CZECHOSLOVAKIA

Boček, Jaroslav. Modern Czechoslovak Film (Artia, Brno, 1965).
Bartošková, Šárka. Československé filmy 1945-1957 I.
          Československé filmy 1945-1957 II. (Československý film, Prague, 1959).
          Československé filmy 1958-1959 (Československý film, Prague, 1960).
          Čs. film 1960/65 (Čs. Filmový ústav, Prague, 1966).
          Čs. film 1966/68 (Čs. filmový ústav, Prague, 1970).
Boček, Jaroslav. La nouvelle vague vue avec un certain recul (Čs. Filmexport, Prague, 1967).
Brož, J. and M. Frída. Historie československého filmu v obrazech 1930-1945 (Orbis, 1965).
Brumagne, M. M. Jeune cinéma tchécoslovaque (Premier Plan, Lyons, 1969).
Dewey, Langdon, Outline of Czechoslovakian Film (Informatics, London, 1971).
Havelka, Jiří. Kronika našeho filmu 1898-1965 (Filmový ústav, Prague, 1965).

Der junge tschechoslowakische Film (Westdeutsche Kurzfilmtage, Oberhausen, 1967).
Liehm, Antonín J. Closely Watched Films (International Arts and Sciences Press, New York, 1974).
————. The Miloš Forman Stories (International Arts and Sciences Press, New York, 1975).
Micciché, Lino. Il nuovo cinema degli anni '60 (ERI, Turin, 1972).
Novák, Antonín. Jeunes cinéastes tchécoslovaques (ARJECI, Paris, 1967).
Novotná, Drahomíra. Le cinéma tchécoslovaque (La documentation française, Paris, 1970).
Ropars-Wuillemier, Marie-Claire. L'Écran de la mémoire (Ed. du Seuil, Paris, 1970).
Škvorecký, J. All the Bright Young Men and Women (Peter Martin Ass., Toronto, 1973).
Wolf, Steffen. Der tschechoslowakische Film (Verband der deutschen Filmclubs, Frankfurt, 1965).
Žalman, Jan. Cinema e cineasti in Cecoslovacchia (Orbis, Prague, 1968).

Periodicals

Film a doba 1956-1974 (Orbis, Prague).
Filmové a televizní noviny 1966-1969 (Svaz čs. filmových a televizních umělců, Prague).
Kino 1952-1974 (Orbis, Prague).

BULGARIA

The Bulgarian Art Feature Film: A Collection of Articles (State Film Distribution Enterprise, Sofia, 1970).
The Bulgarian Cinema Today (State Film Distribution Enterprise, Sofia, 1968).
Bulgarian Cinematography—Guidebook (State Film Distribution Enterprise, Sofia, 1965).
Bulgarian Short Films (State Film Distribution Enterprise, Sofia, 1967-1968).
Bulgaria—A Survey (Sofia Press, Sofia, 1965).
Kino-izkustvoto v Bulgaria (Nauka i izkustvo, Sofia, 1960).
Sergio Micheli: Il cinema bulgaro (Marsilio Editori, Padova, 1971).
Marie Ratcheva: Le cinéma bulgare contemporain (Sofia Presse, Sofia, 1970).
Semaine du cinéma bulgare (Assoc. Française des Cinémas d'Art et d'Essai, Paris, 1973).
25 années de cinéma bulgare (Entreprise d'Etat Distribution de films, Sofia, 1969).

Periodicals

Bulgarian Feature Films (published by State Film Distribution Enterprise, Sofia, 1965-1974).
Bulgarian Film (published by State Film Distribution Enterprise, Sofia), 1960-1974.

GERMAN DEMOCRATIC REPUBLIC

Borde, R., F. Buache, and F. Courtade. Le Cinema réaliste allemand (Serdoc, Lyons, 1965).
Buch, Gunther. Namen und Daten—Biographien wichtiger Personen der DDR (J. H. W. Dietz Nachf., GmbH, Berlin, Bonn, 1973).
Bucher, Felix. Germany (Screen Series, A. S. Barnes & Co., New York, 1970).
Cadars, Pierre and Francis Courtade. Le Cinéma nazi (Collection cinemathèque, Eric Losfeld, Toulouse, 1972).

Deuerlein, Ernst. DDR—1945-1970 (Deutscher Taschenbuch Verlag, Munich, 1972).
Fantastique et réalisme dans le cinéma allemand (Musée du Cinema, Brussels, 1969).
Hamburger, Michael. East German Poetry (E. P. Dutton & Co., New York, 1973).
Kersten, Heinz. Das Filmwesen in der sowjetischen Besatzungszone Deutschlands (Bundesministerium für gesamtdeutsche Fragen, Bonn/Berlin, 1963).
Ludz, P. Ch. The German Democratic Republic from the Sixties to the Seventies (Center for International Affairs, Harvard Uty, 1970).
1946-1964 Defa-Spielfilme. Filmografie (Institut für Filmwissenschaft, Berlin, 1966).
Radatz, Fritz J. Traditionen und Tendenzen—Materialen zur Literatur der DDR (Suhrkamp, Frankfurt, 1972).
Rothe, Wolfgang. Schriftsteller und die totalitäre Welt (Francke Verlag, Bern and Munich, 1966).
Sontheimer, Kurt and Wilhelm Bleek. Die DDR (Hoffmann und Campe, Hamburg, 1972).
Ein Taschen—und Nachschlagebuch über den anderen Teil Deutschlands (Deutscher Bundes-Verlag, Bonn, 1969).

Periodicals

Deutschland Archiv. Zeitschrift für Fragen der DDR und der Deutschlandpolitik (Cologne, 1968-1974).

HUNGARY

Aczél, György. Culture et démocratie socialiste (Ed. Corvina, Budapest, 1970).
Aczél, T. and T. Méray. La révolte de l'esprit (Ed. Gallimard, Paris, 1962).
Bory, Jean-Louis. Miklós Jancsó (Dossiers du cinéma: Cinéastes I, Casterman, Paris, 1971).
Fejtö, François. Budapest 1956 (Ed. Julliard, Paris, 1966).
Haudiquet, Philippe. Panorama du cinéma hongrois (Poitiers, 1970).
Levenson, Claude B. Jeune cinéma hongrois (Premier Plan, Lyons, 1966).
Le Nouveau cinéma hongrois (Études cinématographiques, Lettres Modernes, Paris, 1969).
Marcorelles, Louis. Eléments pour un nouveau cinéma (Unesco, Paris, 1970).
Micciché, Lino. Viaggio attraverso il cinema ungherese (Avanti, Rome, 1974).
Nemeskürty, István. Word and Image—History of the Hungarian Cinema (Corvina Press, Budapest, 1968).
Slovník maďarských spisovatelů (Odeon, Prague, 1971).
Ungarische Spielfilme I-II. (Verband der Deutschen Filmclubs, Frankfurt (1968-1969).

Periodicals

Hungarofilm Bulletin (Hungarofilm, Budapest 1960-1974).
A magyar film 25 éve 1945-1970, I (Film Kultura, Budapest, #2, 1970).
A magyar film 25 éve 1945-1970, II (Film Kultura, Budapest, #3, 1970).
The New Hungarian Quarterly (Budapest, 1968-1974).

POLAND

Cieplak, Tadeusz N. Poland Since 1956 (Twayne Publishers, New York, 1972).
Fuksiewicz, Jacek. Le cinéma en pologne (Ed. Interpress, Warsaw, 1973).
Haudiquet, Philippe. Nouveaux cinéastes polonais (Premier Plan, Lyons, 1963).

Janicki, Stanisław. Film polski od A do Z (Wydawnictwa artystyczne i filmove, Warsaw, 1972).
Kinematografia polska v XXV—leciu PRL (Wydawnictva filmove CWF, Warsaw, 1969).
Michalek, Bolesław. The Cinema of Andrzej Wajda (A. S. Barnes and Co., New York, 1973).
Milosz, Czesław. The History of Polish Literature (The Macmillan Co., New York, 1969).
Polish Short Film During 25 Years of Polish People's Republic (Wydawnictwa filmowe CWF, Warsaw, 1969).
Various authors. Andrzej Munk (Études cinématographiques, Lettres Modernes, Paris, 1965).
Various authors. Andrzej Wajda (Études cinématographiques, Lettres modernes, Paris, 1968).

Periodicals

Film (Warsaw), 1952-1974.
Kwartalnik filmowy (Warsaw), 1955-1965.
Polish Feature Films (published by Film Polski, Warsaw), 1965-1974.
Polish Film (published by Film Polski, Warsaw), 1965-1972).

ROMANIA

Bibliografie Internationala Cinema (Arhiva natională de filme, Bucharest, 1967).
Ceaucescu, Nicolae. Exposition on the Programme of the Romanian Communist Party (Romanian News Agency, Bucharest, 1971).
Ciclo del film rumeno (Archivio della Cineteca Nazionale, Centro Sperimentale di cinematografia, Roma, 1970).
Cineasti Romani. Dictionar bio-filmografic (Arhiva natională de filme, Bucharest, 1969).
Le cinéma roumain (Romania Film, Bucharest, 1968).
Le Développement de la cinématographie roumaine après le 23 août 1944 (Archive National de Films, Bucharest, 1960).
Filmografia productiei cinematografice Romanesti 1949-1969, Filme de animatie (Arhiva Natională de filme, Bucharest, 1970).
Filmul documentar romanesc (Editura Meridiane, Bucharest, 1967).
Cantacuzino, Ion: Contribuții la istoria cinematografiei in România 1896-1948 (Editura Academiei Republicii Socialiste România, Bucharest, 1971).
Cantacuzino, Ion: Momente din trecutul filmului românesc (Editura Meridiane, Bucharest, 1965).
Productia cinematografica din România 1897-1970 (Arhiva natională de filme, Bucharest, 1970).

Periodicals

Full-length Feature Films (published by Romania Film, Bucharest, 1965-1974).
The Romanian Film (published by Romania Film, Bucharest, 1964-1974).
Cinema (Bucharest).

SOVIET UNION

Barna, Yon. Eisenstein (Indiana University Press, 1973).
Dovzhenko, Alexander. The Poet as Filmmaker (MIT Press, Cambridge, 1973).

Kino i vremya (from 1961 on, VGFK, Moscow).
Kinoslovar, I and II (Izdatelstvo Sovietskaya Encyklopedia 1966–1970).
Leyda, Jay. Kino (Collier Books, New York, 1973).
Lunacharsky, Anatoly. On Literature and Art (Progress Publishers, Moscow, 1973).
Ocherki istorii sovietskogo kino, Vols. I and II (Moscow, 1959).
Rimberg, John, and Paul Babitsky. The Soviet Film Industry (Praeger, New York, 1955).
Schnitzer, Luda and Jean, and Marcel Martin. Cinema in Revolution (Hill and Wang, New York, 1973).
Sinyavsky, Andrei. For Freedom of Imagination (Holt, Rinehart, Winston, New York, 1971).
Socialist Realism in Literature and Art (Progress Publishers, Moscow, 1971).
Sovietskie khudozhestennye filmy (Annotirovany katalog I–IV; Gosudarstvennoe izdatelstvo Iskusstvo, Moscow, 1961–1968).
Der Sowjetische Film—Eine Dokumentation (Verband der deutschen Filmklubs, Frankfurt a/M., 1966).
Vronskaya, Jeanne. Young Soviet Filmmakers (Allan & Unwin, London, 1971).

Periodicals

Iskusstvo Kino (Moscow).   *Soviet Film* (Moscow).
Sovexport film (Moscow).   *Sovietski Ekran* (Moscow).

YUGOSLAVIA

Brenk, France. Aperçu de l'histoire du cinéma yougoslave (Académie de l'art dramatique, Ljubljana, 1961).
Dvadeset godina jugoslovenskog filma, 1945–1965 (Savez filmskih radnika Jugoslavije, Belgrade).
Filmografija jugoslovenskog filma, 1945–1965 (Institut za film, Belgrade, 1970).
Holloway, Ronald. Z Is For Zagreb (A. S. Barnes & Co., New York, 1972).
Lukić, Sveta. Contemporary Yugoslav Literature (University of Illinois Press, Urbana, 1972).
Novaković, Slobodan. 20 ans du film yougoslave (Festival du film yougoslave, Belgrade, 1965).
Petrić, Vladimir. Razvoj filmskih vrsta (Umetnička Akademija u Beogradu, Belgrade, 1970).
Petrović, Aleksandar. Novi film, 1950–1965 (Institut za film, Belgrade, 1971).

Periodicals

News (published by Jugoslavija Film, Belgrade, 1969–1974).

INDEX OF FILMS

Abbreviations

Bu	Bulgaria	Lit	Lithuania
Cz	Czechoslovakia	Po	Poland
Fr	France	Ro	Romania
GB	Great Britain	Ru	Russia (before 1917)
Ge	Germany (before 1945)	SU	Soviet Union
GDR	German Democratic Republic	Sw	Switzerland
FRG	Federal Republic Germany	USA	United States
Hu	Hungary	Yu	Yugoslavia
It	Italy		

About Love, SU, 322
Abyss, Hu, 150
Academician Ivan Pavlov, SU, 62
Accident, Hu, 171
Adam's Rib, Bu, 138
Adam 2, FRG, 197
Adam Wants To Be a Man, SU, 209
Admiral Nakhimov, SU, 49, 50
Admiral Ushakov I and II, SU, 66
Adoption, Hu, 399
Adrift, Cz, 404
Adventures of Werner Holt, The, GDR, 270
Adventures in Ontario, Ro, 350
Adventures of a Dentist, SU, 323
Adventures of Till Ulenspiegel, The, German-French, 262
Aesop, Cz-Bu, 339, 344
Affair of the Heart or The Tragedy of the Switchboard Operator, An, Yu, 423
Affection, Bu, 343
Against All, Cz, 106
Age of Daydreaming, The, Hu, 386, 388, 402
Agitators, The, Hu, 409
Agnus Dei, Hu, 397
Agony, SU, 323
Ahasver, Cz, 10
Alarm, Bu, 135, 240
Alarm, SU, 71
Alarm in the Mountains, Ro, 143
Alexander Nevsky, SU, 43
Alexander Popov, SU, 62
Alitet Leaves for the Hills, SU, 63
Allaverdoba, SU, 331
All My Countrymen, Cz, 279, 302, 305
Alone, Yu, 245
Always Prepared, GDR, 265
Ambush, The, Yu, 422
Amour à Vingt Ans, L', Fr, 369

Amphibious Man, The, SU, 210
And Behave Yourself, Cz, 298
And Give My Love to the Swallows, Cz, 304
And Quiet Flows the Don, SU, 204
Andrei Rublev, SU, 308-309, 315-316, 326, 343
Andriesh, SU, 71
And the Blind Can See, Hu, 33, 152
And the Fifth Rider Is Fear, Cz, 293
And the Mornings Here Are Quiet, SU, 314
And Your Love Too, GDR, 267
Anna, Hu, 170
Anna Around the Neck, SU, 71
Anna Karenina, SU, 316
Annelie, GDR, 95
Answer to Violence, Po, 192
Appeal, The, SU, 331
Archangel Gabriel and Mother Goose, The, Cz, 108
Aristocrats, SU, 40
Arsen, SU, 40
Ashes, Po, 369, 382
Ashes and Diamonds, Po, 178, 180, 181, 382
As Long as I Live, GDR, 361
Assassination at Sarajevo, The, Yu, 250
Assassination of the Duc de Guise, The, Fr, 11, 12
Asya's Happiness, SU, 310
Ataman Kord, SU, 203
Atlantic Story, Po, 192
At Midnight, Hu, 170
Attached Balloon, The, Bu, 337
Attention Hooligans, Po, 122, 377
At the End of the Road, Hu, 408
At the Photographer's, Yu, 250
Autumn Flowers, Yu, 427
Autumn Wedding, SU, 321
Ave Vita, SU, 330

INDEX OF NAMES